IN DESTINY'S HANDS

Justin C. Vovk

IN DESTINY'S HANDS

Five Tragic Rulers,
Children of Maria Theresa

RALEIGH   TORONTO   LONDON   BANGALORE

www.lulu.com

For information regarding special discounts for bulk purchases, please contact Lulu, Inc., at http://www.lulu.com/en/buy/.

Cover painting (right): Empress Maria Theresia of Austria, by Martin van Meytens (*Akademie der bildenden Künste, Vienna*).
Cover painting (left): Emperor Joseph II, by Pompeo Batoni, (*Kunsthistorisches Museum, Vienna)*, Maria Amalia, Duchess of Parma, by anonymous (*Hulton Archive*), detail of Grand Duke Leopold of Tuscany (later Emperor Leopold II), by Pompeo Batoni, (*Kunsthistorisches Museum, Vienna*), Maria Carolina, Queen of Naples, by Johann Georg Weikert (*Kunsthistorisches Museum, Vienna*), Marie Antoinette, Queen of France, by anonymous (*Musée Antoine Lécuyer, Saint-Quentin*).

Map illustration courtesy of the Cartographic Research Lab, University of Alabama. Redesigned and reformatted by the author.

ISBN-13: 978-0-557-06021-4
ISBN-10: 0-557-06021-4

Library of Congress Control Number: 2009907852

First Edition: October 2009

10 9 8 7 6 5 4 3 2 1

For Mika.

You inspire me as a journalist,

a friend,

and a cousin.

Contents

PART III
The Flames of Revolution
(1780-1793)

PART IV
Empires at War
(1793-1814)

Acknowledgments

I would now like to take a moment and thank those individuals who have helped me during the process of writing this book. There are many of them, so I crave your indulgence.

First, I acknowledge and thank the head of the Habsburg family, His Imperial and Royal Highness, Crown Prince Otto of Austria, for his encouragement and praise of this project. I am also grateful for his assistance in providing resources from which I could gather research. I would also like to thank H.I. & R.H. Archduke Geza of Austria for responding to my queries regarding the Hungarian branch of the Habsburgs.

I would like to express my deepest thanks to Julia P. Gelardi for granting me permission to use in this book a similar format to her own, *Born to Rule*. Writing a single narrative of five individuals is no easy task, and can often have parallels or similar styles to other written works. Julia's contributions to and guidance on this project cannot be overstated. I am most grateful to her for taking the time to review the manuscript at various points in its lifespan and offering insights on how to make it better. I am also thankful for her constant advice, good wishes, and encouragement.

For granting me permission to use material from several of their books, I would like to thank Mellisa Brandt and the Perseus Books Group. I also express the same thanks to Adam Hirschberg and the Cambridge University Press. For allowing me to use his articles on Emperor Joseph II, I thank Dr. Ritchie Robertson of St. John's College, Oxford.

To my colleagues and friends at Chapters in Ancaster, Ontario, your support, assistance, and advice have meant more than you know. I would like to especially thank LouAnne Disher for guiding me through the world of publishing; Frank Soberg for helping to develop the chronology table that laid the foundation for the book; and Laura Llewellyn for assisting me in the distribution process. I also want to say thank you to Gillian Dias, Susan Hay, Sabaina Malik, Todd Gannon, Suzanne Hanvey, Rosanna Brydon, Susie Weir, Kim Rochon, Nikki Pacsuta, Jenna DiNardo, Laura Toito, Nida Malik, Jennifer Stratemeyer, and Dave Trimmer.

I thank my friend and research assistant, Tony La Vella. I am also grateful to my translator, Vanessa Rundle, who was more than gracious in helping me understand pages and pages of French text, both historic and colloquial.

The one individual who has supported me and been beside me since my first days writing is my editor and very dear friend, Cherylyn Donaldson. I cannot count the hours, days, and weeks she has spent with me on *In Destiny's Hands*. She took an interest in every detail, from the storyline itself to the format of my endnotes. There are not words to describe the heartfelt gratitude I feel for all she has done.

I am grateful to the staff at Lulu, Inc., for publishing this book. Their helpfulness in developing, distributing, and marketing it have fulfilled a lifelong dream of mine and opened a door to what I hope will be a long, successful writing career.

I would like to say a thank you to the individuals who have been a blessing to me during this time. My colleagues in the journalism program at Mohawk College have been great friends. I would also like to thank Patty and Roger West, Alexsis Karpenchuk, Ryan Hashimoto, Christine Matthews, Kim Doucette, Marc Murchison, Joshua Brown, Craig Miller, Jason Leach, Frank Borger, Michelle Donaldson, Karen Ash, and Lisa Wilson. From my family, I thank Jessica Price, Caitlin Price, Jonathan Jaques, Miha Žakelj (to whom this book is dedicated), Gašper Vidic, Matija Ferjan, Patricia and Andy Price, Tom Vovk, and Monika Vovk. My grandmother, Erika Vovk, has also been a wonderful companion during this process. Thank you for being our Maria Theresa.

Finally, I want to acknowledge and thank my brother, Steven, and his wife, Jolene, for always being ready to examine a rewrite or offer advice. And to the two people that have never stopped believing in me, my parents Stan and Sharon Vovk, I can only say that the faith you've shown in me has made all this possible. Thank you for always being behind me.

Simplified Genealogy

BOURBON ∽ (FRANCE)

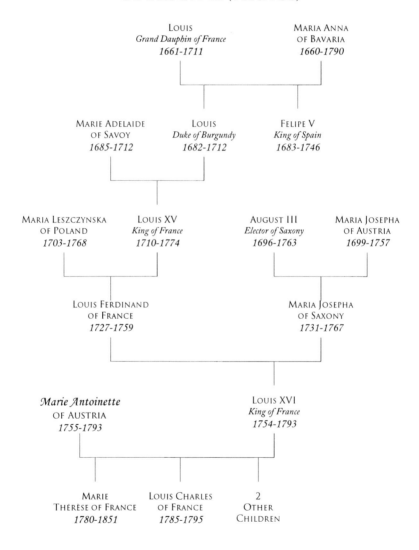

LOUIS
Grand Dauphin of France
1661-1711

MARIA ANNA
OF BAVARIA
1660-1790

MARIE ADELAIDE
OF SAVOY
1685-1712

LOUIS
Duke of Burgundy
1682-1712

FELIPE V
King of Spain
1683-1746

MARIA LESZCZYNSKA
OF POLAND
1703-1768

LOUIS XV
King of France
1710-1774

AUGUST III
Elector of Saxony
1696-1763

MARIA JOSEPHA
OF AUSTRIA
1699-1757

LOUIS FERDINAND
OF FRANCE
1727-1759

MARIA JOSEPHA
OF SAXONY
1731-1767

Marie Antoinette
OF AUSTRIA
1755-1793

LOUIS XVI
King of France
1754-1793

MARIE
THÉRÈSE OF FRANCE
1780-1851

LOUIS CHARLES
OF FRANCE
1785-1795

2
OTHER
CHILDREN

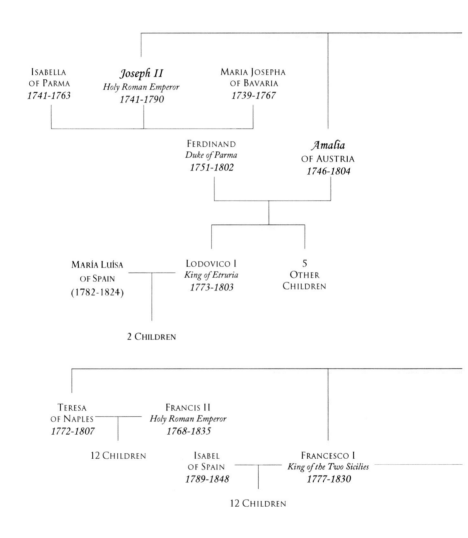

Maria Theresa
Queen of Hungary & Bohemia
1717-1780

ISABELLA
OF PARMA
1741-1763

Joseph II
Holy Roman Emperor
1741-1790

MARIA JOSEPHA
OF BAVARIA
1739-1767

FERDINAND
Duke of Parma
1751-1802

Amalia
OF AUSTRIA
1746-1804

MARÍA LUÍSA
OF SPAIN
(1782-1824)

LODOVICO I
King of Etruria
1773-1803

5
OTHER
CHILDREN

2 CHILDREN

TERESA
OF NAPLES
1772-1807

FRANCIS II
Holy Roman Emperor
1768-1835

12 CHILDREN

ISABEL
OF SPAIN
1789-1848

FRANCESCO I
King of the Two Sicilies
1777-1830

12 CHILDREN

HABSBURG ⌘ (AUSTRIA)

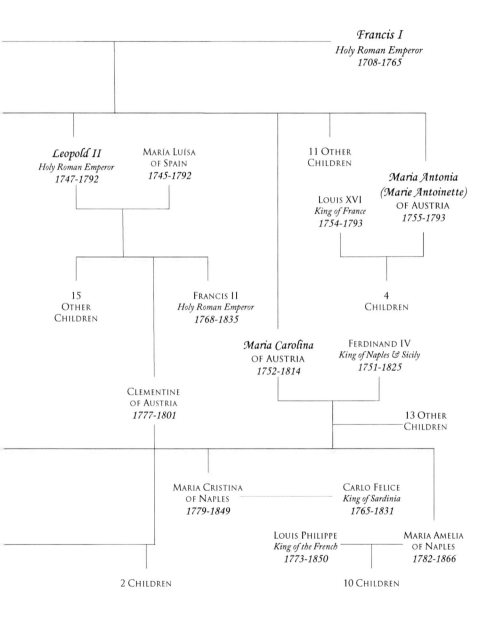

Francis I
Holy Roman Emperor
1708-1765

Leopold II
Holy Roman Emperor
1747-1792

MARÍA LUÍSA
OF SPAIN
1745-1792

11 OTHER
CHILDREN

LOUIS XVI
King of France
1754-1793

Maria Antonia
(Marie Antoinette)
OF AUSTRIA
1755-1793

15
OTHER
CHILDREN

FRANCIS II
Holy Roman Emperor
1768-1835

4
CHILDREN

Maria Carolina
OF AUSTRIA
1752-1814

FERDINAND IV
King of Naples & Sicily
1751-1825

CLEMENTINE
OF AUSTRIA
1777-1801

13 OTHER
CHILDREN

MARIA CRISTINA
OF NAPLES
1779-1849

CARLO FELICE
King of Sardinia
1765-1831

LOUIS PHILIPPE
King of the French
1773-1850

MARIA AMELIA
OF NAPLES
1782-1866

2 CHILDREN

10 CHILDREN

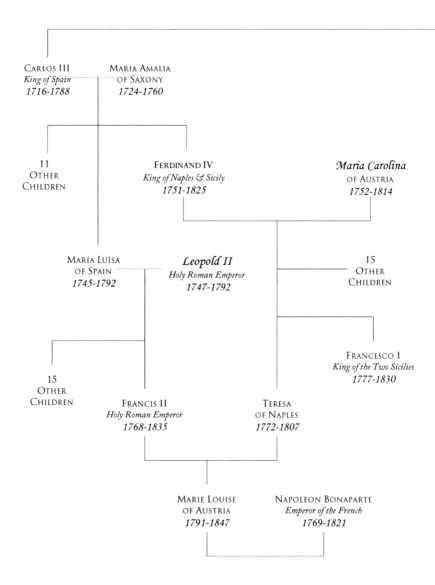

FELIPE V
King of Spain
1683-1746

CARLOS III
King of Spain
1716-1788

MARIA AMALIA
OF SAXONY
1724-1760

11
OTHER
CHILDREN

FERDINAND IV
King of Naples & Sicily
1751-1825

Maria Carolina
OF AUSTRIA
1752-1814

MARÍA LUÍSA
OF SPAIN
1745-1792

Leopold II
Holy Roman Emperor
1747-1792

15
OTHER
CHILDREN

FRANCESCO I
King of the Two Sicilies
1777-1830

15
OTHER
CHILDREN

FRANCIS II
Holy Roman Emperor
1768-1835

TERESA
OF NAPLES
1772-1807

MARIE LOUISE
OF AUSTRIA
1791-1847

NAPOLEON BONAPARTE
Emperor of the French
1769-1821

BOURBON ❧ (SPAIN/NAPLES/PARMA)

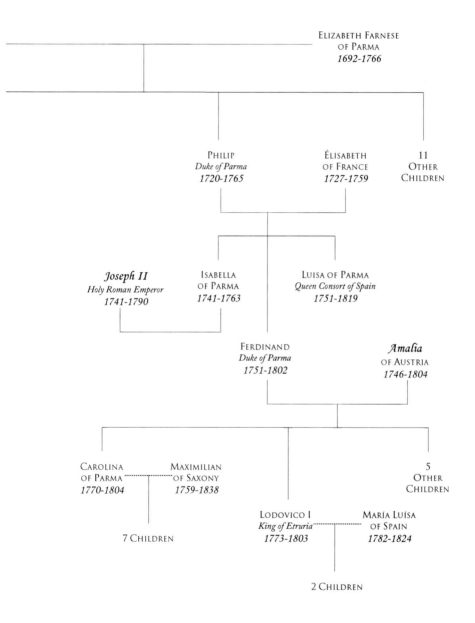

ELIZABETH FARNESE
OF PARMA
1692-1766

PHILIP
Duke of Parma
1720-1765

ÉLISABETH
OF FRANCE
1727-1759

11
OTHER
CHILDREN

Joseph II
Holy Roman Emperor
1741-1790

ISABELLA
OF PARMA
1741-1763

LUISA OF PARMA
Queen Consort of Spain
1751-1819

FERDINAND
Duke of Parma
1751-1802

Amalia
OF AUSTRIA
1746-1804

CAROLINA
OF PARMA
1770-1804

MAXIMILIAN
OF SAXONY
1759-1838

5
OTHER
CHILDREN

7 CHILDREN

LODOVICO I
King of Etruria
1773-1803

MARÍA LUÍSA
OF SPAIN
1782-1824

2 CHILDREN

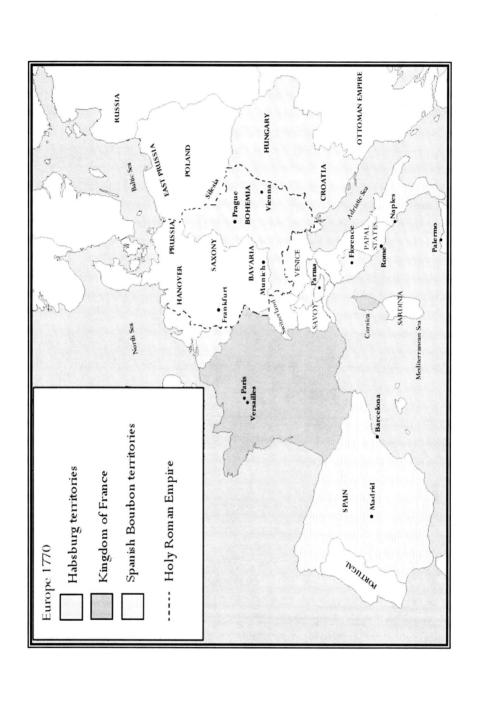

Europe 1770

Habsburg territories

Kingdom of France

Spanish Bourbon territories

----- Holy Roman Empire

RUSSIA

EAST PRUSSIA

POLAND

Baltic Sea

Silesia

Prague
BOHEMIA

Vienna

HUNGARY

CROATIA

OTTOMAN EMPIRE

PRUSSIA

SAXONY

HANOVER

Frankfurt

BAVARIA

Munich

Switzerland

VENICE

SAVOY

Parma

Florence

PAPAL
STATES

Rome

Adriatic Sea

Naples

Palermo

North Sea

Corsica

SARDINIA

Mediterranean Sea

Paris
Versailles

Barcelona

SPAIN

Madrid

PORTUGAL

Main Protagonists

Amalia. Duchess of Parma, consort to Ferdinand, Duke of Parma. Born in Vienna on February 26, 1746, she was the eighth child and sixth daughter of Empress Maria Theresa and Holy Roman Emperor Francis I. Her full name at birth was Maria Amalia Josepha Joanna Antonia. She married Ferdinand on June 27, 1769 (by proxy) in Vienna and on July 18, 1769 (in person) at the Colorno Palace in Parma. See *Ferdinand I.*

Children:
1. Carolina (1770-1804)
2. Lodovico I (1773-1803) ("Luigi," King of Etruria)
3. Maria Antonietta ("Tognina," 1774-1841)
4. Carlotta (1777-1813)
5. Filippo (1783-1786)
6. Antonietta Luisa (1784-1784)
7. Maria Luisa (1784-1789)

Ferdinand. Duke of Parma, 1765-1802. Born on January 20, 1751 in Parma. He was the first child of Philip, Duke of Parma, and Princess Élisabeth of France. Ferdinand married H.I. & R.H. Archduchess Amalia of Austria in 1769 and died October 9, 1802 at Fontevivo. After his death, Parma became part of the new kingdom of Etruria. See *Amalia.*

Ferdinand IV. King of Naples & Sicily from 1759-1816, and King of the Two Sicilies from 1816-1825. The third son of King

Carlos III of Naples & Sicily and Princess Maria Amalia of Saxony, Ferdinand was born on January 18, 1751 at the Royal Palace in Naples. In 1759 his father became King of Spain, making Ferdinand the reigning King of Naples. He married H.I. & R.H. Archduchess Maria Carolina of Austria in 1768. He was forced into exile to Sicily twice, first in 1798 and later in 1805. He returned to Naples in 1814. He died in Naples on January 4, 1825 and was succeeded by his son, King Francesco I. See *Maria Carolina*.

Francis I. Duke of Lorraine, 1729-1737; Grand Duke of Tuscany, 1737-1745; Holy Roman Emperor, 1745-1765. Born as François Stefan on December 8, 1708. He was the ninth child and oldest surviving son of Léopold, Duke of Lorraine, and his wife, Princess Élisabeth Charlotte d'Orléans. He married Maria Theresa in Vienna in 1736 and was elected Holy Roman Emperor in 1745. He was the father of Amalia, Joseph II, Leopold II, Maria Carolina, and Marie Antoinette. See *Maria Theresa*.

Isabella. First wife of Emperor Joseph II. Born on December 31, 1741 in Madrid, Isabella was the eldest child of Philip, Duke of Parma, and Princess Élisabeth of France. She was also a sister of Ferdinand, Duke of Parma. Isabella married H.I. & R.H. Archduke Joseph of Austria (later Emperor Joseph II) in 1760. She died on November 27, 1763 and is buried in Vienna. See *Joseph II*.

Joseph II. Holy Roman Emperor, 1765-1790. Joseph, born on March 13, 1741, was the fourth child and first son of Maria Theresa, Queen of Hungary and Bohemia, and Grand Duke Francis Stephen of Tuscany (later Emperor Francis I). He married Isabella of Parma on September 7, 1760 (by proxy) and later on October 6, 1760 in Vienna (in person). After Isabella died in 1763, Joseph married Princess Josepha of Bavaria in January 1765. See *Isabella, Josepha*.

Children:
1. Theresa (1762-1779) (mother: Isabella of Parma)
2. Christina (1763-1763) (mother: Isabella of Parma)

Josepha. Empress Consort, 1765-1767, of Holy Roman Emperor Joseph II. Born in Munich on March 30, 1739, Josepha was the seventh and youngest child of Charles Albert, Elector of Bavaria, and Archduchess Marie Amalie of Austria. She married Joseph of Austria in Munich on January 13, 1765 (by proxy) and in Vienna on January 23, 1765 (in person). She died in Vienna on May 26, 1767. See *Joseph II.*

Leopold II. Holy Roman Emperor, 1790-1792. The third son and ninth child of Maria Theresa and Francis I, Leopold ("Poldy") was born in Vienna on May 5, 1747. He married H.R.H. Infanta María Luísa of Spain on February 16, 1764 (by proxy) in Madrid, and (in person) on August 4, 1765 in Innsbruck. He ascended the throne upon the death of Joseph II in 1790.

Children:
1. Theresa (1767-1827) (Queen of Saxony)
2. Francis I (1768-1835) (Holy Roman Emperor; later Emperor of Austria)
3. Ferdinand (1769-1824)
4. Marianne (1770-1809)
5. Karl (1771-1847)
6. Alexander (1772-1795)
7. Albert (1773-1774)
8. Maximilian (1774-1778)
9. Joseph (1776-1847)
10. Clementine (1777-1801)
11. Anton (1779-1835)
12. Maria Amalia (1780-1798)
13. Johann (1782-1859)
14. Rainer (1783-1853)
15. Ludwig (1784-1864)
16. Rudolf (1788-1831)

Louis XVI. King of France, 1774-1792. Louis was born on August 23, 1754 at Versailles. He was the third son and fourth child of the Dauphin Louis Ferdinand and Princess Maria Josepha of Saxony. In 1770 he married H.I. & R.H. Archduchess Maria Antonia of Austria. He became King of

France on May 10, 1774 when his grandfather, King Louis XV, died from smallpox. Louis was executed in 1793 during the French Revolution. See *Marie Antoinette.*

Maria Carolina. Queen Consort, 1768-1814, of King Ferdinand IV of Naples & Sicily. Also known as "Charlotte," she was born in Vienna on August 13, 1752. She was the thirteenth child and tenth daughter of Emperor Francis I and Empress Maria Theresa. In 1768 she married King Ferdinand IV, first by proxy in Vienna on April 7 and later in person on May 12 at the Caserta Palace.

Children:
1. Teresa (1772-1807) (Holy Roman Empress; later Empress of Austria)
2. Luisa (1773-1802)
3. Carlo (1775-1778)
4. Mariana (1775-1780)
5. Francesco I (1777-1830) (King of the Two Sicilies)
6. Maria Cristina (1779-1849) ("Mimi," Queen of Sardinia)
7. Cristina Amelia (1779-1783)
8. Carlo (1780-1789)
9. Giuseppe (1781-1783)
10. Maria Amelia (1782-1866) ("Amélie," Queen of the French)
11. Maria Antonietta ("Toto," 1784-1806)
12. Clotilda (1786-1792)
13. Enrichetta (1787-1792)
14. Gennaro (1788-1789)
15. Leopoldo (1790-1851)
16. Alberto (1792-1798)
17. Isabella (1793-1801)

María Luísa. Empress consort of Leopold II, Holy Roman Emperor (1747-1792). Born in Portici on November 24, 1745, she was the fifth child and daughter of King Carlos III of Naples (later King of Spain) and his wife, Maria Amalia of Saxony. She married H.I. & R.H. Archduke Leopold of Austria, first by proxy in 1764, and later in person in 1765. See *Leopold II.*

Maria Theresa. Queen of Hungary and Bohemia, 1740-1780; Empress consort to Francis I, Holy Roman Emperor (1708-1765). Born in Vienna on May 13, 1717, Maria Theresa was the eldest surviving child of Holy Roman Emperor Charles VI and his wife, Elisabeth Christine of Brunswick-Wolfenbüttel. She became queen of both Bohemia and Hungary when her father died in 1740, and the Holy Roman empress when her husband was elected in 1745. See *Francis I.*

Children:
1. Maria Elisabeth (1737-1740)
2. Marianne (1738-1789)
3. Maria Caroline (1740-1741)
4. Joseph II (1741-1790) (Holy Roman Emperor)
5. Maria Christina (1742-1798)
6. Elizabeth (1743-1808)
7. Charles (1745-1761)
8. Amalia (1746-1804) (Duchess of Parma)
9. Leopold II (1747-1792) ("Poldy," Grand Duke of Tuscany; Holy Roman Emperor)
10. Maria Carolina (1748-1748)
11. Maria Johanna (1750-1762)
12. Maria Josepha (1751-1767)
13. Maria Carolina (1752-1814) ("Charlotte," Queen of Naples)
14. Ferdinand (1754-1806)
15. Marie Antoinette (1755-1793) ("Antoine," Queen of France)
16. Maximilian (1756-1801)

Marie Antoinette. Queen consort, 1774-1792, of King Louis XVI of France. Born on November 2, 1755, she was the fifteenth child and eleventh daughter of Maria Theresa and Francis I. Baptized Maria Antonia Josepha Joanna, she was known as "Antoine" she took the French name Marie Antoinette upon her marriage to Louis Auguste, Dauphin of France. They were married, first by proxy, on April 19, 1770 and, in person, on May 16, 1770. Marie Antoinette was executed in 1793 during the French Revolution.

Children:
1. Marie Thérèse (1778-1851)
2. Louis Joseph (1780-1789)
3. Louis Charles (1785-1795)
4. Sophie (1786-1787)

Introduction

October 16, 1793. Dawn. The night's deepening cold had slowly given way to an agreeable, misty morning in Paris. Since before dawn, the streets had gradually been filling with excited, bloodthirsty onlookers. In the silence between the hourly bell tolls, chants from the promenades along the Seine could be heard resounding in the morning air. The government was so overwhelmed by the public response that 30,000 troops were brought in to ensure the peace. As incredible as the crowds along the Seine seemed, even more were assembling at the Place de la Révolution to witness the day's crowning event. Shortly before ten o'clock that morning, the procession began amid shouts of "make way for the Austrian woman" and "long live the Republic!"[1]

Escorted in an open cart like a common criminal, a calm, almost peaceful woman dressed in a white linen gown was moving closer and closer to her ultimate fate. As she awaited her arrival at the scaffold, the thirty-seven-year-old prisoner was utterly alone. Cruel fate had robbed her not only of the man she called her husband for twenty years, but her children too. Her last surviving child, a little girl, had been coldly ripped from her mother's arms and locked away in a dungeon with her aunt while they waited for their fates to be decided. Who was this woman, and how did she come to know such a life? She was none other than the once innocent and beautiful Queen Marie Antoinette of France, the youngest daughter of the Holy Roman Empress Maria Theresa.

Marie Antoinette was one of the most famous queens in history, but she was also the youngest of a very special group of Maria Theresa's children. The Empress had sixteen children throughout the course of her life, but only five of them were born to rule. Most of her children did not live extraordinary lives. In fact, most did not live until adulthood. But destiny had a very specific plan, because five of them would be thrust into the spotlight of an entire continent. These Habsburg children would collectively rule over more than half of Europe at the height of their power and would become the most controversial leaders of the eighteenth century, shaping the course of history for generations to come.

These five siblings were the Holy Roman Emperor Joseph II (1741-1790); Amalia, Duchess of Parma (1746-1804); Grand Duke Leopold of Tuscany (who later became the Holy Roman Emperor Leopold II) (1747-1792); Queen Maria Carolina of Naples & Sicily (1752-1814); and Queen Marie Antoinette of France (1755-1793). This book follows the course of their lives from their childhoods in Austria to the five countries they were destined to rule. They all shared the same experience of becoming a monarch, but they were bound even closer by their mother, one of the most famous women rulers in history, Empress Maria Theresa. Everything from the finer points of their childhood educations to their conduct as rulers was scrutinized by their mother's watchful eye. This would dramatically shape the people they were destined to become.

Fate would also play a vital role in placing these five special siblings on a throne in Europe. Each of them would come to their role by accident, but guided by their mother's powerful hand; even though Joseph was expected to become emperor, he did so in such an irregular fashion that his fellow kings did not know what to make of his accession. Joseph, Amalia, Leopold ("Poldy"), Maria Carolina ("Charlotte"), and Marie Antoinette ("Antoine") would grow up reflecting the different facets of their mother's personality, but no one individual would inherit all of her traits. Between the five of them, they would be known as despotic, scandalous, cold, ambitious, and naïve.

Their lives were not only defined by their mother, but also by the tragic circumstances that overtook them. Within the rarified circle of royalty in Europe, trials and tribulations were hallmarks. But these five siblings each met with tragic, often heartbreaking, events that earned them pity, sympathy, and sometimes even scorn. Two of them were considered to have been the victims of fate, but the other three have been criticized for bringing misfortune upon themselves.

Their stories are set against the backdrop of such historically significant events as the Enlightenment, the French Revolution, and the Napoleonic Wars. France's descent into revolution was a flashpoint that helped bring down the happiness of all five of Maria Theresa's special children. The death of Queen Maria Carolina in 1814 also marked the end of the European order that was known up until that point. The continent—its reigning houses, its politics, and its prejudices—would be nearly unrecognizable after Napoleon engulfed it in the flames of war. And as we will see, these five imperial siblings played no small part in that reformation that forged the world as we know it today.

Special attention should also be paid to the differences in rank between these five siblings. Marie Antoinette and Maria Carolina were queens; Joseph was an emperor; Amalia was a duchess; and for most of his life, Leopold was a grand duke. As divergent as these titles sound from one another, they meant relatively the same thing. Amalia's title as Duchess of Parma was relative to the way her country was ruled. In this case, it was by her husband Don Ferdinand, Duke of Parma. This term in no way diminished her role as a reigning consort. Even until the early twentieth century, Europe possessed many duchies that were considered just as sovereign and independent as any kingdom or empire.

At its core, this book follows the personal lives of Joseph, Amalia, Poldy, Charlotte, and Antoine. As such, it has not been written as an historical account of their reigns. These are the stories of an imperial mother, her five reigning children, and the tragic fates they met, all as a result of their quests for glory. Their lives were also intimately connected with the political events of the day; no one can deny or overstate the importance of the French Revolution in Marie Antoinette's destiny. As much as these five siblings shaped their own lives, so to did the tumultuous events that surrounded them. To that end, a certain degree of leeway has been taken in writing about the relevant political circumstances surrounding their lives. Austria, the Habsburg dominions, and the Holy Roman Empire are particularly important.

Ultimately, the central figure that links these five individuals is their mother, Maria Theresa. She was the most powerful female ruler in the first half of the eighteenth century, and reigned during some of its most turbulent years. By the time Joseph was born in 1741, Maria Theresa was the reigning Queen of Hungary and Bohemia,* a title she inherited from her father. These thrones made up the backbone of what was known as the Habsburg monarchy, a swath of territories, kingdoms, and other states personally owned by Maria Theresa's family. Added to this later was her election as the Holy Roman Empress. These roles that Maria Theresa filled during her lifetime had a dramatic impact on the lives of her children. Some time, therefore, has been given to discussing her character and the circumstances surrounding her reign.

Readers are about to see the erratic course these five lives will follow. Each of them was born into spectacular prestige, wealth, and splendor, but some of them would know the lowest poverty and the cruelest humiliation. Some would die in exile; others would die forgotten and alone. Each of them would have the distinction of playing prominent roles, not only in the royal families they married into, but also in the fates of their countries.

Almost all of them would die to mixed reactions, remembered first and foremost by their contemporaries as the Children of Maria Theresa. But it is up to each individual person to judge for themselves whether or not what history has said about these monarchs is true, or whether they were merely pawns in their mother's game to fulfill her own dynastic ambitions. Did destiny truly have a part in their tumultuous lives, or were they solely responsible for the circumstances they experienced in their respective courts of Vienna, Parma, Florence, Naples, and Versailles?

---

* Bohemia was a kingdom that existed until 1918. It makes up the western half of the present day Czech Republic.

PART I

Destined to Reign

1741—1765

Queen, Empress, Mother

The winter of 1741 was an especially hard one for the people of Austria. Bone-chilling cold and food shortages devastated the unfortunate population. The government was disorganized, and social services had virtually fallen apart. Unrest and panic were rampant and threatened to destabilize the entire country. It is in the midst of this chaos that the story of Maria Theresa's five special children begins, with the birth of the eldest of the group, the future Holy Roman Emperor Joseph II. As the firstborn son of Maria Theresa, Queen of Bohemia and Hungary, and her husband, Grand Duke Francis Stephen of Tuscany, Joseph would one day hold the most vaunted position in Catholic Europe. Like his four special siblings, he came to the throne in a most unexpected way, and at the relatively young age of twenty-four. Joseph was born (weighing a staggering sixteen pounds) on March 13, 1741 at the Schönbrunn, his parents' majestic palace in Vienna. When he was born, he joined an older sister, Archduchess Maria Anna ("Marianne," b. 1738).

When he was baptized that evening in the marble chapel at Schönbrunn with the names Joseph Benedikt August Johann Anton Michael Adam, Vienna was truly *en fête* over the birth of an heir. The British statesman Horace Walpole, who was in Vienna at the time, reported back to his superiors in London of the festive atmosphere in the city: "On Sunday came the news of the Queen of Hungary being brought to bed of a son; on which occasion there will be great triumphs, operas and masquerades."[1]

At the time of Joseph's baptism, Austria was engulfed in what became known as the War of the Austrian Succession of 1740-1748, a conflict that had great ramifications for Joseph and the House of Habsburg.

Austria was faring badly in the war, the causes of which stretched back for decades into the reign of Maria Theresa's father, Charles VI. As the Holy Roman Emperor, Charles reigned over an empire that stretched from France to Poland, and from the Adriatic to the Baltic and North seas. As the head of the House of Habsburg, Charles also personally owned one of the most impressive collections of territories in history. His dominions included present-day Austria, Slovenia, Hungary, Croatia, the Netherlands, Belgium, Luxembourg, Liechtenstein, the Czech Republic, Slovakia, as well as parts of Italy, Romania, Ukraine, Bulgaria, Poland, and Germany.

When Charles VI died in October 1740, his vast empire faced a crisis. The Habsburg monarchy "lacked a political identity: it was a collection of duchies and kingdoms, each with its own historical tradition, constitutional structure, economic framework and ethnic peculiarity."[2] And since Charles had no sons to succeed him, he left this disparate dominion to his eldest daughter, Maria Theresa. Many believed that, as a woman, Maria Theresa would be unable to rule such a far-flung inheritance. To help shore up support for his daughter, the Emperor drafted the Pragmatic Sanction, in which the other major European powers agreed to allow Maria Theresa to succeed her father in exchange for lands and territories. But within a matter of weeks of the emperor's death, the monarchical powers all but tore up the Pragmatic Sanction in an undignified scramble to gain a piece of Maria Theresa's inheritance for themselves.

Four months before Joseph was born, in December 1740, a militarily powerful league made up of France, Spain, Bavaria, Saxony, and their allies launched a massive assault on the Habsburg lands. At the same time, Maria Theresa (who rightfully inherited the thrones of Bohemia and Hungary) was faced with a crisis of imperial proportions. The Holy Roman throne upon which her father had sat was an elected position, not a hereditary one. Each emperor was chosen by the rulers of the largest member states, who were known as the Electors. To make matters worse, women were forbidden from ruling because of an ancient German tradition known as Salic Law. This meant that if Maria Theresa wanted to become empress, she would need to have her husband Francis Stephen elected emperor. And since Bavaria and Saxony—who were both powerful electorates—sided against Queen Maria Theresa and Francis Stephen, their hopes of obtaining the election were dashed.

During these turbulent first years of Archduke Joseph's life, the situation for his parents only got worse. Maria Theresa was humiliated when the Elector of Bavaria, Charles Albert, declared himself emperor with the help of his allies. The final straw for the Queen came when she was publicly betrayed by one of the Holy Roman Empire's most influential figures, King Frederick II of Prussia, more famously remembered as "Frederick the Great." Since the day Emperor Charles VI died, Frederick placated Maria Theresa with promises of friendship and alliance, so much so that Francis Stephen commented to the Prussian ambassador in early 1741, "Really the King is behaving like a father to the Queen and myself and we shall never be able to repay our obligations to him."[3]

With the wool pulled tightly over Maria Theresa's eyes, Frederick II joined the alliance against Austria and marched his army straight into the richest, most valuable province in the Habsburg realm, Silesia. He glibly boasted that his actions *"prevented their occupation* by any other power."[4] The Queen would never reconquer Silesia, nor would she ever forgive Frederick for his treachery and deception. They would remain archenemies until the day Maria Theresa died. The Queen vowed to never take her eyes off defeating the armies of Frederick the Great.

For nearly four years, the War of the Austrian Succession raged across Europe and spelled trouble for Austria. A joint army from France, Bavaria, and Saxony managed to conquer Bohemia for a brief period and seized its capital, Prague. When the city fell, Maria Theresa penned an emotional letter to her governor in Bohemia: "Prague is lost...this is the moment to save your country and your Queen; otherwise I shall be poor indeed."[5] At one point, Bavarian forces managed to capture Linz, putting them only a mere hundred miles from Vienna. A diversion of troops from Upper Austria to Bohemia was the only thing that saved Vienna.

The tide finally turned in 1745 when Charles Albert of Bavaria, the self-proclaimed Holy Roman emperor, died. With her enemies confused and the electors unsure of their next move, Maria Theresa swung into action and struck a deal. In exchange for allowing Frederick the Great to keep Silesia, the Prussian king would support the election of Francis Stephen as the next Holy Roman emperor.

The coronation was held in the ancient city of Frankfurt in 1745. After kneeling on a velvet cushion before the electoral archbishops, Joseph's father (now Emperor Francis I) bequeathed his title as Grand Duke of Tuscany in favor of his children. Cries of "Long live the Emperor Francis I.!" rang throughout the streets of Frankfurt.[6] Maria Theresa would later describe it as "the happiest day of her life."[7]

Maria Theresa's new position as queen-empress thrust her into the European spotlight. She was now the most powerful woman on the continent, wielding power like no other matriarch. The new role of Joseph's parents meant a dramatic change in the archduke's life. Maria Theresa was determined to see her son elected King of the Romans, the title given to the imperial heir. Having Joseph crowned king in Frankfurt would pave the way for him to take over the reins of one of the largest empires Europe had ever known.

CB

In the tumultuous years before she ascended the imperial throne, Maria Theresa continued to give birth to a succession of children: Maria Christina ("Mimi") in 1742, Maria Elizabeth in 1743, and Charles in 1745. On February 26, 1746, another girl—Maria Amalia Josepha Joanna Antonia—was born. Despite her long names, this archduchess would always be known as Amalia.

The use of the prefix Maria was a tradition for all Habsburg women since the 1600s. It was a way for the family to show their veneration "of the Virgin [Mary], the magna mater Austriae, as she was spoken of in a singular blend of reverence and familial claim."[8]

Less than a year after Amalia's birth, another child was born that would join the rarified group of Maria Theresa's special reigning children. On May 5, 1747, the Empress prepared to give birth at Schönbrunn. Like with her other children, the Empress was forced to deliver her baby practically in public thanks to the strict Austrian court etiquette to which she herself was a slave. Next to her apartments, in the ornate Mirror Room, were hundreds of aristocrats who held the Rights of Entry. For centuries, individuals with these rights were actually permitted to be in the room with the birthing mother. When Maria Theresa came to the throne she abolished this practice, and banished the courtiers to an adjacent room.

Now those same courtiers, wearing the traditional Spanish dress Charles VI had adopted, complete with red stockings, black shoes, plumed hats, and lace-trimmed jackets, anxiously awaited the birth of the empress's next child. Eventually, the gold-trimmed double doors flew open. Emperor Francis I, beaming with a wide grin on his round face, stepped through and proudly announced the birth of a son. The courtiers congratulated him, but were forbidden by tradition from kissing the hand of the Empress for another four days.

At his baptism, the baby was given the names Peter Leopold Joseph. Peter was for Peter the Great, father of the baby's godmother Tsarina Elizabeth; Leopold was for his maternal great-grandfather, Emperor Leopold I; and Joseph was for his maternal great-uncle, Emperor Joseph I. This new addition to the Habsburg henhouse came to be known as "Poldy," the German diminutive of Leopold.

Officially, the little boy was referred to as the Archduke Leopold. Each of his three names had illustrious forbearers, and were appropriate for this future grand duke and emperor since they were the names of three emperors, two of the Holy Roman Empire and one of Russia. The choice of Peter as the infant's first name was not an obvious one, and came as the result of the friendship between Maria Theresa and Tsarina Elizabeth of Russia. These two women shared a close friendship as well as a unique bond; they both ruled the only two empires in Europe at the same time; Elizabeth became empress only a few months after Maria Theresa ascended the throne. Leopold's mother considered the tsarina "her dearly beloved friend and sister."[9]

⍥

The environment that the young Archduchess Amalia grew up in was less restricted and regimented than the one her brother, Joseph, was forced to endure. His position as heir meant he was kept on the tightest of leashes, but Amalia was given much more latitude in her early years.

That did not mean her family life was perfect, nor was her parents' marriage an entirely blissful one. For all her beauty, wealth, and power, Empress Maria Theresa found herself unable to keep her husband's attention. The Empress was forced to tolerate an endless stream of women who shared her husband's affections; his relationship with the Princess von Auersperg, a lady of the court, was no secret to anyone. A visitor in Vienna admitted that "the Emperor makes no secret of his passion for her." Even the imperial children knew about their father's love for women. "The Emperor is a very good-hearted father," said Archduchess Maria Christina, "one can always rely upon him as a friend, and we must do what we can to protect him from his weaknesses. I am referring to his conduct with Princess Auersperg."[10]

In spite of Francis's unfaithfulness, he and Maria Theresa had a marriage that seemed to work. They were passionately in love, and managed to overlook this one area for the good of their relationship. The mistresses that paraded in and out of Francis's bedroom actually helped showcase one of Maria Theresa's greatest traits: her devotion to the Roman Catholic faith. Nathaniel Wraxall, a frequent visitor to Vienna, observed that the empress's faith made her "very virtuous in her conduct, true to her marriage vows, and never has an impure thought, has but little patience with the indiscretions of others."[11]

The Empress willingly forgave her husband's infidelities because she passionately believed in being an inscrutable Christian role model for her children, especially her daughters. She felt so strongly about the role of women in marriage that she once told her daughters that "they are born to obey and must learn to do so in good time."[12] Her devotion to God was one of the defining characteristics of Maria Theresa's life, one that she worked diligently to leave as a legacy to her children.

Maria Theresa was not without her own faults. There was a marked difference in the way she treated her children. Her favorites—Charles and Mimi—received lavish affection, but the others were often criticized and compared to their older siblings. The Empress believed that by making her children keenly aware of their own faults, it would help improve them as future rulers. As Maria Theresa would one day discover, this type of parenting rarely worked.

For Amalia, life with her brothers and sisters in the 1740s was a whirlwind of family activities amidst a variety of fairytale-like homes. In winter, the imperial family ensconced themselves in the forbidding Romanesque palace known as the Hofburg. Located in Vienna, the Hofburg was the most lavish of all the imperial residences. Built by an ancient German dynasty in the thirteenth century, it "looked a bit like a medieval fortress."[13] It boasted eighteen different wings and contained no less than 2,600 rooms. At any one time, several thousand servants waited on Maria Theresa and her family at the Hofburg.

In the summer, the family ventured to the less imposing but equally majestic Schönbrunn Palace on the outskirts of the city. There, Maria Theresa was able to indulge her love of decorating. Rooms were done in the Rococo style with "lacquer mirrors, vellum miniatures and tapestries." The empress also relished in decorating parts of the palace in the Far Eastern style. She once declared that "all the diamonds in the world" could not compare to "what comes from the Indies."[14] The famous Habsburg historian Gordon Brook-Shepherd believed the Schönbrunn was truly unique: "Unlike its great architectural and political rivals, Versailles or Potsdam, it remained also a home."[15] The children also loved playing in Schönbrunn's unusual menagerie, which included a camel, a rhinoceros, a puma, red squirrels, and a variety of parrots.

ℭℬ

The close of the 1740s saw a rapid change of fortunes for Francis I and Maria Theresa. The War of the Austrian Succession was ended after eight long years. In the last weeks of April 1748, a continental congress was held in the Imperial Free City of Aix-la-Chapelle. There, surrounded by princes, politicians, and diplomats, Francis I and Maria Theresa were hailed as the undisputed rulers of the Holy Roman Empire. This recognition by their enemies cemented the Habsburgs' place as one of the pre-eminent powers in Europe.

Once the war ended, the Emperor and Empress continued to expand their family with the arrivals of Maria Carolina (b. 1748), Maria Johanna (b. 1750), and Maria Josepha (b. 1751). Sadly, Carolina died shortly after being born. One courtier recalled the tragic scene that took place: "On Tuesday, towards night, Her Majesty gave birth to an Archduchess who died a few minutes afterwards, baptized, however, by a lady among the assistants."[16] But by December 1751 the Empress was *enceinte* again. This time, a beautiful baby girl was born on August 13, 1752. Delivered at the Schönbrunn, the baby was given the names Maria Carolina Louise Josepha Joanna Antonia.

This archduchess's regal names were fitting for this daughter of an empress and a future queen. Maria was for the Virgin Mary; Carolina was for her maternal grandfather, Emperor Charles VI; Louise was for the baby's godfather, King Louis XV of France; Joseph was for none other than her older brother; Joanna was for St. John the Apostle; and Antonia was for St. Anthony of Padua. This bright-eyed baby would be known to her intimates all her life as "Charlotte," a name the Empress always cherished but never chose for any of her daughters. The rest of the world would remember her as the famous Queen Maria Carolina of Naples and Sicily.

The choice of Louis XV for the baby's godfather was a bold move, especially since France had sided against Austria during the War of the Austrian Succession. But the decision also made sense because, like all of her siblings, Charlotte was half French.

Before her parents got married in 1737, her father was known as François Stefan, Duke of Lorraine. When Charles VI brought François Stefan to Vienna in 1723 as Maria Theresa's future husband, King Louis XV became anxious that a marriage between a Habsburg archduchess and the Duke of Lorraine would spell trouble for France. Louis XV wanted to prevent Lorraine from allying itself to the Habsburgs, so he did what all rulers seemed to do, he struck a deal. Louis XV ordered his minister, Cardinal Fleury, to inform Emperor Charles VI that since Lorraine was a French principality, if François Stefan wanted to marry Maria Theresa he would have to renounce his claim to the duchy. To further entice Charles VI, Fleury offered French support for the Pragmatic Sanction if he could convince François Stefan to renounce Lorraine.

François Stefan was understandably shocked by such a demand. There was a heated debate on both sides, and before long, partisan lines starting forming. Tired of waiting, Charles VI's most trusted adviser, Count Bartenstein, told François Stefan point blank: "No renunciation, no archduchess."[17] He eventually agreed, married Maria Theresa, and took the name Francis Stephen. He was also compensated with the Grand Duchy of Tuscany. The loss of Lorraine did not diminish the impressive royal bloodline that the now-Emperor Francis I possessed. His father Léopold, Duke of Lorraine, was a direct descendant of Charlemagne. And his mother, Princess Elisabeth Charlotte d'Orléans, was a granddaughter of King Louis XIII. In time the Emperor, who never learned German and only spoke French, sought to inspire Maria Carolina and her sisters with pride in their French heritage.

ೞ

For Archduke Joseph, growing up meant a strict regiment of schoolwork and practical education orchestrated by his ever-ambitious mother. In the same way she was passionate about her role as a queen, empress, and mother, Maria Theresa was just as strident in training her son for the day he would become emperor. Joseph's education was therefore extreme, covering a wide range of subjects. The Empress dictated a strict curriculum for him on everything from military tactics to the concept of Austria and its greatness. Count Bartenstein (now Joseph's tutor) made the archduke read a text on medieval Austrian history that was six thousand pages long.

Joseph's education reinforced his superior place within the family, which only aggravated the competitive atmosphere among the children. Visitors to Schönbrunn or the Hofburg were startled to find the Habsburg children in open war with one another, throwing priceless pieces of artwork and fighting on the marble floors. Joseph and his brother Charles were especially violent towards one another. One particular fight began when Charles mocked Joseph for only being the son of a queen, while he was the son of an empress.

To Maria Theresa, her children were far too unruly at times. When the time came for them to visit with her one-on-one, a much stricter and more disciplined atmosphere prevailed. Maria Theresa took time on a regular basis to talk with her children in private. High on the list of topics was reminding Joseph and his siblings to always believe "in three things: their religion, their race, and their destiny. They were never to forget that they were Catholics, imperialists, and politicians."[18]

The younger children were indulged in these interviews, but Joseph was grilled about the progress he was making in his studies, both academic and religious. Maria Theresa was an intensely devout woman, and firmly believed that "each day must begin with prayer and the first and most necessary thing for my son is to be certain with a submissive heart of God's omnipotence, to love and to fear Him, and to develop from true Christian practice all other duties and virtues."[19] As a child, Joseph was "confined to the daily task of reading the legends of the saints," the Holy Scriptures, and stories from the Bible.[20] This constricting environment soon birthed in the fearless and stubborn archduke a lifelong antipathy towards anything associated with religion. This was unfortunate for Joseph, because Maria Theresa's deep faith in and love for God was one of the defining attributes of her life and one of her most profound legacies.

2

"The Empress and Her Children Are the Court"

Compared to the other royal families of Europe, the Habsburgs enjoyed a relatively peaceful family life. All was not perfect though. Maria Theresa's third son, Archduke Leopold, was earning a reputation for being her most frustrating child. As a toddler, Poldy resented the lavish affection that was showered upon his older siblings. His "quarrelsome" and "truculent" behavior toward his relatives only grew worse as he got older.[1]

A sickly, sensitive child, his intransigence often got the better of him, resulting in pouting and temper tantrums that grated even on the Empress's steely nerves. Maria Theresa was appalled by Poldy's behavior, once describing him as "lazy and corrupt."[2] By the time he was eight, he was "sulky, arrogant, deceitful, rough, and apparently unfeeling." In short, he was "the most unpromising youngster imagineable."[3]

One of the people who helped fuel Leopold's behavior was none other than his own sister, Mimi. The Empress's favorite daughter, Mimi was an arch intriguer who set about tormenting Poldy and her other siblings. She regularly tattled on her brothers and sisters to the Empress, who readily agreed with her daughter's judgments. Mimi, who was "highly intelligent, quick, shrewd, [and] humorous," constantly exasperated Leopold.[4] When he finally could take no more of his sister's antics, he publicly denounced her at Court for her "scolding ways, her sharp tongue and, above all, her habit of 'telling everything to the Empress'."[5]

Leopold's unwholesome character preyed intensely on Maria Theresa's mind, forcing her to consider several radical options. One possibility was to have him take up an honorary position in the military. The Empress explained to Poldy's tutor, Count Francis Thurn, that "the science of arms" was "the only way in which a prince of his birth can become useful to the Monarchy, shine in the world and make himself especially loved by me."[6]

This military training never materialized. Nor did the suggestion that Leopold be entered into the Catholic seminary. His only hope, Maria Theresa reasoned, was to see him one day married off to a suitable royal bride. Around this time, the Duke of Modena was scouring Europe to find a husband for his daughter and heiress, Beatrix. This worked out fortuitously for Maria Theresa, who was more than happy to see Leopold paired with the wealthy and beautiful Princess Beatrix.

As Empress Maria Theresa began planning Leopold's future, she was pregnant again for the fourteenth time. In 1754, she delivered a son, Ferdinand. By the next year, she was pregnant again. By now she had become an expert in childbearing, so much so that during the first stages of labor she continued to work at her state papers. "My subjects are my first children," the Empress often said.[7] She echoed this sentiment later when she declared, "I am the general and chief mother of my country."[8]

The Empress continued to work at her papers until the last possible minute. On the evening of November 2, 1755 she gave birth at the Hofburg to "a small, but completely healthy Archduchess."[9] At her baptism, this baby girl was given the names Maria Antonia Josepha Joanna, but her family would always call her "Antoine." History would immortalize her as Queen Marie Antoinette of France.

There was an ominous sense of foreboding in Vienna the day Antoine was born. Catholic Europe was engrossed in the Feast of All Souls, also known as the Day of the Dead. Churches, palaces, and other building were draped in black as the people solemnly remembered their departed loved ones. Even more disconcerting was the tragedy that befell the infant's godparents, King José I and Queen María Ana of Portugal, the very same day. A devastating earthquake had struck Lisbon, killing 30,000 people. These would be the first of many ominous signs associated with Maria Antonia.

With the addition of Antoine in 1755, Maria Theresa's brood had truly become a private little army, with some considerable gaps in age. Joseph was fourteen, Amalia was nine, Poldy was eight, and Charlotte was four. The following year, the Empress delivered her last child, Maximilian ("Max"). Maria Theresa and Francis I played vital roles in continental politics, radically shaping the lives of their children. But as we shall see, their own personalities, combined with their individual relationships with their mother, would shape even more the rulers these five special children were destined to become.

⌇

As a mother, Maria Theresa took a different approach to dealing with each of her children. Nowhere was this contrast more obvious than in the tenderness she showed to little Antoine compared to the strict martinet she was with Archduke Joseph. She insisted on military-style education for Joseph, who rebelled against the "unmerciful cramming" he was forced endure.[10] Once, frustrated by her son's unwillingness to do what he was told, Maria Theresa threw her hands up in the air and complained: "My Joseph cannot obey."[11]

Joseph caused no end of stress to his mother. By his teen years, the archduke

> became mercurial. The empress was not blind to her oldest son's problematic personality. He was intelligent yet listless like his father and obstinate like his mother. His relationship with his siblings was no less easy, for Joseph had a tendency to be sarcastic toward them, even in front of strangers. Maria Theresa urged his tutors to mold him into an ideal prince, firing off instructions on how to deal with the heir, who enjoyed "being honored and obeyed" and found "criticism…well-nigh unbearable. Tending to indulge his whims," Joseph was found to be "deficient in courtesy and even rude." No matter how hard Maria Theresa tried to curb her oldest son's obduracy and indifference, he was always to do things his way and cause his mother anxiety.[12]

Joseph's difficult personality earned him the nickname "*Starrkopf*" ("Stubborn One") from the Empress. But he also inherited much of his mother's intelligence. Along with his sisters Marianne, Amalia, and Elizabeth, Joseph attended Maria Theresa's salons, where "reflections on the world, on courts, and the duties of princes, were the usual topics of conversation."[13]

Noticeably absent from these sessions on enlightenment was Emperor Francis. It was much to the Emperor's credit that his children enjoyed a tranquil family life, but Joseph did not see it that way. Francis was an utterly devoted father, but there was never a question that the real power rested with the Empress. Joseph resented the titular role his father had assumed, believing him to be little more than "an idler surrounded by flatterers."[14] But Francis I was also legendary for his joie de vivre and zest for life. By letting Maria Theresa exercise most of the power, Francis was given more time to spend with his children and pursue his love of outdoor activities. No one was happier with this arrangement than Francis himself, who once quipped to his wife's ladies-in-waiting: "Don't mind me. I am only the husband; the [Empress] and her children are the court."[15]

Like her older brothers and sisters, Maria Carolina's early years were spent at her parents' spectacular palaces. In addition to dividing their time between the Hofburg and Schönbrunn, the imperial family also enjoyed spending time at their estate in the picturesque town of Laxenburg in Lower Austria.

Laxenburg became the family's residence when the Habsburgs first purchased the town's Old Castle in 1333. In the first years of her reign Maria Theresa had two new palaces built nearby, the Blauer Hof and the Neues Schloss. Eventually the grounds were redesigned after an English landscape garden. A series of artificial ponds were later constructed, and another palace, Franzensburg (named for Emperor Francis I), was built on one of the islands.

It was at Laxenburg that Charlotte was able to see her parents rid themselves of the strict court etiquette that plagued them in Vienna. The Laxenburg palaces were so small that the throngs of courtiers who normally followed the Emperor and

Empress were forced to find rooms in the town itself away from the imperial family.

Maria Theresa and Francis I preferred raising their children in this type of atmosphere, one that was free of rank and title. Charlotte and her siblings were strongly encouraged to associate with "ordinary" children outside their royal circle. The Emperor and Empress did likewise by relaxing the rules of protocol and allowing people of merit into the court.[16] Maria Theresa believed it was important for her to be "accessible to all. She had accustomed the peasantry to accost her in her walks; she had visited to inquire into and relieve their wants."[17]

One of those "ordinary" people who visited Vienna during this time in Charlotte's life was none other than "the little child from Salzburg," Wolfgang Amadeus Mozart. Invited to Schönbrunn along with his father and sister, little Mozart performed splendidly on the harpsichord and the piano. After he finished playing, he ran up to Maria Theresa, "put his arms round her neck, and kissed her heartily." Mozart's father Leopold later wrote to a friend, "Their Majesties received us with such graciousness that, when I shall tell of it, people will declare that I have made it up."[18]

CB

Compared to her siblings, Archduchess Amalia received very little love or attention from her mother. From a very early age, she and the Empress had a strained, almost indifferent relationship. That Maria Theresa loved her daughter was never questioned, but she did not always know how to express it. The attention Amalia received was usually in the form of a criticism or a comparison to one of her sisters.

One author has observed that, compared to her brothers and sisters, "Amalia...was a much less threatening figure; she was not so clever, not so interesting, not so pretty, not so graceful— and for all these reasons she was not much loved by Maria Teresa."[19] Living under her mother's watchful eye undoubtedly left Amalia feeling very aware of her own shortcomings. But despite falling behind her sisters in favor with the Empress, by the time she was a teenager Amalia sparkled in Viennese society. She was also highly sought after as a possible royal bride. The famed Italian virtuoso Metastasio raved about her "enchanting voice" and "angelic figure."[20]   Even one of Maria Theresa's biographers, John Jenkins, could not help but praise Amalia for being so "surpassingly bright in mind and person."[21]

Many foreign princes visiting Vienna found themselves smitten with Amalia, including the young and handsome Prince Charles of Zweibrücken. Amalia did not know it at the time, but Charles was passionately in love with her, and was biding his time until he could formally propose marriage.

Unlike Joseph, Amalia received a light education that centered mostly on the "need to appear and perform gracefully at court functions." A particular emphasis for the archduchesses was placed on the works of Gluck, Wagenseil, Joseph Stephan, and Johann Adolf Hasse.[22] The Habsburg girls were educated far more in art and history than in geography or mathematics. They were taught "penmanship, reading and French, with a scant hour or two a week devoted to studying maps and reading stories." While the boys were trained in fencing, the girls took up needlework.[23]

The other emphasis that was placed on all the archduchesses was the need for docility and complete obedience. Francis I made sure that his daughters read such works as *Les Aventures de Télémaque* by François Fénelon, which "underlined the importance of females of industriousness and dexterity" in addition to "modesty and submission." As for Maria Theresa, she was "quite unequivocal" when it came to the "necessity for total obedience and submission from the archduchesses."[24]

αβ

By 1760, Archduke Joseph of Austria was a teenager on the verge of manhood. In an era when death at a young age was commonplace, he was becoming famous for his robust constitution coupled with a tenacious personality. He was also considered one of the handsomest princes in Europe, with "an abundance of light brown hair, falling in curls over his shoulders, with an expressive, animated countenance, an aquiline nose, and a fine set of teeth."[25]

With a son becoming a man, Maria Theresa realized she would have to move quickly if she wanted to see Joseph matched up with a suitable royal bride. Ever the ambitious mother, she envisioned a spectacular future for her son. Maria Theresa was determined to see Joseph marry a princess who would make a glittering empress one day, but this was easier said than done.

Europe in the late eighteenth century was a political chess game of alliances and intrigues. A hundred years of warfare between the monarchical powers divided the continent. Prussia and Britain—traditional powerhouses and traditional enemies— became formal allies and reshaped the balance of power in Europe in what became known as the Diplomatic Revolution of 1756. Austria, Spain, and France, eager to preserve their own interests, banded together for the first time. It is interesting to note that this new political order brought a clean division between Catholic and Protestant Europe.

This new triumvirate caused a raucous reaction in Europe. The union of Austria and Spain under the Habsburgs was still a recent memory, but an alliance with France was an unprecedented move. The British minister in Vienna quickly confronted Maria Theresa about this change of foreign policy. "I am far from being French in my disposition," she told him, "and do not deny that the court of Versailles has been my bitterest enemy;...[but] I have little to fear from France." The British minister retorted, "Will you, the empress and archduchess, so far humble yourself as to throw yourself into the arms of France?" "Not into the arms," she shot back, "but on the side of France."[26]

During the ensuing peace process, Maria Theresa and her male counterparts—King Carlos III of Spain and King Louis XV of France—discovered that they each had large families with many children. It cannot be said for certain who first suggested the idea, but these three influential rulers agreed to the marriages of their royal children. Known as the Family Pact, this one piece of paper drafted and signed in Madrid, Versailles, and Vienna would single-handedly determine the destinies of Maria Theresa's five reigning children.

The Archduke Joseph was the first of his siblings to have his life impacted by this document. In searching for a wife for Joseph, Maria Theresa was anxious to see him marry a member of King Carlos III's family. The Habsburgs once ruled Spain, and the Empress dreamt of seeing these two reigning houses reunited. Carlos III was motivated less by imperial ambition and more by fatherly affection. This legendary king conveyed an aura of cold majesty, but he was actually a very warm, caring man. His motivation in signing the Family Pact was to see his children well established in life; he called it an *"affaire de Coeur*, not an *affaire politique*."[27]

Like Empress Maria Theresa, King Carlos III was a person of remarkable talents and ambitions. By the time he was forty, he had already graced three European thrones. A son of the first Bourbon king of Spain after the Habsburg line died out, the former Infante Carlos was called to take over the reins of power in Italy, first as Duke of Parma in 1732. After successfully leading an army to victory against the Austrians in the War of the Polish Succession of 1733-1738, Don Carlos became the first modern king of Naples and Sicily in 1735, taking the name Carlo VII. But when his half-brother, King Fernando VI of Spain, died childless in 1759 he returned to Madrid to reign as King Carlos III.

Carlos also had a large family that could (and would) be easily married into the other reigning houses of Europe. When he signed the Family Pact, Carlos hoped to arrange happy and prosperous marriages for his thirteen children. He also represented the interests of his brother Philip, Duke of Parma. If success was measured by connections, the scope of Carlos III's family gave him the monopoly on Europe. He was the father of two future kings and an empress, and was destined to be the grandfather of an emperor, an empress, two kings, and five queens. In the company of such distinguished relatives, Carlos's niece, the renowned Princess Isabella of Parma, was considered a perfect wife for Joseph of Austria.

The Etiquettes of Greatness

Olive-skinned, with raven hair and deep, dark eyes, Isabella of Parma was born on December 31, 1741 in Madrid. Her mother, Princess Élisabeth of France, was the favorite daughter of Louis XV. Her father, Don Felipe, was a Spanish infante who became the Duke of Parma in 1748 and took the name Philip. Isabella's childhood was happily divided between the courts of Madrid, Versailles, and Parma.

The complex marriages between Europe's royal families meant that Isabella was a granddaughter of Louis XV, a niece of Carlos III, and a granddaughter of Spain's King Philip V. Her exotic beauty and royal bloodline made her an irresistible daughter-in-law for Maria Theresa. The Empress's ambassadors arrived in Parma in 1760 to formally request Isabella's hand in marriage. After she met with the ambassadors and received the proposal, Isabella declared: "I am exceedingly flattered by so distinguished a preference over the other Princesses of Europe, as their Imperial Majesties have shewn [sic] in chusing [sic] me for the wife of their eldest son."[1]

Maria Theresa was delighted when Isabella accepted. Her ambassador to France, the Comte Mercy d'Argenteau, commented that, "at eighteen her [Isabella's] attainments would have been thought remarkable in a clever young man."[2] But Joseph, ever the rebellious and independent youth, had very strong feelings about the match. He wrote to his friend, Count Salm: "I will do everything to win her respect and confidence. But love? No. I cannot play the agreeable, the amateur. That goes against my nature."[3]   All that changed the day he was presented with Isabella's portrait. He was instantly enchanted by this "dark-eyed Italian of remarkable beauty." Eventually, "everything he heard about her confirmed his resolution to marry nobody else."[4]

The wedding—held on September 7, 1760 at the sand-colored Romanesque cathedral in Padua—was, of course, a proxy ceremony. Doing two ceremonies was the accepted practice at the time, because it let Isabella travel to Vienna with her new rank and titles. Standing in for Archduke Joseph as groom was Prince Wenzel Liechtenstein, a member of the Austrian court.

Isabella was faced with a tremendous responsibility being placed upon her shoulders. She was expected to be the Holy Roman empress; to continue a dynasty; and to cement a new era of peace for the continent. This seemed overwhelming to the nineteen-year-old princess. "What should the daughter of a great prince expect?" she once asked. "Born the slave of other people's prejudices, she finds herself subjected to the weight of honours, these innumerable etiquettes attached to greatness...a sacrifice to the supposed public good."[5] Isabella understood all too well "the sadness [that] Princesses endure in having to marry into foreign countries."[6]

Within days of her marriage, the exquisite Isabella left Parma forever, escorted by "a fleet of splendid Austrian equipages" provided by Joseph's parents.[7] Waiting to greet her at Vienna's gates was her new father-in-law, Emperor Francis I. As the bridal procession wound its way through the city's narrow streets, the people were in awe of the more than six hundred golden carriages filled with dignitaries, ladies-in-waiting, members of Isabella's household, and personal belongings. Their destination was the hunting lodge at Laxenburg where Joseph and the Empress were anxiously awaiting their arrival.

When Joseph and Isabella finally came face to face, it was a moment of outward formality; he stiffly bowed and she fell into a deep curtsey. But inwardly, when Joseph laid eyes on Isabella he was swept off his feet. He knew from her portrait that she was beautiful, but when he saw her for the first time, he fell deeply in love with her stunning features.

The "official" wedding took place on October 7, 1760. Despite being enamored with Isabella, Joseph was still nervous on his wedding day. "I am more afraid of marriage than of battle," he said.[8] The ceremony was held at the Church of the Augustine Friars. A forbidding medieval cathedral in the heart of Vienna, it was the traditional parish of the imperial family. Once the Archbishop declared the couple husband and wife, Joseph, dressed in the stylish black and red of the Habsburgs, and Isabella, wearing a voluminous white dress, left the church in a gold and silver state carriage. It took hours for the incredibly long procession to move through the city because of the thousands of people lining the streets to witness the blessed event.

In the days that followed, celebrations "went on for days, balls and banquets and gaudy outdoor displays [were] following one another in giddy succession."[9] After the ceremony, Empress Maria Theresa gave her opinion to her husband: "I am completely happy. The weather, the festivities, everything, in short, was all that could be desired. I quite forgot that I was a King. I was so happy as a mother."[10] How misleading the day's events—and her feelings—would prove to be. There were few indications, if any, that things would go wrong.

Already after a few weeks of marriage, it became obvious that there was a great chasm separating Joseph and Isabella, but this was not necessarily a bad thing at first. Their differences complimented one another. Maria Theresa wrote a few days after the wedding that they had "gained a charming daughter-in-law in every respect."[11] The entire imperial family was taken with Isabella. But Joseph's marriage marked the beginning of a difficult and tumultuous period in the archduke's life. The sad irony was that neither Joseph nor his young bride knew how very brief their time together would be. Isabella would not even live long enough to become empress.

The eighteenth century saw smallpox spread through the reigning houses of Europe like wildfire. There was not a king, queen, prince, or princess who had not lost someone to this dreaded disease. The imperial House of Habsburg was no exception to this.

During the family's stay at the Hofburg in January 1761, Maria Theresa's favorite son Charles died of smallpox. The local newspapers reported the sad news that "his Royal Highness was seized unexpectedly with a new and violent paroxysm last Saturday after midnight... He died with courage, resignation, and calmness." But the papers also cut right to the heart of the issue, saying that "Maria Theresia was all the more prostrated by this loss because it was just this son she loved best of all, and especially more than the Crown Prince, as he had always been so much less self-willed, and more obedient to his parents."[12]

In the midst of their grief, the Emperor and Empress were now confronted with a succession crisis for the second time in their reign. It centered on the tiny nation of Tuscany, in faraway Italy, where neglect and natural disasters threatened to wreak havoc on this ancient and beautiful country.

Since 1530 the legendary Medici family controlled Tuscany, ruling as grand dukes. When the last Medici ruler died childless in 1737, Emperor Francis I was given ownership of the country when he renounced his claims on Lorraine. He and Maria Theresa reigned there for three years, but returned to Vienna after the death of Maria Theresa's father, Emperor Charles VI. Francis's election as Holy Roman emperor prevented him from ever returning to Tuscany's capital, Florence, to rule. This worked out badly for the Tuscan people, because the governing of their country was left to inept ministers who drove the economy into the ground.

Once he became emperor, Francis had planned for his son, Charles, to rule in Florence as grand duke when he died. But now that Charles was gone, the candidature of Archduke Leopold looked ideal. By now he was fourteen, and had matured into a smart, thoughtful young man with a good dose of common sense and much of his mother's political intuition. His parents decided that he would replace Charles "as his father's Lieutenant in Tuscany during his life, and to succeed as [Grand] Duke at the Emperor's death."[13]

The teenage Poldy found himself in a position where everything in his life was about to change. He was no longer just an extra son, a back-up heir in the event something happened to Joseph. But now he was expected to rule his own country one day. His relationship with his father got a new lease on life as well. Maria Theresa may have groomed Joseph, but as the heir to Tuscany, Leopold became the object of Francis's added devotion and care. A closeness began to enter their relationship that had not existed before.

Now that Poldy was being given his own country to rule when he came of age, there was no possible way he could still marry Princess Beatrix of Modena. She was her father's sole heiress, and Modena's laws demanded she have a husband who could carry on the family's rule. Since Leopold was now being prepared for Tuscany, another more suitable bride would have to be found. Since her son was destined to become a reigning grand duke, Maria Theresa wanted to see him paired with a wife of appropriate rank and prestige. The decision of Leopold's wife fell on one of the elder daughters of King Carlos III, the Infanta María Luísa.

All of these monumental decisions went forward with little or no input from Leopold himself. His mother and the King of Spain decided his future. Maria Theresa took a leading role in the negotiations over the marriage contract between Leopold and María Luísa. As an Austrian archduke, Leopold had a claim to the hereditary Habsburg lands, but María Luísa was sixth in line to the Spanish throne. The high infant mortality rate of the Spanish royal family meant there was a possibility she might be called upon to take the throne. This was an unpalatable option for King Carlos, who feared that a return of the Habsburgs to the Spanish throne would shift the balance of power in Europe away from the Bourbon dynasty. In the end, it was decided that María Luísa would have to forfeit her claims to Spain. This was not extraordinary, since a "formal renunciation was frequently asked of departing princesses in order to prevent a foreign dynasty from trying to acquire the family throne if the male succession failed."[14] In a counter offer, King Carlos (who already had a distant claim on Tuscany) demanded that since his daughter was forced to give up her place in the succession, Leopold *must* marry her otherwise he would forfeit the grand duchy.

As the head of a powerful dynasty, Maria Theresa never liked being dictated to by other rulers. She always swallowed her pride, however, when it was necessary. The process of the marriage contract was long, but she and Carlos III reached an understanding on all the most important issues. The dates were decided as well: the proxy wedding would be in 1764, but the actual ceremony would be put off until 1765. Within only a few short years, these young royals would be bound together, uniting two of the most powerful reigning houses in the world. But in the process, the Habsburgs would face their greatest crisis in a quarter of a century.

❦

Because of their closeness in age, Maria Carolina ("Charlotte") and Maria Antonia ("Antoine") had a strong bond with one another; the two archduchesses "were raised almost as though they were twins."[15] But there were still some noticeable differences between the sisters. The future Queen of Naples possessed strong features for a child, and she was not considered as beautiful as Antoine. Charlotte was "large, raw-boned and bulky...with a pinched face and a severe expression." Added to this was a high-spirited and headstrong personality that became a constant source of frustration for Maria Theresa.[16]

Since Charlotte and Antoine were the youngest daughters in the imperial family, neither of them spent much time in the public spotlight. In their young minds, this was ideal because it meant more time undisturbed in their own little world. They played in the sprawling nursery at the Hofburg and picked flowers in the lush gardens surrounding Schönbrunn.

During their early years, the archduchesses made friends with many of the other children at court. They became especially close with two princesses from Hesse named Charlotte and Louise, nieces of the reigning Landgrave of Hesse-Darmstadt, Louis IX. The Hesse girls often accompanied their Habsburg friends on play dates and other adventures. As teenagers and eventually young women, these four princesses would remain devoted friends, corresponding often. Antoine addressed them in her letters as her "dear Princesses." Never one to hide her feelings, Antoine did not mince words when it came to her friend Princess Charlotte: "All your family can be quite sure of my affection, but as for you, my dear Princess, I can't convey to you the depth of my feeling for you."[17]

The time that the archduchesses Charlotte and Antoine shared, both with friends and alone, meant a tremendous amount to these future queens. Until their deaths, both women stayed deeply committed to each other. Antoine recalled that her sister Charlotte taught her "that loving relationships with delightful female contemporaries could be like bastions in an unkind and puzzling world."[18] Not until her arrival in France a decade later did Marie Antoinette truly understand the power of these words.

In private, the sisters got into all sorts of mischief that left Maria Theresa confounded. They spent their time "playing childish tricks, making improper remarks, and longing for unsuitable and unreasonable amusements."[19] The differences in their personalities meant Maria Theresa had to deal with her daughters differently when they acted up. Antoine, naturally docile and obedient, needed little more than a stern warning; but Charlotte, the rebel archduchess, was forced to live under stricter conditions. She was lectured to say her prayers, attend lessons, and obey her governesses. More than once was she threatened by her mother with the words: "I warn you that you will be totally separated from your sister Antonia" if the antics continued.[20]

Maria Theresa was not the only person frustrated by Charlotte. "Willful and impetuous, convinced that she had been born to rule," the Archduchess was a strong force for her governesses to contend with.[21] The Empress was constantly occupied with "high political interests," and so would sometimes go for eight to ten days without seeing her children. To make up for her absence she "maintained a daily, punctilious correspondence" with her children's instructors.[22] Eventually the overworked governesses aimed at making themselves loved by Charlotte and her sisters. They engaged in the "blameable practice of indulgence" that was "so fatal to the future progress and happiness of infancy."[23] Sometimes it was just easier to bow to Charlotte's indomitable will than to resist her.

❧

Once he was married, Archduke Joseph would tell anyone who would listen that he was "unsurpassed in happiness" in his life.[24]

He told Maria Theresa, "My wife becomes ever more dear in my eyes."[25] Not only did he have a wife he adored, he also told his parents he was going to be a father. But for Isabella, Vienna was losing the glitz and glamour that had once been so appealing. Her life began turning from an enchanting fairytale into a maddening existence.

Great Britain's Queen Victoria aptly described royal marriages a century later when she said: "All marriage is such a lottery, the happiness is always an exchange—though it may be a very happy one—still the poor woman is bodily and morally the husband's slave. That always sticks in my throat. When I think of a merry, happy free young girl—and look at the ailing, aching state a young wife is generally doomed to—which you can't deny is the penalty of marriage."[26] Sadly for Isabella, this was a lottery she had lost. Her happiness had been traded off by her relatives for the hope that she might wear the imperial crown one day.

At first, Isabella "was never for an instant at a loss in Vienna,"[27] but her dark personality was beginning to show its true colors as a result of the type of life she was being forced to live. Her homes were now the palaces in and around Vienna. For a young, vibrant woman who was used to the cozy familiarity of the Parmesan court, Austria's stately palaces must have seemed cold and forbidding. Even more disheartening for Isabella was that, instead of her and Joseph being given a palace of their own, they were expected to live under the same roof as Maria Theresa and the rest of the imperial family.

Isabella's mental state began to crumble under the weight of her growing unhappiness. Hormones during her pregnancy exasperated her intense moods. Her thoughts became macabre and gothic and she claimed to be hearing voices. Maria Theresa and Francis I were horrified when she told them, "Death speaks to me in a distinct voice that rouses in my soul a sweet satisfaction."[28]

These disturbing thoughts went hand-in-hand with Isabella's manic personality. She was "neurotic to the extreme in her introspection," but at the same time possessed a keen ability to adapt to the moods of people and places. She was also deeply insightful and able to analyze people with great ease, especially her own husband. According to Isabella, Joseph was "not primarily emotional," but instead "often puts down caresses or words of endearment for flattery or hypocrisy unless one has established a sure claim to his esteem....Given esteem, friendship [with Joseph] follows as a matter of course." She also realized that when it came to Joseph's efforts to assert himself against the domination of his mother, it left him "cold, suspicious, and at times a little overbearing."[29]

With her husband often tied up in government business, Isabella spent most of her time in the care of doctors, especially during the final stages of her pregnancy. She suffered constant headaches, forcing her to withdraw into a prolonged confinement. Isabella occupied herself by writing essays and dissertations, many of which still exist in Austria's state archives today along with more than two hundred of her letters. Most of her papers were philosophical, covering a broad range of topics including education, the nature of masculinity, the superiority of all things French, and the failings of Italy. Growing up, Isabella had been extremely close with her mother, and the two lived for a time at the court of Versailles before joining her father in Parma. This instilled into the princess a deep love of all things French and an antipathy toward Italian life and culture.

When Isabella was with Joseph, she found him difficult to tolerate because of his overbearing and controlling nature. To compensate for her husband's shortcomings, she sought consolation in the company of her sister-in-law, Mimi, with whom she was far more at ease than with Joseph. Isabella came to harbor deep romantic feelings for Mimi, but as a true byproduct of Maria Theresa's court, the archduchess could never even acknowledge that aspect of their relationship.

The two women spent most of their time together, earning them the comparison to Orpheus and Eurydice. Isabella's "self-professed fascination" with Mimi only exacerbated the favoritism issue within the family.[30] Mimi became Isabella's closest confidante, but even she was not immune from her sister-in-law's dark thoughts. "Death is good. Never have I thought of it more than at present," she told Mimi.[31]

The root of Isabella's obsession with all things morbid and gothic can be traced back to the death of her mother Élisabeth, Duchess of Parma, from smallpox in 1759. When she was told that her mother had died, Isabella dropped to her knees and prayed for God to tell her how much longer she would live. A nearby clock chimed four times, so she thought she only had four days left. When the fifth day came, she assumed it would be four weeks, then four months, then finally she resolved she would not live to see her twenty-second birthday. This belief became the very foundation for her entire personality. To understand Isabella's obsession with death is to understand the very essence of who she was. Joseph never realized this and remained completely oblivious to his wife's state of being. For him, she was his remedy for all the worries of life. Once Isabella adapted herself to Joseph's moods, it blinded him completely to her dark personality.

One happy event that did take place in the midst of all these morose tribulations was the birth of Joseph and Isabella's first child—in March 1762—at the Hofburg. The delivery was difficult for the Archduchess, who had never been well during her pregnancy. The high hopes of the court were dashed, though, when the doctors announced that it was a girl, Theresa; the Empress had decreed that all first-born granddaughters were to be named after herself.

The sadness in Vienna that it was not a boy in no way diminished Joseph's love for his daughter and wife. On the contrary, little Theresa brought great joy to the imperial family. She also strengthened the bond between Maria Theresa and Isabella. The Empress found in her daughter-in-law a kindred spirit, another woman of great intelligence and wisdom. "The Empress is such a very good friend herself," Isabella once wrote.[32]

With his baby girl healthy and his wife recovering from the difficult labor, Joseph returned to his state duties. For the first time in his life he focused on the greater political responsibility being placed upon him. The young prince eagerly took on as many tasks as possible in an effort to better prepare him for the day he might be elected to the throne. One of those tasks included securing for himself a place on the *Staatsrath*, Austria's Council of State. Maria Theresa disapproved of her son's appointment to the council, which was little more than a vestige from the War of the Austrian Succession. He soon discovered that the council members had no real authority, and served only to clear out the departmental problems of the Empire. During the council sessions, Joseph was unimpressed by the "long and usually futile debates" that took place. "The endless speeches and long-winded explanations, were so far above me that I understood neither their import nor their relevance," he said.[33]

As Joseph's role in Austrian politics increased, so too did the fights with his mother. In many ways Joseph mirrored the Empress, which no doubt led to their constant battles over every imaginable issue. The Enlightenment was a particularly hot-button issue between mother and son. Joseph "consciously brought [the principles of the Enlightenment] into play, and then Maria Theresa resisted them stubbornly, bitterly sometimes, sometimes despairingly." Maria Theresa was horrified that her son "eagerly embraced the Enlightenment's principles, which she perceived as antithetical to his salvation and that of her subjects."[34] She did find some merit in Joseph's views, but the empress was also a pragmatist and knew that concessions to the old regime had to be made. Change, Maria Theresa was well aware, could not take place overnight. Joseph, on the other hand, was less diplomatic. By trying to make too many changes too fast, he would threaten to nearly tear the Holy Roman Empire and the Habsburg dominions apart one day.

4

"I Have Lost All"

*A*s Austria's imperial family prepared to celebrate Arch-duchess Theresa's first birthday in March 1763, Isabella discovered she was expecting her second child. But as the English author and statesman Nathaniel Wraxall noted: "neither the feelings of a mother, the attachment of her husband, nor the prospect of her own elevation to the highest dignity of the German Empire, could dissipate her habitual melancholy."[1] In fact, she did not care at all to become empress, saying: "I am not interested in that; I have no desire to be Queen of the Romans."[2]

Her thoughts continued to be consumed by death during her second pregnancy. She repeatedly told Mimi that she would not live long enough to give birth. When Mimi reminded her that her health was good, Isabella reaffirmed her belief that she would not live out the year. And when one of her ladies-in-waiting pointed out that by dying, Isabella would be leaving her first daughter behind, she remarked: "Do you think, then, that I shall leave you my little Thérèse? You will not have her more than six or seven years."[3]

In the summer of 1763, Isabella's obsession with death came to the fore again when the imperial family was returning from Laxenburg. As her carriage reached the top of a hill overlooking Vienna, she turned to her traveling companions and ominously declared: "Death is waiting for me there."[4] Joseph remained oblivious to the reality of his wife's existence. She was still his refuge in an overwhelming and burdensome world, but all of that was about to change. Isabella's dark predictions were about to prove tragically prescient.

In the last month of her pregnancy, she contracted that deadly predator that stalked the royal houses of Europe like a hungry lion, the dreaded smallpox virus. In her mind this was the end. She firmly believed she would succumb to the infection before giving birth. At first, her premonition seemed to be proved wrong and she began to recover, but the ordeal was so traumatic that she went into premature labor. On November 22, 1763 she delivered a daughter who died moments after being born. Isabella named her Christina in honor of her sister-in-law.

As Isabella struggled to recover, Empress Maria Theresa nursed her with the utmost tenderness "as if she had been her own child,"[5] but the trauma of giving birth while having smallpox was more than the archduchess could bear. Her life and death struggle began four days later. The imperial family gathered around Isabella's bed as she fought for her life. Maria Theresa wrote to her chancellor: "We are approaching the tragic end of an angel. All my joy, all my rest, died with this charming and unparalleled daughter."[6] As the sun set on November 27, 1762, Isabella took her last breath. When she died, Joseph collapsed at her bedside, exhausted with grief. Looking up at Leopold, his eyes filled with tears, he told his brother: "I have lost all. I wish you from all my heart as good a wife as mine was, but may the Lord protect you from a similar misfortune."[7]

Isabella's body, along with an infant-size coffin containing the body of Archduchess Christina, was ceremoniously taken to the imperial crypts from the Hofburg where they had rested in state for three days. The streets of Vienna were lined with silent mourners who wished to pay their last respects to the woman they hoped would one day be their empress. The imperial family, looking somber and dignified in black, walked the entire route behind the carriage bearing the coffins. The bodies were laid to rest in the Maria Theresa Vault of the imperial crypt, a group of ten linked catacombs where the Habsburgs had been buried for centuries.

The Austrian imperial family was devastated by Isabella's death. A month after the funeral, Maria Theresa wrote to her cousin Maria Antonia, Electress of Saxony: "This loss is closest to my heart. I loved her as my friend, my trusted one, everything."[8]

Joseph no longer knew how to cope with life. His brothers and sisters tried to comfort him as best they could. Mimi's attempt to console him was a dismal failure. Hoping to end his misery, she showed him letters Isabella had written to her claiming she never really loved Joseph, not the way he loved her. Mimi hoped this revelation would bring her brother back to some sense of normalcy, but it had the more understandable effect of driving him deeper into his grief. Archduke Joseph began to cut all his emotional ties with the outside world. His remedy to the pain was to feel nothing at all.

One person he continued to be close with was Isabella's father Don Philip, Duke of Parma. Joseph poured out his heartache to Philip a few weeks after the funeral:

> I never feel more consoled than when I am alone in my room, looking at the portrait of my beloved wife and reading through her writings and works. Since I have spent the whole day with her, I often think I see her before me; I speak to her, and this illusion comforts me...I have preserved all the slightest scraps of paper left by this adorable woman...I want to be able to show the whole world what a companion I possessed in her and how much she deserves to be mourned...I defy anyone to find a better marriage....
>
> I see my child perish in my arms, my wife expire, father and mother overcome with grief, all my family in despair, my dear father-in-law so emotionally afflicted, all Vienna in tears, all Europe sorrowing;...What a loss for humanity is a princess! what damage it does to the whole state, the whole family and unhappy me![9]

As Joseph wept for his wife and second daughter, Maria Theresa went to work trying to secure a second future for her distraught son. She threw herself into having him elected King of the Romans to succeed his father, Francis I.

The death of Isabella ended any hope of an heir being produced in the foreseeable future. Knowing full well her enemies would surely use this as an opportunity to wrestle the throne away from the Habsburgs, Maria Theresa resolved to do everything within her power to keep the crown within her family for another generation. After months of debate, the Electors voted unanimously to make Joseph the imperial heir. In March 1764, Joseph, Leopold, and their father traveled to the most German of cities, Frankfurt, for the coronation.

Frankfurt, the ancient city on the Main River, had been a thriving center of Germanic culture for nearly a thousand years. Since A.D. 855, German kings and emperors had journeyed to Frankfurt to be elected, and were crowned in nearby Aix-la-Chapelle. Joseph's ancestor, Emperor Maximilian II, began the tradition of imperial coronations in Frankfurt with his own in 1562. The ceremony remained unchanged for 200 years, and Joseph would be the next Habsburg crowned there.

The imperial coronation of 1764 was the last great display of royal panoply before the French Revolution. It brought together hundreds of royals, aristocrats, and clergy from across Germany and Austria until the city of Frankfurt overflowed. Attending the event were the entire Council of Electors including King Frederick II of Prussia; the Archbishops of Trier, Mainz, and Cologne; and the Electors Charles Theodore of the Rhine, Maximilian III of Bavaria, and Frederick August III of Saxony. Royal delegations also arrived from the dozens of other states that comprised the Empire.

The ceremony, on April 3, 1764, was a painful one for Joseph, who detested pomp and etiquette. Dressed in purple and white robes, he stood rigidly during the lengthy coronation in the magnificent *Römersaal*, with its high arched ceilings and vivid Gothic architecture. When the time came for Joseph to kneel on a crimson dais to be crowned by the three electoral archbishops, hundreds of royals watched with eyes locked on him, whispering to one another of the great spectacle of seeing a new King of the Romans.

For the men who were old enough to remember Francis I's coronation twenty years ago, the arrival of his son to be crowned was a momentous event that was hailed with the highest expectations. Joseph was only four when his parents were elected, and "at that time all happiness had been wished and prophesied, and to-day it was seen fulfilled in the first-born son; to whom everybody was well inclined on account of his handsome youthful form, and upon whom the world set the greatest hopes, on account of the great qualities that he showed."[10]

One of the guests at the coronation was the poet Johann von Goethe. The impressionable young writer vividly described how Emperor Francis I's robes "of purple-coloured silk, richly adorned with pearls and precious stones, as well as his crown, sceptre, and imperial orb, struck the eye with good effect." But Goethe drew a sharp contrast between the Emperor and Joseph. While Francis "moved...quite easily in his attire," evoking an image of imperial splendor, Joseph "dragged himself along" through the ceremony. According to Goethe, "the crown...stood out...like an overhanging roof" on Joseph's head.[11]

No sooner had the coronation ended than Empress Maria Theresa began pressing the issue of Joseph remarrying. It was imperative, she explained, that as the future emperor, her son must have an heir. Still in Frankfurt and completely heartbroken, Joseph felt that the only woman who could even come close to Isabella was her younger sister, Luisa of Parma. She was already betrothed to Carlos III's heir, the Prince of the Asturias, so when Maria Theresa asked to have Luisa released from the marriage contract, the Spanish king refused. When Joseph was told he could not marry Luisa, he wanted nothing to do with any future wedding plans. He placed the matter of his second marriage solely in the hands of his parents.

Maria Theresa worked long and hard to find a suitable wife for her son, but Joseph wrote to her constantly from Frankfurt begging her not to make him remarry:

Unless it be as proof of my love for you, dear mother, I will never marry again. The days which have just passed have torn open my wound cruelly. The image of my adorable wife is so deeply graven on my heart that at every moment it seems to me that she might return to me. When a courier is announced, I find myself half expecting news from her. And to think that it is all over. When I tell you that I am weeping as I write these words, you will understand the exceeding greatness of my sorrow.[12]

A few days later Joseph wrote to his mother again. He desperately tried to plead his case to her: "My election occurred on March 27, four months to a day since the departure of that dear spirit [Isabella]. On the twenty-ninth it was four months since I was separated from all of her that was mortal, and that was the day of my public entry into Frankfort [sic], What a difference it would have made if these ceremonies had been graced by the presence of my Queen. Forgive me dear mother, if I grieve you by these words, But have pity on a son who is deeply attached to you, but who is on the verge of despair."[13]

Maria Theresa's heart went out to her son, but her love as a mother was outweighed by her unfailing sense of duty. She knew it was vitally important that Joseph remarry, and that he produce an heir. The selection of new wife for Joseph became a high stakes political game in Vienna. Members of the Austrian court were nominating candidates who served their own interests. Mimi was strongly in favor of Princess Cunegunde of Saxony because she was passionately in love with the Cunegunde's brother, Prince Albert.

Maria Theresa's ambition led her on a hunt for a princess who could bring a certain level of significance with her. It just so happened that the Elector of Bavaria, Maximilian III, was eager to find a husband for his spinster sister, Princess Josepha. The thought of her son marrying Josepha was bittersweet for the Empress because the princess's father was none other than Charles Albert, the one-time Holy Roman emperor who sided against Maria Theresa in the War of the Austrian Succession.

The youngest daughter of Charles Albert, Princess Josepha was born on March 30, 1739 in Munich. As the youngest in a family of seven, Josepha spent her whole life stepping out of the spotlight in favor of her older siblings who were destined for lofty positions. Her brother Max became elector when their father died in 1745; one of her sisters married the Elector of Saxony; and another married the reigning Margrave of Baden-Baden.

When it came to putting this Bavarian princess on the list of candidates, Maria Theresa had to swallow her pride, and she hoped that Joseph would pick one of the other potential brides. They included the Infanta Benedicta of Portugal and Princess Elizabeth of Brunswick. For Joseph, his second marriage was of little importance. He had begun to come out of his mourning after returning to Vienna, but his bookish tendencies and workaholism were becoming more obvious. The Emperor and Empress were left at an impasse.

By April 1764, Maria Theresa had narrowed the list from four to two. The newly crowned King Joseph was forced to choose between the rotund, overweight Cunegunde of Saxony or "the short, thickset and pimpley" Josepha of Bavaria. The Empress even arranged for both women to be brought to Vienna so Joseph could meet them face-to-face. Both meetings were dismal at best. Afterwards, Francis and Maria Theresa were anxious to know their son's decision. "I prefer not to marry either," he told them bluntly, "but since you are holding the knife to my throat, I will take Josepha."[14]

The Empress could not help but express her misgivings about the engagement to her daughter Mimi:

> You are to have a sister-in-law, and I a daughter-in-law. Unfortunately, it is Princess Josepha. I hated settling this affair without my son's co-operation. But neither to me, nor to the Emperor, nor to Kaunitz [the state chancellor] would he express any preference....And the worst of it is that we must pretend to be pleased and happy. My head and my heart are not at one on this subject, and it is difficult to retain my equanimity.[15]

In the end, Maria Theresa gave her public approval to the marriage for the sake of the monarchy. After all, Princess Josepha was the daughter of a Holy Roman Emperor, however brief his reign might have been. King Joseph's marriage to his predecessor's daughter solidified the Habsburgs' seat on the imperial throne indefinitely because of the Austrian blood that coursed through Josepha's veins on her mother's side.*

Joseph was beside himself with loathing for his Bavarian bride and resented her with every fiber of his being. Writing to Don Philip of Parma, Joseph said she was "twenty-six years old, has a small squat figure, and is without youthful charm." He went on to cruelly describe her as having "red spots and pimples on her face; her teeth are hideous. She had no qualities, in fact, which would have persuaded me to resume the marital state in which I had once been so happy."[16]

By January 1765, all the plans had been finalized and the wedding was schedule to go forward. Maria Theresa hoped the ceremony would help lift the somber mood that prevailed at the court since the death of Isabella. In a desperate attempt to inject a little joy into the occasion, she found twenty-five young

---

* Josepha's mother, Archduchess Marie Amalie, was Maria Theresa first cousin. This made Joseph and Josepha second cousins.

couples to be married en masse with her son in the courtyard outside Schönbrunn. During the ceremony, held in the palace's Private Chapel, King Joseph was "mad with despair." The stunning Baroque architecture, marble pillars, and gold statues could not help dissolve the "funerally gloomy" atmosphere.[17] The glamour and pomp of the celebrations were little more than a façade to conceal a mourning king and an unloved queen.

During the ceremony and reception that followed, Archduke Leopold stood at his brother's side. But once his role in Joseph's second nuptial was finished, Leopold began preparing for his own wedding, which was scheduled for just a few months away.

Leopold and Joseph took one last opportunity to enjoy each other's company because, after his wedding, Leopold was bound for Florence. The plan was for him and his new wife to rule as representatives of Francis I. The two brothers spent much of their time alone, walking and talking in the streets of Vienna. The Empress was bothered by the amount of time they were spending together because, as she put it, Joseph did not always treat his younger brother with "the superiority and aloofness that Nature and your birth dictated." What Maria Theresa failed to realize was that Leopold had matured beyond his years. When the brothers were out together, this maturity made Joseph seem "rather [Leopold's] younger than his elder brother."[18]

Their mother's objections over etiquette did not stop Joseph and Leopold from bonding. Beginning in 1765, they would write to each other almost every week for the rest of their lives. This amounted to a staggering several thousand letters, published in numerous volumes. It was only in these correspondences that Joseph seemed to show any kind of real emotion. He wrote in one of this early letters to Leopold, "I embrace you with my whole heart and beg you to be persuaded that, though a hundred leagues distant, I love you and shall always esteem you beyond all expression."[19]

Sadly, this closeness would not last long. Within five years an irreparable chasm would separate the pair. They would continue their correspondence, but it would never be the same. On Leopold's part, the once-close relationship he had with his brother would begin to fade away. In its place would be a one-sided, placated association.

❦

By the summer of 1765, much to Maria Theresa's satisfaction, the preparations were in place for the much-anticipated wedding of Archduke Leopold to the Infanta María Luísa of Spain. Leopold wrote to a friend of the great delight his upcoming wedding was having on his entire family: "Never since I came into the world have I seen Their Majesties in such good humour and so gay. The joyful mood casts its rays on us all, and I can say that I have never been so happy as I am now."[20]

In a change of tradition, the wedding was being held in the town of Innsbruck, set against the backdrop of the mighty Tyrolean Alps, instead of in Vienna. Surrounded by towering snow-covered mountains and verdant green valleys, Innsbruck offered its own charm and beauty than the capital could not. The ceremony was held there because María Luísa's father worried that if his daughter was married in all the splendor of Vienna, she would "acquire a distaste for the comparatively quiet life of Florence" in which she was destined to reign at Leopold's side.[21]

At the end of July, the imperial family prepared to leave for Innsbruck, but there was an ominous sense of foreboding the morning they departed Vienna. Standing at the doors of Schönbrunn to say goodbye to her parents was Antoine, just shy of her tenth birthday. She was there with the other members of the family who were not attending the wedding, the younger children and Queen Josepha. Even at so young an age, the future Queen of France could feel something was wrong.

Suddenly at the last moment before he left, Emperor Francis paused, jumped off his horse and on some strange impulse, ran back to his youngest daughter for one last long embrace. Francis took Antoine on his knee and, with tears in his eyes, hugged her over and over again. "Adieu my dear little daughter," he said. "Father wished once more to press you to his heart."[22] Not until many years later did she believe her father had some strange premonition about "the great unhappiness that would be her lot."[23] Later, when the Empress asked Francis about it, the only explanation he could offer her was, "I wished to embrace this child once more."[24] Archduchess Maria Antonia would never see her father again.

From Vienna, Leopold and Francis traveled to the town of Bozen (part of modern-day Bolzano in northern Italy) to meet María Luísa; the Empress and the rest of the wedding party traveled on to Innsbruck. A fleet of legendary Spanish ships escorted the infanta from coastal Barcelona across the Mediterranean and into the Ligurian Sea where they docked in Genoa. From there, the cortège headed north to Bozen.

At twenty years of age, María Luísa was two years older than Leopold. Simple and unpretentious, loyal, inclined towards kindness and generosity, María Luísa was "a blue-eyed beauty of great liveliness and charm."[25] Her lovely dark curls rolled down her back, framing her narrow face and high cheekbones. Her long, pointed nose, typical of the House of Bourbon, accented her gentle smile. In personality, the infanta and the archduke complimented each other. Where he could be cold and withdrawn, she was naturally warm and kind.

Upon Leopold's arrival at Innsbruck with his father and fiancée, a twenty-day drama began to unfold. During the trip to Bozen, he caught a chill. By the time he rejoined his family it had become full-blown pleurisy. Four days later, on August 4, 1765, Leopold and María Luísa were married at the Hofkirche, the Gothic imperial church of Innsbruck. Wedding guests watching the ceremony were seated between eight marble pillars lining walls that were decorated by twenty-eight bronze statues of the greatest heroes in Habsburg history. Like a daunting monolith, the black marble cenotaph of Emperor Maximilian I stood in the middle of the church. As the archbishop conducted the ceremony, Leopold stood at the golden altar struggling to breathe, his lungs inflamed by pleurisy and cutting off his air supply. Sweat rolled down his face as he fought to recite his wedding vows. As soon as they were declared husband and wife, his attendants rushed the archduke off to bed.

What should have been one of the happiest days of Leopold's life was instead filled with anxiety and fear. The crowds gathered outside the Hofkirche to wish the couple all the happiness were disheartened to see Leopold being rushed into a carriage. The Empress, standing at María Luísa's side for support, was consumed with grief and worry over her son's health. By the next day his condition had worsened. He was suffering from a serious fever and appeared to be at death's door. Leopold spent his first days as a husband surrounded by physicians who were helpless to act while he endured coughs, chills, and excruciating chest pain. María Luísa and the rest of the family held a silent, prayerful vigil at his bedside as a priest prepared to offer him the Last Sacraments.

After two terrible weeks, the anxious atmosphere at Innsbruck came to an end when Leopold showed signs of recovery. Within a few days the doctors declared he was out of danger. The sad irony was that no one realized this was only the beginning of the great trials the Habsburgs were about to face.

Towards the end of August, Leopold showed enough of an improvement that his parents decided to go ahead with some of the celebrations that had been planned for the wedding. While Maria Theresa and the archduchesses held a dinner party at their Innsbruck palace, King Joseph and Emperor Francis attended the opera on the night of August 18, 1765.

The Emperor had been feeling unwell during the entire visit, which he blamed on the mountain air: "Oh! If I could once quit these mountains of the Tyrol!"[26] Francis believed he could manage his health well enough to accompany Joseph that night. His sister, Princess Charlotte of Lorraine, was the abbess at a convent in Innsbruck and begged the Emperor to be bled, but he refused, saying, "I must go to the opera, and I am engaged afterward to sup with Joseph."[27] During the performance, Francis began complaining of discomfort. The weighty emperor rose to his feet and stumbled out of the imperial box. Clasping a nearby curtain for support, he collapsed "as if struck by lightning."[28] Joseph shot up out of his chair and ran to his father's side. Taking his father in his arms, Joseph's eyes filled with tears. It was too late. Emperor Francis I died of a massive stroke.

A frenzied chaos swept over the Innsbruck opera house when it was realized that the Emperor was dead. Messengers flew from the theatre to break the tragic news to the Empress and her daughters. In one of the few dramatic moments of her life, Maria Theresa "displayed the kind of grief that had once characterized her ancestor, Juana [the Mad] of Spain."[29] That night, she locked herself in "her own room [and] plunged herself into terrible grief and cried upon her bed for hours.[30]

Prince Albert of Saxony, a member of the court who had accompanied the family to Innsbruck, recalled the night the Emperor died: "Never shall I forget that evening; the Archduke [Leopold] ill in bed; the Archduchesses prostrate with grief."[31] The next day when Maria Theresa finally worked up the courage, she poured out her grief to her children in Vienna:

> Our calamity is at its height; you have lost a most incomparable father, and I a consort—a friend—my heart's joy, for forty-two years past! Having been brought up together, our hearts and our sentiments were united in the same views. All the misfortunes I have suffered during the last twenty-five years were softened by his support. I am suffering such deep affliction, that nothing but true piety and you, my dear children, can make me tolerate a life which, during its continuance, shall be spent in acts of devotion.[32]

The empress sent a similar message to Leopold, who was still recovering from his attack of pleurisy: "Nothing but complete acceptance of God's will can help me beat this blow. You have lost the best and tenderest father. I have lost everything, a tender husband, a perfect friend, my only support, to whom I owe everything. You, dear children, are the sole legacy of this great prince and tender father; try to deserve by your conduct all my affection which I now reserved for you alone."[33]

Joseph was similarly grief-stricken. Although he did not know it at the time, he would have the heartbreaking distinction of watching both his parents die in his arms. In a letter to his sisters in Vienna, Joseph reaffirmed his mother's words, telling them that they "have lost the best of fathers and the best of friends."[34]

The sudden death of Emperor Francis I sent shockwaves across Europe. He had always been healthy and strong with a zest for life, so his death at fifty-six came completely by surprise. The Empress held a brief court in Innsbruck to make the formal announcement and accept the condolences of the courtiers. Even in her despair, Maria Theresa's generous spirit came to the fore when she invited her husband's longtime mistress, the Princess von Auersperg, to mourn with her. "How much we both of us have lost!" the empress told her.[35]

The emperor's remains were taken by ship upriver to Vienna where his body lay in state for three days. The trip back was a painful one for Maria Theresa, who wrote: "I am letting myself be dragged back to Vienna, wholly and solely to assume the guardianship of nine orphans. They are greatly to be pitied. Their good father idolised them and could never refuse them anything. It will be changed times now. I am exceedingly anxious about their future, which will be decided in the course of the next winter."[36]

At the end of August, Europe assembled to bid farewell to Emperor Francis I. Crowds numbering in the thousands packed the streets of Vienna to catch a glimpse of the imperial family. The Empress was dressed completely in widow's black, a tradition she would keep for the rest of her life. After a moving and emotional state funeral, Emperor Francis I was laid to rest in the imperial crypt alongside his family.

As a lasting tribute to his children, Francis wrote a moving letter entitled "Instructions to my Children both for their Spiritual and Temporal Lives." It touched on his endearing love for them and his hope that they would live strong Christian lives:

T'is to prove to you after my death that I loved you during my lifetime that I leave you these instructions, as rules by which you may regulate your conduct, and as precepts from which I have ever derived benefit....

[God] alone can give us not only our eternal heritage, which is our real happiness, but our only true satisfaction in this world.... It is an essential point, and one which I know not how to impress upon you strongly enough, never under any circumstances whatsoever to deceive yourselves about what is wrong, or try to think it innocent....

I herewith command you to read these instructions twice yearly; they come from a father who loves you above everything, and who has thought it necessary to leave you this testimony of his tender affection, which you cannot better reciprocate than by loving one another with the same tenderness he bequeaths to all of you.[37]

These last words of the Emperor made a profound impression on the lives of his children, especially Charlotte and Antoine.

These two future queens of Naples and France would cherish their father's memory for the rest of their tumultuous lives.

PART II

An Empire Divided

(1765—1780)

One Empire, Two Crowns

Maria Theresa's world was completely shattered by the death of her husband. The intensity of her grief can clearly be seen in her letters and journal entries from the weeks and months that followed. "All that I have left is my grave," she wrote to her old friend, Countess Sophie Enzenberg. "I await it with impatience because it will reunite me with the sole object that my heart has loved in this world and which has been the object and goal of all my deeds and sentiments. You realize the void in my life since he has left."[1]

The empress's obsession with her husband's death went so deep that she recorded in her prayer book the exact length of his life, down to the hour: "Emperor Francis, my husband, lived 56 years, 8 months, 10 days, and died on August 18, 1765, at 9:30 P.M. So he lived: Months 680, Weeks 2,958 ½, Days 20,778, Hours 496,991. My happy marriage lasted 29 years, 6 months, and 6 days."[2]

Scarcely had Emperor Francis I been buried before Joseph's true colors began to show themselves. Calling himself Joseph II, Maria Theresa's ambitious twenty-four-year-old son declared to his widowed mother that he was ready to take his place as emperor. But the formidable Maria Theresa was not ready to hand over the throne just yet.

The Holy Roman Empire faced an impasse. Joseph was the rightful heir to the imperial throne, but Maria Theresa was the reigning sovereign of the Habsburg monarchy and its crown lands. The Council of Electors, who recognized Joseph's claim to the throne as King of the Romans, called an emergency diet in Frankfurt to decide what should be done. In November 1765 they reached a decision and gave Empress Maria Theresa an ultimatum: share the throne with Joseph or abdicate.

Unwilling to surrender any of the power she had worked so hard to achieve, Maria Theresa was forced to accept this compromise. On November 18, 1765, a co-regency of the Holy Roman Empire and the Habsburg monarchy was declared between Joseph II and Maria Theresa. The Empress made the announcement that she and her son "have decided for a co-regency of our entire hereditary kingdoms and lands."[3] But she made it abundantly clear that she was agreeing to this arrangement "without surrendering the whole or any part of our personal sovereignty over our states, which will be kept together and moreover without the least actual or apparent breach of the Pragmatic Sanction."[4]

As the new emperor, Joseph inherited a long list of proud and majestic titles that included:

> Holy Roman Emperor, Apostolic King of Dalmatia, Croatia, Slavonia, Galicia, and Lodomeria; Archduke of Austria; Duke of Burgundy, Lorraine, Bar, Styria, Carinthia, Carniola, Brabant, Limburg, Luxemburg, Geldern, Württemberg, Upper and Lower Silesia, Milan, Mantua, Parma, Piacenza, Guastalla, Auschwitz, and Zator; Grand Prince of Transylvania; Margrave of Moravia, the Holy Roman Empire, Burgau, and Upper and Lower Lusatia; Prince of Swabia; Prince-Count of Habsburg, Flanders, the Tyrol, Hennegau, Kyburg, Görz, and Gradisca; Count of Namur; Lord of the Windisch March and Mecheln.[5]

The happiness that should have gone hand-in-hand with Joseph's accession was overshadowed by the intense friction that began taking hold at the Austrian court in the winter of 1765-1766. The old ministers supported Maria Theresa, but the young idealists threw their lot in with Joseph II. The Empress continued to be at odds with her son's views on the Enlightenment, which she believed was full of "erroneous views, from those wicked books whose authors parade their cleverness at the expense of all that is most holy and most worthy of respect in the world, who want to introduce an imaginary freedom which can never exist and which degenerates into license and into complete revolution."[6]

This clash of personalities only exacerbated the love-hate relationship Joseph had with his mother. This was a source of deep anguish for Maria Theresa, who had so many high hopes for the type of man Joseph could become. She expressed her anxieties in a letter to him: "What is at stake is not only the welfare of the State, but your salvation, that of a son who since his birth has been the one purpose of all my actions, the salvation of your soul."[7]

Another point of contention for Emperor Joseph was his second marriage, which was proving to be a disappointment. There was no trace of the happiness and bliss he had experienced with Isabella. Partly still embittered over her death, and resentful of having to marry a woman he did not love, Joseph was terribly unhappy and treated Josepha with utter disdain. He almost completely ignored her, and those times when he did speak to her, he was so cruel that "she would turn pale, tremble, stammer, and sometimes burst into tears."[8] He often called her ugly, and heaped other insults at her. Joseph frequently reminded his wife of her failings, and defiantly refused to have a child with her. "I would try to have children, if I could put the tip of my finger on the tiniest part of her body that was not covered by boils," he said.[9]

Empress Josepha became a pariah in Austria. According to one historian: "Josepha was anything but pretty. She was two years older than Joseph, but many of the Viennese vowed she was old enough to be his mother, and some thought the Elector of Bavaria had cheated the groom by sending an aunt instead of a sister. The Viennese had no use for a Queen who was not pretty, and were unable to conceal their disappointment."[10]

Josepha's position brought her little respect, and she lived a solitary life devoid of any real friends. She spent most of her time in her apartments alone, crying. Her strained relationship with Joseph II meant the imperial court wanted nothing to do with her for fear of the Emperor's wrath. Even Mimi could not help but sympathize with her sister-in-law, saying, "I believe that if I were his wife and so maltreated I would run away and hang myself on a tree in Schönbrunn."[11] The only person who showed Josepha any type of kindness had been Emperor Francis

I, but now he was gone. Whenever she could, Empress Josepha escaped to Baden where she would hold her own private little court and throw lavish dinner parties, but they were "usually unhonored by the presence of her husband."[12]

Rather than accept responsibility for his wife's misery, Joseph threw himself into his new role as emperor. Indignant towards his wife and mother, he saw women in power as nothing but hindrances. During that first year of the co-regency, Joseph seemed to bounce from one conflict to the other. When he was not fighting with his mother, he was harassing his wife. When he grew tired of Josepha's tears, he returned to state business, but no concession Maria Theresa made ever seemed to be enough for him.

As she approached middle age, Maria Theresa felt overwhelmed by her son's unending hostility. She found him to be "sharp, hypercritical...curmudgeonly and unpredictable."[13] Desperate to make peace, the Empress sent her son a heartfelt note: "I offer you my whole confidence, and ask you to call my attention to any mistakes I might make....Help a mother who for thirty-three years has had only you, a mother who lives in loneliness, and who would die when she sees all her efforts and sorrows gone to waste. Tell me what you wish and I will do it."[14]

☙

After the dramatic state funeral for Emperor Francis I, Archduchess Amalia watched as her mother surrendered to her grief. So ruined was the once great and powerful empress that as a symbol of her mourning, "she cut off the hair of which she had once been so proud," covered her apartments in "sombre velvet," and wore only "widow's black for the rest of her life." Empress Maria Theresa was only a shadow of "the strong, young mother" who once claimed that "had she not been perpetually pregnant [she would have] ridden into battle herself."[15]

From this point on in her life, everything about Amalia's mother was "dark and mournful." It became clear to her children that Maria Theresa was projecting her profound feelings of hurt and loss onto them. She became "universally dissatisfied" with their behavior. In time, she developed a deep resentment and reproach to anyone who could still enjoy life.[16] Living without Francis was so unbearable for Maria Theresa that she longed for the "barren waste of Innsbruck where I had concluded my happy days, because I can enjoy no more; the sun itself seems dark to me. These three months seem to me like three years..."[17]

Maria Theresa's perennial mourning made life difficult for the archduchesses, who once told a courtier they would gladly have a tooth pulled to break the tedium of their mother's court. Amalia, who had rarely been in her mother's good graces to begin with, had an especially difficult time coping with Maria Theresa's depression. But her sisters Elizabeth and Mimi continued to enjoy their mother's unbridled favor.

In April 1766, Mimi shocked and horrified her sisters when she actually took advantage of their mother's grief to secure for herself a future of her own making. Mimi was passionately in love with Prince Albert of Saxony, but it was a well-known fact that this lower German princeling was hardly worthy of marrying the empress's favorite daughter. When Francis I died, Mimi realized she could manipulate her mother into doing whatever she wanted. In this case, she used her position to approve her wedding to Albert.

Mimi's marriage was hard on the Empress's already taxed emotional state. Maria Theresa told her daughter on her wedding day: "My heart has received a blow which it feels especially on a day such as this. In eight months I have lost the most adorable husband...and a daughter who after the loss of her father was my chief object, my consolation, my friend."[18] If it were not enough for Amalia to watch her sister act so shamefully, it was even worse when the Empress elevated Albert's status by giving him the Duchy of Teschen as a wedding gift, and appointing the couple as the governors of the Austrian Netherlands.* Mimi's favor with the Empress evoked "the jealousy of her sisters for whom less romantic fates were reserved."[19]

With her husband dead, her favorite daughter married, and her son trying to force her out of government, Maria Theresa resolved that "nothing...would interrupt her sedulous policy of planning her children's marriages."[20] She possessed "a lively

---

* Upon their marriage, Albert and Mimi became the Duke and Duchess of Saxe-Teschen. They will be referred to by these titles from this point forward.

desire to see them well established in the world."[21] But for Amalia this was disastrous, because she had already fallen in love.

❧

Leopold and María Luísa were forced to part ways with Maria Theresa and the imperial family when they departed Innsbruck for Vienna in August 1765. Before she left, Maria Theresa composed a long, emotional letter to Leopold in which she touched on the many challenges that lay ahead of him:

> I find it necessary to put into writing the rule, which we maintain at our court..., and of which were are very pleased. In a distant and young court it is so much more necessary to take precautions, and to take note of morals, without which one could fall into large disadvantages, doubts, cabals, uncertainties, which in this case...could cause the largest misfortunes...It is our tenderness and care, which makes us dictate these orders, and I want to believe, that not only will my dear children observe, but that they will follow them exactly and not act differently....
>
> Your temperament is weakened; you do not trust too much and think that you are less forceful than others. But if you take good advice, if you live moderately, if you do not hide anything,...I hope to see you remain a strong and robust prince....
>
> This same instruction extends to your wife and the rest of the family. On this occasion alone you can and must act as the husband and chief of your house, without showing any kindness [to your ministers]. Your wife swore to you at the altar to be obedient and submissive; it is only on this occasion that you will act as Master, on all others you will be a tender, true, and friendly husband.[22]

This letter made a profound impression on Leopold, and he spent the weeks that followed contemplating his mother's words. He had ample time to do this on the long journey to Florence, the capital of his new grand duchy of Tuscany. His father's death meant Leopold was now the reigning Grand Duke. Accompanying him and María Luísa were only a handful of Austrian advisors (handpicked by Maria Theresa), several Florentine ladies-in-waiting, and Leopold's childhood instructor and friend, Count Francis Thurn.

After two long weeks of traveling, out of Upper Austria, over the Brenner Pass, and on to Italy, the couple arrived in Florence in the early morning hours of September 13, 1765. At their new home, the Pitti Palace, Grand Duke Leopold and his wife were greeted by Francis I's aging ministers. A massive triumphal arch at the palace was built in their honor and kept illuminated by floodlights all night. Among the crowd of politicians welcoming Leopold was a member of the British Legation in Florence, Sir Horace Mann, who would become a familiar face at the Tuscan court. Only hours before the Grand Duke arrived, Mann had reported back to his superiors in London the mood of the people: "We are at the Eve of the Great Duke's arrival, and nobody knows what he is to do."[23]

In the days leading up to Leopold's arrival, there was a genuine sense of uncertainty among Florence's smart set. Tuscany had not had a grand duke for two generations, leaving some to wonder what the son of Maria Theresa would be like as a ruler. By the morning of September 14, confusion and uneasiness had been transformed into heartfelt excitement. The buildings in Florence were draped with the nation's red-and-white flag marked with the Tuscan crest, and portraits of Francis I and Maria Theresa were hung from buildings. Later that morning, Leopold and María Luísa appeared on the balcony of the Pitti Palace before a crowd numbering in the thousands. Upon witnessing the devotion of the people for the Grand Duke and Duchess, Horace Mann happily reported that the "Florentines seem very pretty sensible of their good fortune in having a Prince again to live among them, after thirty years' bondage under inexperienced Lorraine ministers and others so little fit and desirous to contribute to their welfare."[24]

Within a few days of arriving in Tuscany, Leopold (who was only eighteen at the time) was confronted by no less than one ministerial crisis, flooding in the provinces, and a famine that was crippling Florence. Leopold threw himself entirely into pulling his country of out the trenches with the goal of raising it to a place of prosperity. But he was still hampered by his sullen, melancholy personality, which at times bordered on suspicion and paranoia. He was forced to rely heavily on the input of his ministers, and the advice that came directly from Maria Theresa in Vienna. The Empress wrote to her son weekly, reminding him that he was "a German prince" above all else and should even institute German as the official court language. She could also be tender in her letters, and exhorted him: "Prove yourself a good Son to the Holy Father in all matters of religion and dogma. But be sovereign...in governmental affairs."[25]

More independent than many of his other siblings, Leopold did not always heed his mother's advice. There were numerous times when Maria Theresa threatened that if he did not follow her orders, his reign would fail. The Grand Duke chose not to respond to those letters, which caused Maria Theresa to complain "bitterly" to the people around her. Instead, she resorted to using her informal spies to check up on Leopold's progress, including Francis Thurn's own wife.[26]

Leopold and María Luísa's new home was the famous Pitti Palace, but "this severe, almost forbidding, building" left a lot to be desired.[27] It was built on the south side of the Arno River in Florence, and was an empty, cavernous old building. Its oldest wings dated back to 1458 and were decaying and in bad need of repairs. One contemporary described Pitti as nothing more than "a very noble pile...which makes it look extremely solid and majestic."[28] Leopold and his wife had their work cut out for them when they moved in. With a royal suite of only fourteen rooms, little artwork or other furnishings, and only one tiny room for bathing, it would take great effort in the years to come, especially on María Luísa's part, to turn it into a home.

From the moment he set foot in Tuscany, Leopold tried as best he could to become a conscientious ruler, giving much of himself to his new subjects. Far from being content to just be an idle grand duke, he tackled as many of the country's immediate problems as he could. He "found it [Tuscany] a weak and disorganized state fallen into the decay which often befell provinces which were not the centers of a court life and an active policy."[29] To help relieve the devastating famine in Florence, he redirected Tuscany's already-limited resources and paid large sums out of his own pockets to peasants who were starving. María Luísa, who herself was a kind, compassionate woman, supported her husband wholeheartedly and likewise gave to the city's poor and starving. Praised as a "model of feminine virtue,"[30] the Grand Duchess arranged for charity relief and medical treatment for those in need.

In those difficult early days of his reign, Grand Duke Leopold's "good sense and benevolence soon taught him that the monarch's prosperity depended on that of the people, his power on their affection, and his real dignity on the union of both."[31] This concept of the strong relationship that needed to exist between a ruler and his people made a profound impact on Leopold's life, especially when he would be called upon to be emperor one day.

Nearly a year after arriving in Tuscany, the welcome news came that María Luísa was expecting a baby. There was great anticipation over the Grand Duchess's impending *accouchement*, since Joseph II declared he would have no more children. He made his position clear to Maria Theresa: "My mind is made up, dear mother. I believe, that I am doing well by God, by the state, by myself, by you, and by the world."[32] Maria Theresa hoped and prayed the baby would be the much-coveted son and heir.

The pregnancy proved difficult for María Luísa who, true to her nature, never complained. The model of a strict Catholic upbringing, she wholeheartedly embraced pregnancy and motherhood as the role of a proper God-fearing woman. Once she entered her confinement, she was placed under the strictest orders to rest. "An Heir to the House of Austria, expected so soon, ought to be waited for with care," her doctors constantly reminded her.[33]

On January 14, 1767, María Luísa delivered a daughter named Theresa, "to the great disappointment of this place [Florence] and Vienna." Horace Mann, the British minister in Florence, reported that Empress Maria Theresa "wanted a grandson to console her under the despair she is in [over her fights with] the Emperor." It was no secret to the public that many people wished Archduchess Theresa were a boy. "Only a Princess!" became a popular phrase bandied around Florence in the winter of 1767.[34]

The birth of a girl instead of a male heir bothered Maria Theresa more than it did Leopold. He was intensely happy to be a father, and his subjects shared in his joy. They honored Theresa's arrival with "a grand festival, combining splendour with charity...and other acts of generosity."[35] María Luísa was only twenty-one, after all, and there was still plenty of time to have a son.

During his first year in Tuscany, Leopold found himself increasingly committed to the welfare of his subjects. Maria Theresa was proud to see her son taking the burdens of ruling so seriously, but when a previously unknown addendum of Emperor Francis I's last will and testament was uncovered, it threw Leopold's world into chaos.

The will claimed that Francis had deposited two million *florins* into a Tuscan bank account to be used on the country's behalf. In early 1768, Leopold received a letter from Emperor Joseph II claiming that he was struggling to lower Austria's national debt. His solution was simple: Leopold should send the money their father had left in trust for Tuscany to help Vienna. According to Joseph, their father's will stated he was the universal heir, and "the cash in the Tuscan treasury belongs to me."[36]

Leopold was shocked by his brother's request. He had hoped to use the money to drain the malaria-infested swamps in Maremma. Joseph, quick to remind Leopold of his allegiance to Vienna, wrote: "it matters more to the sovereign of Tuscany that a good and salutary financial operation should establish and support the Austrian Monarchy and put it in a position to protect him than a hundred drainings of the Maremma."[37]

The Tuscan government was outraged by Joseph's demand for the money. They explained to Leopold that Tuscany was already an "extremely poor principality...and were firm in their refusal to grant the Emperor's request."[38]

The Emperor did not react well to this refusal, and was quick to tell his brother, "the state has great need of the cash, therefore I must remind you to send it immediately."[39] Leopold refused to be dictated to, which led to an exchange of hurtful letters that flew back and forth between Vienna and Florence. Maria Theresa was appalled by the behavior of both her sons, telling Count Francis Thurn that their letters had "an arrogance and an impetuosity which was not reasonable."[40]

The situation placed a tremendous strain on Leopold, who was still prone to bouts of moodiness and depression. The entire fiasco proved almost too much for the young grand duke's nerves.

He became anxious and withdrawn and did everything he could to avoid the issue. He tried to delay responding, and purposefully forgot to answer some of Joseph's letters. He eventually sent the money, but not without a compromise. The Emperor only received just over a million *florins*, and he was forced to pay Leopold four percent interest on that money for the rest of his life.

The Empress tried to make peace between her sons, but the damage between them had been done. Leopold would never feel the same way about his brother again. Instead, one day he would hate Joseph with every fiber of his being.

For many years, Maria Carolina's life had remained comfortably isolated from the rest of the world. Along with her sister Antoine, this archduchess known affectionately as "Charlotte" lived a life of splendor and imagination in the nurseries at Schönbrunn, Laxenburg, and the Hofburg. Nearly inseparable, Charlotte and Madame Antoine (as she had been nicknamed) only grew closer as they got older.

To observers, there was a strong dynamic in Charlotte's relationship with Antoine. The former was clearly dominant and the latter dependent. This is hardly a surprise, given Charlotte's "strong, forceful personality." The Empress admired her daughter's spirit, claiming that of all her children, Charlotte was the one who took after herself the most.[41] In beauty and stature, she eventually began to take after her attractive sisters, leaving behind the severe German features that plagued her in early childhood. Both Charlotte and Antoine "shared the same big blue eyes, pink and white complexions, fair hair and longish noses," but for some reason, according to the Empress, Charlotte was just not as beautiful as her younger sister.[42]

In 1767, when Charlotte was fourteen, her sister-in-law, the Empress Josepha, died unexpectedly from smallpox. She was given a modest state funeral, and afterwards was buried in the imperial vault, but Viennese society hardly noticed her passing. Maria Theresa mourned the sad life she had led in Vienna, but Joseph II was inappropriately grateful to be released from his awful marriage. Unbeknownst to anyone at the time, Josepha's death would set into motion a series of events that would reshape the course of history and seal the fates of Amalia, Maria Carolina, and Maria Antonia.

Always the dynastic matchmaker, Maria Theresa had worked ceaselessly since the death of her husband to set her daughters up for the game of the century, fulfilling the Habsburg family motto: "Others have to wage war [to succeed] but you, fortunate Habsburg, marry!"[43] At the time of Josepha's death in 1767, the Empress was left with five daughters to be married: Elizabeth, Amalia, Josepha, Charlotte, and Antoine. These five sisters "represented an incalculable political capital." The last in this group, Antoine, was only twelve and not considered of any great importance; her name was mentioned only in passing on the same level as some of her French contemporaries.[44]

By October, all five archduchesses would have their fates decided for them. The same strain of smallpox that had killed the Empress Josepha swept through the Habsburg family like wildfire. Elizabeth, the famed beauty of the imperial family, was horribly disfigured and taken out of the marriage race. Even Maria Theresa contracted the disease and nearly died from it. "All of Europe had been horrified by the ravages smallpox had wrought on the Habsburg Court in 1767,"[45] one historian recalled, but after Maria Theresa recovered, she would be faced with a monumental decision.

She had been "determined to secure" for her unmarried daughters the two Ferdinands—King Ferdinand IV of Naples and Ferdinand, Duke of Parma. When it came to deciding between her daughters, "their individuality was of no concern at the moment." The marriages were for "the sake of the alliances they symbolized," not a love match. The Empress found herself in negotiations again with Carlos III of Spain since Don Ferdinand of Parma was his nephew and King Ferdinand of Naples was his son. The two monarchs decided that the sixteen-year-old Archduchess Josepha, who was "delightfully pretty [and] pliant by nature," would become the next Queen of Naples by marrying King Ferdinand.[46]

Just days prior to Josepha's departure for Italy, Maria Theresa made a decision that literally sentenced her daughter to death. Josepha accompanied her mother to the imperial crypt to pray for the Virgin Mary's blessing on the bridal journey. The tomb containing Empress Josepha's body was not properly sealed, and within two weeks the archduchess was dead from smallpox. Her mother, who had survived the illness that same year, built up an immunity and was thus spared.

Maria Theresa was now faced with a dilemma of international proportions: Carlos III insisted on a new bride for his son "without hesitating, or losing a minute."[47] The empress was down to three daughters, but whom would Carlos III deem acceptable to marry into his family? Would he accept any of them?

"I Remain True to My Dear Vienna"

The untimely death of Archduchess Josepha in 1767 put Maria Theresa in an unenviable position. King Ferdinand IV of Naples was still expecting the "speedy arrival of a young wife"[1] to replace Josepha, but the Empress could not bring herself to choose which daughter to send off to faraway Naples. In a letter to King Ferdinand's father, Carlos III of Spain, Maria Theresa outlined her position: "I grant you with real pleasure one of my remaining daughters to make good the loss…I do currently have two who could fit, one is the Archduchess Amalia…and the other is the Archduchess Charlotte who is also very healthy and a year and seven months younger than the King of Naples."[2] Unable to part with one daughter over the other, Maria Theresa left the final decision to Carlos.

If it had been up to Maria Theresa, she would have had Charlotte marry King Louis XV's grandson and heir, the Dauphin of France, Louis Auguste. The Empress felt a connection to the French king since he was the archduchess's godfather. Charlotte, who showed great promise and ambition, would be a fitting granddaughter-in-law for the famed Louis XV, but fate, it seemed, had other plans. King Carlos III informed Maria Theresa that Ferdinand of Naples had indeed chosen Charlotte to be his wife, ending forever any thought of her one day becoming Queen of France. This one choice by the outlandish and eccentric King Ferdinand sealed the fates of three of Maria Theresa's daughters.

To avoid the headache of renegotiating the complex marriage contract, Charlotte's name was merely substituted for Josepha's. As the soon-to-be queen came to terms with a future in Naples, the Spanish ambassador informed Maria Theresa that King Carlos's nephew, the Duke of Parma, had chosen Amalia to be his wife. It was up to the Empress to tell her daughter of the fate that awaited her in Parma. Little did Maria Theresa realize how truly strong-willed Amalia was, and the ensuing fight between mother and daughter would devastate their relationship.

⚙

"A fierce and deadly winter desolated Florence in the opening months of this year," wrote one contemporary at the beginning of 1768.[3] Quick on the heels of record-breaking cold temperatures and snowfall was the arrival of the dreaded Bubonic plague in Tuscany.

A French ship docked at Livorno was believed to be the source. Several French ministers on board died slowly from the dreaded disease shortly after they arrived. Fearing an epidemic, Leopold ordered the ship back to its homeport, escorted by a pair of Tuscan warships to ensure they did not return. By the spring, the fear that had gripped Florence at the thought of the plague was quickly forgotten as the annual Carnival season arrived.

The festival was one of the highlights just before Lent leading up to Easter celebrations and the Holy Week. Florence came to life with parades, musical performances, masquerades and gala parties. In intensely Catholic Italy, participants of this centuries-old tradition enjoyed the many pleasures they were about to sacrifice for Lent in honor of Christ's sufferings. As grand duke, Leopold was expected to host the most lavish parties of the season, but María Luísa was now nine months pregnant with their second child, and naturally stayed out of the spotlight.

In February, however, she ventured out of her confinement and made a rare public appearance. She visited the famous Via del Corso in the afternoon. That night, arm-in-arm with her husband and wearing a checkered mask, she attended an early performance at the theatre and then visited a masquerade ball.

Shortly before midnight, Leopold and María Luísa returned to the Pitti Palace. A few minutes later, the court doctors were called because the Grand Duchess was in the first stages of labor.

María Luísa's most intense pains began early the next morning on February 12, 1768. They were surprisingly light and lasted only a few short hours. Unlike her mother-in-law, the Grand Duchess of Tuscany was not forced to deliver her baby with hundreds of courtiers gathered outside. Only a handful of Austrian ministers and some of Florence's respected aristocratic ladies awaited the birth of the child.

For Leopold, pacing back and forth across the salon floor must have seemed like an eternity. Finally, the doctors came running out and announced that María Luísa's ordeal had ended. Leopold anxiously asked the doctor about the baby. Overcome by emotion, he told the Grand Duke he was the proud father of a "healthy, well-formed" son.[4] As Leopold ran to be at his wife's side, the court chamberlain announced the joyous news to the fatigued men and women waiting in another room.

Leopold was understandably proud and relieved when his son was born. María Luísa had given him an heir to the Habsburg Empire that was strong and healthy. That evening, the baby was baptized in an intimate candle-lit ceremony in the Pitti Palace's chapel. As he was being held at the baptismal font, he was given the names Francis Joseph Charles. These names were in honor of the archduke's two godfathers, Emperor Joseph II and King Carlos III, and Francis was for Leopold's father. It was fitting that this future emperor be named for two emperors and a king.

"There were great rejoicings in Florence" at the arrival of an heir.[5] Three days of gala parties and fireworks were planned to celebrate Francis' birth. Joseph II was overjoyed for his brother, and wrote to him: "Boldly present as many children to the Monarchy as you can. If they are like you, there will never be too many of them."[6] From the day Francis was born, Joseph took an almost obsessive interest in every area of his nephew's life. Nothing was off limits, and over the next twenty years he would have a deciding vote in every major area of Francis's life.

Leopold's son was the first Habsburg heir to be born since Joseph, and many saw his birth date as a good omen, February

12, 1768—exactly thirty-two years to the day since Maria Theresa married Francis of Lorraine. The symbolism was not lost on the Empress. When news of the baby's birth reached her in Vienna, she was beside herself with happiness. She ran into the Hofburg's imperial theater, still dressed in her nightgown, interrupted the play, and shouted: "My Poldy's got a boy! and just on my wedding anniversary, that's quite polite of him, isn't it?"[7]

A month later, tiny Archduke Francis was declared the heir assumptive to the House of Habsburg in an impressive and outlandish ceremony.* Horace Mann described the upcoming ceremony to his friend Horace Walpole:

> On the Emperor's Birth-day and Name-day [March 13], the Great Dutchess [sic] is to be relevée de ses couches. The young Prince is to be invested on that day with the Toison d'Or, with which the Secretary of that Order is on his way hither, from Vienna. By this mark of distinction, they acknowledge him to be the Heir of the House of Austria, to whom it is given at their births.[8]

The baby appeared strong and healthy to everyone who saw him. When Joseph II visited Florence in 1769, he reported on Francis's development to Maria Theresa: "The Archduke is darling; big and fat. He walks fairly well without leading string and at once recognized my brother, calling him 'papa'."[9] Two days later, Joseph proudly reported that Leopold's son "speaks several words and fears nothing."[10]

Now that the all-important male heir had arrived, and with the grand ducal family comfortably settled in Florence, it was time for a coronation. This was the sort of event Leopold was used to; it brought back fond memories for him of Joseph's coronation as King of the Romans in 1764. María Luísa was no stranger to royal coronations either. As a child of thirteen, she watched as her father was crowned King of Spain.

The event took place at the magnificent Basilica di Santa Maria del Fiore in Florence in June 1768. Since Leopold was the first grand duke of a new dynasty, the Tuscans planned a

---

* The title "heir assumptive" made Francis second in line to the Habsburg throne, next only to his father Leopold. His place in the succession of the imperial throne was not guaranteed. Although it was a formality, Francis would still need to be elected emperor.

"universal jubilation…of all the people" because it represented that they were no longer dependent on a foreign power.[11]   As Leopold made his way down the cathedral's great hall to be crowned, he made a striking impression on the hundreds of people packed tightly inside, watching silently in hushed reverence.   His flowing coronation robes seemed to glow as it reflected the colored light shining through the cathedral's stained-glass windows.   Seated in a special box near the altar was María Luísa.   It was almost impossible to tell that she was pregnant again.

Leopold's coronation in 1768 marked a turning point in his reign.   The Tuscans rallied around their sovereign like never before.   Leopold's oath of allegiance to Tuscany at his coronation sent the people into paroxysms of joy and adulation for their Austrian grand duke.   He took this opportunity to accelerate his plans for reform.   He flattered his ministers by taking "copious notes" on all that was discussed, and earned public trust by getting rid of Maria Theresa's chief agent in the country, Botta Adorno.[12]   By the late 1760s, Grand Duke Leopold was "engaging in reform more advanced than Vienna's."[13]   He even took it upon himself to learn Italian.

ᥫ

The disastrous string of events leading up to Charlotte of Austria's marriage to King Ferdinand IV of Naples was enough to make the young bride quiver with fear.

She "had heard enough about Ferdinand to dread…marrying him" and even came to regard the Neapolitan king as bad luck. Charlotte fought the Empress tooth-and-nail over getting married.   She begged, pleaded, cried, and screamed for Maria Theresa to change her mind, but it was no use.   The death of her sister Josepha gave Charlotte pause, and by March 1768 she made herself sick.   She was terrified that she would share Josepha's fate.   But she was suffering from little more than a "slight fluxion," and recovered in time for the wedding to go forward as planned.[14]

The proxy ceremony took place on April 7, 1768 at the Church of the Augustines in Vienna.   It was the first state function that the Habsburgs had attended since the death of

Emperor Francis I, and helped to punctuate the morose, melancholy routine that consumed the Court.

Charlotte's brothers played key roles in the wedding. Joseph walked her down the aisle, and her younger brother Ferdinand stood in as the proxy groom for the King of Naples. Empress Maria Theresa, who wore a black widow's dress and veil, watched the ceremony from a pieu reserved especially for the imperial family. When the nuptial mass ended, the Empress rose and tearfully embraced her daughter. At the tender age of sixteen, Maria Carolina was now the reigning Queen of Naples, and the youngest queen in the world.

Once the ceremony was over, the imperial family returned to Schönbrunn, but there was little time to celebrate because Charlotte had to leave for Naples that afternoon. As the family gathered in the palace's expansive stone courtyard, it would be the first of three times in as many years they would watch one of the archduchesses leave Austria to marry an unknown foreign husband. The family, with the Empress looking somber and dignified in the center, was surrounded by hundreds of courtiers, aristocrats, and ordinary citizens who had come to say goodbye to the young queen. Maria Carolina's departure from Austria was especially difficult on her thirteen-year-old sister Maria Antonia. As the royal carriage was pulling away from the palace, Maria Carolina, wearing a flowing blue and gold traveling dress, jumped out at the last minute. Hoisting up her dress, she ran back and gave her adored Antoine "a series of passionate, tearful embraces."[15]

Maria Carolina spent her bridal journey reflecting on her life and writing letters to the people that had meant so much to her. One of the most memorable individuals that she wrote to was her former governess, Countess Marie Lerchenfeld: "Write to me everything you know about my sister Antoine, down to the tiniest detail, what she says and does and even what she thinks...Beg her to love me, because I am so passionately concerned for her."[16] This natural sibling concern between Maria Carolina and the future Marie Antoinette would never change, even though both women were aware that they might never see each other again.

Preparation and introspection were common themes on the Queen's journey to Italy. Maria Theresa began with Charlotte a tradition of writing letters giving motherly advice and criticism to her daughters as they ventured out into the world. The tone in many of her letters was considered harsh, even mean, to casual observers, but the Empress believed the only way to get her point across to her daughters was to be brutally honest.

In the first of a long correspondence with her royal daughter, Maria Theresa told Charlotte "that marriage was the greatest happiness," and that she must try to understand her "ill-educated but well meaning husband, King Ferdinand."[17] But when she could have forged a deeper bond with Maria Carolina through her letters, the Empress used cutting words, hoping to stir her to greatness: "To my astonishment, I have observed that you say your prayers without the proper piety. Reprimands mean nothing to you and only lead to harsh words and bad temper." She went on to tell her daughter that at times she found Maria Carolina to be "thoughtless, irritable and rude."[18]

Maria Theresa was not unable to sympathize with Charlotte's position. She was terrified as her sixteen-year-old daughter left home to live among strangers with no idea of what the future might hold. The Empress wrote to her: "I know all too well the burden and the danger bound up in such affairs to which you will lend yourself if you allow yourself to be drawn into them."[19]

The Empress also tried to give Maria Carolina hope about her future husband: "Although an ugly prince, he is not absolutely repulsive...at least he does not stink." Not exactly inspiring words. She also made it a point to emphasize the need for Maria Carolina to blend seamlessly into Neapolitan society. Knowing full well her daughter's love for all things Austrian, the Empress cautioned her: "Do not always be talking about our country, or drawing comparisons between our customs and theirs. There is good and bad in every country....In your heart and in the uprightness of your mind be a German; in all that is unimportant, though in nothing that is wrong, you must appear to be Neapolitan."[20] These were powerful words because, in her heart, Maria Carolina would always and forever remain an Austrian.

The Queen's bridal journey was filled with many distractions—balls, banquets, concerts, and other festivities—to keep her occupied at stops along the way. She traveled a similar route as Leopold did when he left for Tuscany. At Innsbruck, she stopped briefly to visit the site of her father's death. As she moved further away from Vienna and her mother's lands, Maria Carolina's heart sank. Only when she arrived in Bologna were her spirits lifted. Waiting there for her were Leopold and María Luísa. The Grand Duchess had arranged with her brother, King Ferdinand, for them to stay on in Naples to help Queen Maria Carolina settle into her new life. It would truly be a family affair when they arrived in Naples.

In Bologna, the Tuscan court awaited Charlotte's arrival for nearly six hours in the pouring rain with no food, but according to one witness, the "unusual rejoicings that followed were ample compensation." And the Queen later recalled that her brother's "warm reception made her feel right at home." Some members of the British legation in Florence, who were present at this heartfelt reunion, were immediately struck by the strength of the Queen's character. Maria Carolina especially impressed the English minister, Horace Mann. "She is a most amiable little Queen," he wrote. He also praised her "extreme delicacy and good sense."[21]

From Bologna, Charlotte continued to pen letters home to Austria. "I remain true to my dear Vienna," she wrote to Countess Lerchenfeld. "Things are more beautiful here than there, but for me they lack the charm and strong attraction of Vienna."[22] Grand Duke Leopold also took the time to report to the Empress how Charlotte was handling the journey: "The disposition of the Queen is excellent; she has a good heart, she willingly accepts advice, being anxious to do right, but she is impetuous, a little hasty and thoughtless, and has as yet too little experience of the world."[23]

After a few days in Bologna, the bridal party continued on their long journey to southern Italy. They traveled through Florence, Siena, and Ronciglione before heading on to Rome where they attended a private mass in St. Peter's Square. The last stop before reaching the Neapolitan border was the town of Marino. There, on the eve of their departure for the border, both Charlotte and Leopold took the time to compose final letters reflecting their thoughts, hopes, and fears about the days to come. The Queen chose to write to Countess Lerchenfeld: "I am well, but my heart is sad, for I am so near the place of my destination…. More than ever I long to go back to my fatherland, and see my family and my dear countrymen again. Please tell my sister that I love her dearly."[24]

Charlotte may have inwardly feared her future, but to the people around her she conveyed a strong composure and devotion to duty that was a hallmark of Maria Theresa. Writing to their mother, Leopold could not help but express his love and admiration for his younger sister for the way she was conducting herself: "She is so excited, that sometimes she hardly knows what she is saying… Her deportment…is good. Of course, she is so young…she has never been trained to be Queen of Naples."[25]

On May 12, 1768, two days after Leopold wrote that letter, the bridal procession reached the ancient Roman town of Terracina along the Neapolitan border. Protocol required Maria Carolina's Austrian suite to return to Vienna, but the young queen threw such a violent fit that her brother was afraid she would faint. Once the Grand Duke was able to calm her down, she gave a heartfelt speech to her Austrian escort that reduced them all to tears. This was only the beginning of her heartache. In only a matter of days, she would experience anxiety, grief, and devastating depression all because of the man she was forced to now call her husband, the bizarre King Ferdinand IV of Naples.

The Two Ferdinands

Maria Carolina's first meeting with King Ferdinand IV was scheduled to take place in the town of Portella, but not before making a brief visit to the home of the Austrian ambassador. There, she was presented with a casket overflowing with magnificent jewels and diamonds, a gift from Ferdinand. Waiting to welcome Charlotte at the ambassador's residence were the King's court chamberlain, the Prince of San Nicandro, and the new head of her household and her chief lady-in-waiting, the Duchess of Andria.

When Charlotte, her brother and sister-in-law, and her new Neapolitan suite arrived in the remote hill town of Portella, they were received at a grand pavilion that had been constructed for Ferdinand's own parents nearly thirty years before. Ushered in by Leopold and María Luísa, Charlotte was introduced to the Herculean, bear-like King Ferdinand. Dropping on one knee, she kissed his hand, but was quickly raised to her feet by the King. There was only a brief interlude at Portella before Ferdinand took his queen by the hand and escorted her into another carriage, this one bound for the palace at Caserta where they would be married in person.

Ferdinand's life had been vastly different from Charlotte's. The second son of King Carlos III of Spain, he was born on January 18, 1751 in the seaside city of Naples, capital of the kingdom of the same name. Born during his father's reign as King of Naples, Ferdinand came to the throne in 1759 at the age of eight when Carlos became King of Spain. Like his brothers, Ferdinand was strong and robust, thanks in part to the Saxon blood of his mother, Queen Maria Amalia. In the words of the Margravine of Anspach, "tall and muscular, active in his undertakings," Ferdinand was "formed for a long life."[1]

The boy-king of Naples led a free-spirited childhood under the watchful eye of the country's Spanish-appointed regent and prime minister, Bernardo Tanucci. Described by one contemporary as "one of the most extraordinary men of the age, by the rank to which he had raised himself," Tanucci did everything in his power to keep control of Naples for himself.[2] He "therefore set himself the task of making Ferdinand of no account. He instructed the tutor of the king to teach him as little as possible."[3] Ferdinand was not brought up the way a king was expected to be, but his childhood was content. From dawn until dusk, he went on long hikes, played outdoor sports, and wrestled with servants in his palaces. By the time his minority ended in 1767, he detested responsibility in all its forms. He even had a stamp made up with his signature on it that he gave to Tanucci. This carefree attitude actually worked in Ferdinand's favor when it came to his subjects. The working classes of Naples, called the *lazzaroni*, were intensely loyal to him, making him one of the most popular rulers in Europe at the time.

All these thoughts and more must have raced through Maria Carolina's mind during the long carriage ride from Portella to Caserta. It was painfully obvious to her that her husband's manners were boorish and unrefined, but she could also see a kind and good-natured side to him. Writing to Countess Lerchenfeld, Charlotte recalled that everything about Ferdinand "is all much better than I was told." But she also admitted, "I must tell you and confess that I don't love him except from duty."[4]

There was a tremendous excitement in Naples leading up to Maria Carolina's arrival. Not since Louis XIV married the Maria Teresa of Spain nearly 160 years before had a Bourbon monarch taken a Habsburg princess as his wife. The only thing that overshadowed this anticipation was the thrilling prospect of a daughter of Empress Maria Theresa as the new Queen of Naples.

After twelve long hours, Charlotte, Ferdinand, and their group arrived at the stunning Royal Palace in Caserta shortly before midnight. Breathtakingly lit by floodlights, lanterns, and floating candles, this Baroque palace stood out like a vision of royal magnificence in the heart of Italy. Built by Ferdinand's father in 1752, Caserta was reportedly the largest palace in eighteenth-century Europe, dwarfing even the legendary Versailles in France. Its 1,200 rooms were supported from floor to ceiling by marble pillars and decorated with solid gold frescos and statues.

Waiting at the palace to welcome Queen Maria Carolina was a handpicked group of courtiers and ministers, including the ambassadors from France, Spain, and Austria. Just before the stroke of midnight, Ferdinand and Maria Carolina were hastily married in the palace's chapel. Inspired by Versailles in France, the chapel's gold and marble ceiling crested in a frescoed dome at the top. Flooded by candlelight, the King and Queen of Naples recited their vows and became husband and wife.

The honeymoon that followed was an overwhelming ordeal that left Charlotte dazed and frightened. She described her wedding night as being so horrible that she momentarily considered suicide: "One suffers real martyrdom, which is all the greater because one must pretend outwardly to be happy. I would rather die than endure again what I had to suffer. If religion had not said to me: 'Think about God,' I would have killed myself rather than live as I did live for eight days. It was like hell and I often wished to die." Charlotte's torment over her marriage stirred her heart to Antoine's fate: "I pity Antoinette, who still has this to face. When my sister has to confront this situation, I shall shed many tears."[5]

María Luísa tried to console Charlotte as much as possible, but as the reigning queen, protocol limited the time she could spend with the Grand Duchess, who was considered of lower rank. For the five brief days the court would spend at Caserta, Bernardo Tanucci planned a whirlwind schedule of activities. On her husband's arm, and accompanied by Leopold and María Luísa, Charlotte reluctantly attended fireworks displays, concerts, balls, and operas in honor of her wedding.

Nearly a week later, she and King Ferdinand made their first entry together into the city of Naples on May 19. They rode in a decorated state carriage through the city "with royal pomp in the full light of a lovely day." Charlotte's worsening depression was countered by the maddening joy of the crowds crying out her name in the clogged streets. True to her obedient and dutiful nature as Maria Theresa's daughter, the downcast queen wore a brave face as she waved to the people. In spite of Charlotte's great unhappiness, the "scene was worthy of the occasion, and the ensuing celebrations of the royal marriage were prolonged for several months."[6]

The city of Naples that Charlotte went to live in was a far cry from the glamorous and sophisticated Vienna that she had known as a child. With a population of 400,000 people, Naples was the fourth largest city in Europe. Despite the size of its capital city, Princess Michael of Kent described it as being "without doubt among the most backward countries in western Europe."[7]

Situated on the lower half of the Italian peninsula, Naples was one of the southernmost countries in all of Europe, stretching out into the depths of the Mediterranean. Napoleon called it the land "at the end of the world,"[8] but one historian went even further, describing it as "one of the remotest corners of Europe, but one of the most attractive, for Nature and History together have endowed it with all the fascination of the grand, extraordinary, and romantic."[9]

Naples was famous for being a "land of music, poetry, and epic traditions, blue skies, bright seas. Vesuvius, that mighty volcano, with fertile vines twisting at its base;...Naples, that capital of 'the garden of Italy,' with its antique and magnificent temples, its devotional works of art."[10] It was also a land of incredible contrasts where the aristocracy and clergy lived in extravagance, but the lower classes were desperately poor. Nearly ninety percent of the population was believed to be illiterate.

The natural beauty of Naples and its people did not make Charlotte's first months there any easier. In a country she did not know, married to a husband who did not understand her, she was soon overwhelmed by unhappiness and a sense of suffocation. Grand Duke Leopold and Grand Duchess María Luísa provided little comfort to the distraught Queen who, in her despair, began lashing out in fits of rage at the people around her. Writing to his father, Ferdinand described one particular dinner with his wife when "she became a fury....calling to all the servants who are maids, who could see nothing but that she was screeching like an eagle."[11]

Maria Theresa's ambassadors kept a close eye on Charlotte, and it did not take long for the Empress to catch wind of her daughter's behavior. She immediately sent off one of her most brutal letters, chastising Charlotte for her actions:

> Recently you have acquired the habit of being rude to your ladies-in-waiting. You are bad-tempered while they are dressing you; I cannot forgive this rudeness in you and I shall never forgive it.... You must never be lazy, for indolence is dangerous for every one and especially for you. You must occupy your mind, for this will prevent you from thinking of childish pranks, from making unsuitable remarks, and from longing for foolish amusements.[12]

For the pain that such a letter caused Charlotte, it was perhaps the best thing that could have happened to the indolent young queen. It awakened a fire within her, one that would give her the strength to withstand the difficult years to come. Maria Carolina resolved within herself to no longer sit idly by in her new country. Her life, she concluded, would be what she made of it, and refused to be an unhappy token wife, even if she were a queen.

Once Charlotte decided to assert herself, she accepted her fate as a wife, queen, and eventually a mother. In her times alone with Grand Duchess María Luísa, she learned how to be a caring and supportive wife to her husband. Then, in a self-possessed way, she began to flatter King Ferdinand and then dominate him if he displeased her. She found this self-fulfilling method both effective and very much to her liking because, in the words of one historian, "Ferdinand was born to be ruled by others."[13]

Once Charlotte learned to master both her husband and her own volatile emotions, her life in Naples began to settle down. She even started enjoying the national celebrations for her wedding. At the center of public attention for the first real time in her life, there were strong differences between Charlotte and Ferdinand that were obvious to everyone. The British ambassador, Sir William Hamilton, noted that "as Their Sicilian

Majesties and the Great Duke and Duchess have been continually in the eye of the public, every one is struck with the contrast in the behavior of His Sicilian Majesty and that of the Queen and Great Duke." Charlotte amazed everyone, including herself, when she began to sparkle in Neapolitan society only a few weeks after her arrival. "The affability and goodness of the Queen of Naples gives unusual satisfaction here," Sir William wrote in June.[14]

The celebrations, festive though they were, reflected the strict court etiquette of Spain that had been enforced in Naples during the reign of Ferdinand's father, then later when Bernardo Tanucci took over the regency in 1759. By the time Charlotte became queen, her adopted country was still struggling to find its national identity. According to Bernardo Tanucci, "for several years there has been nothing but chaos and no system of well-ordered government." As a result, "Naples remains a Spanish province, or a kingdom in a small state of pupilage."[15]

When the official period of celebration concluded at the end of summer, Charlotte was forced to bid an emotional farewell to Leopold and María Luísa. She was left to stand on her own two feet, but it quickly became clear that she would do so splendidly. Her campaign to win the affections of her husband and the Neapolitan people reaped quick rewards. After less than a year, she proudly wrote to Countess Lerchenfeld, "I passionately love my dear country and my good countrymen." King Ferdinand was likewise "dazzled by this very self-possessing young woman." True to form, Maria Theresa believed the queen was successful in Naples because she followed the Empress's instructions "to the letter."[16]

In early 1769, Queen Maria Carolina was visited by her brother, Joseph II. The Emperor was taking a tour of Italy, and arrived on the first day of March and stayed at the Austrian ambassador's palatial Mediterranean villa in Portici, a few miles outside of Naples. Charlotte, who vividly remembered her brother's critical and sometimes cruel personality, was anxious about how he might react to her life in Naples. Those fears included her unorthodox husband, King Ferdinand. But Joseph managed to surprise his nervous sister. Much to her relief, the

Emperor's easy-going manner struck a note with the uncomplicated Ferdinand. The two rulers became fast friends, and were soon calling each other "Don Pepe" and "Don Fernando."[17]

Joseph II was astounded by the contrasts he saw in Neapolitan society, which included Charlotte's new home, the capital city's Royal Palace. It was bland, colorless building in the heart of Naples, and was a far cry from the stunning residence at Caserta. Built to show Spanish architectural supremacy, the palace failed to impress even the most casual observers. Joseph was shocked when he saw the palace's interior. "The palace of Naples contains five or six frescoed and marbled rooms," he wrote to Maria Theresa; "filled with chickens, pigeons, ducks, geese, partridges, quails, birds of all sorts, canaries, dogs and even cages full of rats and mice, which the king occasionally sets free and enjoys the pleasure of chasing." Sights like these confirmed the Emperor's opinion that his sister was married to "an indefinable being." He concluded that even if Ferdinand's childhood education had not been neglected, "he could never have reached distinction."[18]

One thing Joseph did observe was how "deeply in love" Ferdinand was with the Charlotte, who was now taking advantage of her position and her growing influence at court. Joseph reassured Maria Theresa of his sister's progress: "Dazzled by the grandeur of the court, the honors paid to her, the beauty of the country and the freedom she enjoys, she will become more and more accustomed to it. I am quite at ease about her fate." He also praised his sister for not having "the slightest germ of coquetry."[19]

When the time came for Joseph to return to Austria, it was a difficult moment for brother and sister. Ferdinand, true to his childish and immature nature, only made it worse for his wife by making fun of her when she began crying. Joseph recalled how she "was on the point of getting very angry, and it was only after preaching to her in German that…she mastered her feelings and said nothing." He then "preached to the King to leave her alone today and not torment her."[20] When all was said and done, the Emperor summed up his visit by saying to his mother that, "apart from a little childishness," Maria Carolina's behavior "was excellent."[21]

CB

There was an intense desire on Maria Theresa's part to see her children married off to relatives of King Carlos of Spain. She was thoroughly satisfied with the way Leopold and Charlotte's marriages were turning out. The Habsburg matriarch therefore had the highest hopes when Archduchess Amalia was chosen to marry King Carlos's nephew, the young and immature Don Ferdinand of Parma.

Born in the city of Parma on January 20, 1751, Ferdinand was the only son of King Carlos III's brother, Philip, Duke of Parma; and his wife, Princess Élisabeth of France, the favorite daughter of King Louis XV. Ferdinand was also the brother of Emperor Joseph II's first wife, Isabella. In 1765, Don Philip died in a tragic hunting accident after being trampled by his own horse, then was ripped to pieces by his hunting dogs. Ferdinand, only fourteen, became the reigning duke. Before he reached his majority, Parma was governed by a regency council led by the country's French prime minister, Guillaume du Tillot. Appointed by Louis XV himself, Tillot followed in the footsteps of Bernardo Tanucci in Naples and did everything in his power to keep control of the country for himself. In the meantime, Ferdinand—already somewhat mentally deficient— was left to amuse himself as he saw fit. Emperor Joseph once described Ferdinand's upbringing by saying that "if the King of Naples had been educated like this, it would have succeeded infinitely better than with the duke, and I would much prefer to spend eight days with the King than with him."[22]

The decision to have Ferdinand and Amalia marry was not Maria Theresa's alone, but was largely the result of her ambitious state chancellor, Prince Wenzel Kaunitz. The Prince, who had worked at the Empress's side for nearly thirty years, first entered the imperial service as a courier who brought the news of the Archduke Joseph's birth to the courts of Europe. He worked his way up through the ranks, first as an attaché, then an ambassador, and eventually he became Austria's first state chancellor after successfully negotiating the peace treaty with France in 1756. Kaunitz had a keen ability to assess any problem and immediately come up with a solution, but he was also fiercely ambitious and constantly looked for ways to expand his own influence in Europe. The Empress came to rely on his expertise in foreign affairs immensely, and he was just as loyal to her. When a decision needed to be made for whom the Archduchess Amalia would marry, Maria Theresa turned to Prince Kaunitz without a second thought.

When the time came to tell Amalia of her upcoming nuptials, a dramatic scene ensued in the Empress's apartments at Schönbrunn. Amalia declared she would not marry Ferdinand because she was already "violently in love" with Prince Charles of Zweibrücken, a low-ranking Bavarian prince who frequented the court of Vienna.[23] They planned to get married, Amalia defiantly snorted, whether Maria Theresa liked it or not. Out of the question, the Empress replied. Prince Charles, who was smart and attractive, was considered a very eligible bachelor, but Maria Theresa was dead set against the match. Her daughters who were born to obey, she reasoned, and they had an obligation to marry into prosperous reigning families and further Habsburg supremacy in Europe. In Amalia's case, her marriage to Ferdinand would cement the grand alliance with Spain that began with the marriages of Leopold and María Luísa and Maria Carolina and Ferdinand.

One of Maria Theresa's biographers described the tragedy of Amalia's fate in Parma compared with Mimi's happy marriage: "She had been in love with a quiet young man, Duke Charles of Zweibrücken, and she implored her mother to let her marry him. She thought that she, too, like her sister Marie Christine, should be allowed to choose her own husband. But Amalia was not as strong as her sister, and she was forced to *yield* to her mother's wishes."[24]

Amalia was enraged with every fiber of her being at having to marry a man she did not love, let alone even know. She had little recourse but to fall in line and obey her mother. The Empress was the undisputed head of Austria's imperial family, and to disobey her was an unspeakable act that was wholly unheard of. In the words of one historian, Maria Theresa "sincerely loved her children. She nevertheless also had a domineering streak to her and wished to impose her ideals on her offspring," even if it meant a loveless marriage.[25] In doing so, the Empress created an insuperable chasm between her and her daughter.

Of all Maria Theresa's daughters, her relationship with Amalia was the most strained. The archduchess possessed a "violent self-will" that grew even more intense after being told she had to marry Ferdinand of Parma.[26] She became "permanently embittered" against the mother who already barely loved her.[27] Amalia was deeply hurt by her mother's decision, which was the complete opposite of when she allowed her sister Mimi to marry Albert of Saxe-Teschen.

Echoing Mimi's own dismal attempt to comfort Joseph when Isabella died, the Emperor only made Amalia feel worse when he tried to cheer her up about her marriage. He told her that, if for no other reason, he was in favor of the match because Ferdinand was the brother of his first wife Isabella. Undoubtedly this only added to Amalia's anger and resentment.

Maria Theresa took special interest in the ongoing negotiations over the marriage contract between her daughter and Don Ferdinand. The fact that Amalia was marrying a reigning duke meant she automatically forfeited her imperial status as an Austrian archduchess and a princess of Hungary and Bohemia in favor of a much lower rank. The Empress was keenly aware that her daughter's "rank as Duchess of Parma was much below that of her younger sister, the Queen of Naples; while as to their future homes there would be no comparison."[28]

On June 27, 1769, Amalia became the Duchess of Parma in a proxy ceremony at the dramatic gothic Church of the Augustine Friars. The wedding's gloomy, depressed atmosphere harkened back to Joseph II's nuptials with Josepha of Bavaria. Amalia, wearing a white lace-trimmed French dress, stood at the altar showing no signs of emotion. Standing next to her, dressed in full imperial finery, was her brother, Archduke Ferdinand, playing the role of proxy husband.

The next day, the imperial family gathered in Maria Theresa's apartments to watch the Duchess of Parma surrender all her rights as a member of the Austrian imperial family. With her right hand on a Bible, Amalia repeated after the priest as he spoke the oath of renunciation. She relinquished all claims through her mother to the Habsburg lands and the thrones of Hungary and Bohemia; and any claims to the Duchy of Lorraine through Emperor Francis I. That night, a formal dinner party was held at Schönbrunn to celebrate the wedding. More than

500 invited guests dined and danced in the palace's magnificent ballroom, famous throughout Europe for its gold-leaf artwork and floor to ceiling mirrored walls. Floating candles and crystal chandeliers kept the ballroom lit until late into the night. Maria Theresa insisted Amalia dance with all the members of the "family clique," the ambassadors from Austria, Spain, and Parma.

Two days later, on July 1, Amalia, Duchess of Parma, was carted off in a carriage bound for Italy. For the second time in a year, the imperial family gathered on the front steps of Schönbrunn to say goodbye to an archduchess. As the court chamberlain announced it was time to leave, Amalia fell into a deep curtsey at her mother's feet. Maria Theresa gently raised her daughter up and kissed her on the forehead. Like Charlotte before her and Marie Antoinette after her, Amalia would never see the Empress again.

Amalia's future preyed heavily on Maria Theresa's mind. On the eve of her departure, the Empress sat down and penned a letter for her daughter to read en route. Perhaps for the first time, she wrote to Amalia with sincere affection. Instead of criticizing her, she praised her for the good qualities she knew the Duchess possessed, but also reminded her to be wary of her shortcomings:

> My dear daughter.

> These pieces of advice...come from an affectionate heart, and because I have some experience in life, they can be useful to you. I wish nothing but to see you happy, as you earn this by the goodness and gentleness of your character, by your steady and virtuous behaviour....

> You possess an unusual amount of patience and a very good-natured character. These great qualities you must keep and train further, because they will be of use to you in your life....

> You are a stranger and a subject, you must learn to conform; even more because you are older than your husband, you must not seem to dominate...you know we are subjects of our husbands and we owe them obedience....It is not your affair to reign, so leave these cares to others and do not burden yourself with them....

I give you my blessing and will not stop to the last breath praying for you and loving you affectionately.

Your loyal mother
Maria Theresia.[29]

As her carriage sped out of Vienna, tears ran down Amalia's face as she read her mother's letter, but it would be one of the last times that mother and daughter would connect emotionally. Their relationship would remain a difficult one for the rest of their lives.

For nearly three weeks, Amalia read, contemplated, and chatted with her traveling companion, Emperor Joseph II, on the interminable carriage ride into the south. In the same way that Leopold had accompanied Maria Carolina to Naples, so too did Joseph go with Amalia to be with her during those first critical days in Parma. Suffocated by intense heat and uncomfortable conditions, the tiny bridal cortège plodded through Carniola (present day Slovenia), Venice, and Modena before finally arriving at its destination: the quaint, unassuming Parmesan town of Colorno.

At Colorno, only fifteen kilometers north of the city of Parma, Joseph and Amalia were welcomed by Don Ferdinand and Guillaume du Tillot, the prime minister who had infused the court with a strong dose of French culture. Tall, thin, wealthy, powerful, a very liberal politician, Tillot was vigorously opposed to Ferdinand's marriage to Amalia. As a committed Francophile, he would have much preferred Ferdinand to marry a French princess. But he was overruled by King Carlos III, who commanded that Amalia be welcomed to Parma in a manner befitting her rank as the new first lady of the land.

Only a few hours after setting foot on Parmesan soil, Amalia and Ferdinand were married in person on July 18, 1769. Of all her children's marriages, Maria Theresa would suffer the most aggravation from this one. But it was also this marriage that would produce one of Europe's most surprising kings in the turbulent years ahead.

At her wedding, held in the Private Chapel at the tiny palace in Colorno, Amalia looked outwardly composed as she took her vows, but inwardly she was boiling over with rage. Her wedding gown, made of white satin, was cut in the traditional French style studded with jewels and a long train. Following the custom set by the House of Bourbon, the dress was donated by Ferdinand's family.

Among the guests present was Joseph II, who walked his sister down the aisle. He watched the wedding from a special position just behind the couple, along with the Austrian ambassador. When the ceremony ended, Amalia knelt before the Emperor to receive his blessing, which he gave his sister with a warm hug. The newlyweds then made their way into the palace's grand hall to receive the members of the court.

Maria Theresa was not the only ruler who was keeping a close eye on the wedding. The groom's grandfather, King Louis XV of France, took a keen interest in Ferdinand and Amalia's nuptials. "Send me all the details down to the smallest ones," he wrote to Ferdinand.[30]

Not long after the wedding, Joseph took leave of his sister and returned to Vienna. Colorno's remoteness prevented any major wedding celebrations to be held at the palace. Instead, the court headed south to the capital city, Parma, where Guillaume du Tillot arranged festivities to honor the Duchess.

Upon her arrival in the capital, Amalia was seized with anxiety. The new duchess, very much used to the grandeur of Vienna, was horrified by the relatively small scale of the city of Parma. One biographer compared "the little capital of Parma, in the midst of the wide, hot plain stretching away towards the Alps and the Apennines, with the great city of Naples, its blue sea and enchanting scenery, of which the old proverb says, 'See Naples—and die'."[31] The people of Parma, though, gave their new duchess a hearty welcome. Buildings were decorated with the Habsburg eagle alongside the Bourbon fleur-de-lys. In windows, portraits of Maria Theresa were hung. So new to this rural world, the images of Amalia's mother were a stark reminder of the woman who had sentenced her to this fate.

Every welcome Amalia received caused her heart to sink deeper and deeper. Her new home, for example, was the uncomplicated Ducal Palace; an extravagant but tiny and unwelcoming building that seemed more like a dilapidated villa than a royal residence. Inside, the walls and ceilings were covered by frescos from the Renaissance that, while artistic and breathtaking, conveyed a sense of coldness and sterility. Even worse were the Duchess's own apartments, which were just as ornate but painfully small and left her little privacy from Parma's nosey courtiers.

To make matters even more difficult, Amalia found that Prime Minister Tillot was the undisputed master of the land. She was horrified that even though her new husband was the reigning duke, he was kept in strict submission to Tillot, and Amalia was told to fall in line with a minimum of fuss. From the moment she arrived, she was expected to follow Tillot's orders without question. A devoted subject of Louis XV, the prime minister tolerated no opposition whatsoever to the paramount influence of France. And having been led around by Tillot for years, Don Ferdinand saw no reason to change this. After all, his mother had been a French princess, and in the broad scheme of things, Guillaume du Tillot had brought much needed reform to Parma. But what neither Tillot nor the Duke counted on was the intense, volatile personality of Amalia.

In only a short time, both men realized their new duchess had the fury of a warrior. "She is a perfect Amazon," wrote one historian.[32] Amalia's anger at having to marry Ferdinand manifested itself in the most extreme way. To say that the Duchess of Parma was a martinet would not be an exaggeration. Much of her anger was directed at Maria Theresa, but in a strange twist, Amalia also deeply admired the way her mother overcame her male adversaries to claim the imperial crown. She determined, therefore, to assert herself as a Daughter of Maria Theresa. She vowed to dominate her husband and take the rule of the country for herself.

By the late 1760s, the future seemed rather bleak for the nation of France. The king, Louis XV, had once been hailed as "*le Bien-Aimé*" ("the Beloved"), but his once glamorous reign had fallen into a shadow of lethargy and moral apathy. Even worse was the loss in 1763 of France's colonial possessions in Canada and the Americas, marking the end of the country's tenure as an imperial power under the Bourbons. Added to this were staggering national debt, starvation, and an incredibly wealthy yet notoriously corrupt nobility.

Louis XV's unpopularity was so widespread that pamphlets criticizing him were circulating in the Hall of Mirrors at his own palace of Versailles. When a would-be assassin named Robert Damiens slipped into Versailles and made an attempt on the King's life in 1757, the law required only the most severe punishment. After being tortured, Damiens was executed. Louis himself was against this horrific act, but had to follow the law. The reaction in Paris was outrage and anger, and only further discredited the royal family. Maria Theresa's ambassador to France, the Comte Mercy d'Argenteau, observed that by 1769 the "monarchy is so decadent that it would not be regenerated except by a successor of the present monarch who, by his qualities and talents, would repair the extreme disorder of the kingdom."[33]

With the King entering the twilight of his life, hope for the nation's future naturally shifted to his grandson and heir, Louis Auguste. Given the traditional French title of *Dauphin* as the crown prince, Louis Auguste was born on August 23, 1754 at Versailles. His childhood had been filled with intense tragedy. His father, the previous dauphin Louis Ferdinand, was the King's eldest son and heir until he died of tuberculosis five days before Christmas in 1765. Louis Auguste's mother, Maria Josepha of Saxony, died two years later, leaving him an orphan at the tender age of ten.

The short lifespans of the French royal family prompted Louis XV to begin a search across the continent for a wife for his grandson. It was hoped that if Louis Auguste could marry and produce a son, it would infuse the monarchy with new life and secure the its future indefinitely. Fortunately for King Louis, Maria Theresa was on the hunt for a husband for her youngest daughter, Archduchess Maria Antonia.

For years, the Empress had worked night and day to find a way to ally her family with Bourbon France. She had hoped that one of her older daughters, perhaps Maria Carolina, might sit on the French throne one day. But when Charlotte became queen of Naples and Amalia the duchess of Parma, Maria Theresa's last chance to see one of her daughters become Queen of France was through the marriage of Antoine and Louis Auguste.

The process of arranging such a union was fraught with difficulties. Hoping to avoid the same misery that was unfolding for Amalia in Parma, Maria Theresa gave Antoine a little test. "Over what people wouldst thou like to reign?" she asked her daughter. Antoine replied happily: "Over the French because it was over them that Henri IV. and Louis XIV. reigned,—the Good and the Great."[34] Antoine's answer was everything the Empress could have hoped for.

Their conversation about ruling over the land of Henry IV and Louis XIV was followed by months of waiting and speculation. Living up to its reputation as the most rigidly formal court in Europe, the process for arranging the marriage of the heir to the French throne was steeped in etiquette. It took nearly three years from when Maria Theresa first proposed the idea to when the French representative at the Austrian court, the Marquis de Durfort, formally asked for the hand of the thirteen-and-a-half Antoine for the fifteen-year-old Louis Auguste, which Maria Theresa enthusiastically accepted.

Antoine's mother went into an immediate wedding frenzy. She planned a celebration at Laxenburg to honor the future crown princess, and began intense work with Louis XV and a "small army of advisors" on the incredibly detailed marriage contract, which was quite possibly the most important one of the eighteenth century.[35]

In private, Maria Theresa worked daily on the task of educating and preparing her daughter for one of the most coveted positions in Europe. Until that moment, the Empress never realized how truly lax her daughter's education had been. Her German was poor, and she was almost illiterate in French. As a child, she had been allowed too much time to inculcate with Charlotte. She was never trained in the finer pursuits such as music, art, languages, and literature that were considered necessary for a ruler. But now, all eyes were on Vienna to see what measures the court would take to ensure the success of Maria Antonia, who was destined to be the next Queen of France.

"Farewell, My Dearest Child"

When it came to matters of principle, Emperor Joseph II was more similar to his mother than he cared to admit. Like both of his parents, Joseph was "opposed to the strict court etiquette" that permeated the monarchy. The Austrian court was smothered by the stringent protocol that Maria Theresa's father, Charles VI, had implemented based on the Spanish style. But when Joseph came to the throne in 1765, he "began a vigorous campaign to reduce the elaborateness of Viennese court costume."[1]

Upon first meeting the Emperor, most people were struck by his simplicity and unaffectedness. The famed Hungarian writer Francis Kasinszy recalled meeting Joseph II: "I beheld to my amazement that the Emperor's green coat, with its red collar and yellow buttons, was patched at the elbows. His waistcoat and his breeches were lemon yellow, and he wore white linen gaiters…He detested waste and luxury; he wanted to give an example of simplicity by wearing a patched coat."[2]

Joseph was determined to earn a place for himself among the enlightened rulers of the eighteenth century. He religiously planned reform after reform, and was so eager to accomplish his work, with all its simplicities and enlightened philosophies, which kept him busy from dawn until dusk. He told Leopold of Tuscany, "I am overwhelmed with business and conferences…I rise at six-thirty, go to mass, and am at my desk at eight."[3]

Many times, Joseph forgot that he was not the sole ruler of Austria and the Holy Roman Empire. His youthful energy annoyed Maria Theresa's old ministers, who resented his ambition. He was just as disdainful of them, and publicly announced the contempt he felt for all of them. "None of them have rendered the State any service for years," he said.[4] Joseph's battles with the old regime came from the fact that he was "fiercely idealistic" and "skeptical of the prevailing social order with its ranks and hierarchies." He was also deeply "distrustful of monarchy and contemptuous of aristocrats."[5]

The power Joseph enjoyed as co-regent meant that his reforms did not stop at simplifying the formal dress of the imperial court. Economizing was high on the agenda. Always an opponent of the dredges of wealthy society, as Holy Roman emperor, Joseph II put an end to long-standing court traditions like gambling and hunting, which he called "wasteful manifestations of class priviledge."[6]

Since the day he became co-regent, Joseph tried desperately to be free of his mother's control. He opposed her in every possible manner because he had opinions on everything, even the topics about which he knew nothing. He liked to stir things up, but he also had a hidden, vulnerable side that was prone to flattery. "He loves to shine," Maria Theresa once said. There was an undercurrent of affection and romanticism beneath Joseph's hard exterior. One writer keenly noted that "he feared involvement, and kept both love and friendship at bay."[7] Joseph II's longing to rid himself of Maria Theresa's constant presence to follow his own compass never materialized. Instead, he responded by getting away from Vienna as often as possible. This was one of the great ironies of Joseph's co-regency, that he worked so hard to get away from the only person left in the world who genuinely loved and cared for him.

Using the alias "Count Falkenstein," Joseph took "fact-finding trips to all corners" of his realm. One estimate claimed he "spent nearly a quarter of his time as co-regent" away from Vienna. As the mysterious Count Falkenstein, he wanted to gain a "clear idea" of how his subjects lived and felt under the government.[8] While travelling in cognito, Joseph insisted on remaining in character. Once, when an Italian addressed him as "Your Majesty," he responded: "What majesty? There is no majesty here."[9] Joseph's travels also gave him the chance to show off his talent for languages. He was quite comfortable in French,

German, Italian, and Magyar. As a child, he had even learned a little Bohemian from his instructors.

When he was not traveling under a false name, Joseph gained a considerable reputation for his support of Austria's peasants. On more than one occasion, he was known to personally plow fields alongside the serfs. Moments like these helped endear the young monarch to his people and made his exploits the stuff of local legends. The peasants of one particular village were quick to tell travelers, "Emperor Joseph II *schleppt* here."[10]

Whenever Joseph was in Vienna, nothing about his relationship with his mother was easy. He would pressure her for greater reforms, which led to intense friction. As much as Maria Theresa loved her son, she deeply regretted how "Heaven has appointed" Joseph as her successor, "and excluded from her throne a youth adorned with every quality requisite for governing mankind."[11] The clashes between mother and son were so extreme that Maria Theresa considered forcing her son to abdicate, or abdicating herself. She once told him, "I am ready to give over everything into your hands without keeping the least thing to myself, even entirely to withdraw."[12] Italy was often suggested as a possible locale for retirement, for both Maria Theresa and Joseph.

Since the dawn of her reign, the Empress resolved that neither her late husband nor her son would ever remove from her hands the rule of the Habsburg Monarchy, but for the first time, she was not absolutely certain about her future on the throne. Unlike his father, Joseph refused to play the role of a token consort without any real responsibilities.

The more time Joseph spent as co-regent, the more frustrated he felt. He believed his mother was holding him back from making changes in Austria. His position meant he had primary control over foreign affairs, but that was hardly enough. Abdication and exile seemed like the only way to escape the suffocation of his mother's Vienna. To relieve some of the stress in his life, Joseph wrote frequently and fervently to Grand Duke Leopold of Tuscany. The rift that developed between the brothers over the Austrian debt fiasco had passed, at least where Joseph was concerned. He believed the Grand Duke was his only real friend and closest confidant.

In 1769, tragedy struck Joseph's life again when his seven-year-old daughter Theresa came down with pleurisy. Her life-and-death struggle began in mid-January. As the little archduchess clung to life, her cries could be heard echoing throughout the halls of the Hofburg. As the end neared, she refused to take any food or medicine except from her father's hand. She died in Joseph's arms on January 23, 1769. Theresa's death harkened back to Isabella's disturbingly accurate prophecy that her daughter would not live more than six or seven years. Three days later, her tiny coffin was taken by carriage from the Hofburg to the Maria Theresa Vaults at the imperial crypt. She was laid to rest next to her mother, Isabella, and her sister, Christina.

In the days that followed, Joseph spiraled into a pattern of grief similar to when Isabella died. In front of Theresa's governess, the Marquise d'Herzelles, Joseph collapsed into tears, crying out:

> I have ceased to be a father: it is more than I can bear. Despite being resigned to it, I cannot stop thinking, and saying every moment, 'Oh my God, restore to me my daughter, restore her to me.' I hear her voice, I see her. I was dazed when the terrible blow fell. Only when I had got back to my room did I feel the full horror of it, and I shall go on feeling it for the rest of my life, since I miss her in everything.[13]

Across Europe the death of a great-granddaughter of Louis XV was being treated with "appropriate ceremony." Imperial custom was for the child's belongings to go to the governess, but Joseph asked for his daughter's writings and "her white dimity dressing-gown embroidered with flowers."[14] This latest tragedy in Joseph's life galvanized his more unstable qualities. It pushed him to the edge, and began effacing what was left of his humanity.

♋

Grand Duke Leopold of Tuscany was finding himself in much the same position as Joseph when it came to the meddlesome influence of Maria Theresa. As with the Emperor, she kept Leopold on a tight leash, suffocating him. During the five years he had reigned in Florence, he was plagued by his mother's constant watchful eye and intrusive habits. He had dismissed her ministers and weeded out her spies, but it was not enough. The experience left him deeply suspicious of the people around him, and was only made worse by his moody personality, which had still not improved.

Once, after he had written a particularly miserable letter to Joseph, the Emperor sent him a reprimanding yet loving reply:

> Is it possible, my friend, that...you, whom I should call the most fortunate prince on earth,...regard yourself as unfortunate?...Just compare your situation to that of the rest of us: consider your own country; consider the opinion that Europe in general has of you; think of your domestic good fortune—your wife, your children.... And are you sad? You feel hurt?...Are you dissatisfied with the men with whom you have to deal? Then don't watch them too closely; take firm measures and punish those who contravene them, but stop encouraging this policy of secret talebearing which makes you so mistrustful of the whole human species.[15]

Joseph's words touched a chord with the Grand Duke, but only in part. Leopold had endured all he could and decided to assert his independence from the Empress. He chose to return home to Vienna and confront his mother once and for all.

The visit back to Austria in 1770, which was Leopold's first since his marriage in 1765, helped to focus his mind and strengthen his resolve for the future. Never one to lose a minute, Leopold demanded a meeting with his mother the day he and María Luísa arrived in Vienna. The meeting, held behind closed doors in Maria Theresa's apartments, lasted for hours. Afterwards, both mother and son looked exhausted but seemed satisfied at the outcome.

The arrival of the Grand Duke and Duchess of Tuscany coincided with two important events in the lives of the imperial family. Before dawn on April 21, 1770, Leopold became a father for the fourth time when María Luísa gave birth to a daughter named Maria Anna ("Marianne"). The second important event that took place in April of 1770 was the proxy marriage and departure of Archduchess Maria Antonia for France, where she was destined to reign as Queen Marie Antoinette.

In her last days in her homeland, Madame Antoine received intense and devoted attention from her mother to prepare her to be queen. Maria Theresa arranged for the Abbé de Vermond, a famed French scholar, to come and instruct the archduchess in everything from the French language to etiquette and history. Vermond faced a daunting task. He noted that Maria Antonia was

> cleverer than she was long thought to be. Unfortunately, that stability was subjected to no direction up to the age of twelve. A little idleness and much frivolity rendered my task more difficult. I spent the first six weeks in drawing an outline of the construction of "belles letters." She easily understood when I presented my ideas in a connected form: her judgement was nearly always sound, but I could not accustom her to get at the root of a subject, although I felt she was very capable of doing so. I fancied I could only get her to fix her attention by amusing her.[16]

Vermond was also intensely frustrated by her handwriting, which he observed "is not particularly good...[and] she has acquired the habit of writing inconceivably slow." Despite the difficulties the abbé faced in training the archduchess, he could not help but admit that "she has the most graceful figure; holds herself well; and if, as may be hoped, she grows a little taller, she will possess every good quality one could wish for in a great princess. Her heart and character are both excellent."[17]

It is worth mentioning the differences in the way Maria Carolina and Maria Antonia were prepared to be queens of Naples and France. Charlotte may have ruled over the largest kingdom in Italy, but Naples was hardly the center of culture and high society that France had become. After the reign of Louis XIV, France was one of the undisputed powerhouses in Europe. As queen, Maria Antonia would be at the center of the continental stage, with all eyes on her. She would be expected to set the trends in fashion, food, style, and art. Maria Theresa reminded her daughter: "If one is to consider only the greatness of your position, you are the happiest of your sisters and all princesses."[18]

Even in the midst of such serious training, Antoine continued to misbehave at times. She was, after all, only fifteen years of age. When she began to act "unruly" and "tomboyish" during her instruction, it caused Maria Theresa no end of grief. Growing up, Antoine was the kind of girl "who refuses to concentrate on her studies, prefers romping through forests with her friends, and disrupts parties by giggling behind her fan at the silliness of her elders."[19] But when the time came to assess her daughter's development, Maria Theresa was more than pleased by the progress she saw. She held a private audience with Antoine in the autumn of 1769. The Empress concluded that her daughter was "entirely capable of reasoning and of judgement, above all, in matters of conduct."[20]

On the surface, Maria Theresa may have presented the image of an all-powerful matriarch taking the duty of sending her youngest daughter to France with solemnity, but beneath her imperial veneer, the fifty-three-year-old empress was heartbroken at the thought of saying goodbye to her precious Antoine: "Soon this beloved daughter of whom I am so proud will depart forever. Soon I must give her a last blessing, a last embrace." In their last months together, the Empress "took her daughter on her lap, embraced her, [and] made her sleep in her own room."[21]

As the days flew by and Antoine's departure drew ever closer, Vienna was energized by her upcoming proxy wedding. It would unite the two most prominent royal houses in the world. Aristocrats and nobles attended balls in stately villas; the imperial family threw dinner parties at one of their less-used palaces, the Belvedere; and on April 16, Joseph II and Maria Theresa attended to one final duty. As a matter of both courtesy and protocol, it was required that the King of France formally request the departure of Maria Antonia. The *Gazette de France* described in their April issue the scene that unfolded at the Hofburg: "The court being in full dress, the ambassador of France had a solemn audience with their Royal and Imperial Majesties, when, in the name of the king, his master, he demanded Madame the Archduchess Antoinette as consort for Monseigneur the Dauphin."[22] With the most solemn dignity, Empress Maria Theresa bequeathed her youngest daughter to the care of King Louis XV.

On the evening of April 19, 1770, Maria Antonia married the Dauphin Louis Auguste in a proxy ceremony at the Church of the Augustine Friars. Dressed in a sumptuous clothe-of-silver wedding dress and a golden diamond tiara, Antoine was walked down the aisle by Maria Theresa herself. Following in the tradition of her other sisters' weddings, Archduke Ferdinand stood in for the groom. Maria Theresa and Joseph II watched the ceremony from a raised dais to the right of the bridal couple.

The wedding was intended to Frenchify the young girl; she took the French form of her name for which she would become famous for the rest of her life, Marie Antoinette. She was also now recognized with her new status as Her Royal Highness, the Dauphine of France. More informally, she would be known simply as "Madame la Dauphine."

The following evening, Maria Theresa wrote an emotional letter to Louis XV, telling him that her daughter's "intentions are excellent, but given her age, I pray you to exercise indulgence for any careless mistake....I recommend her once again as the most tender pledge which exists so happily between our States and our Houses."[23]

The next morning, Marie Antoinette left Austria forever. The departure of Madame la Dauphine from her beloved home country was carried out with the greatest state magnificence of Imperial Austria: "Fifty-seven richly appointed carriages, laden with more than twice as many dignitaries and drawn by more than six times as many horses, had filled the Hofburg's majestic central courtyard since dawn. But when the imperial family stepped out of the palace at nine o'clock, the crowds began to separate, making way for Maria Theresa."[24]

The "whole of Vienna" seemed to crowd into the Hofburg's courtyard to bid farewell to the youngest daughter of the Habsburgs.[25] One of Antoine's childhood friends, Joseph Weber, wrote that she "had so completely gained the affection of all who were about her...that, at the time of her marriage, the joy of knowing she was wedded to the Dauphin of France, was entirely clouded at Vienna by the grief which arose from the thought of losing her."[26] And one eyewitness said that the "capital of Austria presents the appearance of a city in mourning."[27]

The thousands of people gathered in the courtyard stood in hushed reverence, their eyes locked on the Empress and the

Dauphine. When the time finally came to say goodbye, Maria Theresa embraced her daughter over and over again. Holding her tightly to her chest, she whispered: "Farewell, my dearest child, a great distance will separate us…Do so much good to the French people that they can say that I have sent them an angel."[28] With that, mother and daughter both collapsed into tears.

Once she had composed herself enough to carry on, Marie Antoinette was ushered into a jewel-encrusted carriage by her brother Ferdinand and the Abbé de Vermond. The scene that followed was heartrending. "With very few exceptions," wrote one author, "she would never see any of them again. Through a wall of glass she stared out at the unsmiling Empress…. With a last, pleading look at her mother, the young woman began to cry."[29] Once the word had been given, the procession began its long journey out of Austrian territory, and Marie Antoinette looked upon the face of her mother for the last time. "I shall never see her again!" she sighed.[30]

More than any of her sisters, Marie Antoinette truly left one life behind as she began another. The Empress insisted her daughter become completely French. That included severing many of the ties she had with her family in Austria. Maria Theresa even recommended her daughter no longer write to any of her relatives: "I do not think that you should write your family, except for special occasions and the emperor, with whom you will reach an agreement regarding this point."[31] She did consent to allowing Marie Antoinette to write to Maria Carolina: "The Queen of Naples will wish you to write to her. I do not see any objection."[32]

Empress Maria Theresa continued the tradition of writing a departure letter to her daughter as she had done with both Charlotte of Naples and Amalia of Parma. The Empress sat down and penned a letter the moment Marie Antoinette left the Hofburg. She had it delivered to the Dauphine when the bridal procession stopped in Freiburg a few days later. Entitled "Regulation to Read Every Month," the letter provided Marie Antoinette with clear directions on how she was to act at the French court: "You must not do anything unusual; On the contrary, you must absolutely lend yourself to what the court is accustomed to doing…. All eyes will be fixed on you."[33]

The Empress's words echoed among her three special daughters, and each one was exhorted to conform, obey, and submit: "The one felicity of this world is a happy marriage: I can say so with knowledge; and the whole hangs upon the woman, that she should be willing, gentle, and able to amuse."[34] That, Maria Theresa believed, was the only true path to happiness in life.

France's Charming Dauphine

The arrival of Marie Antoinette on French soil in 1770 would bring many changes to the country's old and decadent aristocracy. When it came to the subject of their new dauphine, the French court was "fraught with rivalries and vendettas [and] viewed her as a handy pawn in its high stakes struggle for power. On the other hand, a nation on the verge of revolt expected her to breathe new life into its decaying monarch."[1]

The French people saw Marie Antoinette as their hope for the future. In the twilight of Louis XV's reign, their country had reached a place of despair. The old aristocracy remembered with fondness the prosperous reign of the great Sun King, Louis XIV, who, when he "was growing old...took to devotion; Louis XV. tried to dispel his incurable ennui by new sensations."[2] The costly wars sponsored by the current king brought the nation to unparalleled poverty. A recent conflict, the Seven Years' War, and the Spanish, Austrian, and Polish wars of succession bankrupted the country. Poor, working class families had their fathers and sons drafted into the army, leaving the provinces in decay because there was no one to maintain them. All of France hoped and prayed that the daughter of Maria Theresa would revitalize the crumbling Bourbon dynasty and restore the days of the Sun King.

During her two and a half week journey to the Franco-Austrian border, Marie Antoinette was faced with many uncertainties about the future she would face as Madame la Dauphine. Maria Theresa shared her anxieties, and had an "ominous foreboding" about the future. In the days after her daughter's marriage, the Empress spent more time than usual in prayer asking for "the Almighty to avert a disaster that she alone had foreseen." It was a great irony that in Paris, cartoonists claimed that by sending Marie Antoinette to France, "the Empress had blown the lid off Pandora's box."[3] It remains forever in the realm of historical speculation what might have been if either Maria Theresa or Louis XV had decided against the marriage of their heirs.

Awaiting Marie Antoinette just inside the French border was the man responsible for her entire future, King Louis XV. In a moment that would have brought tears of pride to her mother's eyes, Marie Antoinette dropped to her knees to pay her respects to the king. When he took her by the hand and raised her up, she came face to face with "large, full, prominent black eyes and a Roman nose."[4] Unfortunately, Marie Antoinette's husband had not inherited any of those handsome features from his grandfather.

The Dauphin Louis Auguste was fifteen when he and Marie Antoinette came face to face for the first time. This awkward teenager and future king was "nearsighted, maladroit, and grossly overweight." Comte Mercy d'Argenteau pitied Louis Auguste, saying, "nature seems to have denied everything to Monsieur le Dauphin." The unfortunate prince had "thick-lidded, watery blue eyes, a shambling gait, a nervous bark of a laugh, a hoggish appetite, and," because of that, "a corpulent physique."[5] Given the cruel hand fate had dealt Louis Auguste, it is not surprising that he never wanted to be king. He was only in such a position because of the early death of his father and brothers.

Accompanying the King and Dauphin to meet Marie Antoinette were three other members of the court who would come to play meaningful roles in the future queen's life at Versailles. They were the princesses Adélaïde, Sophie, and Victoire—*Mesdames Tantes*—as they were known collectively; these were the unmarried daughters of Louis XV. The ladies were described, in much the same fashion as their nephew the dauphin, as "clumsy, plump old wenches [who never] knew what they wanted to say, and wriggl[ed] as though they wanted to make water."[6]

Madame Campan, once the reader to the princesses and later a member of Marie Antoinette's household, described her recollections of *Mesdames Tantes* in her memoirs. At thirty-eight years of age, Princess Victoire was so overweight that she was nicknamed "Piggy" by her father. Her sister, Princess Sophie, was "remarkably clean" but "horribly ugly," and was therefore known as "Grub." The eldest daughter in this triple entente, Adélaïde, was strong-willed but with "slovenly personal grooming" and a "generally shabby, shopworn appearance." Known to her father as "Rag," Adélaïde was "absurdly proud of her royal rank" as a Daughter of France. She refused to marry a foreign prince and forfeit her status in France.[7] Always following their big sister, Sophie and Victoire did likewise and remained unmarried for the rest of their lives.

Paling in comparison to *Mesdames Tantes* was the most dangerous intriguer of all, the Comtesse du Barry. As Louis XV's mistress, she was the most powerful political force at Versailles and, by extension, the whole of France. Having been brought up at a court where her mother strictly enforced fidelity and piety, Marie Antoinette refused to even acknowledge the comtesse, who held the official role of Royal Favorite. As the future queen and potential new favorite of the King, Marie Antoinette was the first woman to truly threaten the Comtesse's own power base. This made her the Dauphine's staunchest opponent until the day Louis XV died.

That evening there was a formal dinner reception for the Dauphine at Bois de Boulogne, followed by a ceremony that initiated her into the French court. The experience was intense, even jarring. Marie Antoinette was forced to renounce all her connections with Austria in the most dramatic way possible. Stripped naked of the clothes she had brought with her from Vienna, she was redressed with French ones. After dinner, the fifteen-year-old dauphine was required to dispose of all the treasured possessions that accompanied her from Austria, incluuding her beloved puppy. Even her diminutive, "Antoine," was never to be used again.

The pomp and ceremony of Marie Antoinette's startling arrival was followed by the long journey to what would be her home for the next twenty years, the legendary palace of Versailles. The young dauphine was certainly overwhelmed, since the French palace was:

> [An] epic poem in stone dedicated to one man's glory [Louis XIV's]. Even to a girl reared in palaces, Versailles was at once breathtaking and awe inspiring. Schönbrunn with it's 1,100 rooms plus, the Vienna Hofburg slowly growing through the centuries in the heart of the old city, faded into insignificance beside the arrogant splendour of Versailles; an isolated world of privilege and pomp, in which the grandest of courtiers were ready to perform the most menial of tasks if it brought him into the presence of the King, and duchesses fought for the honour of sitting for hours on hard stools in the royal antechamber.[8]

In only a few short days, Marie Antoinette was about to see all the glamour and majesty of Versailles at its finest when she married the Dauphin in person and made her official debut as the Crown Princess of France.

CS

Time and experience had changed the way Grand Duke Leopold felt about his brother Joseph. The Emperor still held deep affection for his brother. And in person, the Grand Duke was still his closest confidant and treated him with kindness and respect. But in private he had very different feelings.

By the 1770s, Grand Duke Leopold detested the Emperor "with an intensity that was unusual even among royal brothers."[9] The fight over their father's last will opened Leopold's eyes to his brother's true nature. It was then he realized the way in which the Emperor used people to fulfill his own ends. Leopold now "understood Joseph too well" to remain close with him any longer.[10]

In private, Leopold became one of the Emperor's harshest critics. He once said that Joseph "likes nobody and thinks only of himself," and that he "says and does everything in order to be praised and talked about."[11] Empress Maria Theresa, though she loved Joseph with all her heart, shared Grand Duke Leopold's feelings. She once summed up Emperor Joseph II by saying ominously, "Imagine what harm such a man can do."[12]

Tuscany's grand ducal family stayed in Austria for the spring and summer after Archduchess Marianne was born. The delivery had been difficult on María Luísa, and she needed time to rest before making the long journey back to Florence. Leopold never wasted a minute, and the second he returned home he continued to work for the betterment of his country and his people. He had the advantage that Tuscany had no military forces to maintain. This meant he was free to use the nation's whole revenue, which was not much, for building up the country's infrastructure. Young, idealistic, and intelligent, he surrounded himself by a respected and capable team of advisors.

In many ways, Tuscany was becoming the envy of Europe, but neither the Grand Duke nor the Grand Duchess ever became trendsetters in Florentine society. In Naples, Queen Maria Carolina was the undisputed leader in the world of fashion, culture, and entertainment. Her parties were famous throughout Italy, but Leopold and María Luísa neither cared for court functions nor held them on any kind of regular basis. Theirs was a truly unique style of rule. While the Grand Duke spent all of his time in administrative pursuits, his wife devoted herself to their growing brood of children. Instead of reviving Florentine society, the Grand Duchess withdrew and isolated herself. Except for a few, intimate friends, no one really knew how unpretentious the Habsburgs of Tuscany could be.

A few days after the youngest daughter of Maria Theresa arrived in France, one of history's most famous marriages was sealed as Louis Auguste and Marie Antoinette were united in matrimony on May 16, 1770. The Duc de Croÿ, a prominent French courtier, was awe-struck at the magnificence that was planned for the event. "The Dauphin does not marry the daughter of the Emperor every day," he said. After all, Louis XV had married an unknown Polish princess, but Louis Auguste was marrying "the daughter of the Caesars."[13]

Marie Antoinette prepared for her wedding on the ground floor of the immense Versailles palace in the white and gold apartments that had once belonged to the Dauphin's mother, Maria Josepha of Saxony. For nearly three hours, her ladies-in-waiting dressed Marie Antoinette in her white and silver brocade dress accented by deep, wide hoops and glistening with studded diamonds. Atop her head sat a diamond-encrusted ringlet and around her neck hung a dazzling pearl necklace that had once belonged to Louis XIV's mother, Anne of Austria. Her bridal finery was nothing short of a "symphony of rose gold and silver sparkling with diamonds."[14] Together with the King and Louis Auguste, who was dressed in an equally resplendent suit of shimmering gold fabric and diamonds, Marie Antoinette made her way to the palace chapel for the wedding ceremony.

Madame Campan recalled the historic entrance Marie Antoinette made into the chapel: "From the first steps she took into the long gallery, she drew six thousand pairs of eyes to her person."[15] Five thousand people had been invited to the wedding, but more than seven thousand had arrived. Outside, many thousands more flooded into the courtyard to celebrate the once in a lifetime experience of the wedding of a dauphin. In the river just beyond the palace entrance, hundreds of onlookers sat in their boats hoping to catch a glimpse of the bride.

During the ceremony, the bride and groom stood beneath a silver canopy. Louis Auguste was characteristically nervous. He stumbled to recite his vows, and trembled when he slipped the ring on Marie Antoinette's dainty finger. One of the guests, the Duchess of Northumberland, noticed that Louis Auguste "appear'd to have much more timidity than his little Wife. He trembled excessively during the service and blushed up to his Eyes when he gave the Ring."[16] After the Archbishop of Rheims declared them married, Marie Antoinette retired to the spectacular Hall of Mirrors where she received the oaths of loyalty from the members of her new household.

Three days later, thousands of French aristocrats gathered in the *salle de spectacles* to witness a sight of their future queen. Beneath diamond chandeliers and gold statuettes, the royal couple danced at their debut ball. Louis Auguste "shuffled" through the dance in obvious discomfort, "blushing and scowling in his usual, unappealing way." In contrast, Marie Antoinette "took the breath of everyone in the hall away." In the words of one witness, she was "so natural and so graceful that the immense hall was filled with nothing but murmurs of admiration."[17]   One of Louis XVI's biographers, John Lewis Soulavie, described the young dauphine on that day as a vision from heaven. She had "an angelic figure; the clearness of her complexion was remarkable, the colours were lively and distinct, her features regular, her shape slender."[18]

Like so much else in the lives of the future king and queen, the wedding was overshadowed by tragedy. On May 30, vast crowds gathered to celebrate in Paris at the Place Louis XV (later the Place de la Révolution). For a reason that still remains a mystery, workmen had dug trenches blocking the courtyard's exits from the Place. Thousands of men, women, and children had come out to watch a massive fireworks display. Suddenly, as people became excited, the push of the crowds forced many people into the pits. Innocent people screamed helplessly as horses and carriages belonging to the nobility, who had also come to celebrate, fell on top of them. When the massacre ended, 130 people had been crushed to death. The Comte de Ségur, who had witnessed the tragedy, remembered the horror of it even fifty-five years later: "Methinks I still hear their cries..."[19]

Marie Antoinette, along with *Mesdames*, was on her way to Paris when news of the catastrophe arrived. Turning her face away from the people around her, the Dauphine burst into uncontrollable tears. The messengers tried to spare her unnecessary grief by holding back the gruesome details, but she saw through them. "You do not tell me all! How many victims!" she screamed. She and Louis Auguste were sickened by this senseless loss of life and wasted no time in helping the injured. Desperate to relieve the suffering of their people, the couple donated a month's allowance to the families of the victims. A few days later, still overcome with grief, the Dauphin sent the following letter to a police official in Paris:

> I have learned of the accident which happened in Paris, and for which I am responsible; I am deeply distressed. They have brought me what the king allows me every month for pocket-money; I can dispose of only that, and I send it to you. Succour the most unfortunate.

I have great esteem, Monsieur, for you.

Louis Auguste.[20]

The next day, the bodies were buried in a mass grave near the Church of the Madeleine. The royal couple spent the remainder of the week in mourning for the victims.

After the wedding and this tragedy, Marie Antoinette worked even harder to win the affection of the French people. Her efforts reaped quick rewards, and her early life at Versailles was filled with many triumphs. When a courtier wished to speak to the Dauphine in German, she replied, "Monsieur, after to-day I understand no language but French."[21] Moments like these won Marie Antoinette instant popularity, and showed how tragically ironic her ultimate fate was.

Her personal relationship with Louis Auguste was improving as well. During the first days of their marriage, the Dauphin barely even spoke to his wife. But after a month, he was beginning to warm up to her. It did not take Louis Auguste long to see her admirable qualities. Comte Mercy d'Argenteau* reassured Maria Theresa of this, saying how Louis Auguste "seems charmed with the Dauphine, and shows a sweetness and complaisance towards her that he was not believed to possess."[22] And later, Mercy admitted how Marie Antoinette "is so graceful, she succeeds in everything; one must admit that she is charming."[23]

The Dauphine's successes met with the greatest approval from both Louis XV and Maria Theresa. The Empress informed Comte Mercy to send regular, secret dispatches to Vienna regarding her daughter's conduct. In one letter shortly after the wedding, Mercy happily reported: "our archduchess has surpassed all my hopes…. The whole court and the general public are full of nothing but praise for her." He went on to say that Louis XV "remains very satisfied with Madame la Dauphine, and is always…complimenting her in a very graceful and touching way."[24]

Maria Theresa praised her daughter, telling her that when it came to Louis XV she must work to endear herself to him; she

---

* His full name and title was Florimond Claude, Comte Mercy d'Argenteau. He is referred to simply as "Comte Mercy," and served as Maria Theresa's ambassador to France.

must prove her worthiness to be queen of France. Maria Theresa knew the greatness and potential that the Dauphine possessed, and encouraged her to that end: "You have something so touching in your whole person that it is hard to deny you anything; this is a gift of God for which you should thank Him, and use it for His glory and the welfare of others."[25]

In the midst of Marie Antoinette's many admirers, there was one person who caused her trouble when she first arrived at Versailles, the Comtesse du Barry. As a result of the pious up-bringing she received at Maria Theresa's side, the Dauphine felt nothing but disdain for Louis XV's mistress. The comtesse, who already came from a shady background, was crass, rude, and abrasive. The very public role she played at the king's side made her and her relationship with Louis XV highly unpopular with the people. Both Marie Antoinette and Louis Auguste, who was just as devout and God-fearing as his wife, considered du Barry an eyesore and an embarrassment to the royal court.

Maria Theresa had encouraged her daughter to look upon Louis XV as her own family now. So when Marie Antoinette saw the King carrying on as he was with du Barry, it was more than she could bear. She described to the Empress how "pitiable it was to see his weakness for Madame du Barry, who is the most silly and impertinent creature it is possible to imagine."[26] To show her disapproval of the du Barry's presence, Marie Antoinette publicly snubbed the comtesse whenever possible. Maria Theresa wholeheartedly agreed with her daughter's moral position, but also understood the damage du Barry could do to her future if she continued to ignore her.

Both the Empress and Comte Mercy implored the Dauphine to talk to du Barry, but she refused. It took nearly two years for Marie Antoinette to finally acquiesce to her mother. "The Empress knows that I will always do what she wants me to do," she told Comte Mercy.[27] When the time finally came in 1772 for her to address du Barry, she uttered only nine words: "There are a great many people at Versailles today."[28] With that simple statement, the comtesse was pacified.

The letters exchanged between Maria Theresa and Marie Antoinette proved to be a lifeline to the Dauphine, and guided her through those turbulent first years. All her guidance, all her support, came from Vienna. These early letters were the beginning of an immense correspondence between the Empress and her daughter that would last until Maria Theresa's death.

The Empress was very specific when it came to the letters they exchanged. Early in their correspondence, she instructed her daughter in the manner in which was to respond to each letter: "At the beginning of each month I will send a courier from here [Vienna] to Paris. You could prepare your letters before his arrival, so that you might send them back with him immediately...You can also write to me by post, but only trivial matters that anyone might know about."[29]

Out of all her daughters living abroad, the Empress would remain in the closest contact with Marie Antoinette, even though they would never meet again. It was one of the great historical ironies of Marie Antoinette's life that as the youngest of the Habsburg archduchesses, she held the highest position among her sisters. The courts that were ruled by Amalia of Parma, Mimi of Saxe-Teschen, and Charlotte of Naples could not compare with the stateliness of France.

☙

The exasperating life that Amalia was forced to endure since her arrival in Italy was taking its toll on the high-spirited young woman. The Parma that the cosmopolitan twenty-three-year-old duchess now called home was little more than a backwaters nation:

> Down the lateral valleys of the Apennines, which cut off Parma from the Mediterranean, several navigable rivers...run down to the Po [River] and the Adriatic.... Centuries of tilling and draining have made it a luscious land. Thickly dotted among the vineyards, the corn and the maize fields, with their rows of mulberry-trees, stand substantial homesteads built for defence around a courtyard, and big, compact villages, with umber-tilled roofs, cluster around a *castello*, or nestle beneath a tall, slim, Lombardo-Romanesque church tower. The long, straight Emilian Way bisects the land, running from Rimini, on the Adriatic, through Bologna, Modena, and Reggio, to Piacenza on the Po.[30]

Parma's rustic charm did nothing to lift Amalia's spirits during her first wretched years there. She might have been less miserable if Ferdinand had been more mature and under-standing. Unfortunately, the teenage duke was too intimidated by Prime Minister Tillot to do anything except occupy himself with the simplest amusements.

Amalia had no illusions about her husband. He was, after all, a simple, weak-minded young man with few if any cultivated interests. One of Maria Carolina's biographers, the famed historian Catherine Mary Bearne, observed that,

> The Duke of Parma proved quite different from the cultivated, well-educated youth described to the Empress and her daughter, and when once he was set free from his studies and married, he turned out to be a remarkably stupid, idle boy, who, like his cousin [King Ferdinand] of Naples, was fond of low company, and delighted to amuse himself by roasting chestnuts and winding up clocks.[31]

The Duke and Duchess were obviously mismatched, and their first years together were terribly unhappy ones. This turbulent time in her daughter's life caused Maria Theresa "endless heartache. As it turned out, Maria Amalia's husband was even less appealing than the unprepossessing Ferdinand of Naples."[32]

To make matter worse, Amalia found that her efforts to follow in her mother's footsteps were failing dismally. As a young queen, Maria Theresa understood that to succeed in ruling she would need the support of the people—both men and women—around her. Amalia did not share this insight. She believed that men contributed nothing to the affairs of state, and sought to shut them out of the political arena altogether. Parma's aristocrats were just as ambivalent to the Duchess as she was to them. They considered her "a dull, cold apathetic girl" who was as unhappy as she was "unpopular at Parma."[33]

In the midst of all her political scheming, Amalia's normally robust health began to wane. She was tired all the time, nauseous from morning until night, and felt an uneasy nervous-ness on most days. When the court physician told the Duchess she was pregnant, it came completely by surprise. Motherhood was not something Amalia had ever envisioned for herself, but soon the idea of raising children to follow in her footsteps took hold. The news that an heir would be born thrilled Ferdinand, who dutifully reported it to his uncle, Carlos III. The King was outraged with the way Amalia was conducting herself, but was temporarily placated and satisfied that dynastic heirs would soon be arriving.

Amalia's pregnancy made Ferdinand more receptive to his wife's agenda, and he proved to be an attentive husband during her *enceinte*. For the first time since their marriage, a connection arose between Ferdinand and Amalia as they anxiously awaited the birth of their first child. As a satellite court of Spain, Parma was still forced to submit to the strict court etiquette that reigned in Madrid. In the last weeks of her pregnancy before her scheduled confinement, Amalia, joined by her husband and their ministers, attended mass daily to pray for the safe arrival of the baby.

On November 22, 1770, Amalia's first child—a girl—was born at the Ducal Palace. Maria Theresa was soon reporting the birth of her latest grandchild to the rest of the family. The watchful empress ensured that her ninth grandchild was properly baptized in the Roman Catholic faith as soon as etiquette allowed. There was a heated debate over the names that would be given to the new princess. Ferdinand insisted upon naming her for someone in his own family, while Maria Theresa was quick to remind Amalia of the Habsburg family law that commanded all first-born granddaughters to be named after herself. True to her self-willed character, the Duchess defied both her husband and the Empress and named the baby girl Carolina, in honor of the infant's godmother, Maria Carolina of Naples. This showed just how far removed mother and daughter had become.

The birth of Princess Carolina changed something in Amalia. She was still determined to take the rule of Parma for herself, but motherhood brought out a gentler side in her brazen personality. Her efforts now took on a decidedly more beneficent tone, directed at the country's welfare. Maria Theresa also redoubled her efforts to establish Parma as a nation of influence. She wrote letters, sent advisors, and even donated large sums of money to the Parmesan court. It was not difficult for the Empress to encourage her counterparts to co-operate, since Ferdinand was a grandson of Louis XV and a nephew of Carlos III. The wealth that poured into Parma after Amalia became a mother brought the nation to a level of prosperity it had not known before.

Amalia would remain Austrian to the very core all her life, but her affection for her mother was almost non-existent less than a year after her marriage. Now that she was a mother and on her way to becoming a strong-willed ruler, this often criticized and unloved daughter began ignoring her mother's advice. The money that the Empress donated meant little to the Duchess and could not be used as a means to control her.

By the time Carolina was born, Amalia had disregarded almost every piece of advice her mother had given her. She managed to cause a scandal by acting without any sense of etiquette. She replaced most of her ladies-in-waiting with handsome young men, giving them the title of "Royal Body-guards." Maria Theresa was by now preoccupied with Marie Antoinette's position in France. As a result, she was becoming increasingly upset by the impact her daughter's behavior was having in Parma. "This will reflect badly on my Dauphine," she wrote.[34]

Emperor Francis I; formerly Duke of Lorraine and Grand Duke of Tuscany (husband of Maria Theresa), c. 1760.

Maria Theresa, Holy Roman Empress, Queen of Hungary and Bohemia, Archduchess of Austria, c. 1760.

A portrait of the Imperial family,
1755. *Left to right*: Francis I,
Marianne, Amalia, Joseph,
Leopold, Elizabeth, Maria
Theresa, and Charles.

ॐ

Maria Carolina
("Charlotte") and her
brother Ferdinand, 1754.

ॐ

Archduchess Maria Antonia (later Marie Antoinette) in 1767. She was widely considered one of Maria Theresa's most beautiful daughters.

Archduchess Amalia, 1765. She was the eldest of Maria Theresa's reigning daughters, but as the Duchess of Parma, she ranked the lowest of all her siblings.

Grand Duke Leopold (*left*) and Emperor Joseph
II (*right*) together in Rome, 1769.

CB

Joseph II's first wife, Isabella of Parma (1741-1763). Isabella's brother was Amalia's husband Ferdinand, Duke of Parma. Her sister, Luisa, became queen consort of Spain.

Archduchess Theresa of Austria (1762-1770). She was the only surviving child of Joseph of Austria and Isabella of Parma.

Schönbrunn Palace outside Vienna,
c. 1760. This was the Habsburgs'
main summer residence.

The Royal Palace of Naples. This was Maria Carolina's
main home in Naples. It paled in comparison to the awe-
inspiring Caserta palace.

The Palace of Versailles, built by Louis XIV. It was the home of Marie
Antoinette and her family from 1770 until 1789.

ℭℨ

King Louis XV of France,
grandfather of Louis XVI. Along
with Carlos III and Maria Theresa,
he was one of the architects of the
Family Pact.

ℭℨ

King Carlos III of Spain (1716-
1788), c. 1760. He was the father
of King Ferdinand IV of Naples,
Empress María Luísa, and King
Carlos IV of Spain.

King Ferdinand IV of Naples and
Sicily at the age of nine. He was
seventeen when he married Archduchess Maria Carolina in 1767.

An Austrian Carnival

Near the end of 1770, Emperor Joseph II began to emerge from his grieving hibernation after the death of his daughter, Archduchess Theresa. But as Joseph returned to his state duties, it was not long before his brief reign was shaken by talk of revolution.

The kingdoms of Bohemia and Hungary had made up the backbone of the Habsburg monarchy for centuries. They were controlled by a feudal system of aristocrats and peasants, but by the beginning of the decade those same peasants were suffering more harshly than ever under their strict noble landowners. The rich were getting richer, and the poor were getting poorer. Maria Theresa expressed her opinions of the situation to her son Ferdinand about how "the peasants are crushed under the excesses of the lords who, in my thirty-six years of rule, have always known how to sabotage changes and how to hold their serfs in bondage."[1]

The situation could not continue forever, and the ensuing crisis would cripple the popularity of both Maria Theresa and Joseph II. What began with protests among the peasants over living conditions and feudal rights transformed into work stoppages, demonstrations, and uprisings. Food supplies quickly dwindled as panic set in across Bohemia and Hungary. Nearly "a quarter of a million Bohemian peasants starved to death" in the "devastating" central European famine of 1770-1772. The imperial family's popularity plummeted when it was discovered that, while the peasants starved, "their landlords amassed huge profits exporting grain to Prussia and Saxony."[2]

Exasperated by the suffering of millions, Joseph relayed the tragedy of the situation to Grand Duke Leopold, telling him how the "cruel drought produced innumerable worms and mice which devour the seed, and I fear even greater misery than last year."[3] In Bohemia, where the famine hit the hardest, growing unrest between the starving peasants and the rich aristocrats exploded to the brink of revolution. The crisis was made even worse by deficiencies in Austria's bureaucracy that delayed any aid from being distributed for two more insufferable years.

To help relieve the agony of her people, Empress Maria Theresa dispatched a commissioner to Bohemia's capital of Prague to assess the situation and offer a solution. But Joseph II was impatient with his mother's plan, telling Leopold: "In Bohemia the need has become so urgent that HM has had to send there a certain [man named] Kressel as commissar. I've been writing and talking about it continuously for nearly six months. No one has been willing to believe it or to act vigorously. We now see the results. *O patientia*, how many times a day I have to invoke you."[4] Kressel quickly reported to Maria Theresa that the situation was dire. He determined that the Bohemian peasants were literally too poor to even afford food.

The rampant starvation forced the Bohemians to their breaking point the following spring. Men, women, and children were dropping dead in the streets from starvation and malnutrition. To ease their suffering, Maria Theresa issued her Robot Patent, which lightened the peasants' financial burdens. In this one patent, she essentially "turned back the clock on a century and a half of illegal encroachment by the landed nobility."[5]

Unfortunately the Robot Patent did little to ease tensions. The peasants' payment obligations had been lessened, but they were still desperate for food and medicine. Finally at the end of their ropes, they revolted in 1775. Several thousand unarmed peasants came together and prepared to march on Prague. Many became frightened as the mob grew angrier and more violent, but the insurrection proved short-lived. More than 40,000 Austrian troops overwhelmed the rebels on a barren field long before they reached Prague. Order was restored, but at a high price. The reputation of the imperial family in Bohemia and Hungary was devastated. This would not be the last time the Habsburgs would face a revolution in the east.

The Magyar and Bohemian people blamed the catastrophe squarely on Emperor Joseph II's neglect of their countries' economies. His relationship with those subjects would never recover. Maria Theresa was the reigning queen of Hungary and Bohemia, but the chaos Joseph had wrought by ignoring those countries, and then waiting to deliver aid permanently weakened the position of the Imperial House of Habsburg within its own lands. To his subjects, Joseph II and the monarchy were one in the same. It would be almost another twenty years before any measurable level of peace would be restored in the east.

☘

After nearly six years as the Duchess of Parma, Amalia was beginning to settle into her role as first lady of the land. She and Ferdinand remained at loggerheads with one another, but their daughter Carolina was a constant source of joy for the young couple. They were devoted, loving parents.

The ducal family, though comfortably off, was never extravagantly wealthy in the way Amalia's brothers and sisters were. Money that poured in from Austria, Spain, and France went to relieve Parma's national debts and combat poverty and illiteracy in the cities. It was also used to help cover the debts Amalia was incurring. She was bent on remaining in as close to an Austrian lifestyle as she could, and "insisted on ridiculous exaggerations of all the habits of the Austrian court."[6] This included throwing lavishly expensive parties, purchasing fashionable dresses, and hiring even more servants for the already cramped Ducal Palace.

Amalia's frivolous spending was matched only by her reputation for being a "political intriguer" with a "sheer zest for the art of manipulation."[7] She continually stirred up dissention among the different factions at the court; no one ever knew whose side she was on. Empress Maria Theresa was appalled by her daughter's behavior. She plied the Duchess with letters exhorting her to submit to her husband, curb her spending, remove herself from state affairs, and devote her life to God. Amalia rarely replied to her mother, and in the few letters she did write to Vienna, she only complained about her life in Italy and showed little remorse for the chaos she was bringing upon her family.

There were always "foolish mistakes to be corrected, [and] offended persons to be conciliated. She did not know how to manage, or to make herself either popular or tolerably happy."[8] She offended the clergy and snubbed the aristocrats, which only hurt her popularity and her reputation even further. "For one so pious and moral as Maria Theresa, to see her own daughter Amalia scandalize herself must have been painful to bear," observed one historian.[9]

Ferdinand and Amalia spent most of their tumultuous marriage at the Ducal Palace in Parma, but their family also came to love the many other castles spread throughout the tiny country. For a few weeks each year, the ducal family moved north to Rezzanello, a cobblestone castle located between Piacenza and Milan. At Rezzanello, the Duchess and her daughter could take long leisurely walks in the lush green forests surrounding the castle. On hot days, the family relaxed by the glistening waters of a pond in the castle gardens.

From Rezzanello, they might go off to one of the countless ancient castles that dotted the countrysides of Parma, Piacenza, and Guastalla. Winter was often spent at Colorno, Parma's answer to Versailles. Its four hundred rooms, marble floors, and open parklands reminded Amalia of her childhood homes in and around Vienna. At Colorno, the ducal family was truly in their element. Ferdinand entertained himself with the priests in the neoclassical San Liborio Chapel, while Amalia held her own private court in the palace's *Sala Grande* ("Great Hall"), reportedly the largest ballroom in northern Italy.

Colorno also gave Amalia the chance to indulge in one of her favorite pastimes, horseback riding. She had developed a deep love for horses as a child, and by the time she was married had become a very accomplished rider.

At her residences, especially Colorno, Amalia loved to throw gala parties. She invited the country's aristocrats, but also opened her homes on these occasions to many of Parma's poor and unfortunate. At dinner, meals fit for a king were served to princes and peasants alike. Amalia's generosity, undoubtedly inherited from her mother, was "one of her engaging qualities."[10]

The British Minister in Florence, Horace Mann, wrote that the Duchess "is as generous as the Empress; France and Spain complain of it, but their remonstrances have had no effect."[11]

Maria Theresa praised Amalia for her generosity, but chastised her for interfering so much in politics. Very little was off limits to the Empress in her letters, including her daughter's marriage. The duchess regularly reported on her husband's endless stream of mistresses, most of whom were peasant women. Maria Theresa had faced the same trial herself with Francis I, and could relate to her daughter's feelings. The Empress encouraged her daughter to take the first step to mend her relationship with Ferdinand: "The more you reveal your feelings and your trust in leaving your husband free, the more devoted he will be. All happiness consists of trust and constant kindness. Foolish love is soon past, but you must respect each other. Each must prove the other's trust friend, in order to be able to bear the misfortunes of life and to establish the welfare of the House..."[12]

Maria Theresa encouraged Amalia to submit whole-heartedly to her husband, but in private, she had very different feelings about her Parmesan son-in-law. Before Amalia married Ferdinand, the only assurances the Empress had received on the Duke's character were what ambassadors told her, along with the three days Joseph spent in Parma in May 1769. When Amalia reported back to her in the weeks after her wedding about the type of man Ferdinand truly was, the Empress was outraged. She told Amalia that the burden of making her marriage work rested on the Duchess's shoulders, but to her daughter Mimi she secretly confided: "I cannot understand how the gentle Isabelle could have such a brother. Some men love mistresses, others gambling, and others horses, but this one—" Her letter abruptly ends, unable to find the words to express her anger over Ferdinand, Duke of Parma.[13]

One of Amalia's greatest detractors at the court of Parma was the country's prime minister, Guillaume du Tillot. He despised her haughtiness, opposed her when she tried to voice her opinions to her husband, and resented her for being Austrian.

A student of the old world school of thought, Tillot believed that the Austrians and the French were mortal enemies and would always be so. Maria Theresa once warned Amalia to be careful of him, saying that he was "considered only a foreigner [in Parma] relying solely on the welfare of the Infante [Ferdinand]" and "has a great number of enemies."[14] By the 1770s this was very much the case. Tillot's pro-French policies were making him unpopular with the people, and his bold edicts limiting the power of the Roman Catholic Church brought the anger of the clergy as well as the ducal family.

In every situation he looked to advance the interests of France and was worried by Amalia's arrival. He greatly would have preferred a French princess to an Austrian one for Ferdinand. Down to some of the smallest details, Tillot ensured Parma had become a subject of France the way Naples had of Spain. During Ferdinand's childhood, the Prime Minister replaced much of the Spanish workforce with French carpenters, tradesmen, artists, and decorators. Even the official court language was changed from Italian to French under his authority. Amalia was a harbinger of change in Parma, and she brought on her heels a renewed interest from Spain, with the power of the Austrian throne behind her. Tillot was now forced to contend with a duchess who was more than ready to replace France's influence with Austria's.

The prime minister was eventually forced out of office in the middle of the decade as a result of the "scandal" and "destitution" that he brought to the country through his devotion to Louis XV and his Franco-friendly policies.[15] Amalia took an active role in bringing down her nemesis. Perhaps for the first time, she formed political alliances within the court and rallied support from among nobles and clergy who had been snubbed by Tillot. Even the Parmesan people had shifted their distrust of foreigners from the Duchess to the Prime Minister. She was now beginning to been seen in a different light. She was a foreigner, yes, but she was one who worked at restoring national pride and the Parmesan sense of cultural identity.

The political crisis over Tillot's administration reached its climax one summer in the 1770s. The ducal family was at one of their country estates when a revolution broke out in the city of Parma. Thousands of people surrounded the Ducal Palace protesting against Tillot, accusing him of being a traitor. Amalia and the government ministers immediately returned to the capital and placed him under house arrest. That afternoon, she appeared on the balcony of the Ducal Palace. When the crowds saw her, they exploded in cheers of loyalty. *"Vive Ferdinand et Amélie!"* they cried. *"Vivent les ambassadeurs de France et les ambassadeurs d'Espagne!"** But the mob's hatred for Tillot was obvious: *"Meure de Tillot et sa canaille! Aux armes, aux armes, Parmesans; ne craignez rien.*[†16]

From his estate in Colorno, Tillot was forced to flee in disgrace to Spain, but he only made it as far as France. "I do not complain of the Parmesans," he said after fleeing. "They think me guilty, and did their duty. Time will come when they will judge me better and render me justice."[17]

Guillaume du Tillot was followed by a quick succession of unsuccessful prime ministers in Parma. In the hopes of stabilizing his nephew's court, King Carlos III appointed a new Spanish prime minister named José de Llano. With French interests no longer paramount in Parma, King Carlos hoped that Llano would bring a new era of Spanish influence. But despite his authority from the King, Llano immediately found himself at odds with Amalia, who was angry at not being consulted about the appointment of a new prime minister. She wrote to one of her ministers, the Marquis Cavriani:

> Your advice on Llano is starting to annoy me, because I know what I have to do [to handle him], and if my advice had been followed...Llano would not be here, and the Infante [Ferdinand] would be the master. But nothing was asked of my opinion [of bringing Llano to Parma], but even if I were asked, no one would believe me, because they think I am too *trop vive*. But great evils require greater remedies. And therefore, I advise you...on Llano, do not give me any more advice, because I will do only what I deem necessary.[18]

In a matter of weeks, Llano was forced from office and replaced by the first Italian prime minister in Parma's modern history, a man named Saccio. The rapid change of governments

---

* ("Long live Ferdinand and Amalia! Long live the ambassadors of France and Spain!")
† ("Death to Tillot and his rabble! With arms, with arms, Parmesans; fear nothing.")

in Parma had an immediate effect on the country. Many of the religious orders that had been suppressed under the Tillot regime returned and enjoyed prosperity under the devout Ferdinand, but academics began to feel persecuted.

Now that Ferdinand had a prime minister in whom he could place absolute trust, he devoted all his time to church ceremonies and raising his family. He was now more content than ever to leave the government in Amalia's hands. By eliminating Tillot, the Duchess of Parma had brought about the very gain of influence she had sought from the beginning.

෴

In the same way that Amalia of Parma dominated her husband, so too did Queen Maria Carolina control her husband, King Ferdinand IV of Naples. Unlike the Duchess though, Charlotte was often gentler and kinder with Ferdinand. And after several years of marriage, the queen had warmed up to her husband. She became "amused rather than depressed" by his "eccentric habits." In her words, Ferdinand had become "a really nice halfwit."[19]

There was never a question of who was in charge. Queen Maria Carolina knew exactly how to control King Ferdinand. She masterfully crafted a smokescreen of melodrama and marital discourse that made him submissive to her will. The royal couple had many volatile fights, but this was because Charlotte knew how to get what she wanted from her husband in just the right way. During their fights, the Queen would orchestrate the situation with such precision that Ferdinand would have to "go and solicit the first chamberlain to obtain permission to return to the nuptial bed, when the angry Queen had banished him from it." The of time needed for a reconciliation was usually determined by Charlotte and her first chamberlain, and was "proportioned to the gravity of the offence."[20] Eventually, the king learned to be obedient to his wife.

Queen Maria Carolina's reputation for being ambitious, clever, and strong-willed, was well earned, thanks in part to her diligent obedience to her mother's advice. Maria Theresa told Marie Antoinette in 1771: "You know how fond I am of your sister Caroline. I must do her the justice to say that, next to you, she has always shown the most genuine attachment to me and the greatest readiness to follow my advice."[21]

By the time she was twenty, Charlotte was very beautiful and used her looks to charm the people around her. Lady Anne Millar, an English noblewoman attached to the British embassy in Naples, praised the queen for having "the finest and most transparent complexion I ever saw." She was also gifted with "a finishing sweetness to her whole countenance."[22] Royalty from across Europe sang the praises of Italy's Austrian queen. Elizabeth, the last Margravine of Anspach, recalled in her memoirs that Charlotte "appeared much better calculated to represent the majesty of a throne [than Ferdinand], and to do the honours of a Court, where she had first imbibed the rudiments of her education. It was natural to her."[23]

The Queen impressed even the men in King Ferdinand's retinue. One of the generals observed that even though Charlotte was "in the prime of youth, her mind was of the most powerful stamp, and her wit of the highest order. By nature she was both proud and haughty, and she nourished within her bosom the most inordinate love of power."[24]

Her love of power should not be confused with being power-hungry. As the "queen of the largest dominions in Italy," she was convinced she was destined to play a part in history.[25] In her mind, "as the daughter of a great Empress, as sister of the Co-Regent of the Hapsburg realm and of the Grand Duke of Tuscany...she expected to play a role in world affairs."[26] Maria Carolina was determined to use her power as queen to increase her nation's influence in Europe by any means necessary.

One of the first things she did was to remove elements of Spanish influence from her kingdom. The Spanish empire was a spent force that could offer little to Naples, but it was clear that Austria and Great Britain were the new pre-eminent powers in Europe. Austria's influence stretched across nearly the entire continent, and Britain's navy was quickly becoming the most powerful in the world. It was only natural for Charlotte to strengthen Naples's ties with Austria; and Britain's fleet could protect them by sea.

The Queen also worked hard to rally the country's "cultured *élite*" to her cause.[27] She threw legendary parties at the Royal Palace attended by the British and Austrian legations, as well as

Naples' most prominent aristocrats. All eyes would be fixed on the King and Queen, dressed in black masks covering half their faces. The royal couple relaxed the strict etiquette at court balls, but guests still danced only at *their* invitation. One of the regular British guests was Lady Millar, who told a friend, "there are many of the Neapolitan nobility, even to the rank of dukes, who are allowed only to see the ball from the upper boxes." It was at her glamorous parties that the Queen cultivated a taste for all things English, thanks to the influence of Sir William Hamilton and his countrymen. Sometimes, there were as many as "three or four sets of English country-dances" in a single night.[28]

In between their galas in the capital, Ferdinand IV and Maria Carolina frequently entertained at their stunning palace in Caserta. There, the court etiquette was relaxed even further, but there were still no rights of entry for dining with the King and Queen. Spanish court customs, which had been the model for Naples, still existed to a lesser extent and prevented anyone from dining at the king's table. Instead, Charlotte did away with tables altogether and lined the ballroom with chairs for an open buffet that allowed for easy mingling. Whenever a buffet meal was served, the King and Queen were content to stand in line waiting for dinner like everyone else. Horace Mann noted that "by a most rigorous order from Spain, he [Ferdinand] cannot admit people to his table, [so now] he has no table at all. He and his Queen, as well as the whole company, eat off their knees."[29]

In the midst of Charlotte's political planning, she and Ferdinand were delighted when they were told the Queen was going to have a baby. The King and Queen both deeply desired to have children. Once, when Ferdinand was hunting at Caserta, he was approached by an impoverished peasant complaining that his wife had just given birth to triplets. "You are too fortunate!" the King cried. "The signora [Charlotte] and I have been married for years and have no children. How gladly I would be in your case!"[30]

Maria Carolina went into labor just before her twentieth birthday. She gave birth to a daughter—Teresa—at the Royal Palace in Naples on June 6, 1772. There was a genuine sense of disappointment from King Carlos III and Maria Theresa that it was not a boy. One of Charlotte's biographers wrote: "After waiting some years for the much-desired heir, Maria Caroline gave birth to a lovely infant; but alas! the perverse little creature was of the wrong sex."[31] This did not bother the King and Queen of Naples. They were blissfully happy to be parents, and dotted on their firstborn child. Ferdinand was kind and gentle with his daughter, and Maria Carolina devoted herself completely to her role as a mother. She would often say that she "was a mother before anything else."[32]

By autumn, Charlotte was once again pregnant. When she told her husband, Ferdinand was thrilled and tearfully embraced his wife. Marie Antoinette of France was happy for her sister, and understood the political importance of having a son. She wrote to Maria Theresa, "I hear that the queen is expecting to be confined. I hope her child will be a son."[33]

CЗ

Maria Theresa spent much of the 1770s struggling with her children. She battled Joseph incessantly; cleaned up Amalia's mistakes in Parma; defended Charlotte to King Carlos III; and guided Marie Antoinette along the treacherous tightrope at Versailles. The one bright spot among her reigning children was Grand Duke Leopold in Tuscany.

Maria Theresa's son and daughter-in-law were the parents of a rapidly growing brood of children. Archduchess Theresa and Archduke Francis were joined in quick succession on an almost annual basis by Ferdinand in 1769; Maria Anna ("Marianne") in 1770; Karl in 1771; Alexander in 1772; Albert in 1773; and Maximilian ("Max") in 1774.

In spite of the differences they had experienced earlier in Leopold's reign, he had earned his mother's respect as both a ruler and a father. Though he himself struggled with some of the tenets of Roman Catholicism, Leopold insisted his children have a proper Christian upbringing marked by humility and modesty. When it came to their religious lives, he told Charlotte of Naples: "In general we have made it a maxim to set up in our children a solid religious foundation based upon persuasion and the true devotion of the heart." And when it came to their character, he worked to ensure they each had "a straightforward, honest, sincere, and compassionate heart, never overlooking even the slightest fault in character,...but passing lightly and indulgently over the slips attributable to youth....We have never flattered them and they have always been told the truth, plainly and forcefully..."[34]

The archdukes and archduchesses of Tuscany led a contented childhood. Leopold wanted them to grow up free from restrictive court etiquette and being able to express themselves. The children were "not brought up in a palace, but in a home." As a result, they were simple and unaffected. But the Grand Duke also expected exemplary maturity from each of his children, especially his sons. He "endeavored to make men of them, not princes, which they already were."[35]

One thing that Leopold took great pains to impart into his children was the concept of royalty serving the people. In 1774 he told the tutors of his younger children:

> The princes must be very aware that they are human beings: that they hold their positions only through the sanction of other human beings; that for their part they must discharge all their duties and cares; and that the other people must have the right to expect all benefits that have been granted to them...True greatness is broad, gentle, familiar, and popular, it loses by being seen at close quarters."[36]

At the Pitti Palace, the boys were divided into two simple, undecorated nurseries, one for the older archdukes and one for the younger ones. Theresa and Marianne had their own equally unassuming nursery. Even the clothes they wore were uncomplicated. Leopold told Charlotte that his "boys, until they are nine, are dressed in sailor suits with large wide trousers, a small jacket at the neck and a round hat."[37]

A strong sense of merriment prevailed in the grand ducal family. All the children were encouraged to "jump, run, use both hands equally, [and] fear nothing." In the summer, Leopold and María Luísa loved taking their family on vacations into the countryside or to the beach on the Mediterranean coast. In the fall when the air was cool and balmy, the children—led by Theresa and Francis—romped and played throughout the Pitti Palace. Leopold told one of his sisters, "we allow them to spend some time each day sliding around in shirts on mattresses spread across the floor."[38]

When it came to education, special care needed to be taken for Archduke Francis. The young boy was destined to become emperor one day, so both Leopold and Joseph agreed he needed to be placed under the care of only the most skilled tutors and instructors. When it came to his children, Leopold understood the role that they played in the future of Austria's monarchy. As a result, he surprised his wife when he agreed to allow Emperor Joseph II a degree of influence over his children's upbringings. In this case, Leopold allowed the Emperor and Maria Theresa to find a suitable tutor for Francis.

In 1774, when Francis was eight, the decision was made on Count Francis Colloredo. An Austrian by birth, Colloredo was a member of the aristocracy and had helped govern the province of Lower Austria for many years. After careful consideration, both Maria Theresa and Joseph II believed he would satisfactorily shape Archduke Francis into a young man who could rule. "I hope Colloredo pleases you," Joseph wrote to Leopold, "although he is not to be judged by preliminaries. It remains to be seen, in a couple of years,… whether he will be as precise and assiduous in following your precepts as I believe he will be."[39]

Colloredo officially began teaching Francis and his younger brother Ferdinand in June 1774. "I like you very much and shall do all I can," Francis told Colloredo. "I have never yet offended God nor lied, and I shall conduct myself prudently."[40] The choice of Colloredo would come to be regarded as extremely prudent. In the years to come, once Francis became emperor and was charged with saving Europe, Colloredo would be his great mentor, advisor, and friend.

 CB

Empress Maria Theresa's health began to decline throughout the 1770s. She was well into her fifties now, and the strain of ruling a vast empire and an equally vast family was exasperating her. She wrote to Marie Antoinette: "my hands and my eyes are failing; I shall no longer be able to write to you but by the hand of another. You will excuse the blots and erasures in this [letter]."[41]

The Dauphine of France was deeply worried about her mother's failing health. When she was told that Maria Theresa was seriously ill during the winter of 1772, Marie Antoinette "dissolved in tears, and [was] unable to say anything except that she was not in a condition to give audience." Comte Mercy, who had witnessed the episode, reported back to the Empress: "She asked for a rosary Your Majesty had given her, and began to pray. Monsieur the Dauphin, who did not leave her, seemed to share very sincerely the grief of his august spouse."[42]

A year later, the Empress had still not recovered completely. She confessed to Joseph in 1773, "my capabilities, my looks, my hearing, my skill are swiftly declining." At times, the aging monarch felt overwhelmed by the way society had changed since her youth. "The irreligion, the deterioration of morals, the jargon which everybody uses and which I do not understand," she said, "all these are enough to overwhelm me."[43]

Maria Theresa's failing health was undermined even further by a new political crisis that emerged in the early 1770s, centered around Poland. For centuries, Poland had been a major European power with a strong ruling dynasty, but by the second half of the eighteenth century it had become little more than a Russian protectorate. Civil war, peasant uprisings, and foreign interference had been destabilizing it for decades. This gave Russia's ambitious tsarina, Catherine the Great, the idea of taking the country for her empire once and for all. She convinced Joseph II and Frederick the Great to agree to a partition of Poland. To keep each other happy, Europe's three eastern powers decided to each take a negotiated piece of the country, which was totally unable to speak for itself. This was the beginning of what became Emperor Joseph II's lifelong mission to expand his realm's borders by force. In the end, Austria walked away from the bargaining table with most of southern Poland, Zator, Auschwitz, and Galicia, and added more than two and a half million people to its population.

Maria Theresa was appalled by the entire scheme. She openly expressed her feelings about it in a letter to Joseph: "I must admit that never before in my life have I been so profoundly troubled. When an unrighteous claim was made on my territories, I stiffened my back and put my trust in God. But on the present occasion...I can get no rest." The Empress was even more candid about her feelings in a letter to her son Ferdinand: "You will be duly informed of the dreary course of the affair....God grant that I may not be held responsible for it in another world: I am haunted by it now. It weighs sharply on my heart and tortures my brain and embitters my days....I pull myself up sharply, or the worry of it all will land me in melancholia."[44]

The strain placed upon Maria Theresa by the Polish crisis and the constant altercations with her son left her feeling drained and worn out. She admitted to Joseph after the partition was resolved that "with the best of intentions, we do not understand each other.... You show too clearly against all old customs and the entire clergy and too free principles in morality and behaviour."[45]

The partition imbroglio did nothing to help the worsening relationship between mother and son. Joseph's "rude and brusque" behavior was a "constant source of aggravation" to Maria Theresa. She described him as "an intellectual coquette" who was "as radical as she was conservative."[46] He constantly hounded her, and when the signs of her age began to press upon her, he overwhelmed her with demands and constant threats to resign from the co-regency, which would effectively rob his mother of her power. Grand Duke Leopold once described the deteriorating situation between his mother and brother by saying: "When they are together, there is [sic] unbroken strife and constant arguments...even in the smallest affairs; they are never of the same opinion and fight with each other constantly over matters worth nothing."[47]

Emperor Joseph II saw his mother as a microcosm of the state of the House of Habsburg. Writing to Leopold, he said: "I reckon that the best pen is hard put to it to dress it up in such a way as to hide the pitiable condition—of uncertainty and irresolution combined with timidity, weakness and pusillanimity—in which the Monarchy, with all its resources and means, languishes and sinks towards its doom."[48]

ை

Now that Amalia had almost total control of the Parmesan government, she was more committed than ever to being her own master. Outside the political arena, she was far more interested in entertaining herself than in her husband or fixing their fractured marriage.

When she could have been taking time to understand and make amends with the dim-witted Ferdinand, Amalia instead spent her time horseback riding, gallivanting at the officer's club in Parma, and gambling away the small fortune that was allotted to her as duchess. When the money started drying up, Amalia pawned the eye-catching diamonds her mother had given her as a wedding present to cover her debts. She made it a point to break with almost every social etiquette that was expected of a reigning consort. She wandered through city streets late at night unescorted, craving amusements; she openly took to love affairs with her male bodyguards; and even dressed in cognito as a man, pretending to be a Spanish prince, when she went shopping.

Unlike the popular Queen Maria Carolina in Naples, Parma's courtiers derided Amalia. They declared her a tomboy, in the extreme, who had delusions of grandeur. Her harshest critics labeled the "Messalina of the eighteenth century."[49] She felt just as much disdain for them, too. They served their own interests, she concluded, and had no concern for the welfare of Parma or its people. Despite the accusations leveled against her, Amalia was deeply passionate about restoring Parma's sense of nationalism that had been stripped away under the Tillot regime. Along with her ministers, she helped cultivate art, literature, and music throughout Parma, Piacenza, and Guastalla.

At the age of twenty-eight, Amalia, Duchess of Parma, was still a young woman with boundless energy. Her attention constantly darted in different directions. But given her unsatisfying marital life, it is not surprising she looked elsewhere for fulfillment. Behind the walls of the Ducal Palace, Ferdinand and Amalia fought constantly. The Duke of Parma was still very immature, lacking in ambition, and offered little to his high-spirited wife. She, in turn, treated Ferdinand in the most reprehensible way. She ridiculed and insulted him constantly. She also publicly humiliated him by canceling orders that he had given. Edicts he issued were even changed to read: "We, my wife and I, order..."[50]

In a letter to her chief minister, Amalia boldly defined her role in Parma: "In my house I give orders, the Infante [Ferdinand] and I unite in this…. Here I possess enough power to command obedience. I am German, and I know what is due to me. Don't forget that. I can make people fear me as well as love me, so I advise you to obey." On the surface, Ferdinand agreed with his wife. He accepted her decisions, and chose not to argue with her commands, but in private, he had a very different opinion of her capabilities. "I am a child," he said, "but my wife is still more so. She has not the talents to rule a land."[51]

Maria Theresa soon became infuriated by Amalia's conduct and reached her breaking point. Desperate to find a way to correct her daughter's scandalous behavior, she wrote to Comte Mercy in 1773: "Perhaps the only way to lead my daughter back to her obligation would, it seems, be to find a person who would be suitable, who could win her trust and lead her, but where is one to find such a person?" With a heavy heart, Maria Theresa concluded: "I see with pain that one will be forced to forget Parma completely in the end."[52]

The only remedy the Empress could think of was to send one of her ministers, Count Rosenberg, to Italy to try and rein in the Duchess. "This is a very serious business," she told Rosenberg. "The errors and unpleasant events…in Parma since the day of the marriage of our Daughter Amalia with the…Duke of Parma are unfortunately known to all of Europe, and are used for stories and laughter."[53] Maria Theresa wrote a twenty-five-page letter for Rosenberg to deliver to her daughter entitled "Rules of the prescribed conduct of the infanta Amalia by count Rosenberg, on the part of the empress Maria Theresa, her mother." In it, the Empress hid none of her feelings from Amalia:

> There is only one sovereign and that is the Infante [Ferdinand], and Madame Infanta [Amalia] is only the spouse of the sovereign.

> When you left for Parma, I always knew you were the wife of the sovereign, and therefore the second person; but most unfortunately I saw that the Infante was never treated as sovereign, and after less than a month, he became first after the Infanta.[54]

It became clear shortly after Rosenberg arrived in Parma that his efforts were useless. The Empress could no longer keep supporting her daughter in light of the Duchess's "political machinations [and] general bad behavior."[55] For all their combined efforts, Maria Theresa and King Carlos III were utterly helpless to aid Ferdinand in establishing a government in Parma separate from the influence of his wife. His age, inexperience, and political apathy, coupled with Amalia's own ambition, made it nearly impossible to form a government that was untainted by her reputation or overcrowded with ministers that were loyal to her.

The Empress tried writing to the Duchess again in the hopes of forcing her into submission by sheer willpower. She told Amalia stories of the outrage at Versailles over Tillot's dramatic exit from the country. And for one brief, fleeting moment, Amalia actually seemed repentant about the way she had been living, but in record time she resumed ignoring the Empress, even in the face of threats of "being constantly watched" by Austrian spies. She made it clear to Count Rosenberg that she no longer wanted to be bothered by letters from Vienna, or Madrid for that matter.[56] For the Empress, Amalia was one "of the many crosses [she] had to bear." Of all of Maria Theresa's children, Amalia "must have undoubtedly caused Maria Theresa the most headache."[57]

By 1773, both King Carlos III and Maria Theresa were forced to sever ties with Parma completely. On a family level, Amalia's "recklessness created an unbridgeable gulf between her mother and her."[58] She was now *persona non grata* in the Habsburg family. Maria Theresa disowned her, stopped all letters, and even forbid any of her other children from communicating "with this unruly sister." She always hoped that her severity would open her daughter's eyes and perhaps be a source of positive distress for the Duchess, prompting her to better herself as a woman, wife, and ruler. The opposite turned out to be true: Amalia "was probably relieved when her mother's severe and tedious letters ceased to arrive."[59]

For the first time in her life, Amalia felt free of her mother's overbearing influence. The Duchess's fortunes seemed to be improving. She and Ferdinand were slowing becoming accustomed to one another; they fought less and actually found they were beginning to tolerate each other's company. A bright spot that helped their marriage at this time was the news that Amalia was pregnant again.

Her doctors encouraged the Duchess to go to Colorno for the birth. The palace there was more modern compared to the damp old Ducal Palace in Parma and provided better amenities to childbirth. On July 5, 1773, a son was born to Amalia and Ferdinand. When the baby was baptized the next day in Colorno's chapel—the same one the Duke and Duchess were married in—he was given the names Luigi Francesco Filiberto. As the heir to the miniscule Duchy of Parma, no one ever expected that this tiny prince was destined to become a king, and a tragic one at that.

☙

Less than three weeks after Amalia of Parma gave birth to a son, Queen Maria Carolina of Naples went into labor with her second child. She delivered a daughter named Luisa after an agonizing birth on July 27, 1773.

Though the Queen was happy to be a mother again, there was nevertheless a sense of disappointment that the child was not a boy. "Again she underwent the peril and labour," recorded one historian, "only to endure a repetition of the same exasperating disappointment." Ferdinand's ministers began looking at Charlotte as little more than "the mother of children, who were 'only girls'."[60]

Nonetheless, the Queen thrived in her role as mother. She proudly considered that to be her first duty, even before being a queen. Charlotte raised her daughters amidst the splendor of the royal palaces in Naples, Caserta, and Portici. There, she made sure that reminders of her beloved homeland surrounded her two daughters. She was very proud to have maintained an Austrian atmosphere within her family.

German was not just an ethnicity to the Queen, it was a state of being. In her private antechambers, she spoke only German, an opportunity she enjoyed because her entire household was Austrian or German. In her entourage there were at least forty-five German maids, pages, and valets. She also appointed Germans and Austrians to positions of authority in Naples. Johann Tischblein and Philip Hackert were commissioned by Charlotte to decorate her palaces in such a way as to remind her of Laxenburg, Schönbrunn, or the Hofburg.

The despotic prime minister, Bernardo Tanucci, was incensed by Maria Carolina's presumption in dismissing and appointing ministers as she saw fit. He labored under the assumption that he was indispensable to the King and Queen and "gloried in the sensation." His power remained unchallenged for years, and he did not consider Charlotte a real threat because "she seemed too flippant to be taken seriously." While the King and Queen were dining *al fresco* one night, Ferdinand retired early to go hunting the next morning. During an after-dinner stroll, Charlotte tripped and fell into the Gulf of Naples with a pair of Austrian brothers she had met earlier that evening. It took the commander of the royal galleys and a team of sailors to retrieve her, which gave rise to malicious gossip and rumors. When King Ferdinand heard what had happened he was furious, but Tanucci "reassured himself that he had little to fear from this high-spirited young woman." Embarrassing moments such as this did not stop Queen Maria Carolina from trying to infuse Naples with some of the glamour of the Viennese court: "With her youthful vivacity and aura of Viennese glamour, Maria Carolina rejuvenated the life of the Neapolitan court. Historians speak of an Austrian Carnival after a Spanish Lent."[61]

One person who never hesitated to sing Charlotte's praises was the British ambassador to the Two Sicilies, Sir William Hamilton. He and Charlotte became fast friends because, like the Queen, Hamilton was himself a strong force in Naples. The ambassador was a veritable institution in the Two Sicilies, having served there for thirty years. Sir Nathaniel Wraxall described him as having "such an air of intelligence blended with distinction in his countenance" that it "powerfully attracted and conciliated every beholder."

Sir William was famous for his "superior intellect [and] philosophical mind,"[62] which attracted travelers and royals alike to his Neapolitan estate. His charisma and joie de vivre made him a close friend of Charlotte's. In the difficult years ahead of the Queen, William Hamilton would become an indispensible friend.

"We Are Too Young to Reign"

At the palace of Versailles, Marie Antoinette lived in a gilded cage. Her whole life was spent in the presence of others, but she always felt terribly alone. She was constantly in the company of an entourage she hardly knew, that was handpicked by Louis XV and the head of her household, the strict and inflexible Comtesse de Noailles. In her position as Madame la Dauphine, Marie Antoinette was waited upon by hundreds of individuals. She had people to manage her household, mistresses of etiquette, financiers, valets, bedchamber servants, priests, and chefs. She "could not make a gesture, take a step, utter a word without triggering a reaction in the attendants who never left her."[1]

Coming from the familial, bourgeoisie Habsburg court, she was overwhelmed by how she was now being treated with the "unremitting solemnity" that had been established "for all Bourbons since Louis XIV instituted his system of etiquette." When it came to her role as dauphine, "the protocol to which the princess was forced to adhere turned her into both an idol and a victim: an idol because her entourage had to worship her like a goddess, but a victim because their staunch service robbed her of whatever privacy she had enjoyed in Vienna."[2]

It did not take Marie Antoinette long to begin missing her native Austria. Despite holding one of the highest positions in Europe, the youngest of Maria Theresa's five special children had the most difficulty adapting to her new homeland. After six months in France, she was still "young, open, volatile, and inexperienced...in the midst of people who hated Austria, and detested any alliance with the imperial house."[3] Writing to her mother, she was quick to declare, "my heart is always with my family in Austria." And she admitted: "I swear to you, that I have not received one of your dear letters without having tears come to my eyes....I ardently wish I could see my dear, my very dear, family for at least one more instant."[4]

To ease her homesickness, Marie Antoinette fought hard to make friends at Versailles, especially with the ladies in her entourage. She ingratiated herself with other fun-loving young women of the court. This group that the Dauphine found herself a part of "loved pleasure and hated restraint, laughed at everything, even the tattle about their own reputations, and recognized no law save the necessity of spending their lives in gaiety, behind a thin and sometimes deceptive screen of decorum, which concealed badly, or not at all, certain caprices which came near to creating scandal."[5]

Louis Auguste, the shy, awkward Dauphin, took no notice of his wife's behavior. As a matter of fact, her barely noticed her at all because he was too shy to even approach her. On a personal level, the couple related as well as could be expected; they were genuinely good friends, nothing more. While Marie Antoinette waited for her husband to mature, she found comfort and acceptance with her new friends. Among them was her playboy brother-in-law Charles, Comte d'Artois. Charles took it upon himself to arrange amusements for the dauphine, who filled her days with pastimes like "chasing butterflies in the palace gardens" and "going for donkey rides in the forests around Versailles."[6] Emperor Joseph II disapproved of his sister's behavior, saying, "If she listened a little less to the people who urge her on...she would be perfect." He believed that her "desire to have fun" was a "weakness" that anti-Austrian courtiers preyed upon.[7]

Maria Theresa was even more anxious than her son when it came to Marie Antoinette's activities. "I see, with grief, the dangers that threaten my child," she wrote to Comte Mercy.[8] In another letter, she confessed her fears over "the stormy circumstances of the court of France, my daughter's situation greatly disturbs me. Her nonchalance, her slight inclination for all serious application, her indiscretion (caused by her youth and vivacity),...furnish me with more than one subject to fear."[9]

The Dauphine's breaking with the rigid traditions of the French court did not stop with her late nights and wild parties. She even accompanied Louis Auguste and the King on their hunting excursions, which was considered the territory of men. These times allowed her to show off her exceptional horse riding skills, which she had honed during her early years in Austria. But when it came to carrying on like the men, Maria Theresa strongly objected to her daughter's actions:

> Riding spoils the complexion, and in the end your waistline will suffer from it and begin to show more noticeably. Furthermore, if you are riding like a man, dressed like a man, as I suspect you are, I have to tell you that I find it dangerous as well as bad for bearing children—and that is what you have been called upon to do; that will be the measure of your success. If you were riding like a woman, dressed as a woman, then I would have less cause for concern. It is impossible to guard against accidents. Those that have befallen others, like the Queen of Portugal, who afterwards were unable to have children, are anything but reassuring....One day you will agree with me, but it will be too late.[10]

Maria Theresa's letter provoked an instant reaction from her daughter. Marie Antoinette assured her: "the King and Monsieur le Dauphin take pleasure in seeing me on horse-back....They have been enchanted to see me in the uniform of the hunt."[11] Knowing she had been beaten on this one issue, Maria Theresa acquiesced: "Since you tell me that the King and the Dauphin approve, then it is enough for me. It is up to them to command you; it is into their hands that I have placed my lovely Antoinette."[12]

The Empress's letter did touch on a point that was a sore one for the dauphine: after four years of marriage, she was still not pregnant. It continued to be a source of deep worry for her. This was never more true than when she learned that her sisters, Amalia of Parma and Charlotte of Naples, were expecting children again. "When shall I be able to say the like?" she woefully asked her mother.[13] More than any of the other five special Habsburg children, Marie Antoinette of France had inherited her mother's overwhelming sense of duty. All that she longed for was to bring honor to her husband, her family, and France, by producing an heir. She also wanted someone to love unconditionally, but her shame at not having a child was about to be overshadowed by one of the most significant events of the 1770s, which had dramatic consequences for her, France, and ultimately, the fate of Europe.

On May 10, 1774, King Louis XV died from smallpox. He had been healthy for years, so when the virus invaded Versailles no one expected him to fall ill. This particular strain of smallpox was so deadly that more than ten courtiers died within twenty-four hours. On his deathbed, the ailing monarch, who had reigned for fifty-nine years, took his first confession in four decades. He repented for his adultery and fornication, and in keeping with his penitence, banished the Comtesse du Barry. "Madame, I am sick, and I know what I have to do," he told her.[14] Marie Antoinette reported to her mother, "Happily the cruel illness left the King's mind clear till the very last, and his end was very edifying."[15]

One contemporary observed that the reign of Louis XV, while "peaceful in general, had preserved a degree of strength imparted to it by the power of his predecessor: on the other hand, his own weaknesses had been preparing misfortune for the prince who was to reign after him."[16]

The unfortunate man on whom this great burden fell was Marie Antoinette's nineteen-year-old husband, who was now King Louis XVI. The royal couple was waiting in Marie Antoinette's apartments when they received the news of the King's death. The sound of the courtiers rushing to pay homage to the new sovereigns was "a terrible noise, exactly like thunder." When they were told the awful news, the couple dropped to their knees and cried out: "Dear God, guide us and protect us. We are too young to reign."[17]

Jacques de Norvins, a French aristocrat, wrote that after Louis XV's death, "mourning could be seen everywhere from the blazing chapel of Versailles and the funeral luxury of the princely residences to the lowliest shops in the suburbs. Everyone took pains to make his clothing look melancholy. All of France went into mourning."[18] Louis XV's funeral at St. Denis was hardly what one would have expected though. It resembled "rather the removal of a load one is anxious to get rid of than the last duties rendered to a monarch."[19]

One of Marie Antoinette's first acts as queen was to extend the banishment of the Comtesse du Barry into full-fledged exile, along with her supporter, the Duc d'Aiguillon. The decision signaled a final, decisive victory for the new Queen against her most dangerous rival. The future looked bright for Marie Antoinette of France. Emperor Joseph sent his best wishes to his sister: "I congratulate you on your husband's accession to the throne."[20]

Now that she was queen, Marie Antoinette had a glimpse of what it must have been like for her mother. She began to understand the efforts the Empress took to secure such a vaunted position for her. She wrote to Maria Theresa shortly after Louis XV's death: "I feel more than ever what I owe to the tenderness of my august mother, who expended such pains and labor in procuring for me this splendid establishment."[21]

Maria Theresa had been preparing her daughter for this moment for years, but when it finally arrived, she had an ominous foreboding about the future. "I am distressed, truly distressed, the burden is too great," she lamented.[22] She under-stood the weight of ruling, and was painfully aware of the shortcomings of both her daughter and son-in-law. The Empress wrote prophetically to Comte Mercy that from now on, her daughter's life "will be either very noble or very unhappy....I think her happy days are over, and sooner even than mine were."[23] She repeated a similar sentiment to her son Ferdinand: "I fear this is the last of your sister's peaceful happy days."[24] Only time would tell whether or not Maria Theresa's worries were justified, but in the meantime she wrote to her daughter drily: "I shall not pay you any compliments on your dignity; it is very dear-bought...you are both very young and the burden is heavy....But all I can advise you is, do nothing precipitately; learn to see with your own eyes; change nothing."[25]

For the moment, fortune seemed to be smiling on the new king and queen. The French people greeted the accession of their new monarchs with overwhelming joy; they called the King "Louis *le Désiré*."[26] France had stagnated for decades under Louis XV, now the people were ready for a young ruler who was in tune with the needs of the people. Queen Marie Antoinette was just as loved by her countrymen. The French poet Jean Baptiste Gresset spoke of "the universal delight, the affectionate acclamations, that preceded, accompanied, and followed" Marie Antoinette wherever she went.[27]

Many of her contemporaries noted that the Queen seemed to be even more popular than the King. When news reached the Empress of Marie Antoinette's popularity, she praised her daughter: "Every one is in ecstasy, every one is wild about you…they expect the greatest happiness. You have revived a nation which was in extremity, and which was alone sustained by its affection for its princes."[28]

During this exhilarating time in Marie Antoinette's life, signs were already visible of the great upheaval that lay ahead. The Republican writer Avenel announced prophetically: *"The Austrian is on the Throne!...* This is the Prologue of the great drama which is soon to begin, when Paris will march upon Versailles to win back France for the French."[29]

Very few people in Paris were against Louis and Marie Antoinette, but in a surprising twist, the only place they were not universally loved was at their own court. Ambitious plots abounded, and seemed to spring up everywhere. Writing to Leopold in Tuscany, Emperor Joseph II hoped, "above all, that our sister will have nothing to do with the intrigues of the court."[30] But in the days following Louis XVI's accession, *Mesdames Tantes*—the Princesses Adélaïde, Victoire, and Sophie— seized an opportunity with their ill-prepared nephew to strike against Austria. They used Louis to appoint a series of new, anti-Austrian ministers, who would push for a break with the Habsburgs. The subsequent appointments of the Comte de Vergennes and the Comte de Maurepas crushed Marie Antoinette. Both were completely against all things Austrian, including the Queen herself.

This inevitably led to the birth of two warring factions at the court of Versailles: those for the Austrian alliance, and those against it. Louis XV had believed in the alliance wholeheartedly, but Louis XVI's rise shed some doubt on its future. The anti-Austrian group worked their strategies against Marie Antoinette. They were "discontented and vindictive" and "became spies upon her [the Queen's] conduct, exaggerated her slightest errors, and calumniated her most innocent proceedings."[31]

After less than a year, Queen Marie Antoinette began to lose some of her famed popularity among her subjects. One of the greatest detriments to her reputation was her brother-in-law, the Comte d'Artois, who was still responsible for her entertainments. In Austria, Maria Theresa and Joseph II began to worry about her as well, especially the amount of time she spent with Artois. Comte Mercy wrote a letter to the Empress confirming many of her fears: "on several occasions it has been noticed that he [Artois] drinks intemperately and is addicted to gambling."[32]

It did not take long for Marie Antoinette to become consumed with entertainments. Her evenings usually began at the opera or theatre, followed by a lavish party or gambling until the early morning hours. Unable to tolerate her daughter's behavior any longer, Maria Theresa sent her a scolding letter:

> What frivolity! Where is the kind and generous heart of the Archduchess Antoinette? All I see is intrigue, low hatred, a persecuting spirit, and cheap wit...Your too early success and your entourage of flatterers have always made me fear for you, ever since that winter when you wallowed in pleasures and ridiculous fashions. Those excursions from pleasure to pleasure without the King and in the knowledge that he doesn't enjoy them and that he either accompanies you or leaves you free out of sheer good nature...Where is the respect and gratitude you owe him for all his kindness?[33]

Shortly after this letter arrived, it was followed by another from the Empress. In it, she sought to reassure her daughter of her motives for being so harsh:

> My dear daughter, here are four points that I recommend to you with all the love of which you know I am capable: Do not say that I scold, that I preach. Say rather: Mama loves me very much and is constantly concerned about me and my well-being. You must believe her and comfort her by following her advice. You will feel easy in this, and in future every shadow that has so vexed you will be banished from my confidence.[34]

173

The people of France, however, were not as quick to reassure the Queen of their love for her. They were slowly becoming offended by Marie Antoinette. The French yearned for serious monarchs who would bring reform and reshape the country, but instead were frustrated by an indecisive king and an apparently shallow queen. In one of the first public displays since her husband's accession, Queen Marie Antoinette joined the court at a horserace. Far from the cries of applause that surrounded her as dauphine, she was instead greeted with very noticeable public displeasure. According to Comte Mercy: "the Queen was not received with the customary applause and indications of joy.... The public sees that the Queen is thinking only of amusements."[35] Slowly but surely, cracks were beginning to develop in the love France had for its Austrian queen.

&

Maria Carolina was facing her own opposition in the form of her father-in-law, King Carlos III of Spain. Unlike in Parma, the King was still a very powerful force in Naples, and always had a close relationship with his son, King Ferdinand.

Charlotte's efforts to rid her country of Spain's authority had a direct impact on the royal family. What began as a matter of simple foreign policy turned into a clash involving two strong-willed rulers. King Carlos took Charlotte's efforts to replace Spanish authority with Austrian authority in her country as a personal attack on him as a father. Though the Queen never admitted to having a personal vendetta against Carlos III, it is understandable why he might have thought that.

Caught in the middle of this battle royal was King Ferdinand IV. Day by day, he was forced to choose between his loving father and his strong wife. Perhaps the cause for the friction between Carlos III and Maria Carolina was the fact that they were actually quite similar. Had they ever united in a given cause, their combined willpower and tenacity would likely have been unstoppable.

The strained relationship between these two rulers enjoyed a respite for a time when Maria Carolina became pregnant again. On a cold winter morning in January 1775, that great moment that Charlotte and Ferdinand had been praying for finally arrived. The labor was long and hard, but the Queen delivered a son in her apartments at the palace in Naples.

Halberdiers flew from the palace to spread the news throughout the capital. In the nearby Gulf of Naples, warships fired cannon salutes in honor of the crown prince, who was given the traditional title Duke of Calabria. That night, celebrations were held across the city of Naples. The British ambassador, Sir William Hamilton, threw a party in his palatial home. At dinner, he toasted the health of the King, Queen, and infant prince. At the baby's baptism, he was named Carlo after his godfather and grandfather, King Carlos III of Spain. In France, the news was "greeted with unselfish joy" by the still childless Marie Antoinette when she heard that her sister had finally produced a son.[36]

Prince Carlo's birth gave Maria Carolina greater influence than ever before, since her marriage contract gave her a seat on the Neapolitan Council of State after she delivered a son. The Queen announced that she was "fully prepared for that event. The public rejoicings had scarcely subsided before she claimed her right to enter the Council" and take an even more active role in governing.[37]

The Neapolitans began to view their queen in an even greater light. She had done her duty to the nation, and her popularity rose even higher. Ferdinand began to view his wife differently too. Now that she had presented him with the much-coveted heir, he was even more open to her influence. He gave his wife greater support in her efforts to bring Naples to a place of power in Europe.

In the years following Prince Carlo's birth, Naples enjoyed "halcyon years of peace and prosperity." The country became famous as a haven for British citizens, thanks to Charlotte's love of all things English. William Hamilton gladly reported to his superiors in London, "Their Sicilian Majesties upon every occasion are remarkably gracious to the subjects of Great Britain."[38]

There was never any doubt that the head of this prosperous government was Maria Carolina. When the famed writer Louis Dutens visited Caserta—the same Dutens who visited Vienna when the Queen was a small child—he noticed the very unique way in which the royal couple functioned. When he was invited into an audience with Ferdinand and Charlotte, Dutens observed that the King "never spoke, or at least very rarely...but the Queen made ample amends for his silence, by the affability and the engaging manners with which she received" her guests.[39]

The peace in her kingdom allowed Charlotte to devote more attention to her family. Teresa, Luisa, and Carlo were soon joined by another girl, Mariana, in November 1775. Charlotte loved her children deeply, and was passionately committed to every area of their lives in the same way her mother had been with hers; their education was of particular importance to the Queen. The world-renowned painter Elisabeth Vigée Le Brun (who later became a close friend of Queen Marie Antoinette) regularly visited Naples. She once observed, "The Queen is a very highly cultivated woman and takes the greatest pains with the education of her daughters."[40]

Once Philip Hackert had finished decorating the royal palaces, Charlotte was so thrilled with his work that she invited him to be the drawing master to her daughters. Hackert was "frequently summoned of an evening to talk with, and instruct them [the princesses] on art and kindred subjects."[41] Never one to hide her feelings, Charlotte went above and beyond expressing her gratitude to men like Hackert. Even King Ferdinand was fond of him, and gave him a personally engraved snuffbox, prompting Charlotte to quip, "I fear he is at the end of his tether, for he never gives presents." The Queen was also fond of giving gold-plated snuffboxes, but was often accused by the Court of being too lavish and spending too much money on frivolities.[42]

For Ferdinand to give anyone a gift, let alone a man, was utterly unheard of, and showed just how strongly influenced he was by his wife. A few years later, he stood behind his wife against his father when an inoculation against smallpox was developed in the mid-1770s. Charlotte was quick to have her family treated because she knew first hand just how deadly the virus could be. But the intensely religious court of Spain disapproved on theological grounds. As the head of Catholic Europe, it was unthinkable for him to inoculate himself against a disease that was otherwise believed to be in God's hands. With a minimum of fuss, Charlotte managed to convince her husband, and their entire family was inoculated.

Medical breakthroughs like the smallpox vaccine helped reinforce the belief in a prosperous and flourishing Naples under King Ferdinand IV and Queen Maria Carolina. Poets, artists, and great intellectuals like Johann von Goethe, who attended Joseph II's coronation as King of the Romans in 1764, flocked to Naples. Goethe wrote to a friend: "Naples at first sight leaves a free, cheerful, and lively impression. Numberless beings are passing and repassing each other: the king is gone hunting, the queen *promising*; and so things could not be better."[43] And a few weeks later he wrote: "Naples is a paradise, in it every one lives in a sort of intoxicated self-forgetfulness."[44]

John George Keysler, a member of the British Royal Society, called Rome and Florence "mean and contemptible" compared to Naples. And Lord Macauley, "who basically disliked everything everywhere," actually found Naples to be praiseworthy. "Rome and Pisa are dead and gone," he said. "Florence is not dead, but sleepeth; while Naples overflows with life."[45] It came as no surprise, therefore, that the egotistical Prime Minister Bernardo Tanucci took it as a personal compliment when "the wise and valiant Prince of Brunswick told the King of England that he found it the metropolis of Italy."[46]

Friendship, Family, and Alliances

For Marie Antoinette, one of her first major public responsibilities as queen took place in 1775. In June, she and Louis traveled to the historic French city of Rheims for their coronation. For Louis and Marie Antoinette, this grand occasion was more than just a ceremony or a display of royal pomp. The King and Queen, who were both devoted Catholics, saw this as a deeply religious event. The Comte Mirabeau called it the "grandest of all events for a people... it is then that Heaven consecrates our monarchs and strengthens in some way the ties that bind us to them."[1]

The symbolism of the location itself presented Louis as the next thread in the tapestry of France's ancient monarchy. Rheims, forged from the ashes of a tribal village by the Romans sometime before A.D. 250, was the site of French royal coronations since the twelfth century. As one of the oldest archbishoprics in France, Rheims reinforced the connection of the King and Queen with the country's religious and royal past. For Louis and Marie Antoinette, there could be no better venue for their coronation.

The ceremony took place on June 11, 1775. Marie Antoinette was dressed in a shimmering gown covered in sapphires, rubies, and other jewels. The long coronation, which lasted for more than five hours, was held at the Cathedral of Notre-Dame. Inside, the church had been transformed "into a kind of Baroque opera house" that was "draped with crimson cloth of gold" for the occasion.[2] According to the Duc de Croÿ: "it was most majestic.... All these ancient costumes were imposing, even more so because one sees them only on this day."[3]

As the first reigning queen to attend a French coronation since 1549, there was no precedent for Marie Antoinette's role during the ceremony.* A specially decorated box was built to the right of the altar so she could see everything clearly, but also so that her silhouette would not obscure the guests from seeing the King.

Wearing a clothe-of-silver robe and a scarlet camisole, Louis made his way up the aisle to the altar. After kneeling on a plush square of plum-colored fabric, the Archbishop of Rheims anointed him with oil from the same phial used by St. Rémy to baptize Clovis, the first King of France, in A.D. 496. When Louis stood after the anointing, he "seemed transfigured by grace." He looked over at Marie Antoinette, who had tears streaming down her face. "An unmistakable air of contentment was then reflected in the monarch's appearance," Comte Mercy told Maria Theresa.[4]

The silence in the cathedral from the hundreds of people gathered inside was awe-inspiring. When the moment came for Louis to be crowned, Marie Antoinette was deeply concerned for her husband's well being. The crown, worth a staggering twenty million *francs*, was so heavy that Louis muttered, "The crown is hurting me," in gasped breaths.[5] The Queen could see her husband was in pain from the weight of his royal mantle. "What is wrong with the King?" she asked one of her ladies anxiously, noticing his discomfort. "Look how ill at ease he seems. Do you think the crown is too tight?"[6]

When Louis was declared the newly crowned King of France, thunderous applause roared from the crowd, a first at Rheims. The applause was reportedly so powerful that it shook the entire cathedral to its foundations. Outside, a crowd numbering in the thousands waved the French and Royal Bourbon flags. Throughout the streets, cannon fire echoed in honor of the king.

The historic event proved overwhelming for Queen Marie Antoinette. Writing to her mother a few days later, she described the joyous event:

---

* Catherine de' Medici (1519—1589) was the last French queen to attend a coronation. She was present at the coronation of her husband, King Henry II (1519—1559), on June 10, 1549.

The coronation was perfect in every way. It seems that everyone was very pleased with the King; all his subjects must have been pleased; great or humble, they all showed him the utmost interest; the church ceremonies were interrupted at the moment of the coronation by the most touching cheers. I couldn't contain my emotion; tears rolled down my face in spite of myself and people took kindly to it. I did my best during the entire trip to respond to the people's enthusiasm…It is at once amazing and most fortunate to be so well received…in spite of the high price of bread, which, unfortunately, continues. It is a remarkable trait in the French character that lets itself be carried away by evil suggestions and then returns to the good right away. It is certain that having seen people treat us so well in spite of their misfortune, we are even more obligated to work for their happiness. The King seemed to be imbued with this truth; as for me, I know that I will never forget the day of the coronation (even if I live to be a hundred).[7]

Marie Antoinette wisely picked up on the fickle nature of the French people after only a year on the throne. Over time, however, her keen ability to sense the pulse of the nation would diminish.

The unconditional love the royal couple felt at Rheims did not last long. The Queen's position was set to become more precarious the longer she reigned at Louis XVI's side. She was also finding herself caught between her husband and her brother, Emperor Joseph II, in the chess game that the alliance between France and Austria had become. She confided her feelings about her situation to Maria Theresa: "I will do my best to contribute towards the preservation of good friendship and alliance; where should I be if there were a rupture between my two families."[8] But the death of Louis XV ended much of the hope and optimism about the future of the union. In a bid to raise Austria's standing at Versailles, the Emperor pressured the Queen for support, but Louis XVI had little intention of involving her in matters of state.

In a letter to Joseph II, the Queen admitted: "I have raised the issue [of anti-Austrian ministers] more than once with the King, but…he does not often talk to me about great decisions. When I reproach him for not having spoken to me on certain subjects, he looks somewhat embarrassed, and sometimes adds that he had not even thought to do so. So I can tell you that political affairs are those over which I have the least control....I allow the public to believe that I have more credit [with the King] than I do in reality, because, if people were not to believe me on this point, I would have less power still."[9]

If the pressure from her family in Austria were not enough to grate on the Queen's nerves, the insecurity she felt among her husband's relatives at the French court must have seemed overwhelming. After five years, Marie Antoinette's relationship with brothers-in-law was growing warmer, but her closeness with *Mesdames Tantes*—the king's aunts Adélaïde, Sophie, and Victoire—was tepid at best. The only two members of the royal family that the Queen had any kind of connection with were her sisters-in-law, Clothilde and Élisabeth, the King's youngest sisters. But even those friendships were hampered by the fact that in 1775 Clothilde married the crown prince of Sardinia and Élisabeth was still a mere child, only eleven.

To make matters worse, five years had gone by and Marie Antoinette had still not given birth to a child. She watched in great pain as her brother-in-law, Louis Stanislaus, the Comte de Provence, married a Savoyard princess and had children of his own. Dejected and feeling like a failure, the Queen often sat alone in her apartments crying, longing for a child.

In Vienna, Maria Theresa understood all too well that her daughter's future (and that of Austria's future with France) hinged on the birth of an heir. Without a son, the Queen's influence with the King and the court was almost non-existent. "The position you are in makes me tremble," Maria Theresa told her.[10] Emperor Joseph shared his mother's concern for Marie Antoinette's welfare. "Her situation with the King is very odd," he wrote to Leopold of Tuscany over the lack of a child. "He is only two-thirds of a husband, and although he loves her, he fears her more." The Holy Roman Emperor and Grand Duke of Tuscany talked often of their sister at Versailles. According to Joseph, "she is empty-headed," and was still "unable as yet to find her advantage."[11]

The birth of Prince Luigi of Parma managed to create an uneasy bridge between Maria Theresa and Amalia. The Duchess was the first of the Empress's daughters to deliver a son, prompting the mother to push for a reconciliation.

She wrote a long, emotional letter that was promptly sent off to Count Rosenberg, her minister in Parma. She ordered him to seek an emergency meeting with the Duchess, then read the letter in her presence. The contents of that meeting were never made known, but a few days letter the Empress wrote to a friend: "A reconciliation with Parma is accomplished."[12]

Once the lines of communication were reopened with Parma, Maria Theresa finally began to ease the embargo she placed upon Amalia with the rest of the family. She even thought that the presence of relatives would help lift her daughter's spirits, "and every now and then she sent one of her daughters to stay with Amalia."[13] But when Mimi visited Parma in 1775, she barely recognized her younger sister. There was no "trace of the glamour, the beauty," she said. "Her beautiful figure was changed, her dress and carriage have changed even more. She is less gay, less discriminating."[14]

The strain of living with so incompatible a husband in such a small and backward country had taken its toll on the once beautiful duchess. This "self-willed and haughty woman did not change in essentials. It was only her appearance and her spirit that broke down under the strain of her wild behaviour."[15] Stress had aged Amalia well beyond her years. Her complexion, once the envy of every woman in Austria, was pale and wrinkled. Her long, chestnut hair was tinged with flecks of grey. Even her moods had become more subdued.

This change in Amalia's lifestyle and personality was passed on to her children. Prince Luigi was a handsome child with blonde hair and blue eyes, but he was shy and withdrawn around anyone other than his family. His tendency to brood and withdraw would last for the rest of his life, especially when destiny would make him an unlikely king. When it came to Princess Carolina, who was five, Mimi wrote that Amalia's "eldest daughter is the most beautiful child one can imagine, but she has a trace of melancholy so that one can only observe her with pity."[16] Melancholy was perhaps the best word to describe the Court of Parma.

Mimi's visit seemed to do little to dissipate the depressing mood at the court. Even with her sister there, Amalia sought refuge in outdoor activities. The peace and quiet helped settle her volatile emotions. She enjoyed riding and hunting ever since she was a little girl. The dense forests surrounding the city of Parma lent themselves to the Duchess's hunting parties. She even commissioned the artist Carlo Angelo dal Verme to paint a portrait of her as the Roman goddess of the hunt, Diana.

Along with hunting and sometimes even archery, Amalia was passionate about her horses. Emperor Joseph II once told Marie Antoinette that the Duchess was as "equally scientific in breaking-in horses" as Charlotte of Naples was "in the art of man training." He noted that "she is constantly in the stables with her grooms, by which she GROOMS a pretty sum yearly buying, selling, and breaking-in,"[17] which helped relieve some of the debts she had acquired early on in her marriage.

In 1778, when Amalia was thirty-two, a frightening accident nearly destroyed her world. One afternoon, three-year-old Luigi was playing in the Ducal Palace with Carolina when he slipped and hit his head off a marble table. Ferdinand and Amalia were terrified that they would lose their only son. This proved to be a turning point, not only in their marriage, but in Amalia's life as well. The anxiety of waiting to see whether their son would live or die introduced a closeness between husband and wife that had never been there before. As hundreds attended daily masses to pray for the prince's recovery, Ferdinand and Amalia held a twenty-four hour vigil at their son's bedside. Luigi's life and death struggle was hard-fought. The toddler was battling a severe concussion with the possibility of a hemorrhage looming ever present. After a long road tinged with heartache, Prince Luigi showed signs of improvement and eventually recovery, but his life would be changed forever.

Soon after the accident, Ferdinand and Amalia noticed disconcertingly that their son seemed dazed and confused from time to time. The Duke and Duchess had to face the heart-breaking reality that Luigi was now epileptic. In time, this had the understandable effect of making the young prince extremely dependent on his family, especially his mother. This tragedy brought the Parmesan House of Bourbon closer, but it intensified Luigi's tendency to withdraw when he was sick. He was never the same after his brush with death, and his already fragile constitution was weakened even further. Amalia never could have expected that her little prince's health problems would one day shape the course of Italian history.

CR

The once strained and difficult relationship between Grand Duke Leopold and his sister Maria Christina had eased to the point that Mimi was asked to visit Florence in 1776. When she arrived at the Pitti Palace, Leopold, María Luísa, and their children were standing on the stone footsteps waiting to greet her. As they welcomed her into Pitti's grand salon, the little archdukes and archduchesses tackled their aunt in paroxysms of joy and laughter. She delighted in being "rolled on the floor" as she played with her nieces and nephews.[18]

As part of her visit, the Duchess of Saxe-Teschen was under strict orders from Emperor Joseph II, who asked her to report on the well being of Leopold's children. In particular, she was expected to report on Count Colloredo, the man Leopold had entrusted with the care of his family. Mimi already disliked Colloredo, and expected her visit would support that opinion. But after only a short time in Florence, she was enchanted by the devotion her nieces and nephews showed to the count:

> When I arrived here I was anything but captivated by Colloredo. I regarded him as a good and genteel person who was not equal to his job. But now that I have watched him with the children, I have changed my opinion and come to consider him remarkably well suited to his post. His mildness and his attachment to the children are unique; they stamp him as the very man for the task. He finds nothing that he does for them difficult, and though he treats them as friends, he carefully maintains his position. He observes them and studies them, and, without obstructing or irritating them, permits them no license. Tirelessly, by day and night, he keeps them neat and comfortable, praises them when occasion warrants, and strives to instill and preserve in them that feeling of honor which is so essential in this world. And the children love him.[19]

Leopold was just as happy with Colloredo as he ever had been. After Archduke Francis had been under the count's care for several years, Leopold wrote: "We have been singularly fortunate in our choice of teachers and persons who surround the children. [They] have always, in conduct and language, acted entirely in accord with our views."[20] There was little doubt from anyone that, of all of Maria Theresa's special children, Leopold of Tuscany's family life was the most content.

❀

A decade on the throne had failed to give King Ferdinand IV of Naples any taste for matters of state. Whenever someone asked his opinion on kingly business, he threw his hands up and remarked: "Ask my wife, she knows everything!"[21] Ferdinand was not without his redeemable qualities. The British statesman Henry Swinburne described him in 1777 as "very good natured and well disposed, as many traits evince. He is boyish and romping, and very fond of amusements."[22] The king continued to give Charlotte free reign over the government, and even had the inkstand removed from his council chambers so he would not be inclined to write anything.

Ferdinand "was incapable of either originating or carrying out any plan." Once, when the Council of State was in an important session, he heard the crack of a whip from the courtyard below. He immediately jumped up, asked the Queen to make whatever decision she thought best, and ran outside to join the activities. On the other hand, Ferdinand IV regularly complained to his father in Spain that Charlotte was a melodramatic prima donna. If she needed to make a particular point, she went about it in the most exaggerated fashion. In one particular fight, she cried out, "for at least a year, whether you die or burst, I refuse to be pregnant." Afterwards she was so angry that she bit Ferdinand's hand.[23]

Unwilling to let this thespian queen hold any more power, Bernardo Tanucci unsuccessfully tried to block Maria Carolina's motions in the Council of State. She responded by using her position to significantly cripple Tanucci's own political power. The aging prime minister tried repeatedly to go against Charlotte, but her growing influence with Ferdinand—and by extension his influence with King Carlos III—meant he was powerless against her.

The formidable pair danced around each other in the political arena for some time, until Tanucci made a fatal mistake. One evening, he went to Ferdinand as the king sat alone in his council chambers. There, by candlelight and shadow, Tanucci made a dramatic plea for the King to banish his wife from the council. The suggestion would be taken under advisement, the king quietly replied. In the morning, Ferdinand told his wife every detail about the meeting. At the next council session, during the opening vows of loyalty to the King and Queen, Maria Carolina jumped to her feet. Her face contorted with rage, she pointed at Tanucci, her hand shaking in anger. After a few moments of intense silence, she leveled the Prime Minister with accusations of treason against the monarchy. She was so worked up that her ladies-in-waiting had to remove her from the council room to recover.

The meeting between Tanucci and Ferdinand was exactly the ammunition Charlotte needed to force the prime minister out of office once and for all. Word of his indictment came one morning in October 1776 while he was still in bed. The Marques de Marco delivered the news to the stunned Tanucci. "I must tell you confidentially that all this has been our Queen's trick," he told him. Tanucci's replacement was an Englishman named Henry Swinburne. The Marquis della Sambuca described him as "a creature...who looks very unlike a genius: his aspect is heavy and inanimate: his first manoeuvre [sic] was very impolitic and blundering, in laying a tax upon oil, which he was obliged to take off."[24]

Bernardo Tanucci's dramatic downfall—similar to the Duchess of Parma's struggle with Guillaume du Tillot—was quickly followed by the arrival of a new member to the royal family of Naples. On a balmy night in August 1777, the Queen gave birth to a healthy baby boy. The royal couple named their second son Francesco, in honor of the infant's maternal grandfather, Emperor Francis I. Prime Minister Swinburne reported the prince's birth to his father: "at a ball at Posilipo, the Queen was taken ill and retired, and not long after, the roar of the cannon announced the birth of a Prince. He has since been christened by the innumerable names of Francis, Louis, Januarius, Jean Baptiste, Pasquale, Balthazar, Melchior, Gaspar, &c., &c."[25]

Since Prince Francesco was the second son, no one ever expected him to play a major role in ruling Naples. But like Maria Carolina, Francesco would come to occupy a throne unexpectedly. The Queen had no idea that she had just given birth to a future King of Naples.

ℚ

Of all his siblings, Emperor Joseph II was always closest with Marie Antoinette, even after she left Austria. They wrote to each other daily, sharing their deepest thoughts and inmost feelings with one another. Joseph was deeply interested in her personal growth, as well as her lukewarm marital relationship with her husband, King Louis XVI.

Maria Theresa was also "desperately worried" about her daughter, since after seven years of marriage there was still no child.[26] It was not outside the realm of possibility for a French queen to be carted off to a convent or sent back to her homeland for failing to produce an heir. The Empress used what strength of will she had left to prompt Joseph II to take action. He announced in 1777 that he "desired to free himself from old prejudices" that prevented an Austrian monarch from visiting France.[27] He decided to visit Versailles to save his sister's marriage.

The Emperor's visit made Queen Marie Antoinette more than a little apprehensive. It was well known that, while she deeply loved and respected Joseph, his talent for ridicule and criticism was famous. As a small child, she remembered the way he so cruelly maligned his second wife, Empress Josepha. He even once rudely announced: "I have three miserable brothers-in-law. The one at Versailles is an imbecile, the one at Naples is a madman, and the one at Parma is an idiot."[28] The young and insecure Marie Antoinette was about to find her entire life under Joseph's critical microscope.

Maria Theresa, who had been ruling alongside the denigrating emperor for twelve years now, knew from first-hand experience the fine line her daughter would have to walk if she wanted to avoid Joseph's wrath when he arrived. "Either my daughter will win over the Emperor by her kindness and charms or he will be impatient," she told Prince Kaunitz.[29]

Regardless of Marie Antoinette's anxiety, she was still excited to see Joseph. She "thirsted with sisterly affection for the sight of her brother, and anticipated with pride the opportunity of presenting to her new countrymen a relation of whom she was proud...and whose imperial rank made his visit wear the appearance of a marked compliment to the whole French nation."[30]   Unfortunately, most of the court loathed the Emperor, and detested the idea of his presence at Versailles. Even one of Joseph's most loyal supporters, Prince Charles-Joseph de Ligne, said he was a man who "governed too much but did not reign enough."[31]   Versailles held its breath until the unpredictable "brother of their beautiful Queen" arrived.[32]

Joseph arrived in France on April 18, 1777 under the name Count Falkenstein. In addition to the anonymity his pseudonym gave him, he also insisted on staying in the town of Versailles at a local inn. This harkened back to his earlier days when he traveled incognito throughout the Habsburg lands staying in villages and hostels. Marie Antoinette "would have wished to have her brother received according to his rank, as a great and powerful monarch," but he would have none of it.[33]   Joseph always said that "it was his custom when travelling, to lodge in a 'cabaret', and...he should not remove himself thence until he left Paris."[34]

When he finally arrived at the palace, Marie Antoinette and her whole household met Joseph on the front steps where there was a heartfelt reunion between brother and sister. Their embrace was deeply moving and brought everyone to tears.

Almost from the moment he arrived, Joseph wasted no time in critiquing his sister's life. The "scornful, brutal style" he took with her can be seen in many of the comments he made: "You are getting older and you no longer have the excuse of youth... What will become of you? An unhappy woman and still more unhappy princess."[35]   Joseph was just as scathing in his opinion of Louis XVI. He told Grand Duke Leopold that Louis was "absolute sovereign only to pass from one form of slavery to another. He is badly brought up; his appearance works against him, but he is honest; he is weak to those who know how to intimidate him and consequently he is ruled with a rod of iron. The man is weak but not a fool. He has ideas, judgement, but is apathetic in body and mind. In sum, the *fiat lux* [let there be light] has yet to come; it is still undeveloped."[36]

Joseph II spent six weeks in France. He spent most of that time lecturing his sister on every facet of her life. He nearly caused a royal scandal while attending her *toilette*,* mocking his sister and her ladies-in-waiting for the amounts of rouge they wore on their faces, comparing "them aloud to the bloodstained Furies of classical mythology." Marie Antoinette was horrified by Joseph's attacks on the long-standing French etiquette to which she had grown accustomed. He retorted ironically that his sister "scarcely seemed to recognize the degree to which his resistance to court etiquette mirrored her own past and present rebellions."[37]

As time went on, Joseph began to enjoy a rare level of intimacy with the King and Queen as his attitude softened. His opinion of Louis had improved to the point that he admitted to Maria Theresa, "I like the King, and if needs be I will fight for him."[38] Joseph chose to spend more time simply enjoying his sister's presence again. He joked that if this "dear and charming Queen" had not been his "little sister," he would surely have married her for the "pleasure of her company." Later, when the pair was alone, Joseph revealed that he had forgotten how sweet life could be until she had re-entered his. "This sister is the woman I love best in the world," he said.[39]

In the times between his audiences with the King and Queen, Joseph continued to cause a stir at the French court. In one day alone, he told the Duc de Croÿ that Austria and France "could make a marriage" between their respective pet elephants; then he dispelled any rumors that he planned to marry the thirteen-year-old sister of Louis XVI, Princess Élisabeth.[40] The Comte de Provence, Louis XVI's younger brother, wrote a disdainful letter to King Gustav III of Sweden detailing Joseph's behavior: "The emperor is mightily cajoling, a great maker of protestations and vows of friendship; but on a closer examination his protestations and his frank air hide the desire to pump one, as we say, and to dissemble his own sentiments,...but mala-

---

* The *toilette* was an almost sacred ritual. Each day, the Queen would be awoken by her Mistress of the Household. Then, every high-ranking lady of the court, from princesses to duchesses to countesses, would each take a turn dressing one portion of the Queen's body. Sometimes, if enough princesses were present, the *toilette* could take several hours.

droitly, for with a little incense, of which he is very greedy, far from his finding you out, you easily find him out. His accomplishments are very superficial."[41]

The greatest damage was done in the collision of ideologies between Austrian and French society. Joseph "did little to dispel the stereotypical image of Austrian crudeness that prevailed at Versailles at the time." As far as the courtiers were concerned, they were "predisposed against her [the Queen's] brother because of his 'erratic foreign policy opposed to French interests'."[42] They also felt that Joseph II's "manners were eccentric" and "his frankness often degenerated into rudeness." But despite these criticisms, he was praised for speaking "much and fluently; he expressed himself in [French] with facility, and the singularity, of his expressions added a zest to his conversation."[43]

When the time came to say goodbye, Joseph and Marie Antoinette knew it would be almost unbearable. He told their mother: "I quitted Versailles with grief, having become veritably attached to my sister. Her emotion on my departure was great, her self-control admirable; it required all my force to find legs wherewith to go away."[44] The Queen was just as saddened by her brother's departure. "My dearest Mother," she wrote to the Empress. "It is plain truth that the departure of the emperor has left a void in my heart from which I can not recover. I was so happy during the short time of his visit that at this moment it all seems like a dream."[45]

Weeks after Joseph had left, the heartache of leaving his most beloved sister still caused him deep sorrow. "I parted from the queen with much pain," he told Mimi; "she is indeed a charming woman."[46] Joseph's parting from the French court was less difficult, with no love lost. He believed they were "jealous of his talents, fearful of his future ascendency in Europe, and hostile to the interests of the house of Austria."[47]

Surprisingly, Joseph's visit actually went a long way to reversing the unfavorable image of Austrians in France, but it had little to do with Joseph's interactions and attitudes towards the French aristocracy. In fact, he refused to conform to the etiquette and protocols of the society. Instead, the success came from the Emperor's serious readings of French Enlightenment authors like Rousseau.

Joseph II's apparent support of the Enlightenment caused his admirers to blindly follow him in whatever pursuits he chose, and mistakenly assumed he was a "philosopher king." The irony in such a title was that Joseph really had little interest in the *philosophes*. Although he did meet with some of them in Paris, he dealt a major blow to many of his admirers on the return trip to Vienna. His route home took him through the gates of Ferney in Switzerland, where Voltaire was expecting him. The famed writer had planned a spectacular dinner party to honor the Holy Roman Emperor and even hired peasants to sit in overhanging trees to provide a worthy ovation for the imperial ruler. To the unending embarrassment of his retinue and the detriment of his reputation, Joseph never showed up at the dinner. Commenting on his slight of the *philosophes*, he shrugged it off, claiming, "his own business of sovereign would always prevent his ranking himself amongst the adepts of that sect."[48]

Once he had returned to his own dominions, Joseph continued to look for ways to expand Austrian territory and influence. His efforts after the partition of Poland led him into a friendship with Catherine the Great. The two became fast friends, and she was often in awe of the Emperor. She wrote to her son, Grand Duke Paul, that Joseph II "likes talking, he is learned, he wants to put everyone at their ease, one has no idea what he looks like if one hasn't seen him, his portraits don't look like him at all.... He eats only once in 24 hours, he goes to bed early and gets up early, he eats what he is given and drinks only water.... He likes talking and knows a lot of things."[49] Catherine the Great would quickly get the chance to see Joseph II in action, because Europe was about to be engulfed in yet another war.

The flashpoint for this latest crisis in the winter of 1777-1778 was Bavaria. The country at that time was one of the most powerful electorates in the Holy Roman Empire. The elector, Maximilian III ("Max"), had known for many years he would die childless. When Max finally died on December 30, 1777, Europe's rulers made an undignified scramble for a piece of prime Bavarian real estate.

Caught in the middle of this clash of the titans was the Austrian imperial family. Emperor Joseph II pushed for an

191

immediate invasion of Bavaria, and did not mince words in a letter to Austria's state chancellor, Prince Kaunitz:

> I have just received the news that the elector of Bavaria has played on us the trick of dying…This is my first idea: since we've agreed on the principal point, namely that we should mutually recognise [sic] the rights we believe we have, and since it is [now] only a question of their greater or lesser extent; as there is no time to discuss the matter, we should take possession of lower Bavaria.[50]

The Emperor believed that gaining Bavaria was "a true *coup d'état* and an addition to the monarchy of inestimable value."[51]

Filled with apprehension, Empress Maria Theresa watched as her son pushed the Holy Roman Empire to the brink of war. She was "extremely worried" about his "militaristic intentions." She knew Joseph's claim on Bavaria was "weak," and believed that "'a universal conflagration' was a heavy price to pay for 'a particular convenience'."[52] "I do not see clearly the justice of the title by which we pretend to lay claim to Bavaria," she wrote.[53] And she told her son bluntly that the "present situation, far from offering a happy, open, and peaceful prospect, overwhelms me…. I have never seen any such enterprise prosper…"[54]

At the beginning of January 1778, Emperor Joseph II decided it was time to take possession of Bavaria. He ordered 15,000 troops into Lower Bavaria to secure the territory. He told Grand Duke Leopold that his "troops will take possession. In the first case we shall seize upon what belongs to us, in the other, as emperor, I will declare the fief vacant, and occupy it till arrangements are made among the claimants." Joseph believed the "circumstances of Europe are favorable" for an invasion because "the attention of all the world is occupied elsewhere, and I flatter myself that this stroke will succeed without war, and the acquisition, though it be not complete, will still be a fine one, as it will have cost nothing."[55]

Once it became clear that Austrian troops were firmly entrenched in Bavaria, Joseph wrote proudly to Leopold: "Our decision was a good one, and will bring as much solid advantage as honour and renown."[56] Unfortunately for the Emperor, his reign, and Austria's imperial family, he could not have been more wrong. His overconfidence was about to lead to a "series of blunders" that would be witnessed on a continental level.[57]

"Only in Tears"

Faced with an impending war, the Austrian imperial family was divided over Bavaria. Maria Theresa and many of her children refused to sanction Joseph's actions. As he turned to the rest of Europe for support, the Emperor found his fellow rulers were hanging him out to dry. King Louis XVI declared France neutral, and the Holy Roman Empire's electoral states refused to support their emperor.

To exacerbate matters, Maria Theresa's old nemesis, King Frederick the Great of Prussia ("Fritz"), declared himself the protector of Bavaria. "*I* do not like to appropriate to myself what belongs to another," he said.[1] Fritz made himself a lightening rod for everyone who opposed Joseph's invasion. He wrote to his minister at Versailles, Count von Goltz, hoping to rouse France out of its neutrality and enlist King Louis XVI's support against Austria. "This is the moment," he said, "to display all your strength, it is necessary that the deaf should hear, the blind should see, the apathetic should act."[2]

Owing to the great strength of her character, Empress Maria Theresa spoke out against the invasion of Bavaria. She composed a heartfelt letter to Joseph boldly declaring her disapproval of the entire situation:

> It is a question of nothing less than the ruin of our dynasty and Monarchy, and even of a total revolution in Europe....
>
> I should be unworthy of the name sovereign and mother if I didn't take measures appropriate to the circumstances...I will gladly commit myself to anything, even if it tarnishes my reputations.

People can accuse me of senility, weakness, pusillanimity. Nothing will stop me rescuing Europe from this dangerous situation.

If war breaks out, place no more reliance on me. I shall withdraw to the Tyrol, to finish my days there in the deepest retirement, where my only occupation will be to lament the unfortunate fate of my House and my peoples, and to try to end my unhappy days in a Christian manner.[3]

The Emperor still refused to withdraw his forces. Reluctantly, Frederick the Great finally went to war against Austria, plunging the Holy Roman Empire into civil war. On July 8, 1778, Fritz personally led the Prussian army into Bohemia. "It was a day of terror," one Austrian veteran said; "I venture not to describe the sensation produced at the imperial head-quarters by the first account of the march of the Prussians into Bohemia."[4]

When war finally broke out in July 1778, Maria Theresa was frantic. The invasion by Prussia prompted the "elderly and incapacitated" empress to write to Comte Mercy: "We are at war. It is what I have been dreading since January; and what a war! With nothing to gain and everything to lose....I do not know how to live. Nothing but my faith sustains me."[5] A few days later, she wrote a telling letter to her son Ferdinand about the strain the conflict was placing on her:

This is stronger than I am. I am broken-hearted. I tremble at every door that slams, at every carriage that passes quickly, at every woman who walks in haste. I preach to myself; I try to find myself such I was thirty-six years ago but I was young then, I had a husband, who took the place of everything to me. Weakened by my years and my reverses, my health no longer sustains me; my soul alone through religion resigns itself and acts, but does not revive me.[6]

The Empress was now sixty and could no longer hide her failing health behind a mask of devotion to duty. Her son's suzerain war was taking a heavy toll on her.

By the end of July, all seemed to be over for the Austrians. Not only were Fritz's soldiers better trained and better equipped, they had nearly 40,000 more soldiers than the rag-tag army Joseph was leading. Maria Theresa, a loyal Austrian to the core, rallied to the imperial cause. She sent out an urgent order for all available troops from across the Empire to rally in eastern Austria and prepare to march to war. In his memoirs, Prince Charles-Joseph de Ligne wrote of the call Maria Theresa sent out: "From the Black Sea to the Ocean, from the Adriatic and the Lake of Como to the Rhine, all the troops of Austria were put in motion."[7] Once all the numbers were in, the Empress had 160,000 troops to place in Fritz's path. Joseph ordered his soldiers to retreat and regroup with the army the empress had assembled.

As Joseph and his generals planned their final battle with Fritz's army, Maria Theresa was racked with anxiety. She sent a desperate plea to Marie Antoinette to use her authority as queen to help stop the war: "Save your house and your brothers. I shall never ask the king to involve himself in this unfortunate war, but only to make some protestations.... [France] will never find a friend or ally...more sincerely attached than we."[8] Marie Antoinette promised to do everything she could to help. "I have every motive for acting," she wrote back to the Empress, "for I am quite persuaded that the glory of the King and the good of France are concerned in this, *without reckoning the welfare of my dear country!*"[9]

CB

Queen Marie Antoinette's heart went out to her family and her former countrymen, but the French court paid little attention to the War of the Bavarian Succession in the early months of 1778 because every royal, aristocrat, and dignitary was consumed by the biggest piece of news to hit Versailles in years: Marie Antoinette was finally going to have a baby.

When Maria Theresa was told, she was overcome with joy. "You send me great and unexpected news!" she wrote to her daughter. "May God be praised! And may you, my beloved Antoinette, be strengthened in your splendid position by giving France an heir."[10]

For the next nine months, she was watched endlessly. Every move she made was dotted over because, in the eyes of the court, she was possibly carrying a future king of France. Maria Theresa was also more than happy to instruct her daughter on every possible aspect of parenting: "Particularly in the first year, everything depends upon the care that children receive: I am speaking of sensible and natural treatment, not swaddling them too tightly, not keeping them overly warm and not overfeeding them with gruel and food."[11]

The Queen's health during her *accouchement* was excellent. She ate and exercised regularly, and was getting enough rest each night. She proudly declared by the end of May that she was becoming "amazingly fat." Once it appeared that her pregnancy was going smoothly, she decided it was time to make the announcement public. In a move that was typical of her generous character, she gave 12,000 *francs* to relieve the suffering of people in the debtors' prison of Paris. Marie Antoinette was very specific about who got the money: it was first and foremost to be anyone who was imprisoned for debts owing to the care of their children. She explained her decision by saying, "I gave to charity and at the same time notified the people of my condition."[12]

The months of waiting finally ended on a frigidly cold day in December 1778. More than two hundred people gathered at Versailles to await the much-anticipated delivery. For more than eight hours, they waited as Marie Antoinette endured excruciating contractions. "The Queen showed great courage," Comte Mercy reported to the Empress.[13]

The delivery was especially traumatic because French court etiquette allowed people holding the Rights of Entry to actually be in the room as the queen was giving birth. Excited men and women pressed in around Marie Antoinette, nearly suffocating her. One group of courtiers could not get a clear view of the birth so they climbed on a couch. Others shimmied up curtains or planted themselves on the massive windowsills.

A few minutes later, the doctors announced the Queen had given birth to a healthy baby girl. Exhausted from the labor and suffocated by the throngs of people, Marie Antoinette saw the room begin to spin wildly and passed out. "Give her air!" one of the doctors shouted. "Warm water! She must be bled in the foot!" Realizing the Queen's life now hung in the balance, a deafening silence fell over the room. As the doctor carefully made an incision in Marie Antoinette's heel, "the blood streamed out freely, and the Queen opened her eyes. The joy which now succeeded to the most dreadful apprehensions could hardly be contained."[14]

As she held her new baby daughter in her arms, Marie Antoinette whispered: "You were not wished for...[but] you are not on that account less dear to me. A son would have been rather the property of the State. You shall be mine; you shall have my undivided care, shall share all my happiness, and console me in all my troubles."[15]

A twenty-one cannon salute announced the birth of a daughter, who was duly named Marie Thérèse, in honor of the Empress (who was also the godmother). As the eldest daughter of the King, she was given the illustrious title Madame Royal. The official dispatch from Versailles announced, "a Princess has been born into the world at half-past eleven this morning."[16] Nathaniel Wraxall was in Vienna when the news reached Maria Theresa that she was a grandmother for the twenty-fifth time. He wrote in his memoirs about the atmosphere at the Court, and the reaction of the Empress:

> After nine years of sterility, her [Marie Antoinette's] pregnancy was an event which inspired this Court with the liveliest joy. All the labors of the Empress Queen, and of her minister Prince Kaunitz, by blending the Austrian and Bourbon families, to extinguish the long hereditary animosities of the two Crowns, remain still incomplete while there is not a Dauphin. The Queen of Naples, and the Archduchess of Parma, who are married to two other princes of the House of Bourbon, have both performed this essential service to the state, and produced sons. Maria Theresa has omitted no exertions on her part, to ensure the like benediction on her youngest daughter. As the means which she conceived to be most effectual, she has wearied Heaven with prayers, and prostrated herself before a variety of saints and altars, to obtain so great a boon.[17]

Neither Marie Antoinette nor her husband allowed their happiness to be quashed by anyone else's disappointments over the fact that it was not a son. The birth of a Daughter of France was still a joyous event, and the King and Queen celebrated the arrival of their first child with their whole hearts.

Once the excitement at Versailles began to dwindle, Marie Antoinette happily reported to her mother: "My health is entirely re-established. I am about to resume my ordinary life, and consequently I hope to soon be able to announce the fresh hopes [of a Dauphin] to my dear Mamma."[18]

Their desire for the much hoped-for heir did not diminish the fact that Marie Thérèse was the joy of her parents' lives. After only a few months, she was developing into a healthy, intelligent baby. When her daughter was only eight months old, Marie Antoinette proudly wrote to her mother: "The poor child is starting to walk quite well in her dress *à paniers*. She started saying 'papa' a few days ago; her teeth are not out yet, but you can feel all of them. I am very pleased that she has started naming her father, this is one more tie that binds him to her."[19] The Empress wrote back to the Queen: "What you report to me of your dear daughter causes me great joy. Yet I must confess that I am insatiable; she needs a companion, and he should not be long in coming."[20]

❦

By the end of July, the Austrians were being thoroughly trounced by their Prussian counterparts. The small Austrian frontier militias in Bohemia were being quickly overwhelmed and annihilated.

Maria Theresa was terrified for the welfare of Joseph as his army moved closer to the Prussian troops. She poured out her heart to him in an emotional letter:

My dear son.

I beg you to take care of yourself; all the news that we receive, makes us shudder with horror; Fritz is boiling with rage, and he will vent his anger in all directions. Since his army appears to him full of bad will, he orders executions on a large scale, he promises his soldiers that they have permission to pillage the invaded territories; this is outrageous. By no means do I expect a favorable answer…

I take you into my arms and will pray for you as much as I can, in my feeble position. Adieu.[21]

As his army headed north, Joseph saw firsthand the heavy toll the war was taking on the Bohemian people. Starvation was running rampant for the second time in less than a decade. The Emperor described the tragic scene in Bohemia to Grand Duke Leopold: "War is a horrible thing—the ravaging of fields and villages, the lamentations of the poor peasants, in short the ruin of so many people, the ferment one is caught up in day and night."[22]

By the end of the summer, the tide began to turn in Austria's favor. Although the Prussian army had great success at first, they quickly became stalled in the Sudeten Mountains that stretched from Germany to Poland. After a few weeks in the mountains, Fritz's troops were plagued by desertions, starvation, and disease. With his options exhausted, he ordered his troops to retreat in September 1778.

For Maria Theresa, this victory was the best kind. Her son was safe, never having faced the Prussian army in open battle; and her archenemy Fritz was humiliated for all of Europe to see. Eager to end quickly what was left of the war, the Empress arranged for mediation from France and Russia. For the last time before the French Revolution, the great rulers of Europe assembled together to end the War of the Bavarian Succession.

This time they converged upon the city of Teschen near Silesia in November 1778 to begin the long process of negotiating a peace between Prussia, Austria, and Bavaria. The talks lasted an insufferable six months. "Never did there exist so strange a Mixture of Warfare and Negotiation," was how the British envoy in Vienna described the conference.[23]

Hostilities finally ended on May 13, 1779 when Austria and Prussia signed the Treaty of Teschen The war was arguably one of the most pointless conflicts in modern European history. Nathaniel Wraxall recalled in his memoirs, "No campaign in the course of the present century has more disappointed expectation, produced fewer events, or been attended with so inconsiderable an effusion of blood."[24]

Not everyone was disappointed in the war's outcome though. The day the treaty was signed held special meaning for Maria Theresa: it was her sixty-third birthday, and she could think of no better way to celebrate than through the restoration of peace to her empire.

The Empress "declared that no event of her long reign had ever caused her such unmingled satisfaction as the peace of

Teschen."[25]   To Joseph's eternal displeasure, the settlement forced Austria to return to Bavarian control all the territory seized in the conflict except for the "essentially worthless" Inn District.[26] As far as Joseph II was concerned, the Treaty of Teschen left him with only "a morsel" of what he had wanted, and for months afterwards he seemed inconsolable. He had such lofty goals for this campaign, but he was miserable when it all came crashing down. Maria Theresa tried as best she could to comfort him:

> My dear son!
>
> …One has to have the courage to make sacrifices for others and to judge righteously. Once we were a Great Power, but not anymore. We have to bend our head; at least we should rescue the ruins and the nations, who still remain with us, and whom we were so fortunate to rule. In spite of our losses we insisted to maintain our former high living standards. Begin your accession to the throne by re-instating peace, order and prosperity to those, who really deserve it. You yourself will rejoice in the happiness of others, even if it should be on account of your personal greatness. I know your heart and depend on it. Save your nations, and in this way you will gain more fame than through the claims, a conquerer [*sic*] is entitled to…
>
> I take you into my arms…[27]

In the years to come, the pointless War of the Bavarian Succession came to be known as the Potato War, because Prussian and Austrian troops survived on the fronts by living off the potato crops of the unfortunate Bohemians peasants. This was Emperor Joseph II's last major campaign as Co-Regent of the Habsburg Realm. The next time he would lead Austria into battle, he would do so alone.

⅋

As the Treaty of Teschen was restoring peace to the Holy Roman Empire, Charlotte of Naples was waging a battle of her own. Malaria had infiltrated the Court of the Two Sicilies, cutting straight to the heart of the Queen's family, with devastating consequences.

Her eldest son, four-year-old Carlo, Duke of Calabria, fell ill with the infection in December 1778. His life and death struggle began on the night of December 17. The toddler was racked by a high fever and excruciating pain. There was nothing "more terrible than the combination of accidents which contributed to make the scene of the death of the Hereditary Prince of Naples more horrible. The Queen did not suspect his danger till the moment the physicians declared there were no hopes, at which news one of the women, calling to the King, dropped down in convulsions; her companion fell into the same state, and they could not be removed out of the Queen's hearing."[28]

Henry Swinburne, the Neapolitan Prime Minister, remembered that Maria Carolina was "plunged into the greatest affliction" when her son died.[29] Carlo brought great joy to his parents' lives. Witnesses described him as "a very fine boy, of promising expectations, to whom his mother was passionately attached."[30]

Charlotte blamed her son's death on the incompetence and poor training of the Neapolitan doctors. Instead of giving little Carlo an emetic or something similar, which would have saved him, they made the fatal mistake of bleeding the child. Afterwards, he was too weak to survive.

The devastated Maria Carolina placed her son's tiny body in a child-sized coffin and had him buried in the royal crypt at the cathedral in Naples. This was the first time that Maria Carolina was faced with the death of a beloved child, but sadly for the Queen of Naples, it would not be the last.

℘

The War of the Bavarian Succession was only one of many hardships Maria Theresa faced during her decades on the throne. In the last years of her life, she was dogged by assassination attempts by young revolutionaries and university students, but she refused to meet these threats with anything less than absolute courage and strength of character. After one failed attempt in 1772, she wrote to one of her governors describing how little she let these things bother her: "If one wishes to carry out such an act, one does not write about it and allow time for investigation. All this convinces me that one should not make this affair more important than it is...This does not worry me and I have not acquired any grey hairs because of it."[31]

Courage and fortitude became necessities for Maria Theresa in her final years, partly because of the loneliness she experienced. Joseph II, still bereft over the loss of the Bavarian war, had practically abandoned his mother and Vienna, in favor of his adventures across Europe. "I wish that these journeys would once and for all come to an end," she wrote to Marie Antoinette. "It becomes worse every year, and increases my sorrow and anxiety at a time when in my age I need aid and consolation."[32]

One of the bright spots in Maria Theresa's life continued to be her grandchildren. Her relationship with Charlotte and Amalia's children was improving, and she was tenderly close with Leopold's son, Archduke Francis. Just before his twelfth birthday in 1780, the Empress sent her grandson a touching letter:

> My dear grandson: the twelfth of this month is the happiest day of my life. It was the day of my more-than-happy marriage and of your birth, the first grandson whom God gave me and who so well lives up to our hopes by his qualities of heart and his diligence. Continue, my dear grandson, to apply yourself and follow the counsels of those who have you in their care, and to imitate your dear parents. We shall celebrate this day together in our hearts; I shall think of Florence and you think of Vienna, and we shall describe to each other all the hours of the day....I am always your faithful grandmother
>
> MARIA THERESA.[33]

The Empress was especially fond of all of Leopold's children, and asked to be kept up to date on the tiniest details of their lives, even their height. At the beginning of October, Maria Theresa wrote to Leopold: "I have received the measurements for all your dear children, Theresa and [Alexander] are surprisingly big for their ages, Karl and even Francis and little Marianne are too."[34]

To fill the rest of her time, Maria Theresa worked tirelessly at her state papers. In her off hours she constantly visited her husband's grave, and even had a chair brought into the crypt so she could spend long hours there. Every afternoon, she spent three or four hours there writing, knitting, or praying.

On October 20, 1780, Maria Theresa celebrated her fortieth anniversary as Queen of Hungary and Bohemia, but in her heart, she knew that her time was coming to an end. A sad pall hung over the final days of her long life. She wrote dejectedly to a confidante: "It often comforts me to know that the years...that are gone will not return, and that every moment brings me closer to death."[35]

The only joy Maria Theresa seemed to find was in taking care of her children. She was especially concerned about Marie Antoinette's fate, because of all her special daughters, she was the only one who had not yet produced a son, prompting here to write: "These are the only happy moments of my sorrowful existence; the lovely Queen of France contributes a lot to it, but we must have a Dauphin."[36] Maria Theresa later admitted to her daughter, "Yesterday I was all day more in France than in Austria."[37]

At the beginning of November, Maria Theresa, ignoring her doctor's orders, participated in the annual Habsburg family pheasant hunt. Already in poor health because of age and stress, she caught a terrible cold. Within days, she was suffering racking coughs, chest pains, and had difficulty breathing. Her fever made her so hot that her bedroom windows were kept open night and day. The Empress's days were long and difficult, and her nights were agonizing because she could not sleep. When her condition appeared critical, Joseph summoned as many of his siblings as he could. Marianne, Elizabeth, and Max were already holding a vigil, and Albert and Mimi flew from the Austrian Netherlands to be at their mother's side. Of the five special children, only Joseph II could be present at the Hofburg for the death vigil.

The night of November 29, 1780 marked the final hours in the life of Empress Maria Theresa. "God has asked for my life. I feel it," she told Joseph.[38] Iron-willed during her twilight moments, she refused to take any kind of drugs or medication to ease her suffering. "In a few hours I shall appear before the judgment seat of God and would you have me sleep?" she asked with her characteristic fortitude.[39]

In her last hours, she summoned her family into her room. She spoke of her life, her successes and failures, and her children. "I have always tried to do my best," she said. "I trust in the mercy of God."[40] She composed a final letter to Leopold, and spoke of the grief that the news of her death would cause the Grand Duke and Duchess. "You are Christians and virtuous," she wrote, "this comforts me.... God receives you. I give you both and your dear ten children my blessing."[41] And when she spoke of Marie Antoinette, her "voice softened and her eyes filled with tears."[42]

For a long while, she sat in silence. Her children kept their eyes fixed on their mother. Eventually, she looked at each of them and said: "Never think...that my heart is in any way changed towards you; it is only that I have given you to God, all that I have most valuable in the world, and that which is alone hard for me to leave. This is the reason why I look upon you in silence."[43] One by one, she called them to her side, blessed them, kissed them on the forehead, and gently dismissed her daughters, saying, "retire into another apartment, and recover your spirits."[44] Tears ran down Joseph's face as he realized he was saying goodbye to his mother forever.

She was now finding it nearly impossible to breath lying down, so she had Joseph help her onto a nearby couch. "Your Majesty is lying uncomfortable," he said. "Yes," she replied, "but well enough to die."[45] A few moments later, she was gone.

For three days, Maria Theresa's body lay in state at the Hofburg. Draped across her coffin were the Austrian and Habsburg flags. On top rested her trademark pearl encrusted crown that she always wore atop her black widow's veil. On the cold morning of December 3, 1780, the funeral procession made its way from the Hofburg to the Capuchin Church. The streets of Vienna were lined with thousands of spectators watching the solemn occasion. The English minister to Vienna recalled that after "the death of the empress every thing in this capital wears the face of heartfelt affliction."[46] In keeping with her greatest wish, Empress Maria Theresa was buried next to her husband in the imperial crypt.

Europe deeply mourned the loss of Maria Theresa. Writing in French to Emperor Joseph II, Catherine the Great offered her condolences: "*Monsieur mon frère. L'âime vivement affectée du malheureux événement dont je viens d'apprendre la nouvelle*."[47] Maria Theresa was one of the longest reigning sovereigns in Austrian history, and arguably the most successful. Perhaps most ironically of all, she was the only female to ever rule the House of Habsburg. The annals of King George III ranked her "in history among the illustrious sovereigns of her time," and her biographers hailed Maria Theresa as "*the most blameless and beneficent sovereign who ever wore a crown*."[48] Her life-long enemy, Frederick the Great, gave the most sincere words upon hearing of the Empress's passing: "I shed sincere tears on her death.... I have waged war against her, but I have never been her enemy."[49] It comes as little wonder, then, that she "ruled Europe by the power of her genius; she...had no equal amongst the sovereigns of this century..."[50]

Joseph mourned her loss more deeply than anyone, in spite of the fact that he fought with Maria Theresa more than any of her children. But writing to Leopold after the funeral, he expressed profound sorrow: "I am so overwhelmed by the horrible ceremony that I can only send you a single word. This is the most *cruel* experience imagineable."[51] In Florence, the Grand Duke made sure appropriate mourning was ordered and "all publick [*sic*] and private amusements are prohibited."[52] Queen Maria Carolina was overcome by this "severe sorrow and calamity;"[53] and Marie Antoinette was "deeply afflicted by her death."[54] She wrote to Joseph: "Stricken with this awful misfortune, it is only in tears that I can write to you. Oh, my brother! Oh, my friend! no one remains to me but you, in the country which will always be dear to me...Remember, that we are your friends, your allies; love me. I embrace you."[55]

Marie Antoinette of France wanted to honor her late mother in "appropriate, regal style." The French court ordered massive quantities of "sumptuous velvet [and] satin clothes in somber mourning colors."[56] Madame Campan, who was one of the Queen's most trusted lady-in-waiting, recalled that Marie

---

* ("My dear brother. I am deeply afflicted by this most unhappy news that I have just been informed of.")

Antoinette was heartbroken. Campan wrote that in the days that followed, she "never ceased talking of the courage, the misfortunes, the abilities and the pious virtues of her mother."[57]

PART III

The Flames of Revolution

(1780—1793)

14

The Philosopher King

*F*rederick the Great rightly said that the death of Maria Theresa "commences a new order of things.... As for the emperor, the son of this great woman, I have seen him, and he appeared to me too enlightened to rush rashly into enterprises. I esteem him, but I do not fear him."[1]

After the Empress's funeral, many were hopeful that a new era of liberalism and progressive policies would begin under Joseph II. The historian Robin Okey observed that there was such an air of anticipation when he ascended the throne that many throughout Germany and Austria were brimming with excitement: "Few men have taken up the reins of government amid such expectations as Joseph II...The German epic poet Klopstock had dedicated his *Hermannsschlact* to him in 1769 and hailed him as the Charlemagne of learning. The philosopher Herder had called on him to give a German fatherland to those who yearned for it. Frederick of Prussia, no friend of the Habsburgs, spoke of the beginning of a new order."[2] Undoubtedly, Maria Theresa's death "placed on the throne of Austria, with undivided power, one of the most remarkable personalities of the time."[3]

Joseph himself was like a prisoner finally being released from his confinement. Now that he was free from his mother's overbearing influence, he could rule as he saw fit. At the top of his agenda was enacting many of his long-awaited reforms. He was often deeply frustrated by how slowly his mother initiated reforms, and upon her death he was ready to institute a whole new series of changes, the likes of which Austria had never seen. "He was anxious to elevate and educate his subjects, declaring that it was his great ambition to rule over freemen."[4] Many of the reformations he prepared had been under consideration during his mother's lifetime, but were never implemented. They were rather broad because he wanted to wash away the last remnants of his parents' rule.

During her reign, Maria Theresa issued approximately one hundred new edicts each year. Now that he was emperor, Joseph issued around seven hundred. To some extent, this "flurry of activity" stemmed from his pent up frustration after having spent fifteen years as a "superfluous figurehead" in the co-regency. Joseph ensured many of his first reforms were the ones that the Empress refused to confront.[5]

The Austrian people were looked to their emperor to lead the country into the nineteenth century, but the illusion of Joseph as a philosopher king quickly began to crumble, especially in Vienna. Society life during the Josephinist era stagnated almost immediately, and the aristocrats grew tired and bored. Francis I and Maria Theresa may have been pious, but they were also famous for their gala parties. Emperor Joseph II detested high society and shunned entertaining altogether. He even refused to have a coronation, both as the imperial ruler and as the King of Hungary.[*]

In place of parties, Joseph threw himself entirely into his work. In one of his most ambitious projects, he strove for administrative unity in the diverse Habsburg lands. He began working on a plan that would not come to fruition for many years, but when it did, it would leave a definable mark on Central Europe.

Even though Joseph was widely considered one of the "Enlightened Despots," his radical and far-reaching reforms were more a reflection of his own personal philosophy rather than the altruistic principles of the Enlightenment itself. He was convinced of his own unassailable position as sovereign, and made his decisions without heeding the wisdom of his advisors. Opposition came against his reforms from many of his mother's old ministers. In such instances, the Emperor's "spiteful

---

[*] Joseph had a long-standing aversion to Hungary, stretching back many years. He refused to even be acknowledged as the King of Hungary, despite the fact that he was the rightful monarch.

penchant" for humiliating any who disagreed with him was more than evident.[6]

In 1781, Joseph caused a monumental stir across Europe when he unexpectedly emancipated all of Austria's peasants. In this one sudden move, he abolished serfdom completely throughout the Habsburg lands. However, the outcome of Joseph's actions had unexpected and profound consequences. He believed in the morality of the emancipation, but it left the newly liberated peasants with serious financial hardships; many were unprepared to be given their freedom. As a result, a serious labor crisis occurred throughout Austria, Hungary, and impoverished Bohemia. The poorer peasants were forcibly removed from their properties and became landless laborers, wandering the countryside searching for work. In Prague, angry peasants rallied outside the palace of the imperial governor. As armed cavalry fired shots into the air to disperse the mobs, portraits of the Emperor were burned and destroyed by the people. For the second time in less than a decade, Joseph II had forced his subjects to starve and die.

As messengers from Hungary and Bohemia brought news of the unrest in the north and east, Joseph could not understand his subjects' ingratitude. In his mind, the serfs had their freedom, what more could they want? They had their freedom, yes, but little else. Within a year of Maria Theresa's death, Austria and the Habsburg realm were already beginning their descents into chaos.

❧

As Joseph II of Austria shocked the continent by freeing his empire's serfs, Europe's great powers were beginning to involve themselves in a new conflict less than two years after the end of the War of the Bavarian Succession. The united Thirteen Colonies in America had been fighting against the British for their independence since 1775, prompting a political chess game among Britain's adversaries. Great Britain was bound up in an alliance with Prussia, but most of the major players on the continent were hostile to King George III and the Court of St. James.

France, Austria, and Spain each sent support to the Colonies in the form of troops, supplies, and money. The consequences of this support proved disastrous for Marie Antoinette and the French monarchy. Pressured by his advisors to deal a crippling blow to Britain, Louis XVI raised taxes and began ruining France's fragile economy by supporting the war in such a direct manner. Since 1771, there had been "an annual deficit of 22 million livres, and a standing debt of 205 millions."[7] The French people started deeply resenting King Louis XVI and Queen Marie Antoinette. They could not understand why their sovereigns were bankrupting the country on a war half a world away. France's involvement in America's revolution against Britain was the first step towards that country's own revolution against the Royal House of Bourbon.

In Florence, Grand Duke Leopold did not want to miss the chance to expand his country's influence, and hit Great Britain hard. But unlike his contemporaries, this son of Maria Theresa was much more calculating in his involvement.

Instead of direct support, Leopold sent his special minister, Philip Mazzei, to assist the Colonies in Virginia. He saw much more success than Louis XVI, as can be seen in a letter from Mazzei to Leopold in May 1781 where he describes how the open dialogue established with Virginia was proving "advantageous to the states of Your Royal Highness."[8] Unlike France, Tuscany was spared the disastrous consequences of direct involvement in the American War of Independence.

◯ℨ

Only a short time after the birth of Marie Thérèse, who was more commonly known at court as Madame Royal, Marie Antoinette was pregnant again. This *enceinte* was kept a closely guarded secret, and only a few close friends were told. This decision proved wise in the end. Early in the pregnancy the Queen injured herself entering a carriage and lost the baby eight days later. Louis spent the entire morning at his wife's side, consoling her, and the couple wept together, not as king and queen, but as husband and wife. Neither he nor Marie Antoinette realized that in just a short time their mourning would be transformed into joy.

By the spring of 1781, Queen Marie Antoinette was pregnant again. She lost so much of her hair that she was forced to rely on a wide collection of wigs to maintain her image.[9] Other than this abnormality, her pregnancy was coming along very well. She wrote to her old friend, Princess Louise of Hesse-Darmstadt: "My health is perfect; I am growing very large. I have great faith in [having a son], and I do not doubt of its coming true."[10]

On the morning of October 22, 1781, Marie Antoinette awoke just as her contractions were starting. To make sure that no crisis occurred this time during the delivery, all the courtiers were sent to one of the adjacent rooms. Only the physicians, Louis, and members of the royal family were allowed into the delivery room.

Marie Antoinette's second delivery lasted only a few short hours. At half past one in the afternoon, the baby was born. Everyone in the room kept solemn faces until the sex of the infant was announced. As Marie Antoinette looked around at her family and saw their grave expressions, she was certain it was another girl. Bracing herself for the news, she told them: "You see how reasonable I am. I do not question you." The room remained silent as Louis slowly walked up to his wife's bedside with the newborn infant wrapped in his arms. Tears streaming down his face, he whispered, "Monsieur le Dauphin requests permission to enter."[11] With an indescribable look of joy on his face, he handed his wife their son. "Madame," he said, "you have fulfilled my wishes, and those of France."[12]

Once Marie Antoinette had seen her son, Louis presented him to the expectant courtiers waiting outside. One eyewitness recalled the moment when it was announced that a son had been born:

> The joy was overwhelming; all heads were turned. You saw them laughing and crying alternately. People who did not know one another, men and women, fell upon one another's necks; and even those who were least attached to the queen were carried away by the universal delight. It was same when, half an hour after the birth, the doors of the queen's chamber were thrown open, and Monsieur le Dauphin was announced.... There were acclamations of joy and clapping of hands, which penetrated to the queen's chamber and assuredly to her heart.[13]

The Dauphin was baptized that afternoon at three o'clock in Versailles' chapel. King Louis said that the first thing for his son was to "be made a Christian." As the Cardinal de Rohan poured streams of water over the baby's tiny forehead, he was given the names Louis Joseph, for his father and uncle. Angélique de Bombelles, a close friend of the Queen's, was present at Louis Joseph's baptism. She wrote to her husband that the "cries of the people outside of the chapel at the moment the child entered, the happiness on every face, moved me so much that I could not keep from tears."[14]

Always the doting uncle, Emperor Joseph wasted no time telling the rest of the family the joyous news. From Vienna, he wrote to Grand Duke Leopold about how "the news of the happy delivery of the Queen of France and the birth of a Dauphin absorb all my time."[15] And a few days later, he happily reported: "The Queen continues to be doing well" after the delivery.[16]

A universal exuberance gripped France after Louis Joseph was born. The excitement was so intense it may have even surpassed the acclaim of Louis XVI's coronation in 1775. "In the streets one meets nothing but fiddles, and singing and dancing," wrote Angélique de Bombelles. "I call that touching; and in fact, I know no more amiable nation than ours."[17] The person who undoubtedly experienced the greatest joy was King Louis. Tears filled his eyes whenever he looked at his son, and he talked about the Dauphin whenever an opportunity presented itself or "he could find somebody willing to listen to him."[18] The arrival of a son utterly transformed Louis XVI.

As the weeks and months passed after Louis Joseph's birth, cracks began to appear in the ultimate happiness of Marie Antoinette. Despite her giving France a dauphin, she was still the subject of slander and innuendo. A priest in Maine was telling his parishioners that the "queen pillages on all sides; she even sends money, it is said, to her brother, the emperor."[19]

Strangely enough, Louis XVI still enjoyed the popularity of most of his subjects. When the royal couple made a public appearance in Paris in 1781, Louis was greeted with cheers, but Marie Antoinette was met with cold silence. This was the first step in France's long, inexorable march towards revolution. Louis was still viewed with some level of dignity and respect, but the blame for the nation's mounting problems rested solely with the Queen.

At this point in her life, Marie Antoinette paid little attention to the growing public resentment towards her. Instead, she was deeply worried when she began to notice that her son was "a sickly child," whose health was becoming troubling.[20] Louis Joseph no longer seemed the robust, healthy child he had been at birth. His appearance began to change and become misshapen. No one was prepared for the possibility that the Dauphin of France was suffering from a rare and deadly tuberculosis of the spine.

⁓

In the aftermath of the unrest in the Habsburg crown lands, Emperor Joseph II turned his attention to the future of the monarchy. This time, his eyes were fixed solely on his nephew, Archduke Francis.

As a future emperor, it was imperative for Francis to marry and have a son. So when Joseph began a tour of the Holy Roman Empire in 1781, he took this opportunity to begin searching for a wife for his nephew. He found many princes and dukes who were eager to have one of their daughters marry a nephew of the emperor. Joseph's search led him to a small duchy in the Swabia region of southwest Germany called Württemberg. Catherine the Great recommended he visit the country after her son Paul married one of the Duke of Württemberg's daughters. When Joseph arrived in the capital city of Stuttgart, the reigning duke, Frederick II, gave him an imperial welcome and introduced him to his youngest daughter, Elizabeth.

Upon meeting the Duchess, who was fourteen, Joseph promptly reported his opinions of her to Grand Duke Leopold: "She is not beautiful and will never be pretty. She is tall for her age, slender, well-formed, has pretty enough eyes, is blond, has a large mouth, and possesses a sweet and alert expression."[21] Joseph's comments about her lack of beauty notwithstanding, Elizabeth was by far the most promising young woman he had seen.

Joseph was not the only ruler keeping a watchful eye on Elizabeth's marriage prospects. Catherine the Great, whose daughter-in-law was Elizabeth's sister, hoped that a marriage between Elizabeth and Francis would create a new Austro-Russian family pact. But Frederick the Great was "setting heaven and earth in motion" to prevent such an alliance.[22] Fritz even persuaded the Queen of Denmark to try and snatch Elizabeth for her son, the crown prince.

In a letter to Joseph in January 1781, Catherine warned him of his competition:

> This year appears to be destined for events, with treaties and marriages of all sorts. The Queen of Denmark* wants to pair [her son] the Prince Royal with the younger sister of my daughter-in-law. My opinion has been asked for; I said that the youth of the Prince made it possible to think about it more than once, and that I did not believe the parents of the Princess are pressing her to marry. But I have abused the patience of Y[our].I[mperial].M[ajesty].; I ask you to excuse it.[23]

Fritz was determined to do everything in his power to keep Elizabeth from becoming a Habsburg. When her parents rejected the idea of her marrying the Danish crown prince, Fritz dispatched his own great-nephew, Prince Frederick Wilhelm, to Mömpelgard to "woo the fourteen-year-old princess. But Elizabeth tearfully informed her parents, when asked, that she would never marry the Prussian Prince."[24] After more than six months of philandering against Joseph II and Catherine the Great, Fritz finally threw in the towel of opposition.

Once Elizabeth's parents accepted the proposal that was made on Francis's behalf, Joseph immediately sent off a letter to Florence letting Leopold know what had transpired: "I believe I have thus made a stroke of state and simultaneously procured for the young man [Francis] the best and most agreeable woman whose existence is known to me." Leopold, who had long perceived his son as belonging to all of Austria, wrote back on behalf of himself and María Luísa: "we feel that our children are also yours and the state's, and that consequently it is for you to

---

* The queen that Catherine was referring to was Juliana Marie, Queen-Regent of Denmark, who took over the reigns of power when her stepson, King Christian VII, went insane in 1772.

dispose of them in a manner that seems to you useful and advantageous to the Monarchy."[25]

As Joseph made arrangements to have Elizabeth brought to Vienna, Leopold of Tuscany was being faced with the equally daunting task of how to tell Francis that his future wife was already picked out for him. Leopold wanted to let the matter rest for a time, since Francis was only twelve. However, he preferred his son to hear the news from his parents rather than from the gossip at Court. After wrestling with the issue for several months, he and María Luísa broke the news to their sensitive son gently. When they summoned him into María Luísa's apartments to tell him, they were surprised at how well Francis reacted, and within a few weeks, he seemed to forget altogether.

Upon Joseph II's return to Vienna after his tour abroad, he immediately went back to his state papers in a flurry of reforms. Austria was unprepared to deal with the alarming rate at which he was trying to change the country so soon after Maria Theresa's death. Joseph seriously upset the religious balance of the Holy Roman Empire when he issued the Patent of Toleration in October 1781.

For centuries, non-Catholics in Austria—especially Jews— had been persecuted by the state. Even Maria Theresa once wrote that "no Jew shall be allowed to stay here (in Vienna) without my written permission."[26] The Patent was intended to end such bigotry and extend religious freedoms to non-Roman Catholics living within the Habsburg lands, specifically towards Jews, but also to Protestants and the Greek Orthodox Church. It even allowed Jews who were living in the cities to leave the slums and ghettos in search of safer homes.

At the time, the Patent was extremely controversial, as Jews and non-Catholics alike were very much stigmatized. Maria Theresa responded to Joseph's tolerant ways in 1777 by declaring: "To my great grief I have to say that there would be nothing more to corrupt in respect of religion if you intend to insist on that general toleration of which you maintain that it is a principle from which you will never depart....I will not cease praying myself...that God may protect you from this misfortune, the greatest which would ever have descended on the Monarchy...you will ruin your state and be guilty of the destruction of so many souls."[27]

Naturally, the Patent was extremely unpopular with Catholics, in large part because of the tolerance it granted to Jews. Throughout European history there had been a strident distrust of non-Christians. In the Middle Ages, events such as the Crusades and the Moorish strongholds in the Iberian Peninsula reinforced this distrust. For his controversial patent, Joseph II soon found himself being called "emperor of the Jews" by Catholics and non-Catholics alike.[28]

He continued to create dissention in Austria, Hungary, and Bohemia by curtailing the powers of the Roman Catholic Church and secularizing the clergy. Joseph was "making the bishops take oaths of obedience to him, reorganizing episcopal sees and seeing that they were given to the natives of the country concerned."[29] Over the next five years, he took control of 738 of 2,047 abbeys, seventy-percent of which were in Hungary alone.[30] "Since it was reckoned that the Church had held three-eights of Austrian land...the economic effects of this release of capital was considerable," but Joseph did not stop at repossessing the land.[31] In a move that was seen as a direct attack on Catholicism in the Habsburg realm, nearly 27,000 monks and nuns were "obliged to choose between a more productive career or retirement on a government pension."[32]

As the rights of Catholics continued to be stripped away, Emperor Joseph II extended more liberties to other religious groups. He removed the restrictions that prevented them from buying property, joining guilds, or even attending university. In the meantime, the dominant position of the Catholic Church was further undermined by the creation of the Commission on Spiritual Affairs (CSA). When the CSA got within arm's reach of controlling the Church, and as the Emperor continued to dismantle many of Austria's monasteries, the Vatican realized it was time to intervene if they hoped "to mollify Joseph."[33]

His "anticlerical, liberal innovations" prompted an official visit from Pope Pius VI in July 1782.[34] Queen Maria Carolina begged Joseph to treat the Pope properly, but he only remarked: "Voltaire wrote that one should kiss the feet of the Pope in order to bind his hands, and I shall follow the spirit if not the letter of this advice."[35]   The Pontiff was received "courteously but with none of the outward marks of reverence due to him."[36]   It was a "sufficiently cold reception," and "even the Pope's presence did not interrupt the execution of his [Joseph's] plan."[37]

Even as the symbolic head of Europe's eastern Catholic dominions, Joseph II ardently refused to be influenced by the Vatican, despite making some "minor concessions on religious toleration."[38]   However, the Pope's arrival stirred the hearts of Joseph's Catholic subjects and gave Vienna a renewed sense of energy.   Joseph told his sister Mimi: "During these last days there has been an extraordinary crowd in front of his [the Pope's] windows.   It was a wonderful sight, such as I have never seen before and never expect to see again.   It is impossible to say how many people were there."   Even a Protestant man named Bourgoing wrote: "The presence of the Pope has had an amazing effect.   I am not a Catholic and I am not easily moved, but I must confess that the sight touched me deeply."[39]

Once the Pope departed Austria, Joseph II's ulterior motives for his actions against the Church revealed themselves.   He wanted to create "a modern state as effective as Prussia."   To reach this goal he was forced to maximize the "productive capacity" of his subjects.   He believed there was no point in having "able-bodied, potential workers" confined to monasteries or serf lands, or disbarring people from employment because of religious restrictions.   One historian argued that Joseph's "edicts of toleration were meant to make his non-Catholic subjects available for the service of the State."[40]

As much as Joseph believed in the State serving the people, he was an equal proponent of people serving the State.[41]   In his mind, "the good of the state is always indivisible."[42]   He relaxed many of the censorship laws in Austria, but it did not appease his subjects, who were becoming increasingly disillusioned with their enlightened monarch.   One account suggests that once Joseph had allowed for public debates and freedom of speech, he himself was the brunt of much criticism.

Liberals and intellectuals initially praised Emperor Joseph II for the new freedoms he brought to his people, but as his reign neared the five-year mark his support began to wane.   Despite the size of the Habsburg lands, Joseph wanted his to be a uniform nation like France.   He seemed to so easily forget that his realm was so large that it bordered France in the west, Russia in the East, Prussia in the north, and the Ottoman Empire in the south. These boundaries meant that Austria, Hungary, and the other lands under Joseph's rule covered roughly one-third of the continent. He was hard pressed to find uniformity among such a diverse mixture of ethnicities, languages, and religions.

In the 1780s, Joseph decided once and for all to do away with the aristocratic systems in the Habsburg realm that he detested so much. The only way he could see this happen was to unify the crown lands into a single state over which he and his government had absolute control. He believed that "in the Habsburg Empire peoples are a complication in the history of the dynasty," and not the other way around.[43]

Not for the first time, a Habsburg ruler wanted to amalgamate all their lands into a single nation under one flag. To smooth the process along, Joseph opted for two official state languages. Latin was to be used in Hungary and Bohemia, and German in the rest of the empire. What he failed to realize was that few people, if any, wanted a uniform state. The most distant countries in the crown lands were the ones that were the most fiercely committed to their independence and national identity. In the west, Belgium and the Austrian Netherlands resented Joseph's sudden interference in their state affairs. Hungary and Bohemia—still embittered over the Emperor's brazen attitude toward their nations—felt they were losing even more of their cultural identities.

This new policy Joseph was adopting also divided the Austrian imperial family. The governors of the Austrian Netherlands at the time were the Emperor's sister Mimi, and her husband Albert, Duke of Saxe-Teschen. The Duke and Duchess were equally upset when Joseph suddenly began interfering in the Dutch government. One of Joseph II's biographer's wrote of the arrangement with the Netherlands: "So much was the Government regarded as separate that Maria Theresa considered the appointment of her favourite daughter, [Maria] Christina, and her husband to the joint viceroyalty as securing her a permanent establishment; and, in writing to her sister,…she always wrote as though they were the heads of two nearly equal houses."[44]

Joseph's popularity plummeted in Belgium and the Netherlands, but the people there were still loyal to the memory of Emperor Francis I and Empress Maria Theresa. Mimi wrote to Prince Kaunitz: "the blood of Maria Theresa which ran in her veins, and the upright and gentle character of her husband, had so won the affection of the people that the present troubles had not shaken their attachment."[45]

The very fact that Joseph made these unwise decisions shows just how out of touch he really was with his people by this stage in his life. Commenting on the task before him to a secretary at the French embassy, he admitted: "it is a hard job to rule nations so remote from the centre and so diverse in character; one can only guide them with an iron chain." [46] This statement marked a gradual descent in Joseph's personality into a more belligerent frame of mind. The lack of gratitude he perceived from his subjects was beginning to put a strain on his bombastic personality, which was beginning to give a distinctive flavor to his increasingly unstable reign.

The reforms that he dedicated his life to were being hampered by his own excessive haste and severity, his tendency to micromanage, and his workaholism. Joseph was known for sending out letters encouraging civil servants to work night and day out of devotion to the state. These letters highlighted the growing insensitivity he was developing towards his subjects. Once, when there was a timber shortage in Austria he ordered that dead bodies be sown into linen sacks instead of coffins. There was such widespread outrage across the country that he was forced to withdraw the edict immediately.

Public rejection on this scale marked a turning point in the reign of Emperor Joseph II. It rendered him permanently disillusioned and bitter towards the general public. His resentment of his people is clear in a memo he wrote to Prince Kaunitz:

> Since I daily observe that the ideas of the living are, alas! so material that they think it infinitely valuable for their bodies to rot more slowly after death, and to remain a stinking carrion for longer: I do not care how people want to be buried; and you will therefore explain that when I have shown the rational causes, the utility and practicality of this kind of burial, I shall compel nobody who is

unconvinced by it to be rational, and that as far as coffins are concerned, everyone may provide for his dead body as he pleases.[47]

By 1785, Joseph's mental state was bordering on megalomania. He saw himself as a knight in shining armor destined to save his people from the chains of the old regime through the ideals of the Enlightenment. This belief went so far that he actually kept a horse saddled and ready day and night in the event of any type of disaster so that he could be present to rescue his subjects from their misery.

When parts of the Danube flooded that year, Joseph was quick on the scene. But he was shocked that the homeless peasants blamed him for the disaster. The victims believed that his attacks on the Church had brought the wrath of God on Austria. He merely shrugged his shoulders and rode off on his horse.

Without a doubt, the 1780s signaled a crash in the popularity of Emperor Joseph II. As he became more insensitive to the needs of his people, they in turn became angered and tired of his supposed enlightened despotism. According to one modern historian: "Sincerely devoted to his people's welfare, he forced on them unwanted (though often salutary) reforms, and received little thanks. No wonder that he became morose and suspicious."[48]

Rather than face the internal problems of his empire, he committed himself to doing everything possible to expand Austria's borders. He lived his life wanting nothing more than to increase the territories of his house in the hopes of unifying Germany under the Habsburg banner. Joseph II was a strong believer in the idea of a united Germany, and once declared, "I am Emperor of the German *Reich*."[49]

Introduced into the empire's unstable mix at this time was war in northwestern Europe. It was a conflict that exploded after years of tensions in the Benelux region between the Holy Roman Empire and the Dutch Republic. From 1784 to 1785, Austria was entangled in what became known as the Kettle War.

The Netherlands during the Josephinist era were divided into the Dutch Republic in the north, and the Low Countries (more commonly called the Austrian Netherlands) in the south. After the Treaty of Westphalia in 1648, the Dutch had sealed off the Scheldt River from the Austrian Netherlands, cutting off trade and shipping routes. Emperor Joseph II "attempted to revive the idea...that Belgium should recover its former eminence in trade" by recapturing the Scheldt from the Dutch.[50]

In October 1784, three Austrian vessels led by the warship *Le Louis* departed Antwerp to seize control of the Scheldt in Amsterdam. Instead of capturing the river quickly and quietly, the Austrians were humiliated. The Dutch had their own ships waiting in Amsterdam. Their lead ship, the *Dolfijn*, fired a single shot that ricocheted off a kettle on the deck of the *Le Louis*, hence the name "Kettle War". Terrified (and grossly incompetent), the *Le Louis*'s captain immediately surrendered. With the Emperor's flagship in their control, the Dutch added insult to injury by capturing one of Austria's nearby fortresses.

When Joseph received the news of the surrender, he turned red with anger and immediately sent for his advisers. On October 30, he sent a formal declaration of war to the Dutch Republic. The next day, he sent an incensed telegram to Leopold of Tuscany about the situation brewing in the Netherlands: "My dear brother, I believe that because of the public news my stories with the Dutch are known to you, of their insolence as they fired three shots at my buildings and occupied it, just as they did at sea [with the *Le Louis*]."[51]

To stall for time, the Dutch hesitated sending any reply. By mid-November, they had amassed a fleet to attack Antwerp. The commander of the Dutch forces, Prince Frederick III of Salm-Kyburg, prepared a fleet of Friesian ships. But before another shot could be fired, the war was over. Prince Frederick's ships were forbidden to leave their port under an ancient treaty with Britain. After the *Le Louis* and its crew were returned to the Empire, Austria and the Dutch Republic agreed to a ceasefire.

Emperor Joseph had always hoped his sister, Queen Marie Antoinette, would provide French support in the Kettle War. But the Queen protested, saying it was not her place to interfere with France's international relationships. After the ceasefire was declared, it was revealed that France had supplied the Dutch Republic with weapons and ammunition.

Franco-Austrian relations took a heavy blow over the Scheldt Affair, but it would not be the last time. The 1780s saw a massive decay in the relationship between Austria and France. But Joseph II still tried to take advantage of Marie Antoinette's position as queen to further his own goals. He compelled her to "prove her devotion to the august house and family [of Austria]."[52] The relentless demands he made on Marie Antoinette of France were a source of strain on the young and sensitive queen. The relationship between the two powers began deteriorating to the point of "floundering" now that the alliance's two main architects, Louis XV and Maria Theresa, were dead. King Louis XVI's ministers began to tread carefully when it came to Emperor Joseph. One of the King's officials commented to the French ambassador in Vienna, "We have stopped the progress of the Emperor…and that's not easily forgiven."[53]

03

Trials and tribulations had forced Ferdinand, Duke of Parma, to finally grow up after nearly two decades of marriage. The more solemn tone his wife had adopted and the near-death experience of his son, Prince Luigi, had made a deep impact on the once boorish duke. He still had some of his childish qualities, but spending time in the presence of his wife had made him wiser and more politically attuned. By the time he was in his late thirties, Ferdinand was growing into a man. He was actually maturing at a faster rate than his uncle, King Ferdinand IV of Naples.

In their marriage, the Duke and Duchess of Parma continued to grow closer. They still had many differences to overcome, but they were beginning to come together in devotion to Parma. Amalia had always been a bold and daring woman, but now Ferdinand, who once held no pride in his nation or his position, was taking up a wiser mantle. Fatherhood had also forced him to put his childish ways behind him.

The improvement in Amalia's marriage was marked by the arrival of more children. Carolina and Luigi were joined by two other sisters, Maria Antonietta ("Tognina," b. 1774) and

Carlotta (b. 1777).* Like her older siblings, Tognina was very quiet and withdrawn. She was also very artistic with a gift for both music and painting. Wanting to nurture her daughter's talent as much as possible, Amalia arranged for the famed painters Giuseppe Baldrighi and Domenico Muzzi to instruct Tognina.

The family's home continued to be centered on the Ducal Palace in Parma. Once a "rambling congeries of buildings," it had become a home to the close-knit ducal family.[54] Over the years, it was expanded several times. Most prominently, a casino was built onto its left wing. This was later expanded to include two older noble houses, and eventually became connected by a series of archways to the church of San Paolo, which became the ducal chapel in 1787. These new additions suited Ferdinand and Amalia well, since the Duchess enjoyed gambling at the casino, while her husband spent many hours praying with the bishops in the chapel.

The Court of Parma was vastly different than Vienna, Versailles, or even Naples. It was small and bourgeoisie, where the ducal children stayed intimately close to their parents, not unlike the way it had been during Amalia's childhood. The education of the princes and princesses was of the utmost importance to their parents. The Duke and Duchess particularly favored their two eldest children, Carolina and Luigi, who were given monastic instructions with their father. But it was Tognina who took a keen interest in the matters of God.

As heir to the throne, Prince Luigi's health was always in the forefront of his mother's mind. His long golden curls and rosy cheeks masked a body that was in poor condition. His epileptic seizures became crippling, but with his parents by his side, he rallied through each episode. The strain of watching her son suffer was more than Amalia could bear at times and her nerves began to fall apart.

Now that her mother was dead and buried, there was no one left to support Amalia, Duchess of Parma. She and Joseph II had drifted apart, and once Maria Theresa disowned her, she was cut off completely from her brothers and sisters elsewhere in

---

* Amalia had also given birth to three other children: Filippo (b. 1783), Antonietta Luisa (b. 1784), and Maria Luisa (b. 1787). Tragically, these children died from smallpox before they were two years old.

Europe for a time. The Parmesan envoy in France did make regular reports to the Duchess, but her relationships with Marie Antoinette and Maria Carolina were lukewarm at best, and she was not even on speaking terms with Mimi anymore. The closest tie Amalia and Maria Carolina had was between their husbands, the two Ferdinands, who would write to one another. As she went through the many trials in her family, Amalia undoubtedly longed for the strength, support, and influence of the mother that she had chosen to forsake for so many years.

"The White Elephant"

The 1780s was a decade that marked a dramatic change in fortunes for each of Maria Theresa's five special children. Grand Duke Leopold and Queen Maria Carolina continued to enjoy great popularity; Amalia, Duchess of Parma, was coping with family hardships; and Emperor Joseph II was seeing his empire crumble under his unsuccessful reign.

Like Joseph, Queen Marie Antoinette was entering a difficult phase in her life. Within a few short years, France would reach the point of no return. But before that happened, the Queen's popularity continued its steady decline. Her decadent, extravagant lifestyle was causing her to be unfairly portrayed as a power-hungry madwoman whose spending habits were bankrupting the nation.

The newest storm brewing on France's turbulent political horizon would infamously be remembered as the Affair of the Diamond Necklace. It would once and for all galvanize the loathing of the French people against their Austrian queen and irreparably damaged the reputation of the Bourbon monarchy.

The twisted plot all began with a famed Parisian jeweler named Charles Boehmer who had been the personal jeweler to the French royal family for years. During Marie Antoinette's early years on the throne, she purchased from him frequently. When she did so, she paid only out of her own purse. Now that she was a mother with a family to take care of, her tastes became more modest and demure. After receiving jewels as gifts from Louis in 1782, and having redressed some diamonds herself, she declared "her jewel-case rich enough, and was not desirous of making any addition to it."[1]

Choosing to ignore the Queen's insistence for modesty, Boehmer decided to take advantage of his position with the royal family. When King Louis XV was alive, he had commissioned Boehmer to make the most extravagant necklace imaginable for his beloved du Barry. Boehmer acquired some of the most spectacular diamonds in Europe; when the necklace was complete, modern estimates placed its worth at $93,000,000. Nearly 650 flawless diamonds weighing more than 2,800 carats were hung in rows and dangling from tassels. It was widely considered to be the most elaborate single piece of jewelry Europe had ever seen. But when Louis XV died and the du Barry was banished, the necklace was all but forgotten. Boehmer found himself nearly bankrupt from making it, and finally decided in 1782 to offer it to Marie Antoinette. But when she laid eyes on it, she refused it, claiming, "that the state of her finances did not admit of her expending such a sum on so useless a purchase."[2]

Boehmer refused to take no for an answer. He spoke to numerous members of the Queen's household, but no one was willing to try and solicit the necklace to her. Eventually he persuaded Louis XVI's first gentleman to show it to the King, "who admired it so much that he himself wished to see the Queen adorned with it, and sent the case to her."[3] Indignant that her husband would purchase such an extravagant necklace in her name, Marie Antoinette adamantly protested. Once she had discussed with Louis why it was so inappropriate to spend that kind of money on such a frivolous item, she made sure it was returned to Paris.

Nearly a year passed without any further talk of the necklace. In 1783, Charles Boehmer resurfaced and again tried to solicit the King's business. A series of attempts to sell the necklace at other European courts failed, and eventually the Queen recommended that if the deal was "not that bad" then the King should buy it as a future wedding gift for one of their children. She could not bring herself to ever wear it, explaining that she was "unwilling that the world should have to reproach her with having coveted so expensive an article." In the end, Louis declined the necklace for the final time, claiming "their children were too young to justify such an expense."[4]

Unable to find a buyer, Boehmer found himself hopelessly in debt and desperate for money. He used his position as Jeweler to the Crown to obtain a private audience with Marie Antoinette. With Madame Royal at her side, she watched as "Boehmer threw himself upon his knees, clasped his hands, burst into tears, and exclaimed, 'Madame, I am ruined and disgraced if you do not purchase my necklace. I cannot outlive so many misfortunes. When I go hence I shall throw myself into the river.'"[5]

Queen Marie Antoinette was unmoved by the jeweler's plea, nor was she duped by his efforts to play upon her emotions. Instead, in one of the most uncharacteristic displays of her life, she lashed out at him and proceeded to put him in his place for his shameful appeal and his unprofessional manner. "Not only have I never ordered the article which causes your present despair," she exclaimed, "but whenever you have talked to me about fine collections of jewels I have told you that I should not add four diamonds to those which I already possessed. I told you myself that I declined taking the necklace; the King wished to give it to me, but I refused him also; never mention it to me again." From that point on, Marie Antoinette refused to even see Boehmer for fear of his "rash character." In time she began to hear rumors that the "Boehmer had disposed of his 'white elephant' [the necklace] to the Sultan of Turkey that it might adorn the shoulders of a favourite slave."[6]

As the Diamond Necklace Affair began building to its dramatic climax, another mystery cropped up in the life of Marie Antoinette of France. She had given birth to Marie Thérèse in 1778 and Louis Joseph in 1781, and by 1783 she was pregnant again. What makes this pregnancy unique to all her others was that history seems to have forgotten it. The memoirs of her ladies-in-waiting and other members of her household make no mention of it at all. The only reference that is ever made to it is between Marie Antoinette and Joseph II in two letters from 1783. Joseph wrote in September, "I await with infinite impatience...the news of your pregnancy."[7] A few weeks later, Marie Antoinette told her brother: "My pregnancy and health are marvelous."[8]

These were the last references Queen Marie Antoinette made about her pregnancy. Her next letter to Joseph in

December 1783 made a vague reference to her health and the well being of her children, but she never mentioned anything about her pregnancy again. Perhaps the stress of the necklace affair forced the Queen to miscarry, but as far as history is concerned, the outcome of Marie Antoinette's pregnancy of 1783 remains a mystery.

In March 1784, when the Queen's pregnancy would have been long behind her, the necklace affair reached a pivotal moment. A con artist named Comtesse Jeanne de Lamotte heard about the trouble the necklace was causing at Versailles. She developed a scheme to discredit the monarchy and get the multimillion-dollar piece of jewelry for herself. Lamotte's pawn in the affair was the Cardinal Louis de Rohan, a French aristocrat and former ambassador to Vienna who was loathed by Marie Antoinette for his unscrupulous conduct. Rohan, whose name would come to be synonymous with the Diamond Necklace Affair, was held in low regard by most of Maria Theresa's children; Grand Duke Leopold of Tuscany said he was "without religion or morals."[9]

Lamotte and Rohan began prying the lid off of a Pandora's box that could never again be closed. The pair would unwittingly help to bring down one of the most powerful dynasties in history.

❧

As scandal and innuendo surrounded Marie Antoinette, Emperor Joseph II was being immersed with similar frustrations in his own dominions. In the northwest, the Dutch Republic continued to attack Austrian establishments in Belgium and the Netherlands. In the east, a new threat had arisen in the form of the Ottoman Empire.

At that time, most of the Balkans was under Turkish rule. The Sultan, Abdul Hamid I, was eager to take more of Europe for himself, but Joseph II and Catherine the Great refused to let any more of their territory fall into his hands. Ottoman incursions, coupled with the Dutch revolutionaries, threatened to completely destabilize the Habsburg monarchy. Joseph had become so despondent with the situation that he announced: "Nothing in the world could be more advantageous for the

Monarchy than if a gigantic earthquake were to plunge all the Turkish provinces into the ocean and thus create a coastline from Dalmatia to the Dniestr [river]. In that case I would gladly renounce all further acquisitions and Hungary would be like Belgium and Holland."[10]

In the midst of the anarchy that threatened Joseph's rule, there was one bright spot. He took it upon himself to care for the most valuable resource his empire possessed: his nephew, Archduke Francis. Once Leopold became Joseph's successor, the process began of grooming Francis to take the throne. His childhood in Florence was spent much in the same way his uncle's had in Vienna, surrounded by tutors, advisers, and instructors. Francis had a decidedly Italian education, which was considered highly unsuitable for a future Holy Roman emperor. Joseph and Leopold agreed that a proper training in Vienna was needed to prepare the archduke to rule.

In June 1784, Leopold and Francis left Florence for Vienna after the archduke turned sixteen, arriving at Laxenburg on the last day of June. They were met by Joseph, who was overjoyed at the presence of his brother and nephew, who had never even seen Vienna. There were tours of the capital, visits to the imperial estates, and meetings with important government officials. But perhaps the most important meeting for Francis took place on July 1, when he came face to face with the slender, graceful, and eager-to-please Elizabeth of Württemberg. The Duchess had already been living in Vienna for two years when Francis arrived, and even though they had only just met, they were smitten with one another.

Leopold's presence was required back in Tuscany almost immediately, so he left his son in the hands of Joseph and Elizabeth. The Emperor immediately took a proactive role in his nephew's education, but true to his nature, was deeply critical of Francis's shortcomings. Joseph wrote a lengthy memo regarding the archduke's education:

When we consider that he is seventeen years of age, and compare him with others of the same age, we are at once struck with the conviction that his physical development has been completely neglected; that he is stinted in his growth; that he is very backward in bodily dexterity and deportment; in short, that he is neither more nor less than a spoiled mother's child, who considers all that he does himself as infinitely important and hazardous, and never takes into any account what he sees others doing or suffering for him. The manner in which he was treated for upwards of sixteen years, could not but have confirmed him in the delusion, that the preservation of his own person was the only thing of any importance.[11]

Count Colloredo, Francis's childhood tutor and friend, accompanied him to Vienna to act as his steward. Joseph told him bluntly: "Every person who holds public office and especially we [royals] must be ruled first and foremost by the words 'commitment' and 'duty' and seek to put them into practice in their fullest possible meaning."[12] Joseph made these words the edict by which his nephew was to live by in Vienna. The Emperor cared for his nephew deeply, but he also felt Francis was "dim-witted...whose physical awkwardness made him timid and lethargic."[13]

Joseph developed a strict training regiment of "fear and unpleasantness" to turn Francis from a prince into a leader.[14] Under his uncle's supervision, he was not allowed to "eat, sleep or enjoy himself until he had completed his daily duties."[15] The Emperor isolated Francis from servants and other people in order to make him more self-reliant, since Joseph believed his nephew "fail[ed] to lead himself, to do his own thinking."[16] Joseph's strictness notwithstanding, he and Francis became very close during his time in Vienna. Eventually, Leopold's son would become Joseph II's closest and most beloved relative.

ℛ

The year 1783 proved to be catastrophic for the Kingdom of Naples when a massive earthquake struck southern Italy. The heavily populated region of Calabria, as well as much of Sicily, was devastated; the city of Messina was nearly destroyed. "The cathedral, the royal and archiepiscopal palaces, the hospital, most of the convents, churches, and houses were in ruins;" wrote one author.[17]

In the days that followed, food, medicine, and rescue aid trickled in, but were hampered by the crippling damage done to the countryside. The devastated cities descended into anarchy. Untold "numbers of people were killed, while robbery, violence, and panic increased the scenes of horror which everywhere prevailed."[18]   The suffering of their people horrified King Ferdinand and Queen Maria Carolina.   To assist the relief efforts, they emptied their own bank accounts to help pay for food and medicine. Once that money was used, they personally took to the streets soliciting donations for the survivors.

When this devastating earthquake leveled the Two Sicilies, Charlotte had been working to make Naples a strong, independent naval power. She was anxious to reorganize the marine fleet, which was essential for the country's survival. Naples was surrounded by water on three out of four sides, and its success as a European power rested on its ability to traverse and maintain its territorial waters in the Mediterranean. Charlotte believed a strong navy was essential "for the purpose of protecting the commerce of the kingdom, and defending its coasts against the audacity of the African corsairs."[19]

Naples had traditionally lacked naval and military experts because Bernardo Tanucci always relied upon support from Spain's famous armada. The Neapolitan navy was therefore in desperate need of a gross overhaul. When Emperor Joseph II visited Naples in 1769, even he commented: "if I were King of Naples I would have fewer soldiers, but I would give everything to form a navy." Charlotte urgently appealed to Leopold of Tuscany for "an officer with ideal qualifications."[20] The man she would get would stand by her side for the next two decades, bringing both fame and scandal to the Kingdom of the Two Sicilies.

Sir John Acton was exactly what Queen Maria Carolina was looking for when she asked Leopold to recommend an able sailor to her service. Raised in France, he was a British nobleman and an officer in the Tuscan navy who served in the joint Spanish-Tuscan campaign in Algiers, quickly making his way up through the ranks and into the Tuscan Naval High Command.

The eighteenth century English scholar Edward Gibbon described him as "a very pretty sensible young man,"[21] but he was not without his flaws. One author called him a "foreigner, a soldier of fortune," who was "ambitious and covetous."[22] The Neapolitan ambassador to Great Britain, Prince Caramenico, threw his recommendation in with Leopold's choice for Acton as the man to reorganize the kingdom's navy. After only a few conversations, Charlotte realized that he was the perfect collaborator to help her reform Naples. Once she had persuaded Leopold to transfer Acton to her service, Charlotte appointed him Secretary of State for the Marine. The arrangement between the Grand Duke and the Queen enabled Acton to work in Naples without actually resigning from his Tuscan post.

Charlotte was genuinely impressed with Acton's abilities, especially when he began working his way up in Naples much like he had done in Florence. Within a few years, he was named commander-in-chief of the Neapolitan armed forces and navy. The more time John Acton spent in Naples, the more he earned the favor of the royal family. Queen Maria Carolina came to greatly depend on this British baronet, but as the pair worked more closely together, rumors and innuendo flew about the nature of their relationship. Charlotte was so enthralled by Acton that the pair were accused of being lovers, although it has never been proven. King Carlos III of Spain tried to use the rumors to persuade King Ferdinand to dismiss Acton: "They have turned you into a pasteboard king, you must get rid of Acton at once, or send him out of your kingdom."[23]

Charlotte was horrified when her husband began believing all the rumors about her and Acton. His jealousy, though perhaps unfounded, sent him into a wild rage. Bent on resolving the Acton issue once and for all, the King and Queen shut themselves up in Charlotte's apartments for twenty-four hours, locked in a battle of wills. "I am trying to surprise you together. I will kill you both, and have your bodies thrown out of the windows of the palace!" Ferdinand screamed.[24] Maria Carolina fired back a venomous attack, reminding her husband of his own infidelities. More than a day later, the Queen emerged, exhausted but victorious, and Acton remained in office. He even saw his power and influence increase. Charlotte wrote to Queen Marie Antoinette that she believed Acton was "useful to her people, inasmuch as he was a man of considerable information and great activity."[25]

In Spain, Carlos III refused to sit idly by while his son did nothing to halt the Queen's agenda. Disappointed by the outcome of Ferdinand's confrontation with Maria Carolina, Carlos sent a *charge d'affairs*, a certain Señor Las Casas, to Naples "to persuade her to dismiss Mr. Acton from the business of the state, and from her intimacy." Las Casas was not received well in Naples, and for good reason. He took every opportunity to offend the King and Queen. In a letter to Marie Antoinette, Charlotte "complained bitterly" of the "insulting proceedings" that Las Casas was forcing her to endure. Always ready to take control of any situation, she refused to concede defeat. She tried desperately to convince Las Casas that Acton had only received her favor because of his "superior capacity."[26] When he openly accused her of taking Acton as her lover, she defiantly declared: "I will have his picture drawn by the best painter in Italy, and his bust made by the best sculptor, and both sent to the King of Spain, who may judge whether his is a figure for a woman to fall in love with." "Oh, madam," came the impudent reply, "my master has lived long enough to know there is no answering for the caprices of *des dames galantes*."[27]

Charlotte was outraged and filled with "indignation" by such an "audacious reply." She was early into one of her numerous pregnancies at the time, but was so overwhelmed with rage and anger that she miscarried. When word of the crisis reached King Louis XVI, he intervened with Carlos III on his sister-in-law's behalf. Thanks to Louis, she "obtained complete satisfaction in this affair, and Mr. Acton was continued in his post of prime minister."[28] But the damage had already been done. Acton's critics now loathed him as much as Queen Maria Carolina adored him. They claimed "he had no idea whatever...of the politics of Europe, nor even of the very country which he governed."[29] It would take the Queen nearly twenty years to realize that some of the accusations leveled against her beloved minister just might be true.

In the midst of all these trials on the Neapolitan political scene, Britain's ambassador to Naples, William Hamilton, continued to be a great ally to the Queen and to Prime Minister Swinburne. Hamilton was as much of an attraction in Italy as Maria Carolina herself. People came from all over Europe to see this "eighteenth century dilettante" who was famous for being "a most generous host." When the middle-aged ambassador married in the mid-1780s, his new wife Emma was certainly "not the least of his attractions."[30] Maria Carolina, who was eager to formalize an alliance with Great Britain, "graciously received" Emma Hamilton for an audience. The young woman was rather indiscreet, sharing a number of diplomatic secrets, but she fascinated the Queen. It is easy to see why the two women became fast friends, and in time, they were nearly inseparable.

Emma's honesty and devotion endeared her to the Queen. She became Charlotte's closest friend and confidant, and the two women wrote to each other on an almost daily basis. In the same way that Joseph II and Marie Antoinette wrote long, affectionate letters to one another, so too did Charlotte and Emma. Most of the time, the Queen's letters began with "My very dear Friend" or "My dear Miledy," and usually ended with equally endearing words. In one particular letter, she closed by saying, "Believe me to be ever your sincere and grateful friend, Charlotte."[31] Lady Hamilton was just as fond of the Queen.

After only a few short years as commander-in-chief of the Neapolitan military forces, John Acton had curried so much favor with Maria Carolina that she used her influence to make him Prime Minister of Naples when Henry Swinburne resigned his position to return to Britain. Charlotte regretted the loss of Swinburne, so she did everything within her power to surround herself with allies. In order to grow closer to the remaining English influences at her court, she actively worked at spending more time with Emma Hamilton.

The Queen enlisted Lady Hamilton and Prime Minister Acton's help in ridding her country once and for all of influence from Spain. At the same time, King Carlos III continued waging a war against Action that, at times, was almost unbearable for the Queen. She detailed "the mortifications inflicted by the Court of Spain" to Marie Antoinette. But Maria Carolina also viewed John Acton as "a man whom malevolence itself could not suppose capable of interesting her otherwise than by his services."[32]

16

Overturning the Throne

When the Affair of the Diamond Necklace came about in the 1780s, Louis de Rohan was a politically ambitious man who was not content to remain a princely cardinal for the rest of his life. His sights were set on a much loftier goal, his nomination as Prime Minister of France. Since the position was a royal appointment, he was forced to look for ways to ingratiate himself with Queen Marie Antoinette.

When the Comtesse de Lamotte discovered Rohan's ambition, she used this to her advantage. She claimed that she was in "good standing" with the Queen and in a position to arrange for a return-to-grace for the Cardinal. She told Rohan that Marie Antoinette was considering having him acquire Boehmer's necklace for her, and "that the Queen would take the necklace on condition of paying for it by instalments [*sic*], and at the same time insisted on the purchase being kept a profound secret."[1]

Rohan leapt at the chance to be of service to the Queen. He blindly believed every word Jeanne de Lamotte said. With the Cardinal as her unwitting dupe, Lamotte's intricate scandal to take the necklace for herself deepened. To add another layer of reality to the scheme, she began a fictitious correspondence with Rohan by actually pretending to be Marie Antoinette. Letters between the pair became more emotional and colorful with each exchange. Lamotte managed to convince him "that the queen was in love with him."[2]

Cardinal de Rohan begged the Comtesse de Lamotte to arrange a meeting between him and the queen. Masterfully manipulating the situation, she agreed and hired a prostitute named Nicole Leguay to play the role of Marie Antoinette in the charade. On a warm night in August 1784, Leguay—who already bore a strikingly resemblance to the Queen—met with Rohan in one of the empty gardens around Versailles and persuaded him to embezzle funds in her name.

In the meantime, the relatively unknown Lamotte was "openly and unreservedly" boasting of her close, personal relationship with Marie Antoinette, shocking Paris's social *élite*. She also made sure that Boehmer was aware of her fictitious relationship, and told the jeweler in January 1785 that she had finally convinced the Queen to buy the necklace. The Comtesse claimed that because the Queen did not want to cause a scandal, she would use the hopelessly devoted cardinal, Prince Louis de Rohan. When Rohan finally took possession of the necklace in 1785, he agreed with Boehmer to an installment plan for payment. Later, he took the necklace to Lamotte's estate and gave it to a man whom he was told was a valet of the Queen.

When the time came for Boehmer to receive the first payment, Rohan discovered that the supposed royal bursaries he had been given were worthless. Boehmer went and complained about his predicament to Queen Marie Antoinette herself, who again protested that she had never ordered, let alone received, the necklace. As the jeweler recounted the series of events to her, she was horrified. She cried to Madame Campan, venting her anger squarely at Louis de Rohan: "This hideous crime must be laid bare. The whole of France and Europe shall know that the Roman purple and the title of prince only conceal an out-of-elbow, vulgar cheat who dares to try and compromise his sovereign's spouse."[3]

On August 15, 1785 the Cardinal was arrested by royal order and imprisoned in the Bastille. During his interrogation, the secrets of the scheme were made clear to him. When he learned the true nature of the plot, "his Eminence...was so affected, that he was obliged to have a glass of water brought him before he could recover himself."[4] Three days later, French authorities apprehended Jeanne de Lamotte along with some lesser accomplices.

Marie Antoinette was outraged, and believed that Rohan had masterminded the entire episode. In her opinion, only he was unscrupulous and devious enough to engineer such a scandal. The King and Queen decided to keep the matter quiet until it was absolutely necessary to make it public. In a letter to Joseph II about the affair, Marie Antoinette wrote: "Everything has been concerted between the King and me; the ministers knew nothing of it until the moment when the King sent for the cardinal, and interrogated him in the presence of the keeper of the seals and the Baron de Breteuil."[5]

King Louis was eager to resolve this attack on his wife's credibility as quickly as possible. In September, he announced to his ministers: "We have not been able to see without just indignation that an august name, dear to us in many ways, has been boldly taken, and that the respect due to the Royal Majesty [the Queen] has been violated with unheard-of insolence."[6]

On May 13, 1786, the very public trial of the Cardinal de Rohan and the Comtesse de Lamotte began in Paris. "I am anxious that this scandal, with all its details, should be thoroughly cleared up in the eyes of the world," Marie Antoinette wrote to Joseph.[7] The ultimate outcome was hardly what she, or the monarchy, had hoped for. Adding insult to injury, Rohan was acquitted of all charges. The jury decided he was just a pawn in the hands of the Comtesse. Jeanne de Lamotte was not so fortunate. She was found guilty and sentenced to be whipped, branded, and locked up in the prostitutes prison *Salpêtrière*. In London, *The Times* reported that the necklace was later disassembled and its pieces sent to Holland and Portugal.

Public speculation about the trial swooned across Paris. The people believed the Queen had orchestrated the entire event and tried to use Lamotte to discredit and destroy Rohan. These rumors were reinforced after the trial by Marie Antoinette's very public disappointment at the Cardinal's acquittal. Suspicions towards her deepened when Rohan was deprived of his clerical and royal titles, his style as Serene Highness, his status in French society, his position at court, and his eventual exile to the Abbey of *la Chaisse-Dieu*. Jeanne Lamotte managed to escape *Salpêtrière* and flee to England, but the Queen's critics believed that she helped her escape.

If the French monarchy were an opera, then the Diamond Necklace Affair would be its closing act. It served one last time to strip the House of Bourbon of any credibility in the public eye. "The French monarchy received a shock from which it never recovered," said one historian.[8] Instead of clearing Marie Antoinette's name, the trial damaged her public image even more. History remembered "that unutterable business of the Diamond Necklace" as the "Largest Lie of the Eighteenth Century..." And Prince Talleyrand, one of the greatest diplomats in French history, prophetically warned: "Pay attention to this wretched Necklace-affair; I should not be in the least surprised if it overturned the throne."[9]

By the middle of the decade, the kingdom of France was standing on the edge of a knife. The First Estate, the upper echelon of French society of which the monarchy was a part, lived off the work of the peasants, called the Third Estate. Heavy taxes levied for the pensions of retired courtiers and the economic disaster of supporting the American war outraged the people, especially now that they believed Marie Antoinette orchestrated a multi-million dollar scandal. There would be no rapprochement between the royal family and the people.

At the time of the necklace imbroglio, Queen Marie Antoinette was pregnant again. This latest *enceinte* was much more difficult than her previous ones. On Easter Sunday in March 1785, a twenty-two cannon salute announced that she delivered a healthy son at Versailles. That afternoon, the infant prince was baptized and given the names Louis Charles. It was the tradition among the French royal family that all the sons and grandsons of the king be named Louis. The baby's second name, Charles, was in honor of his godmother, Queen Maria Carolina of Naples.

Motherhood consumed nearly all of Marie Antoinette's time. Marie Thérèse, Madame Royal, was her parents' little princess. She learned many lessons at her mother's side, but "in her manners and turn of her mind" she was the spitting image of her father. Her character was "a mixture of goodness and rusticity."[10] Marie Antoinette insisted on teaching her daughter generosity and kindness. From a very early age, Madame Royale was taught by her mother to have a "desire to succour the unfortunate." Marie Antoinette "incessantly talked" about the suffering of the poor and the need for people of class to help alleviate their burdens.[11] On more than one occasion, she made her daughter personally distribute her own money that she had saved for the impoverished French people.

As the Queen taught Marie Thérèse how to be a loving human being, King Louis instilled in her piety, courage, and conviction. Devotion to God was especially important in their family. When Marie Thérèse had her First Communion, her father told her "that religion is the source of happiness, and our support in the troubles of life."[12] The King and Queen of France imparted the same love for God that Maria Theresa had insisted upon for her own children.

The princes Louis Joseph and Louis Charles received a more stately education. They were instructed by the most scholarly minds in France, but the health of the little dauphin continued to be a cause for worry. The most casual observers could see the differences between Marie Antoinette's two sons. As the Dauphin suffered and languished in a frail body, Prince Louis Charles was the embodiment of health and vivacity.

Unlike her brother and sisters in Italy, Queen Marie Antoinette did not give birth to many children, but the few she did have she loved with all her heart. Only a few months after Louis Charles was born, the Queen, now thirty, became pregnant for the last time. On July 8, 1786 she gave birth to a daughter named Sophie. From the day she was born, Princess Sophie was different than her siblings. She was immediately described as being "ailing" and "malformed," and did not live long.[13] She died just before her first birthday of a rare form of tuberculosis.

The baby's body lay in a clear coffin under a jewel-encrusted crown and a purple velvet pall in the grand salon of the Petit Trianon, a private chateau at Versailles used by Marie Antoinette. After an intimate and emotional funeral, Sophie's body was taken by carriage to the necropolis of the French royal family, the Basilica of St. Denis in Paris. There, Marie Antoinette's dead daughter was laid to rest amongst her ancestors while her grief-stricken mother and family mourned. Louis XVI's sister, Princess Élisabeth, wrote to a friend that, upon seeing the Queen after Sophie died, "what we did most was to weep over the death of my poor little niece."[14] Like any mother, Marie Antoinette was overcome with sorrow when her little girl died. "She might have been a friend!" she cried.[15]

The death of Princess Sophie marked the beginning of the end for Marie Antoinette and her family. The nation showed little sympathy for their grieving monarchs. Outcries and accusations of everything from financial rapacity to open treason began to surround Versailles. France's Austrian queen was at the center of almost every allegation, insult, or crude joke. Marie Antoinette began living her life under the constant suspicion by the public that she had engineered the necklace fraud, using Louis de Rohan and Jeanne de Lamotte as pawns in her scheme for power. According to the angry people of Paris, she had no doubt funneled the money from the scam to Emperor Joseph II to help in his innumerable military campaigns.

With the passage of time, the King and Queen began withdrawing from public view. Marie Antoinette and Louis XVI were beginning to slip into their own world, oblivious to the tides of change that were sweeping across their nation. They were blind to the fact that the "symptoms of the Revolution were already discernable. They were apparent in the disorder that reigned high and low, in the struggle of rival ambitions fighting for mastery, in the multiplication of scandals, in the pamphlets that mocked and slandered the King and Queen," not to mention "the incessant efforts of the factions who sought the downfall of the House of Bourbon with such bitter enmity and deliberately set themselves to degrade it."[16]

By the later half of the 1780s, anger against the monarchy continued to rise. The kingdom "hurried on towards the Revolution. Royalty had lost its last scrap of prestige."[17] Tragically, the royal couple was not in touch with reality enough to see that unless something was done to slow the progress of revolutionary ideals, it would destroy their lives forever.

Unlike Queen Marie Antoinette, Grand Duke Leopold of Tuscany's family remained relatively free of tragedy and complication. Much of the contrast can be traced to the differences between the French royal family and the Tuscan grand ducal family. Whereas Marie Antoinette's children were in front of the whole world at Versailles, with every part of their lives under scrutiny, Leopold's children grew up in a warm, cozy environment where they were nurtured and cared for by two attentive parents.

Unlike Marie Thérèse, Louis Joseph, and Louis Charles, who had a loving yet formal and strict relationship with their mother, Leopold's children came to admire their father for his kind and goodhearted nature. This was especially true for Archduchess Theresa, who at the age of twenty-one fell in love with Prince Anton of Saxony. From a dynastic point of view, it was a suitable match. As a son of the Elector of Saxony, Anton came from a proud royal family. But what appealed to the down-to-earth Theresa the most was that, besides the fact that Anton was devoted to her, he stood little chance of ascending the Saxon throne. Like her father, Theresa was content to lead a quiet life with her family. Leopold approved of the match, not realizing that his daughter would one day become Electress of Saxony, and later, its first queen.

The wedding took place in September 1788 in Florence. Breaking with tradition, a proxy wedding was not conducted. The Archbishop of Florence married the couple in the city's Basilica di Santa Maria del Fiore. A month later, they renewed their vows at a candlelit ceremony in Dresden. Though he kept a stone-faced exterior, it was bittersweet for Leopold to see his eldest daughter marry and leave the family to start one of her own. The Grand Duke and Duchess consoled themselves with the fact that Theresa was not the victim of an arranged marriage. Having married off his daughter to an amiable man, Leopold anticipated the arrival of grandchildren.

Princess Theresa was already twenty-one when she got married, but Leopold and María Luísa continued to expand their family. By the time of Theresa's wedding in 1788, Leopold was the father of fourteen children. His first eight children— Theresa, Francis, Ferdinand, Marianne, Karl, and Alexander— were joined by Joseph (b. 1776), Clementine (b. 1777), Anton

(b. 1779), Maria Amalia (b. 1780), Johann (b. 1782), Rainer (b. 1783), Ludwig (b. 1784), and Rudolf (b. 1788).*

When it came to this next generation of Habsburg, Emperor Joseph II took more than a passing interest. Not content to train Archduke Francis, Joseph became intimately concerned about how his nieces and nephews were being raised. In 1787, he wrote Leopold a letter about the children's education that bordered on an interrogation. Leopold, ever the cool head, replied with reassuring words:

> Please be assured that, far from having put into the heads of my children that they must have...the airs of archdukes and archduchesses, we have constantly directed their education and our talks and discussions to the end that they might fully understand the need to fit themselves for eventual employment according to their respective abilities and [understand] that they will grow up to be merely ordinary private individuals and servants of the state.[18]

Family was a high priority in Leopold's life. In a gesture of peace and magnanimity, he sought to heal many of the wounds between his sister, Mimi, and himself by allowing his son Karl to spend half of every year in the Austrian Netherlands with his aunt and uncle. The Duchess of Saxe-Teschen's visit in 1776 started the process of reconciliation, but in the years that followed, the siblings worked at growing closer. They wrote to each other weekly, exchanging news about their countries and their families.

As the undisputed Habsburg patriarch in Italy, Leopold kept Mimi up to date on everything that was going on in Tuscany, Parma and Naples. He wrote to her in 1789: "My children, thank God, are doing well, Theresa had the measles, but [they were] extremely benign. She contracted it by nursing her husband who had it."[19] With no children of her own, Mimi continued to be a devoted and trusted friend to Leopold's children. She regularly visited Theresa and Anton in nearby Saxony, passing along to Leopold as much information as she could. "I thank you for the news you have given me about

---

* Grand Duchess María Luísa had given birth to 16 children, but two of them—Prince Albert (b. 1773) and Prince Max (b. 1774)—died as children.

Thérèse in Dresden," Leopold wrote in response to one of Mimi's letters.[20]

Leopold and María Luísa's family bliss was not destined to last, because worry over the health of their sons would haunt their waking hours. After Archduke Rudolf was born, Leopold became disheartened when he discovered his normally robust children were suffering from excruciating headaches, dizziness, and disorientation. His beloved sons, the next generation of royals for Austria, were showing signs of that dreaded disease, epilepsy.

As their sons grew into free-spirited individuals, Leopold and María Luísa kept the truth of their children's condition to themselves. As a hereditary disease, it could be passed on to the next generation of Habsburgs. Some of the children, like Karl and Rainer, were lucky enough to have only a mild form of epilepsy. But others, like Archduke Francis, would pass it on to their children. The condition that affected Francis and his brothers was to have a devastating impact not only on their family, but on the future of the Habsburg monarchy and the Austrian Empire itself that was to follow in the next century.

"Anguish and Deep Despair"

After Austria's humiliating defeat in the Netherlands, Emperor Joseph II had no choice but to make peace with the Dutch Republic. The Treaty of Fontainebleau was signed, ending the short-lived Kettle War. As the governors of the Austrian Netherlands, Mimi and Albert were asked to represent Joseph in the negotiations. By the end, Austria had been forced to concede so much territory that the Emperor exploded with anger.

Echoing her mother's sentiments from the War of the Bavarian Succession, Queen Marie Antoinette was desperate to see peace restored to Europe. When Joseph finally signed the treaty, she was relieved: "I give you my compliments, my dear brother, on your signing of the peace treaty with the Dutch."[1]

This most recent failure showed Joseph that he needed to rule with more of an iron fist. In a letter from 1787, he re-defined his personal mission in life: "It is necessary to be sincere at court and severe in the field; stoical without obduracy; magnanimous without weakness; and to gain the esteem of our enemies by the justice of our actions."[2]

In January 1788, an event took place that helped lift the tense mood that pervaded Vienna. The city was energized by the news that Joseph's nephew, Archduke Francis, was finally marrying Elizabeth of Württemberg. The six years that Elizabeth spent in the Austrian capital had earned her the love and admiration of the people. She was intensely popular and famous for her kindness and generosity. She also brought with her prestige as the sister-in-law of Catherine the Great's son, the future Tsar Paul I.

Francis and Elizabeth were married at the traditional Capuchin Church with only a few close relatives in attendance. The groom's uncle, Albert of Saxe-Teschen, stood as best man; Joseph's brother Max—now the Archbishop-Elector of Cologne—performed the ceremony; and Francis's friend and tutor, Count Colloredo, walked Elizabeth down the aisle. Leopold and María Luísa were unable to attend because of pressing state business in Tuscany, but they had Joseph report on the ceremony and the festivities that followed. The event stirred up excitement across Europe. Leopold's sisters living abroad did not hesitate to send their best wishes to Vienna. Even King Louis of France wrote to Joseph, "I receive with great pleasure the sign of friendship, you give me" by including the details of the wedding.[3]

No sooner were Francis and Elizabeth married than Emperor Joseph turned his attention back to his military campaigns. This time, he began to look eastward to fulfill any territorial ambitions he may still have had by 1788. He continued to be a close friend of Catherine the Great, and began meeting with her on a frequent basis. The Empress was equally fond of her Austrian counterpart. The cordial relationship they shared opened a door that allowed Joseph to lead Austria into an alliance with Imperial Russia, placing the Holy Roman Empire on the verge of war with Russia's longtime enemy, the Ottoman Empire.

Both Russia and Austria shared borders with the Ottoman Empire, which occupied nearly half of the Balkan Peninsula in the eighteenth century. Austria's territories at the time extended as far south as Bosnia and Herzegovina, colliding with Turkish-held Montenegro, Albania, and Serbia. Catherine's empire was in a similar position because the Ottomans in Romania flanked Russia's western border.

Joseph II viewed his alliance with Russia as more for show than force. He believed it was a useful and formidable weapon to keep Turkey and its new sultan, Selim II, in check, rather than necessarily for conquest. He "had little interest in acquiring their sparsely populated, disease-ridden territories."[4] Eventually Joseph voted to join Russia's campaign against the Ottomans, but held off on making a formal declaration of war for some time. He took the time to build up thousands of troops along the Turkish border.

Several weeks went by without any action from Joseph. Then suddenly in the spring of 1788, with his "armies now being ready for action, the emperor issued his declaration of war." He was deluded into thinking that another conflict would help Austria's predicament, but even before the first offensive began, the war was "debilitating and unpopular." In Vienna, "the morale of the cultural elite was severely eroded; fears of conscription led many aristocratic families to leave Vienna, and there were widespread feelings of disillusionment with Emperor Joseph, a sense that he had betrayed the promise of an enlightened reform movement."[5]

When Austria carried out its first offensive in the Austro-Turkish War of 1788-1791, it did so with untrained soldiers and poor supplies. Their first target was Belgrade. Joseph wanted to liberate the city, which had been under mostly Ottoman control for centuries. The linchpin of the operation was the support of Russia, who flanked the Turks on the eastern front. When Russian reinforcements never arrived, the Austrian troops were vanquished. The Turkish garrison guarding Belgrade battled with a ferocity that no one ever expected.

The failed siege of Belgrade was "little short of a fiasco...when compared with the hopes with which the campaign opened, its results were miserably small."[6] This crushing defeat would be only the first of many for Austria during the war, and would sound the death knell of Emperor Joseph II's reign, and eventually, his life.

CB

Queen Maria Carolina of Naples had followed in her mother's footsteps in more ways than one. She ruled her kingdom with little interference from her idle husband, but she was also the mother of a very large family. By the late 1780s she had been pregnant twelve times, but Italy's low standard of living meant that she was forced to watch four of her children die in infancy. Her eldest surviving children—Teresa, Luisa, and Francesco— were followed in quick succession by a pair of twin girls in 1779, Maria Cristina ("Mimi") and Cristina Amelia. After them came

Gennaro in 1780, Maria Amelia ("Amélie") in 1782, Maria Antonietta ("Toto") in 1784, and Clotilda in 1786.*

The loss of four of her children was heartrending for the Queen, who was an intensely devoted mother. But this bleak period in her life was made easier by the arrival of more children. In July 1787, the ships docked in the Gulf of Naples fired a twenty-one cannon salute signaling the birth of a daughter, Enrichetta.

In Spain, King Carlos III, who was now seventy-one, was so enchanted with the arrival of more grandchildren that he put his own resentment of Charlotte aside. He promised her that if her next child were a son, he would present her with the distinguished Golden Fleece and Grand Cross of Carlos III. Within weeks of the King's offer, Charlotte was pregnant again. Her third son was "duly born" on the night of August 26, 1788 shortly after the King and Queen returned from the theater. In a move hinting at a reconciliation between Maria Carolina and her father-in-law, the Queen consented to making Carlo "the first of the seventeen names he was given at the christening."[7]

No sooner had Prince Carlo been born than Ferdinand and Charlotte began considering marriages for Teresa, Luisa, and Francesco. With her eldest son approaching marriable age, the Queen found herself contemplating the possibility of uniting the royal families of Naples and France through the marriage of the Duke of Calabria and Madame Royal. Charlotte's motherly scheme to get the young couple together relied as much on Marie Antoinette as it did herself. In a letter to the Queen of France, she poured her heart out explaining how she wanted to be even closer to her dear sister through the marriage of their children. More than that, it would help unite two reigning houses and strengthen Bourbon-Habsburg influence in Europe.

Touched though she was by Charlotte's offer, Marie Antoinette politely declined. She preferred Marie Thérèse to marry Louis-Antoine, Duc d'Angoulême, her first cousin and son of the Comte de Provence. Marie Antoinette knew that if her daughter married him, she "would not lose her rank as daughter of the Queen." She also refused to inflict upon her daughter the "feelings of deep regret, in case she should be married to a

---

* Maria Carolina's children that did not survive infancy were Carlo (1775-1778), Mariana (1775-1780), Cristina Amelia (1779-1783), and Giuseppe (1781-1783).

foreign Prince, to take her from the palace of Versailles at seven years of age, and send her immediately to the Court in which she was to dwell; and that at twelve would be too late; for recollections and comparisons would ruin the happiness of all the rest of her life."[8]

With France no longer being an option, Charlotte was forced to look elsewhere for a bride for her son. And what of her eldest daughters, Teresa and Luisa? In the end, it was none other than the paternal Grand Duke Leopold who would help to unite the royal families of Austria-Tuscany and Naples. But the talk of marriage in Naples came to a crashing halt when catastrophe struck the House of Bourbon in the winter of 1788.

C3

When Austria failed to capture Belgrade, Emperor Joseph II prepared for a second major offensive, this time against Turkish-occupied Romania. But with his eyes fixed on the east, he did not realize that a new enemy was arising in the north. Stepping into the conflict was a tenacious and dynamic new king in Prussia, Frederick Wilhelm II.

Fierce, proud, and a sworn enemy of the Habsburgs, this successor to Frederick the Great was determined to bring down Joseph II. Rather than launch a direct assault on Bohemia or Austria, Frederick Wilhelm concocted a masterful plan that would cut off Austrian forces from any support in their upcoming offensive. He convinced Sweden to invade Russia by going through Finland, thereby forcing Catherine the Great to divert the bulk of her forces to the north, leaving Austria to stand alone against the Turks.

To boost the morale of his frightened troops, Joseph himself went to the battlefields. Living under strenuous conditions did nothing for the welfare of the soldiers and took its toll on the Emperor. In the "marshy territory" of the Balkans they encountered "dysentery, typhus, and malaria."[9] By the autumn of 1788, the Austrians had advanced against the Turks and were headed for Karánsebes, part of modern-day Caransebeș in Romania.

In September they crossed the Timiș River, planning to inflict great damage on the Turkish forces there. What the

Austrians got instead was one of the most humiliating defeats in military history. Soon after their arrival at Karánsebes, the soldiers was separated and divided, then in the confusion turned on themselves in what became known as the Battle of Karánsebes. Exhausted, angry, and drunk, a group of soldiers scuffling over a bottle of schnapps furiously fired a shot into the air. The other soldiers thought the Turks were attacking, and opened fire on their own army. Every shadow was mistaken for an enemy soldier as the Austrians annihilated their own army.

The barrage of artillery killed or wounded nearly ten thousand soldiers. When one of the commanders ordered a retreat, Emperor Joseph was on horseback struggling to lead his disoriented troops out of the battle zone. In the confusion, his horse threw him into a freezing river. The spread of malaria and other diseases played havoc with Joseph's constitution. With his army decimated and his health ruined, he was forced to retreat to Vienna. On the return trip, the military doctors gave Joseph the fatal news that he had contracted tuberculosis. When he finally arrived in Vienna in early 1789, no one could escape the undeniable truth. Emperor Joseph II was dying.

ℱ

In the final years of his life, King Carlos III of Spain became burdened by the problems that plagued his family. His favorite son, the Infante Gabriel, died from smallpox in 1788. Then there were the two daughters-in-law. King Carlos was deeply troubled by the behavior of Maria Carolina in Naples, but even more so by the scandalous behavior of his first son's wife, Luisa.

The Princess of the Asturias, as she was titled when she married the Spanish heir, was none other than the sister-in-law of Amalia, Duchess of Parma. She was also the same princess whom Emperor Joseph had once considered marrying when his first wife, Isabella, died. Luisa was a haughty, reprehensible woman who was as different from Carlos III as Amalia was from Maria Theresa. For the King, "love and affection for his family was constant and one of his finest traits,"[10] but the scandal being caused by the women who had married into the Spanish royal family caused him no end of grief.

Sick from a "feverish cold," the King was soon on his deathbed. The final stroke came when he refused any type of treatment. The only remedy the ailing king would accept was to have hot deer's grease rubbed on his body to warm him up. On the night of December 14, 1788, King Carlos III died "with great firmness and piety."[11]

The grief in Spain at his death was "profound and sincere for they [the Spanish people] realized that the one who had checked" Spain's slide towards decay, the man "who had turned darkness into light and brought order out of chaos had left a splendid edifice unfinished, though apparently firmly founded."[12] The death of Carlos III marked the passing of the last surviving signatory of the Family Pact. The children of Maria Theresa, Louis XV, and Carlos III were now the ruling generation of Europe, and would shape the futures of their own children as their parents had for them.

When the news arrived in Naples, Charlotte and Ferdinand were in the grips of their own crisis. While the royal family was at their sprawling palace in Caserta, the Queen and several of the children fell ill with smallpox. Nine-year-old Prince Gennaro died on January 2, 1789. The Austrian ambassador wrote to Vienna: "The royal family and court have lately been in great distress. Scarcely had they had time to recover from the...death of his Catholic Majesty, when the second Prince, the Infant Don Gennaro, died in a few hours, after a sudden relapse, of small-pox, on January 2nd, at four o'clock in the morning. His royal parents, whose especial love his precociously developed intelligence had gained, are plunged in grief."[13]

Having lost two children of his own, Grand Duke Leopold's heart went out to his sister. He described the royal family's perilous situation to Mimi: "In Naples the queen is always sick. She inoculated her daughter Amélie and her last son who is teething, and at the moment, there is a terrible epidemic of the awful small pox in Naples."[14] Only three days after Leopold wrote that letter, Charlotte's infant son, Prince Carlo died from the disease despite his inoculation. The child's final struggle was heartbreaking. His screams were so loud that they echoed throughout the palace's massive halls.

Like any mother, Maria Carolina was crushed beyond words by the death of her children. According to one of her biographers, when Carlo died, she "added to her sorrow by reproaching herself bitterly for having perhaps caused the child's death by having him inoculated when he was too young to bear it or the weather too cold."[15]

Later, Charlotte wrote to her ambassador in Austria, the Marquis de Gallo: "Overwhelmed by anguish and deep despair at the loss of two beloved sons, my fondest hopes, I only have time to assure you that I am still the mother of eight children, and that I shall fulfill to the utmost all the duties of motherhood. It is only to accomplish these that I wish to prolong a life which a thousand sorrows has rendered so distressing."[16]

❧

Emperor Joseph was never again healthy after his brush with death in Romania in 1788. Following his return to Vienna, he was a broken man suffering terribly from exhaustion and tuberculosis. He could no longer hide the reality of his situation. "I am bedridden with a fever and pain in the side," he told Grand Duke Leopold. "The lungs, especially the left one near the heart, are much weakened."[17]

The Habsburg historian Andrew Wheatcroft described the terrible physical condition Joseph was in by the end of the decade:

> The man who had formerly been so vigorous and healthy showed the most unmistakable signs of rapidly failing strength. His eyes became weak and watery; he had sore legs; erysipelas in the head had obliged him, even as far back as 1783, to wear a wig; whilst before that he wore his beautiful fair hair, which had gradually assumed an auburn tinge...with two simple curls and pigtail. His complexion, once so clear, was now of a reddish-brown hue; the smallpox marks [on his face] looked as if deepened, and his hanging cheeks added to the length of his face.[18]

With his health failing and Austria suffering setbacks on the battlefield, the political noose tightened around Joseph's neck. By early 1789, the imperial armies were retreating from Romania. Soon, they were forced to withdraw from Mehadia, and within weeks, the Banat was overrun with Turkish soldiers.

On the front lines, Austrian troops suffered from "epidemics: the lazarettos were filled to capacity, half the army was sick, and thousands of soldiers died." On the home front, there "was open opposition [to the war]...fueled by the enormous economic burden it placed on the population. Food prices had risen drastically and in some cases doubled; bakeries had been looted for the first time in Vienna's history."[19] Protestors marched on the Hofburg, demanding an end to the war.

Unrest was not confined to Austria's capital. Angry at the way the Emperor had ruined Central Europe's economy, the Habsburg dominions exploded in violent revolts. In the Austrian Netherlands, Mimi and Albert watched anxiously as the dreaded stench of revolution flooded Antwerp. The people's fury, held in check by the Habsburgs for more than two centuries, was finally boiling over.

Urged on by their republican counterparts, the Dutch rose up against the imperial regime in May. Terrified, Mimi wrote to Joseph describing the day the citizens revolted:

> People thronging in thousands, with their hats blazoned with the arms of Brabant, made it a day full of terror—all the more so as we had certain information that it was intended to begin that very evening the pillage of the royal and ecclesiastical treasuries, that the minister and those members of the Government who were in ill odour [sic] were to be put to death, and complete independence declared.[20]

On May 30, the insurgents broke into the imperial palace and forced Mimi and Albert to sign an order revoking all of Emperor Joseph II's authority in the Netherlands and Belgium. When he was told about the uprising, the Emperor was "full of indignation" about the "rising impertinence of his subjects, all caused by the timid action of the Government."[21]

As violent as the Dutch insurgents became, the revolts that broke out in Hungary were the most damaging to the monarchy and shook the Austrian hegemony to its very core. Magyar nobles were sitting on the brink of full-fledge revolution. In Bohemia and other eastern states, peasants were leading uprisings. Hoping to quell the revolutionary flames, Joseph issued a decree that the peasants must be paid in direct cash, instead of the customary labor obligations that had been in place until that point. Both the aristocracy and the peasantry rejected this new policy, claiming that the government's barter system was already depleted and lacked money.

Joseph's government was on the verge of abandoning him, and his advisors kept their distance. Prince Kaunitz, the man who had been an adviser to Habsburg rulers for nearly fifty years— the man who had ignited almost every conflict Austria had seen in all that time—could not be found. The Emperor had spent his entire life pushing people away. Now, as he lay dying, he was seeing the ultimate results of his own singular vision. In his darkest hour, Emperor Joseph II was completely alone.

A Pale Sun

The situation in France became perilous by 1789. Food was scarce, money was disappearing, and the people were crying out for change. The demands of his people prompted King Louis XVI to convene the *Etats Généraux* (Estates General) for the first time in almost two hundred years.

The *Etats Généraux* was the closest thing to elected representation France had at the time:

> The 23 million subjects of the king were divided into three estates: the first consisting of the clergy (around 130,000); the second, the nobility (around 500,000); and the third, the commoners (approximately 97 percent of the total population). Unlike the third estate, the first two were exempt from taxation. The third estate was made up of bourgeoisie, or the middle class, and the peasants. Peasants composed the overwhelming majority of the third estate and also carried the heaviest tax burden.[1]

The three estates only came together during periods of intense turmoil for France. Their convening at Versailles on May 6, 1789 signaled that the reign of King Louis had reached a crisis. It showed everyone—the French people, the aristocracy, and the government—how hopelessly out of touch the monarchy was with the rest of the country.

The popularity of the royal family was at an historic low. When Queen Marie Antoinette arrived at the opening of the session, she was hissed and booed by angry spectators. One witness noted that "never has there been a queen of France less loved and yet she cannot be reproached for a single wicked deed." He concluded: "We are certainly unfair towards her and much too hard in judging what are only faults of frivolity and thoughtlessness."[2] "Intensely unpopular owing to her recklessness and love of gaiety rather than to any graver fault, she had come to dislike facing the people, and her heart was sad over her little son, whose only part in the pageant was to lie on cushions in the balcony of the *Petite Écurie* and see the procession."[3] Marie Antoinette was nearly reduced to tears, mustering all of her courage and strength as the daughter of Maria Theresa to keep her composure.

In his opening speech to the gathered assembly, King Louis made lofty statements about his deep interest in the health of the nation and his desire to be his people's closest friend. He naively believed his countrymen were unified with their king in will and purpose. He still believed he could bring France into its most prosperous era. His romantic, ideological words fell on deaf ears. Louis may have been "a good man and a Christian, but not a king. He knew how to love, to pardon, to suffer, and to die, but he did not know how to reign."[4]

The king's speech might have been aimed at inspiring hope and goodwill, but the people had already reached the point of despair. The country was about to be overcome by disaster, signaling the collapse of the monarchy, but not before the French House of Bourbon faced another tragedy.

On June 4, 1789, Marie Antoinette and Louis XVI were devastated when their beloved dauphin, Louis Joseph, died from tuberculosis of the spine. The poor child had been languishing for years, prompting his mother to confide in her diary: "My oldest boy causes me much anxiety. His figure is misshapen; one hip is higher than the other; and the vertebræ [*sic*] of the back are displaced, and project. For some time he has had continual fever, and is very thin and feeble."[5]

The Comtesse Lâge de Volude visited Louis Joseph several months before his death. She described her meeting to the Princess de Lamballe: "We went after dinner to visit the little Dauphin. It was heartbreaking. His sufferings, his patience, his intelligence were most touching.... I could think of nothing but this dear and unhappy child who was dying before our eyes."[6]

For several long weeks, Marie Antoinette watched the heartrending spectacle of her son's life and death struggle. She was at his bedside at the royal estate of Meudon when he finally passed away. At six o'clock the following morning, the Duc d'Harcourt informed the King of the tragic news. "Death of my son at one in the morning," was the simple entry Louis made in his journal that day.[7] The young boy who was heralded to be the next great King of France was gone, replaced with "'a decayed old man,' covered in sores, at the age of seven and a half."[8]

Marie Antoinette's second son, Louis Charles, was now the dauphin and heir to the throne. He and Marie Thérèse wept for their dead brother, who was given a small, tasteful funeral after laying in state at Meudon. The bereft parents could not justify spending large amounts on an expensive funeral, even for their own son, while so many of their people were suffering in poverty. His tiny, child-sized coffin filled "the last vacant niche at St. Denis in the tomb of the Kings of France."[9] After the funeral, the royal family was overwhelmed with grief and retreated to their estate at Marly for several days of private mourning.

The court followed the tradition of wearing black to mourn the dauphin's death, but even in this deepest, most intimate of acts as a grieving mother, Marie Antoinette was vilified by the people. Her black wardrobe associated her in the minds of the French with pure evil. Parisians viewed anyone in black suspiciously, since it was the color of the anti-liberal aristocracy and one of the two colors of the House of Habsburg. Marie Antoinette was horrified when rumors began circulating in Paris that "she had poisoned the Dauphin herself, lest he grow up to favor his subjects' bid for freedom."[10]

Prince Charles-Joseph de Ligne, a loyal supporter of the queen's, was the first to admit, "It is only the wicked who can speak ill of her, and only fools who will believe it."[11] Reviled, hated, and rejected, Queen Marie Antoinette of France was finding herself surrounded by enemies on every side. The court resented her, the public loathed her, and now two of her children were dead. Filled with despair, she wrote to Leopold of Tuscany, "at the death of my poor little Dauphin, the nation hardly seemed to notice."[12]

There seemed to be no end to the insults that were being heaped upon Marie Antoinette. Each day, she requested to be informed of the latest accusations against her. One morning, when a police officer from Paris forced himself to stop reading the list of libels because of how hurtful they were, she told him: "Go on, Monsieur, do not let my tears stop you. It is only natural that I should feel the evil that is spoken of me and the false opinion formed of me by a people I hoped would love me and for whose happiness the King and I are ready to sacrifice everything."[13]

The whirlwind events of the *Etats Généraux*, the death of their son, and the unrest throughout their kingdom denied King Louis and Queen Marie Antoinette any real chance to grieve. The year had brought unparalleled suffering to the people of France. The country was bankrupt because of Louis XVI's support of the wars in the American colonies, the national debt had soared to nearly half a billion *livres*, and heavy taxes and food shortages finally pushed the people to their breaking point.

Riots broke out in the streets of Paris in the summer of 1789, prompting die-hard royalists to fear for the future of the monarchy. Louis XVI's brothers urged him to have troops move in and seize control of the city. Louis, always the gentle soul, refused to add to the bloodshed. He told his brother Charles in July: "My troops will retreat from Paris, and I shall employ milder measures. Talk to me no more of an act of authority, of a great stroke of power; I believe it is most prudent to...yield to the storm...and expect everything from...the love of Frenchmen for their King."[14]

Sadly for Louis, these were useless words. The day after he made those statements, France's infamous Bastille prison fell to rioters in Paris. Across the city, a cry rose up from the masses. "To the Bastile!" they chanted.[15] To the people, the building represented royal oppression in all its forms. It "not only overshadowed the capital, but it darkened the hearts of men, for it had been notorious for centuries as the instrument and the emblam [*sic*] of tyranny."[16] The storming of the most loathed building in France was as the falling of rocks before a mighty avalanche.

Having returned to Versailles, Louis and Marie Antoinette remained oblivious to the riots in the capital; they were still in deep mourning for their dead son. When the Duc de Liancourt told Louis of the events in Paris, the King declared, "But this is a great revolt!" "No, sir," the Duc replied, "it is a great Revolution!"[17] In Louis' opinion, the fall of the Bastille was "a popular insurrection no different from others that Paris had witnessed in the course of the previous centuries."[18] The King and Queen did not realize that the day the Bastille fell, "Paris rose as one man;....and the King was beaten, and forced to make submission; if not sincere, at least complete. The whole history of France was changed by the intervention of Paris—Paris, followed by the whole of France."[19]

Throughout the summer, the country continued its downward spiral towards unbridled chaos. By September, Count Fersen, a Swedish nobleman who frequented Versailles, wrote anxiously: "All bonds are broken, the authority of the King is gone, and Paris is trembling before forty or fifty thousand ruffians (*bandits*) or vagabonds.... The nobles are in despair... Several regiments have revolted....the King and Queen have not escaped it."[20] With the most ominous symbol of the monarchy destroyed, and Paris in open revolt, the stage was set for the most infamous revolution in history to begin.

On the night of October 5, 1789, six thousand worker women congregated at the Hôtel de Ville in Paris to protest the inflationing prices of bread. Within hours, they decided to march on Versailles. When the mob, which had swelled in size en route, arrived at the palace, the soldiers guarding it were useless against their wrath. They were already furious after the six-hour march from Paris. Added to this was the perceived inaction from the king and queen to their demands for bread. After hours of waiting, bands of rioters stormed the palace and began sweeping through looking for the royal couple. Their intent, or so it was claimed, was that they wanted to bring Louis and Marie Antoinette back to Paris to guarantee the increase of food supplies.

The assaults on the palace guards were merciless, but according to Princess Marie Thérèse, the crowd's fiercest rage was for the queen herself. "My mother knew that their chief object was to kill her," she said.[21] Many were calling for her head, while others wanted more unspeakable actions to be done to Marie Antoinette, who was waiting in her bedroom calmly but fearfully.

As the mobs swept through the palace's ground floor, they cried out at the tops of their lungs, "Louis shall no longer be king!" and "The queen's head—Down with the queen!"[22] Even more chilling were shouts of: "We'll cut off her head…rip her heart out…fry her liver…make her guts into ribbons."[23] The people saw her as the "scapegoat for the weaknesses and failures of the monarchy."[24] She had barely enough time to get dressed before a band of marauders arrived at her apartments. She managed to escape through a secret door that led to her husband's rooms.

The terror for the royal family that night was unmistakable. Even more tangible was the suspicion over who incited the revolt: none other than the king's cousin, Philippe, Duc d'Orléans. Descended from a cadet branch of the Bourbon dynasty dating back to King Henry IV, he represented to the people what a successful French monarch could be. If Louis XVI was the embodiment of the worst possible king, then Philippe was the best.

Marie Antoinette believed that, at the very least, the Duc d'Orléans wanted her dead, a sentiment she passed on to her daughter. The future Duchesse d'Angoulême recalled: "the principal project [of the attack] was to assassinate my mother, on whom the Duc d'Orléans wished to avenge himself because of offences he believed he had received from her."[25] While it was agreed that the Duc's animosity towards Queen Marie Antoinette was genuine, it has never been conclusively proven whether or not he instigated the march on Versailles in 1789.

As the attacks raged on, the royal family huddled together in the king's apartments for protection. The crowds in the courtyard outside demanded the King and Queen step out onto the balcony to face their cries. "Let the queen show herself!" they shouted.[26] One of the generals guarding the royal family turned to Marie Antoinette and said, "Madame, the people will not be pacified unless you go." "Then I hesitate no longer," she replied.[27]

When the royal family appeared on the balcony, the marauders refused to allow Marie Antoinette to be humanized, and shouted: "No children! No children!" She was no longer the mother of the nation, but the embodiment of inhuman autocracy.[28] Summoning all her courage as Maria Theresa's daughter, her "proud spirit rose; thrusting back the children she stepped out upon the balcony and instinctively crossing her arms over her breast as she looked onto the menacing crowd below, stood erect and motionless, face to face with the men and women who had sought her life."[29]

The Marquise de Tourzel, the royal governess, remembered that night how the Queen had an "air of grandeur and heroic courage in the presence of danger...[it] had such an effect on the mob that they at once abandoned their sinister designs and [were] struck with admiration." One of the royal attendants claimed, "her courage and noble air disarmed the bloodthirsty tigers." As Marie Antoinette stood motionless on the balcony, the crowds demanded, "To Paris! To Paris!"[30] There was little action the royal family could take. The size of the crowd meant escaping unnoticed was no longer an option. They had no choice but to agree.

At half-past midnight, they filed into a carriage and began the seven-hour journey to Paris. Accompanying them was the Marquise de Tourzel and the King's sister, Princess Élisabeth. As the carriage pulled away from the palace, Marie Antoinette took one long, final look at the palace that had been her home for nearly twenty years. "I know the fate that awaits me," she said ominously.[31]

The carriage transporting the royal family arrived in Paris in the early morning hours of October 6. The King and Queen were allowed to bring 670 servants with them to care for their needs. Princess Élisabeth wrote to a friend: "My date alone will tell you to what a point our misfortunes have come. We have left the cradle of our childhood—what am I saying? left! we were torn from it. What a journey! what sights! Never, never will they be effaced from my memory....What is certain is that we are prisoners here; my brother does not believe it, but time will prove it to him. Our friends are here; they think as I do that we are lost."[32]

Marie Antoinette settled her family into their new home, the Tuileries, but this four-hundred-room palace left a lot to be desired. The interior of this cavernous old building "was dark and depressing, with ancient, faded tapestries and workmen's ladders everywhere." Constructed by Catherine de' Medici in the 1500s, it was connected to the Louvre by a long gallery.

Centuries of neglect had turned it into a dilapidated structure that was now a home for servants, squatters, and prostitutes. During the family's first night, Prince Louis Charles slept in a room with furniture barricading the entrance because the doors did not shut. The next morning he told his mother, "Everything is very ugly here, Maman." Reflecting her own sense of humility, the Queen replied firmly but gently: "My son, Louis XIV lodged here comfortably; we must not be more particular than him."[33]

The Tuileries offered the royal family little privacy. The day after they arrived, Marie Antoinette was confronted by a mob of women in the palace courtyard. One of the women cried, "Love the inhabitants of your good city," to which the Queen replied by saying: "I loved them at Versailles; I will love them just the same in Paris." When another woman called out to her in German, she immediately recoiled and scoffed: "German! I no longer understand it. I have become so thorough a French-woman that I have even forgotten my mothertongue."[34] The crowd burst into thunderous applause. It was an episode that showed her just how truly fickle the French were. Undoubtedly, the sound of their cheers seemed empty to the Queen. It would be one of the last times in her life that the people of France would show her anything close to affection.

To her credit, Marie Antoinette displayed an awe-inspiring strength of character throughout her ordeal. "The Queen...has incredible courage," wrote Princess Élisabeth.[35] It was that courage that gave the royal family the strength to try and live some kind of a normal life at the Tuileries. King Louis fought to maintain the dignities and traditions of the *ancien régime*, but by the end of the year, the revolution was in full swing and had seized all of Paris: "In the tableau of Paris at the close of 1789, the court does not occupy a brilliant place. One might say that royalty, doubtful of itself, is effacing itself voluntarily, and dwindling away. Every day it loses a little more of its prestige. The rays of the royal sun, once so dazzling, are growing pale."[36]

The great hope that Marie Antoinette brought with her to France in 1770 was now only a dim memory. Those individuals who looked forward to her restoring the French monarchy to glory had resigned themselves to its eventual death. The days of Louis XIV, the great Sun King, would never come again. The pale sun of the Bourbon dynasty had all but set as France marched unstoppably into one of the darkest periods in its history.

❦

The fates of revolutionary France and Austria were of great concern to Grand Duke Leopold in Florence. Hungary was continuing its own march towards revolution. The Habsburgs were the rightful kings of that country, but Joseph II's failed reign had pushed the crown council (known as the diet) to consider dethroning the Habsburgs completely.

A venomous cloud of anarchy continued to swirl over Belgium and the Austrian Netherlands as well. "The Low Countries are lost," Joseph told Leopold dejectedly in January 1790.[37] Events were spiraling out of control across the Holy Roman Empire as the Emperor's health continued to decline. Realizing his time on earth was coming to an end, Joseph pleaded with Leopold to come to Vienna and establish a co-regency to restore order: "I adjure you, dear brother, by your friendship for me and your duty to the lands which belong to you…, to come here as quickly as you can…. I could not die in peace, did I not know that the state was in the hands of its chief."[38]

In his reply, Leopold assured his brother he would start for Vienna as soon as affairs in Florence were settled. But his own health had remained fragile over the years. At the time of Joseph's request, Leopold was suffering from a terrible flu, and the "shock" of everything that was happening dealt a blow to his "very sensitive nerves," forcing the grand duke to remain in Florence.[39] In a letter to his sister Mimi, Leopold was more candid about the situation:

> Very dear sister. At the moment, I am expediting the mail, I received your letter and entirely share your opinion about everything regarding the Netherlands [being Joseph's fault]. I have already told you this in all of my other letters….I flatter myself to think that a general war [in Europe] will not take place, even though the King of Sardinia, Spain, and the Duke of Parma make light of it in Italy….H[is]. M[ajest]y. is much worse and it is even feared, that I will not arrive in time to see him. I am in Florence, where a strong

cold as stopped me and forced me to take a couple of days before leaving.... I will leave as soon as I can...I embrace you.

L.[40]

When it came to the issue of establishing another co-regency, Leopold had no intention of sharing in his brother's soaring unpopularity. He told Mimi: "It has been offered to me to make a co-regency, but as you can well believe, I have not accepted."[41]

❧

In his darkest hour, Emperor Joseph II yearned for the family he had worked all his life to keep at a distance. After Maria Theresa died, he sent all of his siblings away. The unmarried archduchesses Elizabeth and Marianne were made the abbesses of convents; Ferdinand had married the heiress of Modena; and Max was the archbishop-elector of Cologne.

By January 1790, the Emperor was at death's door. By then, no one would visit him, not even his own ministers. Self-pity and regret seized Joseph. With nothing but time on his hands, he had little to do but reflect on the failures of his twenty-five years on the throne. In one of the last letters he ever wrote to Leopold, he revealed the true depth of his final misery:

> I confess to you that, humiliated by what has happened to me, seeing that I am unfortunate in everything I undertake, the appalling ingratitude with which my good arrangements are received and I am treated—for there is now no conceivable insolence or curse that people do not allow themselves to utter about me publicly—all this makes me doubt myself; I no longer dare to have an opinion and put it into effect, I allow myself to be ruled by the advice of the ministers even when I don't think it is the best, since I dare not hold out for my view and indeed I haven't the strength to impose it and argue for it.[42]

He was worn out and brokenhearted. His ministers would not and could not carry out his plans, orders, and directives. Prince Kaunitz held out until the bitter end, refusing to see him. In a last act of desperation, Joseph issued one final edict from his sickbed. He formally renounced and withdrew all of his disastrous reforms.

Emperor Joseph ultimately returned to the Roman Catholic faith that he had forsaken for so many years, and even rescinded the Patent of Toleration. This move, while appeasing the Vatican, set back the cause of tolerance in Austria by decades. Not until the reign of his nephew Francis would religious freedoms in Austria begin to reappear. Day after day, the imperial ministers gradually came to visit the Emperor as he rescinded one unpopular edict after the other. But the one issue on which he refused to budge was the war with Turkey. Austria's imperial dignity was on the line, he believed.

The only family member that was with Joseph in those final days was his nephew, Francis. In February the archduke turned twenty-two. As a present, Joseph gave him a diamond-studded dagger to remember his uncle "who will soon be no more."[43] The last week of Joseph's life was filled with heartache. After Francis's wife Elizabeth, who was nine-months pregnant, visited Joseph on February 17, she was "seized with the first most severe pains of approaching labour."[44] The delivery was excruciating, and the baby had to be delivered by forceps, an untested practice in the eighteenth century. When it was announced that the baby was a girl, Joseph took it upon himself to name the infant Ludovica. Afterwards, Elizabeth seemed to be recovering, but she died suddenly in the middle of the night from a hemorrhage.

The Emperor always held a special place in his heart for Elizabeth. When his chamberlain announced the news of her death, he broke down in frantic tears. "Throw me on top of her," he cried over and over again.[45] "And I live yet? Lord, thy will be done."[46]

After battling constant coughing, chest pains, and fever brought on by the tuberculosis he contracted in Romania, Joseph II—the Holy Roman Emperor, the King of Hungary and Bohemia—died on February 20, 1790 at the Hofburg, where his body laid in state for three days. In keeping with his last wish, Joseph was dressed in the uniform of an Austrian field marshal.

The state funeral for the Emperor was a farce. A German diplomat named Hummer-Purgstall described it as an "indecently cheerful occasion."[47] Thousands of people lined the streets of Vienna to say good riddance. Rocks, mud, and other objects were thrown at the coffin as it was taken through the streets. Joseph's body was laid to rest in the imperial crypt, next to his parents.

Though Joseph II was not missed to the extent of either of his parents, reaction to his death was sincere throughout Europe. The city of Frankfurt resembled "a living grave.... The whole magistracy is in deep mourning; the garrison black, everything wound with crape; the imperial recruiting officers, the councillors, ambassadors, and so on, all, all black; it has an exceedingly mournful appearance."[48]

In London, *The Times* reported simply, "The Court will go into mourning this Sunday for the late Emperor, Joseph II."[49] In his *Letters on Mankind*, Johann Gottfried Herder made a moving tribute on Joseph's behalf:

Without having known the Emperor, without ever receiving any benefit from him, I could have wept when I learnt the details of the end of his life. Nine years ago, when he came to the throne, he was worshipped like a tutelary deity, and the greatest things were expected of him, the most useful, wellnigh impossible things; and now they have laid him in the grave like a victim of time. Was there ever an Emperor, was there ever a mortal I should say, who had nobler projects, who took greater trouble, who made more strenuous efforts, who worked with greater zeal? And what a fate was that monarch's, who, confronted with death, was forced not only to renounce the aim he had set himself during his noblest years, but also to disavow, formally, the whole of his life's work, to annul it solemnly, and then to die![50]

Joseph's close friend, Prince Charles-Joseph de Ligne, took the duty upon himself of informing Catherine the Great of his death. He perhaps best described the Emperor's life and ultimate demise:

He is no more, Madame, he is no more, the prince who did honour to mankind, the man who did most honour to princes. That ardent spirit is extinguished like a flame whose substance has burned away; that active body lies between four planks that forbid his action. After watching with his precious remains I was one of four to bear him to the [church of the] Capuchins. Yesterday I was not in a state to render to your Imperial Majesty an account of this sorrow.

Joseph II. died as he lived, with firmness; he ended as he began, with the same methodical spirit.[51]

Leopold was still at the Pitti Palace in Florence at the end of February. Early on the morning of February 25, he received an urgent dispatch. An official state messenger had arrived to inform the Grand Duke that his brother Joseph had died. Leopold was now heir apparent to the imperial throne—only a unanimous election could make him emperor—and the reigning King of Hungary, Bohemia, and the other Habsburg crown lands.

19

Weights of the Crown

*T*he day that Leopold learned of Joseph's death and his accession to the Habsburg throne, he sent off an emotional letter to his son Francis in Vienna: "We are and should try to remain two friends who love each other cordially, have nothing to hide from each other, and contribute together to the well-being of the public and the state. You will accomplish through your strength and youth those things which I can no longer do."[1]

The next letter he sat down to write was a very emotional one. Leopold took upon himself the unenviable duty of breaking the news of Joseph's death to Queen Marie Antoinette:

> My very dear sister. The unfortunate loss that we have recently suffered due to the death of H.M., and that which I have suffered in addition in the death of my daughter-in-law, oblige me to write to you directly and immediately, as soon as I learned the sad news, to keep you informed. I well imagine all of the understandable pain, that this news would has caused you, especially given the personal attachment and friendship, that H.M. had particularly for you. Although I am more than persuaded, that such a loss cannot be repaired, I dare to offer you in me, who in friendship, attachment, [and] true and sincere interest in everything that could interest you in all ways.[2]

Marie Antoinette was saddened by her brother's death. She wrote back to Leopold about how she "was touched by your letter." But about her present situation in Paris, all she could write was: "I do not say any thing to you of our actual position: it is too heart-rending.... It is a war of opinions, and one which is still far from being terminated."[3]

By March, Leopold had no choice but to finally leave for Vienna. From his palace in Pisa, he departed alone; his family would follow later. In Klagenfurt, he was met by Count Colloredo and Archduke Francis, who was still grieving the loss of his uncle and wife. When Leopold finally arrived in Vienna on March 12, 1790, the welcome he received from the Austrian people and the government ministers was lukewarm at best. The city was caught in a whirlwind of confusion after Joseph died.

Leopold immediately set up an office in the Hofburg. This was not an easy time for him. Not only was he still suffering from the flu, he was also terribly lonely without his wife and children. To make matters worse, the state of the government was a wreck, much as it had been for Maria Theresa when Emperor Charles VI died in 1740.

Three days after he arrived in Vienna, Leopold sent Mimi a letter describing the stress he was under. "My health is fair," he wrote. "It is not the trip which has made me suffer so; it is the sad state and situation of the monarchy and the confusion which reigns everywhere throughout the realm."[4] From dawn until dusk, he worked almost nonstop trying to put the Habsburg monarchy back together. After two months of working exhausting hours, largely by himself, Leopold was desperate to be reunited with his family. "In 15 days, thank God, my wife and my family will be here," he said; "at least then I will have some consolation, because for now I am working at my desk from 7 o'clock in the morning until midnight."[5]

On May 16, María Luísa and the younger children finally arrived. Leopold happily reported to Mimi, "I am writing to you today at the moment my wife finally arrived here...and in perfect health with my three girls, my 4 boys will come in three days."[6]

By the end of June, the rest of the children had arrived. So desperate was Leopold to see his family back together that he arranged for Princess Theresa and Prince Anton to come from Dresden and stay at the Hofburg for a while. "Now Leopold and his spouse were happy, surrounded once more by all fourteen of their living children. And the halls of the imperial palace again rang with 'children's shouts of joy'."[7]

With his family reunited, one of the first tasks Leopold undertook was to search for a new wife for Archduke Francis. Unlike Joseph, he did not look for a princess who symbolized a political alliance. He was far more interested in strengthening the bond within his family. Leopold found himself considering a marriage between Francis and Princess Teresa of Naples, the eldest daughter of Queen Maria Carolina.

It took little prodding from Leopold for Francis to agree to the marriage. Eighteen at the time, Teresa was tall, graceful, and possessed beautiful features. Brought up by her exacting mother, she had all the qualities of a future consort. Charlotte prided herself on having raised Teresa "for her calling."[8] To further entice his sister, Leopold proposed a second and third marriage between their children. He suggested his son Ferdinand could marry Teresa's sister, Luisa; and his daughter Clementine would be a fine bride for Prince Francesco, Duke of Calabria.* Charlotte happily agreed because "she was anxious to arrange marriages for those [children] who were growing up, and her dearest wishes were granted when her brother…proposed his second son for her eldest daughter, and his daughter the Archduchess for the Prince Royal."[9]

Maria Carolina's three eldest children were eager to be married, but Francesco was nervous. According to his mother: "There is only one thing that humiliates him: this is the difference in height between them, as his fiancée is four or five inches taller. He hopes to grow, and in order to reach her height, he rides assiduously and takes more exercise."[10]

Once the proposals were agreed upon, Leopold wrote to Mimi, "I have taken two daughters of the Queen of Naples for my 2 sons, and have promised my Marie† to her son."[11] For the rest of the spring and summer, Leopold and María Luísa worked to prepare for the upcoming double weddings. Since Clementine and Francesco were only thirteen, their marriage was postponed for several years. Leopold invited King Ferdinand IV and Queen Maria Carolina to accompany their daughters to

---

* Francesco became crown prince of Naples with the title Duke of Calabria when his brother, Prince Carlo, died in 1778.
† Marie was Leopold's nickname for Clementine.

Vienna for the celebrations. It would be the first time the Queen returned to Austria since her own marriage in 1768.

The weddings were originally planned for July, but a series of unexpected events forced them to be pushed back. Archduke Francis had contracted a serious fever and was gravely ill; and by 1790, Charlotte was pregnant for the fifteenth time. During the final weeks of her confinement, she could not contain her excitement at seeing Vienna again. She sought to continually reassure Leopold of the good choice he made in selecting her daughters: "Louise has become quite different... Happiness has completely transformed her. She has a very good heart and will succeed admirably if she is well advised and guided in the beginning. Theresa is very sensible: she is delighted with Francis's affection...and his solid qualities."[12] On July 2, 1790, Charlotte went into labor, delivering a healthy son. In honor of the upcoming weddings, she named the new prince Leopoldo.

Once the Queen had recovered from the delivery, she and the Emperor agreed for the weddings to take place at the end of summer. "I have also just arranged my family affairs," Leopold wrote to Mimi. "The king and queen of Naples will come here in September with their daughters and we will celebrate here the three marriages."[13]

The archdukes Francis and Ferdinand married the princesses Teresa and Luisa at the Church of the Augustine Friars. As his sons were at the altar, being joined in wedlock with the beautiful daughters of Maria Carolina, Leopold was overcome by emotion. The uniting of the Imperial House of Austria and the Royal House of Naples was conducted with the greatest stately dignity and magnificence. Even in unstable France, Marie Antoinette sent her best wishes to her brother and sister: "You are in the middle of wedding feasts. I wish all the happiness possible to your children."[14]

The wedding celebrations reinvigorated Vienna's high society. For nearly two weeks, fireworks displays, operas, and gala parties enlivened Austria's capital. On September 30, a messenger arrived from Frankfurt with urgent news. After months of debate, the imperial Council of Electors had voted unanimously to make Leopold the new Holy Roman emperor. The announcement sent Vienna into convulsions of unrestrained joy.

Emperor Leopold II and Empress María Luísa's coronation took place on October 9, 1790 in that ancient and dignified German city, Frankfurt. Leopold declared that, rather than being simple and restrained, the ceremony was to be magnificent beyond measure. He wanted it to be a symbol of the empire's renewed strength. The streets were lined with thousands upon thousands of people clamoring to see the great spectacle.

The highlight of the ceremony was when the diamond-and-jewel encrusted imperial crown was placed on Leopold's head in the famous *Römersaal* that had held his parents' coronation fifty years before. María Luísa watched from the imperial box along with Francis and his wife Teresa, and King Ferdinand and Queen Maria Carolina, whom Leopold implored to attend. The Empress's eyes filled with tears as Leopold knelt and was crowned on soil that had been brought from Aix-la-Chapelle, the ancient site of imperial coronations.

Leopold and his family returned to Vienna at the end of October. "Finally we have all happily arrived and in perfect health in Vienna, very content with out trips," he told Mimi.[15] Less than two weeks later, the imperial family was on the move again. This time they were bound for the city of Pressburg (located within modern-day Bratislava) for Leopold's much-anticipated coronation as King of Hungary. This ceremony was not just a display of royal pomp, but it was also an incredible political triumph that speaks volumes to Leopold's tenacity and leadership ability. When Joseph died, the Hungarians were only a step away from dethroning the Habsburgs permanently; they claimed they had "no need of an Austrian king."[16] The fact that Leopold was able to change their opinions of his family in less than a year was nothing short of astounding.

If the Frankfurt coronation was a show of imperial splendor, then the Pressburg ceremony was a pageant of ancient and medieval rituals that were tied into Hungary's rich medieval history. On November 15, the Prince Primate of Hungary placed the Crown of St. Stephen on Leopold's head and proclaimed him the Apostolic King of Hungary. The crown was made of gold, and decorated with holy icons and precious stones. Four golden pendants covered in pearls dangled from either side. His flowing robes were scarlet and purple with gold leaves adorning the collar. At the end of the ceremony, the guests stepped outside to watch as Leopold "galloped up the coronation hill, drew the sword of Saint Stephen, and delivered four strokes in the shape of a cross."[17] The coronations helped rally the people to their new king and emperor. By the autumn of 1790, Leopold II was the undisputed patriarch of an empire stretching across half the continent.

CB

In the turbulent days and months following their removal from Versailles, Marie Antoinette and her family faced a daunting future at the Tuileries in Paris. Soldiers needed to be placed on active duty throughout the palace to keep the royal family safe.

In France, anti-monarchist feelings grew by leaps and bounds throughout the course of the year. The people decided it was time to curb the powers of the king, so the *Etats Généraux* was reorganized into the National Assembly. This was the first form of democratic representation in French history. The Assembly still proclaimed loyalty to Louis XVI, but its core mission was to steer the country towards a more republican political system. Some of its members were moderate, believing that it was their duty to work with the king. Others were more aggressive, and wanted to see the monarchy toppled.

Many royals fled the country in 1790, fearing for their lives at the hands of the violent republican movement that was taking hold. King Louis XVI's aunts, *Mesdames Tantes*, had been living at their Bellevue estate since 1789, but decided to flee to Rome. "You know that my aunts are going," Marie Antoinette wrote to Leopold. "We do not believe that we can prevent them." As public animosity continued to rise, the fate of the royal family was continuously debated, leaving the future uncertain. Writing to Leopold in October, the Queen decried her situation: "Oh my God! If we have committed faults, we have certainly expiated them." She begged her brother to "guard my homeland...from similar perils."[18]

Queen Charlotte of Great Britain was deeply moved by what she saw happening to Marie Antoinette, prompting her to write: "The poor unfortunate Princess, what a bitter portion hers is. I pity both the King and her, and wish anxiously that they meet with some well disposed people to extricate them hourly out of their great horrible distress."[19]

No relief came for Marie Antoinette and her family. In December, she outlined her trials in a long letter to Leopold II:

> Yes, my dear brother, our situation is dreadful....I am in constant terror. After having undergone the horrors of the 5th and 6th October, anything may be expected. Assassination is at our doors. I cannot show myself at a window, even with my children, without being insulted by a drunken mob, to whom I have done no harm, and amongst whom there are doubtless unfortunates whom I have myself relieved. I am prepared for any event, and I can now, unmoved, hear them calling for my head....forgive me, I entreat you, if I still refuse your advice to leave: remember that I am not my own mistress; my duty is to remain where Providence has placed me, and to oppose my own body, if need be, to the dangers of the assassins who would attack the King. I should be unworthy of our mother, who is as dear to you as to myself, if danger could induce me to fly far away from the King and from my children.[20]

The more time Marie Antoinette and her family spent at the Tuileries, the more changed they became. The Queen no longer threw parties or attended the theatre and the opera. Instead, she occupied her time with "prayer, long hours of needlework pursued with feverish activity, alms, good works, [and] charitable excursions through Paris. The Queen of France had become the model of a Christian mother, the governess and teacher of her daughter."[21] She did as much good for the people of Paris as she knew how. She cancelled the debts of the poor, took care of the sick, visited factories, and attended public events, but for all her acts of charity, the French people "never ceased to revile her."[22]

The abuse that was heaped on the King and Queen would have been unbearable had it not been for the unwavering support of their close-knit family. The Duc d'Orléans had sided with the republicans to save himself, taking the name Philippe Égalité, but many of the other members of the royal family threw in their lot with the King and Queen. In some of the darkest moments of her life, Marie Antoinette was supported by none other than her own children.

Princess Marie Thérèse, once described as "sulky" and "ill-tempered," had grown wise beyond her years. The Queen's brother-in-law, the Comte d'Artois, recalled one particularly moving scene in April 1791. King Louis had been ill and hoped to visit one of the royal estates in a more comfortable climate. As the royal family attempted to depart the Tuileries, their carriage was accosted by an angry mob. The Comte d'Artois recalled what happened next:

> It was on this occasion that I saw my niece in her true colours. All the strength that the King and Queen and my sister [Princess Élisabeth] had hitherto drawn from their natural firmness, courage, and piety seemed now exhausted.... My niece...stood alone in the centre of this miserable circle. Her expression, as she flitted from her father's side to her mother or her aunt, showed that she was well aware of her position, but rose above it: tears were in her eyes, but her lips were smiling. Her innocent caresses, her tender thought for us all, and her comforting words were as balm upon all our wounds. When she came to me I clasped her in my arms, and said: 'Oh, my child, may Heaven shower upon you all the happiness that is denied to your unhappy family!'.[23]

Marie Antoinette was comforted in moments like these by the people she loved most in the world, but even that group was dwindling. Shortly after this touching episode, the Comte d'Artois, along with the rest of the king's relatives, except his sister Élisabeth, fled the country. They were bent on gathering an army to march on Paris. The royal family had only each other to rely on, save for a few loyal servants who stayed with them. They were a loving group, deeply devoted to one another and to God, and would remain so until the bitter end.

☙

The coronation ceremonies of 1790 marked a pinnacle in the reign of Emperor Leopold II. Hungary and the eastern states had been pacified and brought back into the imperial fold. Relations between Leopold and the Magyars were on such good terms that the Hungarian Diet voted unanimously to appoint his son, Archduke Alexander, to the vaunted position of Palatine of Hungary. Dating back to the year A.D. 900, the prince-palatine was the highest position in the country after the king. Leopold was deeply touched that his eighteen-year-old son would be given such an honorable position. Leopold declared to the Hungarian people: "I offer you my son, as a pledge of my sincere regard to become a distinguished mediator between us, and to promote our mutual affection."[24] In an official statement, the Emperor said "he would measure the prince's filial devotion by the conscientiousness with which he carried out his duties as Palatine of Hungary."[25]

As the crisis in the east dwindled, Belgium and the Austrian Netherlands were still in revolt. Adding to this ferment were the dangerous revolutionary flames that were spreading from France. When it came to Leopold's position on France, his first priority was the welfare of the royal family.

Leopold offered support to Marie Antoinette, promising to do everything he could to help if she and her family could escape from Paris. He urged her "to work with the National Assembly and accept its draft of a new constitution."[26] But this was easier said than done. "From far away, it is easy to advise prudence and temporizing, but not when the knife is at one's throat," Marie Antoinette told the Spanish ambassador to France.[27]

As Leopold II began sounding out support from Austria's allies, he was faced with another quagmire. The Comte d'Artois and the other exiled royalists were now calling themselves "the émigrés" and began hounding Leopold constantly. As the brother of their queen, they followed him everywhere trying to get him to lead an imperial army into France.

A wise and astute ruler, the Emperor knew that a direct assault would fail, and would be disastrous for the King and Queen. Leopold finally agreed to meet with Artois in mid-1791. When the two men came face to face, it was a heated encounter, rife with emotions. But the Emperor told Mimi afterwards that he was confident that he got his point across: "You ask me about my intentions about the events in France, here it is: I met with the comte d'Artois to persuade him to put his confidence in me to prevent him from making a move which [could] compromise the life and safety of the king and the queen for no reason. I have succeeded in convincing him..."[28]

Unfortunately, he was only partly correct. He did make his point to Artois, but that did not stop the émigré leader from continuing to rally support. Marie Antoinette reported to Leopold: "The times are extremely pressing, and it is wished that you would make a decision promptly. The princes, the comte d'Artois and all those that follow them, absolutely want to act; they do not have their own means to do so and will lose us without your agreeing to help."[29] But in her heart, she agreed with her brother's reluctance to invade, even if she did not like it: "The sudden invasion of foreign troops would cause inevitable disorders. The King's subjects, both good and bad, would infallibly suffer by it."[30]

One of the problems Leopold faced with assisting Marie Antoinette was that he "was not only the brother of the Queen of France but he was also the head of a great power with an ambiguous attitude towards France, alliance or no alliance."[31] Before he took any action, the Emperor wanted "the complete co-operation of all the powers."[32] And by the end of summer 1791, the other European rulers had still not reached a decision about whether or not to join Austria in saving the French royal family. Leopold admitted: "I [am still]...waiting for the kings of Spain and Sardinia, the Swiss and the Empire and the king of Prussia, to be able to make a declaration and to act in concert [with them], in the case of the events in France, which will cause violence."[33]

Though he hoped for the support of Prussia, Leopold realized it would not come easy. The Austrians had not quickly forgotten the role King Frederick Wilhelm had played in helping the Ottoman Empire against them in the war. But if he had any hope of saving Marie Antoinette, he would need the support of the Hohenzollerns. He wrote to Frederick Wilhelm: "I solemnly protest, no views of aggrandizement will ever enter into my political system.... To your majesty in particular, I will act as you act towards me, and will spare no efforts to preserve perfect harmony."[34] This personal plea from Leopold worked. Shocked and impressed by the Emperor's frankness and humility, Frederick Wilhelm agreed to a meeting with him at Reichenbach. For the first time, Prussia and Austria began working towards a real peace between their two countries.

With Prussia as an ally and the rulers of Spain, Sardinia, and Switzerland contemplating a campaign against France, Emperor Leopold took this chance to end the unpopular Austro-Turkish

War. By the end of 1790, the tide of battle was turning in Austria's favor. The armies of Field Marshal Laudon finally succeeded in capturing Belgrade after a siege lasting more than three weeks. But in Vienna, opposition to the war continued to be strong. Determined to bring peace to his empire, Leopold opened the lines of communication with Istanbul to finally end the costly war. But the conclusion of the war and the restoration of peace in Austria would pale in comparison to the tragedies that were about to befall Emperor Leopold II and Queen Marie Antoinette.

"The Most Blessed Monarch"

*L*eopold of Austria continued to be deeply worried about the welfare of his sister and her family in France. The tense atmosphere in Paris nearly exploded in the summer of 1791 when the French royal family made an attempt to escape from the Tuileries. The plan had been to flee to the royalist town of Montmédy, but a series of misfortunes destroyed their efforts and they were captured in Varennes and returned to Paris for the last time. The anger in France was overwhelming, prompting the King and Queen to make a passionate plea to the other European monarchs to intervene.

"It is high time to save our sister and to smother this French epidemic," Leopold told his brother Max.[1] But at the very moment when he could have stepped in, Austria needed its emperor. With the help of King Frederick Wilhelm, Leopold managed to convince the Ottoman Empire to agree to end the war. He told Mimi: "I have pushed the Empire to do the right thing. I am making peace with the Turks, who, at present, will sign [the treaty]."[2] The Treaty of Sistova was signed in Bulgaria on August 17, 1791, ending the Austro-Turkish War. Though Turkey had fared badly by the end, Austria gained only a few meager territories, amounting to "nothing more than the town of Orsova" in southwestern Romania "and two small places on the Croatian frontier."[3]

During this incredibly stressful period in Leopold's life, his family continued to be a source of strength to him. Always loyal, Empress María Luísa remained at her husband's side through it all. His children were his eyes and ears throughout the Holy Roman Empire. Theresa and her husband Anton had since returned to Dresden, where they lived at the court of Prince Anton's father, the Elector of Saxony. After the summer weddings in 1790, Leopold named his son Ferdinand as the new grand duke of Tuscany. This meant Queen Maria Carolina's daughter Luisa was now the reigning grand duchess.

Leopold's other children were given prominent roles to play as well. His son Karl represented the Emperor in the Low Countries; the Archduchess Marianne became the Mother Abbess of the Theresian Convent in Prague; Alexander flourished in his role as prince palatine of Hungary; and in his father's absence, Archduke Francis was appointed regent in Vienna.

Leopold took it upon himself to travel throughout the Empire in an effort to restore confidence in the monarchy. It was during his traveling in the summer of 1791 that tragedy struck. In June, Francis's sixteen-month-old daughter Ludovica died suddenly of influenza. The tiny archduchess was sickly, and "had been mentally ill since birth."[4] Though the child was not her own, Francis's wife Teresa was just as heartbroken as her husband. Echoing Maria Carolina's own loving nature, Teresa plied her husband with letters of love and support in the weeks after Ludovica's death. She wrote in August: "Dear, best Francis, I am writing you again so that you may not remain even a single day without a letter from me. My thoughts are always with you, as your name is ever on my lips and you are in my heart."[5]

☙

With her eldest daughters married and settled in Europe, Queen Maria Carolina was more than pleased at how well their lives were turning out. Teresa and Francis enjoyed a blissful marriage in Vienna; and Luisa and her husband, Grand Duke Ferdinand III, were devoted to one another. The birth of Prince Leopoldo in 1790 only added to the Queen's happiness.

For the most part, Charlotte's family life was blessed. Though smallpox had claimed the lives of eight of her children, the surviving princes and princesses brought great joy to their parents' lives. Charlotte had a close, intimate bond with her daughters, especially Toto and Amélie. When the French Revolution began, Amélie took it especially hard because she had always fancied that she might one day marry her cousin, Louis Joseph. But when he died in 1789, the little princess's hopes of becoming Queen of France were shattered. It would be so many years until Amélie married that some believed she would never do so. The great irony was that she was still destined to sit on the French throne.

While her family gave Charlotte strength, ruling a vast kingdom took its toll on the forty-year-old queen. By 1791 her health was getting worse. She had been pregnant fifteen times, which understandably placed an incredible strain on her. To make matters worse, "she complained of her wretched nerves." Soon, she was suffering from dizziness and rushes of blood to her head. Since she was pregnant again, her doctors took no action because they were afraid it would cause a miscarriage. Charlotte had spent nearly all her adult life pregnant, and looked forward to the end of her childbearing days. "I sincerely hope this will be my last child," she admitted. During this, her sixteenth pregnancy, the Queen was more concerned with the welfare of her daughters abroad than her own impending *accouchement*. The irony was not lost on her that, as she was becoming a mother again, she was about to be a grandmother.[6]

After only six months in Austria, Charlotte's daughter Teresa was pregnant. Her mother, who had the utmost faith in Austria's physicians, watched the archduchess carefully. On December 7, 1791, Teresa gave birth to a daughter named Marie Louise. This first grandchild of Queen Maria Carolina of Naples would become famous as the future wife of Napoleon Bonaparte, and would later supplant her aunt Amalia as the Duchess of Parma.

Maria Carolina promptly sent off a letter to Teresa after Marie Louise was born. She congratulated her daughter on the delivery, and praised her for being "so sensible and brave [during the delivery], for uncontrolled groans do not help pain, and cause those present sorrow and disgust. One must put up with the evil for the pleasure of being a mother."[7]

Charlotte mirrored Maria Theresa in the way she wrote to her daughters, but her letters were of a more loving tone.

Undoubtedly, the greatest joy in her life was her children. In a letter to a friend, she described the happiness they gave her: "Francis [the Duke of Calabria] is well, and on all occasions gives proof of his good heart. I hope he will be the comfort of my old age, and I shall be relieved when all my children are happily settled."[8]

CB

After months of debate, Emperor Leopold was done waiting for the other continental powers to join him against France. The situation in Paris was bordering on anarchy after the royal family's disastrous flight to Varennes. Along with the King of Prussia, Leopold was afraid that if nothing were done, France's brand of violent republicanism would spread to the rest of Europe.

With the help of his daughter Theresa, the Emperor arranged for an emergency summit at the Elector of Saxony's *Bergpalais* in Pillnitz. There, surrounded by Japanese style décor in massive marble rooms, Leopold and King Frederick Wilhelm decided it was now time to take action against France.

Upon hearing of the summit at Pillnitz, the Comte d'Artois and his émigrés showed up uninvited "to plead what he calls the cause of thrones."[9] Louis XVI's brother made a compelling case for a military strike. He managed to convince the King and the Emperor. On August 25, 1791, history was made when the two rulers signed the famous Pillnitz Declaration. The agreement cited the readiness of both Austria and Prussia to intervene in France "to secure a monarchical government, which was equally fitted to the rights of the sovereign and the interests of the nation."[10] Leopold and Frederick Wilhelm agreed, "by mutual consent, with the forces necessary to obtain the true welfare of all. In the mean while they will issue to their troops proper orders, that they be in readiness to go into active service."[11]

Writing to Mimi, Leopold explained his motivation for signing the declaration: "One cannot aid the King and Queen, without the perfect coöperation [*sic*] of all courts, which will be difficult [to get]."[12]

The people of France were enraged by the Pillnitz Declaration, and feared that it threatened to destroy their new-

283

found freedom. They were now more committed than ever to toppling the monarchy. Bands of revolutionary marauders even began making cavalry raids across the French border into Alsace. In September, King Louis XVI was forced to swear allegiance to a new republican constitution.

By the end of February 1792, France was itching for war. The National Assembly declared that if Leopold did not "renounce all intentions and acts against the sovereignty and independence of the French nation, it would declare war."[13] Leopold had grown tired of threats from Paris. He boldly announced to his ministers: "The French wish for war and they shall have it; they shall see that Leopold the pacific knows how to wage it, if wage it he must."[14] Unlike Joseph II, Leopold was forced to contend with very real and very dangerous threats to his crown and his empire. True to form, he met these threats with dignity and temper. No one ever expected that his reign, and life, were at their end.

In the early months of 1792, Leopold's health began to decline. He had been enduring a terrible bout of colic since his visit to Prague in 1791. By the beginning of the new year, his memory was almost completely gone and he had trouble remembering from one day to another.

At the end of February, Leopold began suffering "from excruciating pain in the bowels, accompanied by vomiting." His doctors believed he was experiencing an inflammation of the bowel, and incorrectly assumed that a series of bleedings would cure him. It did provide the Emperor some relief, but only briefly, and he "was soon seized with convulsions" and a high fever on the last day of February.[15] The next day, Archduke Francis wrote a letter to his brother Alexander in Hungary describing some of the details of their father's illness:

> I am writing you a few lines to...inform you that our father was suddenly seized with a violent rheumatic fever early yesterday morning. The fever is accompanied by pains in the side and a chest constriction which makes it difficult for him to breathe. He has been bled three times since yesterday, the blood being spotted and much inflamed. The doctors held a council today, for the illness has not yet subsided. He will be bled again this evening and we hope for improvement thereafter. There is as yet no danger but the matter is serious.[16]

Only a few short hours after Francis wrote this letter, Emperor Leopold II died on March 1, 1792, in the arms of his devoted wife. He was only forty-four years of age. Francis, overcome with his own grief, had to find the strength to tell his brother Karl the sad news: "The greatest misfortune which might befall our family forces me to write to you. Our father died…at four o'clock today, without receiving the last sacrament, but in the arms of my mother. I am too frightened in my monstrous calamity to write any more."[17]

Leopold's death was sudden and tragic. Everything happened so quickly that only one news bulletin was issued, by Dr. Lagusius, the head of the Emperor's medical team:

> His Majesty the Emperor was seized on February 28 with a rheumatic fever accompanied by pains in the chest; the ailment was at once fought with bloodletting and other necessary remedies. On February 29 the fever increased, but three blood-lettings seemed to bring some relief. The following night, however, proved very restless and greatly weakened his powers. On 1 March the Emperor began to vomit, with horrible convulsions, and was unable to retain anything of which he partook. At three-thirty in the afternoon he expired, vomiting, in the presence of Her Majesty the Empress.
>
> Vienna, March 1, 1792
>
> Lagusius[18]

Empress María Luísa was devastated. She had lived her life at her husband's side for over twenty-five years. All she knew how to be was a wife. Leopold's death was an irreparable loss to Austria and the Habsburg monarchy. The Holy Roman Empire mourned the passing of a sovereign for the second time in two years.

Austrians responded by draping Vienna in shades of black and yellow, the two colors of the Habsburg flag. At the funeral, Emperor Leopold's body was placed on a special flatbed carriage. The bells of the Capuchin Church tolled mournfully on that cold, gray morning in March 1792 as the slow-moving funeral procession wound its way through the city streets to the imperial crypts. His body was buried next to his parents and brother.

In Naples, Queen Maria Carolina took the death of her favorite brother as a "crushing blow."[19] Her grief quickly turned to outrage: "Tell me, in God's name, how did they leave my poor dear brother to die without the Sacraments, without telling him of his condition. Delirium, his swollen stomach and four bleedings indicated the inflammation, yet nobody was charitable enough to warn him!... All my life I shall never cease mourning for my brother and friend."[20]

During his brief two years on the throne, Leopold II pulled his empire back from the verge of civil war and helped to fortify it against its enemies. He was "a sovereign, who, within the short space of a single year, relieved the country from foreign war and internal commotion, who baffled a great combination which threatened the independence of his house, and established a throne which at his accession was tottering to its very foundations."[21]

The Viennese newspaper *Wiener Zeitung* wrote a moving tribute to Leopold in his obituary: "Our feelings of pain are tempered by the consoling thought that the virtues of the most blessed monarch have devolved upon his exalted son,...who for some time shared with his father the problems of ruling and who long since has established a claim to the general love of his subjects."[22]

Emperor Joseph II, c. 1770. His idealism
and desire to reform Austria, though well-
meaning, nearly tore the Habsburg monarchy
apart.

Empress María Luísa, wife of Leopold II. She remained her husband's closest friend and confidante during their entire twenty-seven-year marriage.

Pitti Palace, c. 1777. *Left to right:* Theresa, Karl, Clementine, Marianne, María Luísa (holding Joseph), Leopold, Francis, and Ferdinand. *Seated in the front row:* Alexander.

Emperor Francis II, Leopold's son and successor. In addition to being Maria Carolina's nephew, he also became her son-in-law in 1790 when he married her daughter, Teresa.

☞

Amalia, Duchess of Parma, c. 1780. There was a profound contrast between her volatile, early years in Parma, and her subdued, melancholy later years.

☞

Ferdinand, Duke of Parma. It took him nearly twenty years to mature as a ruler. He spent the last years of his life fighting French suzerainty in Italy.

Maria Carolina, Queen of Naples. Of all Maria Theresa's children, she most emulated her mother, both as a ruler and a mother. She was the undisputed ruler of Naples, and also delivered 17 children.

The Royal Family of Naples in 1783. *Left to right:* Teresa, Francesco, King Ferdinand, Queen Maria Carolina, Maria Cristina, Carlo, and Luisa (holding Amélie). Despite giving birth seventeen times, only seven of Maria Carolina's children survived into adulthood.

King Louis XVI, husband of Marie Antoinette. Despite being hampered by timidity and indecisiveness, Louis was a kind and good-natured king.

Queen Marie Antoinette of France, 1779. This image was painted by the most famous female artist of the eighteenth century, Élisabeth Louise Vigée Le Brun.

℃ℬ

Marie Antoinette with her children, Marie Thérèse, Louis Charles, and Louis Joseph, in 1787. Also by Le Brun

Princess Marie Thérèse in 1795. As the daughter of Marie Antoinette and Louis XVI, she was known as "Madame Royale" at the French court.

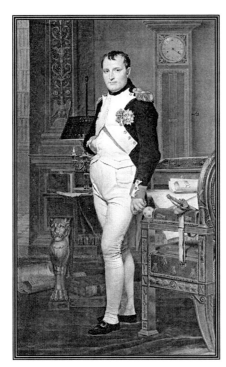

Napoleon I, Emperor of the French. He was directly responsible for the ultimate fates of Queen Maria Carolina and Amalia, Duchess of Parma.

Empress Marie Louise, wife of Napoleon Bonaparte, and their son, Napoleon II.

Marie Louise was the daughter of Emperor Francis II and Teresa of Naples, making her a granddaughter of both Leopold II and Maria Carolina. She was also a double-great-grandchild of Maria Theresa.

Maria Amelia of Naples ("Amélie"), Queen of the French, with her sons Ferdinand Philippe and Louis, 1835

21

Oppressed Innocence

Marie Antoinette's hopes of rescue were dashed one after the other, first with the death of Joseph II, then when Leopold died in March 1792. Only six weeks later, Leopold's wife, Empress María Luísa, "declared she could not survive [without] the husband she had always loved passionately," and died.[1]

The closest relative Marie Antoinette had left in Austria was her nephew Francis, who was quickly named emperor by the Frankfurt diet. He was barely twenty-four when he came to the throne. All of Europe watched with baited breath to see what this young emperor would do, but they would not have to wait long. The flames of revolution were about to spread beyond France and would soon consume all of Europe.

A few weeks after his accession, Emperor Francis II made the bold move of openly allying himself with the émigrés. The ambitious young ruler allowed them to assemble troops on Habsburg soil for an assault on France. This was a dangerous move, one that Leopold II never would have allowed, and it pushed France over the edge. In Paris, die-hard revolutionaries feared that monarchist forces were about to invade. Louis XVI's sister, Princess Élisabeth, who shared the family's confinement at the Tuileries, described the atmosphere in Paris to a friend: "People retail a thousand scraps of news, each of them, still more foolish than the others. They say that Russia, Prussia, Sweden, all Germany, Switzerland, and Sardinia are to fall upon us."[2]

In April 1792, the National Assembly was replaced by a new provisional government, calling itself the Legislative Assembly. The new government had no choice but to act against Austria. They declared that by allowing the émigrés to assemble troops, "Austria had announced, in the most injurious manner, her intention of meddling in the home affairs of France."[3]

Determined to rise up against "the House of Austria," the Assembly needed King Louis's approval to make a formal declaration of war. They incited the people until mobs starting forming around the Tuileries. They harangued the royal family night and day. Louis, completely dejected, feared for his family's safety if he did not go along with the Assembly. Bowing to the pressure, on April 20, 1792 he called for a special session of the Assembly to formally declare war on Austria. The governess for the royal children, the Marquise de Tourzel, recalled how "the King left the Tuileries for the Legislative Assembly with sadness painted on his face."[4]

Queen Marie Antoinette took the news gravely, but calmly. She wrote to her old friend, Comte Mercy: "War has been declared. I must speak of the nation, and say that Austria has never desired to wage war against France."[5] French flags draped buildings throughout Paris as citizens sang *La Marseillaise* and ran through the streets shouting republican slogans. At the Tuileries, the King and Queen were holding a solemn court. Louis XVI, prone to bouts of moodiness, slipped into a deep depression brought on by his guilt over having declared war. For nearly ten days, he did not utter a single word to anyone. As for Marie Antoinette, her clothes reflected her somber mood; she looked dignified wearing dark shades of blue and green.

There were high hopes for this war, but the French military—disparate and unorganized—was no match for the vastly superior armies of Austria, which had been reorganized and strengthened during Leopold's two brief years on the throne. In May, French troops met with disaster when they tried to invade the Austrian Netherlands. The Austrian soldiers stationed there were caught completely off guard, and their army was barely half the size of France's, but they still managed to completely crush their invaders. The French commander had no choice but to retreat. News of the spectacular defeat sent shockwaves throughout the revolutionary armies. Before long, soldiers began deserting their regiments en masse. One group of officers even murdered their general.

The French people, angered at being so thoroughly humiliated, turned their animosity towards Queen Marie Antoinette. Many believed she was anti-French and pro-Austrian. The supposed proof came in the form of open letters to her friends in exile—men such as Comte Mercy or Count Axel Fersen—letters that mentioned battle plans: "the plan is to attack by the Savoy and Liège."[6] The Queen's accusers conveniently forgot the fact that this and other letters were written before France and Austria were at war.

The thought of their queen being a traitor turned the French against Marie Antoinette once and for all. The citizens of Paris were up in arms and ready to exact revenge on her for their losses at the hands of the Austrians. With the Franco-Austrian war in full swing, there was a heated debate in the Legislative Assembly between the right-wing Feuillants and the leftist Jacobins and Girondins about whether or not Marie Antoinette should be allowed to remain in France.

They considered exiling her back to Austria "like the foreign enemy she was."[7] The idea of imprisoning her in a convent was also bandied about. The Assembly, trapped in a deadlock, could not decide on a course of action, so the issue was dropped. As far as Queen Maria Carolina of Naples was concerned, any of these suggestions were better than what Marie Antoinette was already living through. Charlotte was worried sick about her sister and admitted, "I would give my life blood to save her, not to make her the Queen of France again, but that she may finish her sad days in a convent."[8]

Once it was decided that Marie Antoinette would stay in France for the time being, life for the royal family turned from a bad dream into a nightmare. The soldiers guarding them took on a more menacing air, limiting their freedoms and forcing them to endure greater captivity at the Tuileries. They were deprived of some of the most basic necessities, and became subjected to the offensive whims of their guards night and day. The soldiers hurled insults at Louis, and made disgusting remarks in front of Marie Antoinette and the children. Writing to his aunts in Rome, King Louis described their sad life in Paris: "My children are in a languishing state; the queen finds the continuance of her health in the fortitude of her spirit, and I in my resignation to the decrees of Providence."[9]

During the summer of 1792, the King and Queen began to fear for their safety. From time to time, angry mobs would besiege the Tuileries for hours on end. Marie Antoinette rarely spoke openly of her anxieties, but Louis XVI was more candid. He told a friend, "it is impossible for me to believe that the future will be happy."[10] A few days later he confessed to his brother, the Comte de Provence: "my heart is oppressed; all I see, and all I hear, afflicts me."[11] Louis could sense that his life may be in danger. He wrote prophetically to his brother, "but a little while, and I shall exist no longer."[12]

By August, Emperor Francis II had made allies in his war against France. Prussian troops, under the command of the Duke of Brunswick, captured Longwy and Verdun. Not content with these triumphs, the Duke issued an "incredibly violent" manifesto that "threatened to subject the capital [Paris] to total subversion and bring death to its inhabitants if they did not submit to their King." Louis XVI was falsely accused of being in league with the Duke's army, and that he "had colluded with the enemies of the nation. Driven by an irrepressible desire for revenge, the Parisians in the local assemblies demanded the King's deposition and trial."[13]

The Brunswick manifesto sent Parisians into outbursts of rage. Thousands of angry citizens poured into the streets surrounding the Tuileries. The Legislative Assembly, fearing for the King's life, advised Louis and his family to place themselves under government protection and leave the palace. Believing his departure would only lead to more violence, Louis declared he and his family would stay at the Tuileries. For nearly two days, the crowds grew angrier and angrier. In an incredible show of cowardice, many of the soldiers guarding the royal family abandoned their posts and joined the mob outside, leaving only a handful who remained loyal to the King and Queen.

Inside the palace, the terrified royal family huddled together in a few rooms on the upper floors. They covered the windows and barricaded the doors. During the chaos, one of the guards took notice of Marie Thérèse, who was clutching her mother's hand in terror. "How old is Mademoiselle?" the soldier asked

Marie Antoinette. "She is at an age when such scenes cause only too much horror," she replied.[14]

On August 8, the National Guard commander, Galiot Mandat, desperate to protect the royal family, brought in nine hundred Swiss Guards, another nine hundred gendarmes, and nearly two thousand National Guardsmen. The following day, they were told that the storming of the palace was imminent. That evening, as the family was gathered in the King's apartments, a deeply moving scene took place. Nearly two hundred aristocrats arrived at the Tuileries ready to fight for king and country. Armed with swords, muskets, and any other blunt objects they could find, these men were prepared to die for their royal family. But the sight of these noblemen inflamed the crowd's animosity even further.

The mob reached a fever pitch by August 10. Bands of rioters managed to break into the palace, but not before being tackled by the Swiss Guards. Desperate to save the lives of the royal family, the Legislative Assembly sent a representative, Pierre Roederer, to the Tuileries to persuade them to accept government protection. In an audience with Louis and Marie Antoinette, Roederer made his case. "Resistance is impossible. All of Paris is coming," he told the Queen. Turning to the King, he implored: "Sire, there is no time to lose; there is only one thing to do now. We request permission to take you away." Fearful of a repeat of the violent storming of Versailles in 1789, Louis quietly muttered: "Let us go." His wife remained silent, but her face was flushed with emotion.[15]

At eight-thirty that evening, Marie Antoinette and her family left the Tuileries forever. Escorted by Roederer and the Swiss Guards, they made their way through the angry mob and into a carriage bound for the *Salle du Manège*, the great meeting hall of the Legislative Assembly. The Assembly's deputies argued long into the night about what to do with them. After spending three nights in a cramped little room attached to the *Salle*, the family was moved once again. This time, to the dank, tiny cells at the *Couvent des Feuillants*. There, the reality of their situation came crashing down on the Queen. "We are lost, we will die in this horrible revolution," she cried out.[16]

Now that the royal family was in government custody, the decision for their new home was made. Their new residence was an inhospitable commune known as the Temple, so named because it had once housed the Knights Templar. "I always begged the Count of Artois to have that villanous [sic] tower of the Temple torn down," the Queen exclaimed when they arrived; "it always horrified me."[17] The Temple was a menacing fortress dating back to the thirteenth century. Its titanic stone walls were separated by only four artillery turrets. It was more a prison than anything else.

At the Temple, every last bit of dignity the royal family had was stripped away. Their loyal band of servants was sent away and they were confined to old prison rooms on the upper floors. Even during the most personal of duties, no less than two guards constantly watched them. Louis's first valet *de chambre* recorded the indignities the family suffered: "This constant torment [of always being watched] which the Royal Family suffered in not being able to give a loose to any unrestrained expression of their feelings, to any free effusion of their hearts, at a moment when they could not but be agitated with so many fears, was one of the most cruel refinements, and dearest delights of their tyrants."[18]

In spite of these abuses, those who attended the captive royals could not help but be moved by the deep kindness and grace with which they acted. Never was there any complaining of their conditions or loathing for their captors, but always a quiet humility and trust in God's will above all else. Even in the face of their own uncertain fates, Queen Marie Antoinette and King Louis XVI never wavered in their faith in the Lord.

❦

As the eighteenth century drew to a close, tragedy had become a hallmark of the five special children of Maria Theresa. Even in the relative tranquil of Italy, the life of Amalia, Duchess of Parma, was plagued by heartache. She was devastated by the news that both Joseph II and Leopold II had died, and was also worried sick about Marie Antoinette.

One visitor to Parma during this bleak period in the Duchess's life was the famous painter Elisabeth Vigée Le Brun, who was moved by the sad pall that hung over Amalia's life. Dressed from head to toe in black, she had entered into a prolonged period of mourning for her dead brothers. Le Brun expected to find a brazen, flamboyant woman barely entering middle age, but instead she was greeted by a subdued duchess holding court.

Le Brun recalled her first meeting with Amalia: "Her rooms were all hung with black, she looked like a shadow; all the more as she was very thin and pale. She rode every day on horseback; her way of living and her manners were like those of a man. Altogether I was not charmed with her, although she received me extremely well."[19]

The loss of her brothers weighed heavily on Amalia. Her beauty, which was once legendary, had almost completely faded. Her cheeks were sunken in and her chestnut hair had turned almost entirely silver. One bright spot in her life was her children, who remained closely attached to the Duchess even as they approached adulthood. All of that was about to change, however.

Like her sister in Naples, Amalia was determined to marry her daughters off to respectable German princes. Her eldest child, Princess Carolina, had inherited much of her mother's beauty and was eager to be married herself. Amalia made sure Carolina crossed paths with Prince Maximilian of Saxony ("Max"), who frequently visited Italy. When the ducal family visited Saxony in the late 1780s, the couple met again, fell in love, and announced their intention to marry. Amalia was happy that her daughter was marrying into the powerful ruling family of Saxony; Max's brother was Prince Anton, the husband of Carolina's cousin Theresa. But Amalia was concerned by the fact that, as the fifth son of the elector, Max stood little chance of ever inheriting the throne. This was a small issue, though, and Amalia gave her blessing, as did her husband Ferdinand.

After an intimate, candle-lit proxy ceremony at the Ducal Chapel in Parma, Amalia said goodbye to Carolina forever. The formalized wedding took place in May 1792 at the ivy-covered electoral castle in Dresden. Anton stood as Max's best man, and Princess Theresa was Carolina's matron of honor. With her eldest daughter married, Amalia turned her attentions on her son Luigi, who was about to embark on a life of his own. In the process, he was destined to make history.

CB

At the end of September, Georges Danton and his Girondin party seized power in Paris. The moderate Legislative Assembly was dissolved, replaced by the more belligerent, anti-monarchal National Convention, which held its first session on September 20. Less than twenty-four hours later, the Convention voted unanimously in favor of ending the two-hundred-year Bourbon monarchy in France. The dethroned king and his family were given the surname Capet, a reference to one of the country's ancient dynasties. Since Louis was no longer a king, this meant that Marie Antoinette's position as queen had ended.

When the news reached the Temple, one witness recalled how Louis, "having a book in his hand, continued to read, without suffering the smallest alteration to appear in his countenance." He also noticed that the "queen displayed equal resolution."[20] Marie Antoinette's daughter, Marie Thérèse, recalled in her diary the day her parents were deposed: "The Republic was established on the 22nd September; they brought us the news with delight." That evening, Louis and Marie Antoinette were consumed by grief over what had just happened. "We were unwilling to believe it, but it was true," Marie Thérèse remembered.[21]

Reaction to the dramatic downfall of the powerful Bourbon dynasty ranged from shock to indifference. Gouverneur Morris, the American minister to France, recorded in his journal: "Nothing new this Day except that the Convention has met and declar'd they will have no King in France."[22] With their protective royal mantle stripped away, the fate of Marie Antoinette and her family was more uncertain than ever.

By Christmas, any remnants of the Legislative Assembly still sympathetic to the former royal family were consumed by the dangerous radicalism that was growing in the National Convention. The war with Austria was beginning to turn around as French forces succeeded in taking Nice, Savoy, and Frankfurt. Not content with these military victories, the Convention decided to make their rule of France absolute.

In January 1793, Louis was taken from his family to be interrogated and tried for crimes against the nation. There was little doubt from the Tribunal Council—largely made up of leftist Jacobins and Girondins—that he would be found guilty.

Witnessing the unprecedented trial of a king by his former subjects, Gouverneur Morris wrote to Thomas Jefferson: "it would seem strange that the mildest monarch who ever fill'd the french Throne...a Man whom none can charge with a Criminal or cruel Act, should be prosecuted as one of the most nefarious Tyrants that ever disgraced the Annals of human nature." He found it hard to believe that "Louis the sixteenth, should be prosecuted even to the Death. Yet such is the Fact."[23]

On January 20, the chairman of the Tribunal, Pierre Vergniaud, announced, "It is with profound sadness that I declare the penalty incurred by Louis Capet to be, by the vote of the majority of this assembly, that of death."[24] At two o'clock that afternoon, Louis was informed that he would be put to death by the swiftest, most humane way possible: the guillotine at the Place de la Révolution (formerly the Place Louis XV). When the sentence was read, he exclaimed: "Ah! I shall then at length be delivered from this cruel suspense."[25] Marie Antoinette and the rest of the family only found out later that night from the voices of the criers beneath their prison windows.

That evening, the Capet family (as they were now called) had an emotional last meeting in the Temple. It was the first time they had seen Louis in nearly six weeks. Marie Thérèse, now fifteen, was old enough to understand the torment her parents were enduring. "He wept at our grief," she remembered, "but not at the thoughts of his own death."[26]

As he was being escorted back to his cell that night, Louis told his wife that he would come to say goodbye to them the next morning at eight o'clock. Do you promise? his family asked in one voice. I promise, he replied. "Why not at seven o'clock?" his wife implored. "Very well, then: yes! at seven o'clock," Louis conceded.[27] These were his final words to his long-suffering wife. Marie Antoinette, Marie Thérèse, and Élisabeth, who was incarcerated with her brother's family, wept uncontrollably that night, so much so that their cries reportedly reached through the walls.

The sun rose over the City of Lights the next morning, but there was no sign of Louis. Upon returning to his cell the night before, his Father Confessor convinced him that any further goodbyes would only add to his family's pain. Louis confessed to his aide: "I had promised to see them this morning, but I wanted to spare them the sorrow of such a cruel parting: how painful it is to me to have to leave them without receiving their last kisses!"[28]

As the morning went on, the Capets waited in silence, not knowing the fate of their loved one. They listened desperately to hear anything from outside the Temple walls that might indicate the time. Around nine o'clock they heard drum rolls. Later, Marie Antoinette described hear "the movement of men and horses" outside the tower windows. They realized in that dark moment that their king, father, husband, and brother was taking his final march to death.

Across Paris, "the greatest tranquillity [*sic*] prevailed in every street through which the procession passed." As the deposed king made his way through the crowded streets, his prayer aloud was that "the blood you are going to shed may never be visited on France." When he reached the Place de la Révolution on the north side of the Seine, he took his place on the scaffold with "that modest intrepidity peculiar to oppressed innocence."[29]

His family in the Temple waited for another horrific hour. At twenty minutes past ten in the morning they heard more drum rolls, followed by cannon fire and loud cheers and cries of joy echoing throughout the streets. Marie Antoinette knew then that her husband was dead.

"The monsters! They are satisfied now!" Élisabeth cried.[30] According to the Temple guards, Marie Antoinette's reaction to her husband's death was deeply moving. She dropped to her knees and hailed her son as King Louis XVII. After kissing his hand, she tearfully muttered the words: "the King is dead, long live the King."[31]

Gouverneur Morris, overcome by Louis's tragic fate, described how the former king "died in a manner becoming his Dignity." Upon the scaffold, Louis "express'd anew his Forgiveness of those who persecuted him and a Prayer that his deluded people might be benefited by his Death."[32]

Louis's exiled siblings were devastated by their brother's murder. His brother Charles, Comte d'Artois, in Westphalia at the time, was "overcome with horror when he learnt that the greatest criminals the world has ever known had just crowned their numberless sins by the most horrible of all crimes."[33] His sister, Crown Princess Clothilde of Sardinia, poured out her heart to a relative, saying: "He whom we have just lost in so unjust and barbarous a manner is certainly now our protector before God. My only consolation lies in the assurance of his eternal happiness."[34]

In Great Britain, the execution of an anointed monarch was decried as an "abomination" by King George III, who subsequently agreed to join forces with the other European powers to make war against "those murderers in Paris."[35] He wrote that Louis's execution "calls on us to join against that most savage as well as unprincipled nation."[36]

With that as their impetus, the First Coalition against France was formed in 1793. This league of nations was originally made up of England, Austria, Spain, and Holland, but within a few months they were joined by Russia, Sardinia, Portugal, and the German electorates. The members of the Coalition may have initially been apathetic to the French royal family's plight, but after the former king was killed, there was a genuine sense of anger. Europe's monarchical powers were ready to settle scores on Louis XVI's behalf.

Marie Antoinette was utterly broken by her husband's death. Like her mother upon the death of Emperor Francis I, she took to wearing black widow's weeds for the rest of her life. In the days that followed, the ex-queen displayed a dignified resolve that spoke volumes to the strength of her character, largely the result of her childhood spent at Maria Theresa's side. Writing to a friend, Marie Antoinette calmly admitted: "we are aware of the tragedy that has befallen us...our own tragedy is certain, and we wish to go into mourning." As she spent the summer months watching France descend further into its violent revolution, the youngest daughter of Maria Theresa made no secret of the fact that she became "prouder and prouder to have been born a German."[37]

Marie Thérèse remembered her mother falling into a near-catatonic state after her father's death. Marie Antoinette's health began to rapidly decline because she had lost the will to live; all of her hope and strength were gone. The National Convention, knowing full well the ex-queen's days were numbered, commissioned Alexander Kucharski to paint one final portrait of her. When Kurcharski arrived at the Temple, he expecting to find a queen enraged by her dethronement. Instead, he came face to face with a woman who had "aged far beyond her thirty-seven years, a woman whose morbid black headdress, haunted gaze, and hollowed-out features bespeak a condition even more harrowing than death."[38]

In the early autumn of 1793, there seemed to be increased leniency towards Marie Antoinette (and royalist sentiments in general). The Convention was at a loss for what to do with her since there was no precedent in French history for regicide and the subsequent treatment of the widowed queen. No one was certain how to proceed. It seemed increasingly likely that Marie Antoinette would be sent packing to her relatives in Austria rather than continue to be imprisoned, tried, or executed. Marie Thérèse recalled, "the guards thought we were going to be sent away."[39]

After several weeks of uncertainty, plans to exile Marie Antoinette and her family came to a screeching halt. The First Coalition was making headway after driving the French out of Belgium. Incursions into French territory by enemy forces soon sparked rumors of a royalist plot to kidnap Louis Charles and install him as the new king of France. The National Convention decided that "Louis Charles, son of Capet, [was] to be taken from his mother and placed in a separate apartment, the best-guarded one in the Temple."[40]

Two days later, six guards came to the family's cell to remove Louis Charles. His mother so violently opposed the guards that it took them over an hour to tear the boy, sobbing and shrieking, from her arms. "My child! my child, remember, whatever may happen, to be always good, always upright!" she screamed.[41] Marie Thérèse described one of the most painful moments for her mother: "The first thing that [the watchman] did was to take away [my brother's] black suit," of which Marie Antoinette had "said [to him] before he left that she hoped he would not give up his mourning [clothes for Louis XVI]."[42]

The chances of Marie Antoinette and her family being freed faded over time, especially once they were separated. The National Convention faced "a barrage of daunting new threats" in the form of attacks on French borders by the European allies and counterrevolutionary insurgencies in the provinces.[43] Determined to show solidarity to the Revolution and its ideals, the Convention made the fateful decision to put Marie

Antoinette on trial in the same manner as her husband. In the words of the infamous Maximilian de Robespierre, it was "time for patriots to rekindle their vigorous and immortal hatred for those who are called *sovereigns*."[44]

Leading up to her trial, she was ordered to leave the Temple for the Conciergerie, an ancient palace-prison complex on the banks of the Seine. Marie Thérèse wrote of the night Marie Antoinette was moved from the Temple:

> August 2, at two o'clock in the morning, they came to wake us up in order to read my mother the decree of the Convention, which ordered that…she should be conducted to the Conciergerie for her trial. She listened to the reading of this decree without being affected or saying a single word. My aunt and I at once asked to follow my mother, but this favor was not granted.…My mother, after tenderly embracing me and recommending me to be courageous, to take good care of my aunt, and to obey her like a second mother, renewed the instructions my father had given me; then, throwing herself into my aunt's arms, she intrusted [*sic*] her children to her care.[45]

Marie Antoinette summoned all her resources in an effort to not be overwhelmed in front of her captors. It was the last time she saw Marie Thérèse or Élisabeth.

Once at the Conciergerie, she managed to pilfer a piece of scrap paper. She wrote a letter to Marie Thérèse: "I want to let you know, my dear child, that I am all right; I am calm, and I would be altogether so if I knew that my poor daughter were not so worried. I embrace you and your aunt with my whole heart."[46]

Marie Antoinette spent two long months alone in captivity before finally being summoned to appear before the Revolutionary Tribunal at eight o'clock one cold October evening. In her spirit, she knew her time had come, but she defied her captors with her last breath. "So long as France is great and happy, that is all I care," she said, refusing to display any kind of anger or bitterness. When asked if she considered as enemies anyone who caused war in France, she snorted defiantly: "I regard as my enemies all those who do wrong to my children."[47] And when the former queen was asked if she regretted that Louis Charles would never become king, she said that she did "not even regret the loss of her son's throne, if it led to the real happiness of the country."[48]

Once her interrogation was complete, Marie Antoinette was then forced to listen to a protracted list of royalist crimes against the state. The accusations included direct responsibility for famines in the countryside; unjustifiable spending at her private estate, the Petit Trianon; and funneling money to Emperor Joseph II. The evidence was "scant, and the witnesses' testimonies relied shamelessly on inference and hearsay." When it was time for Marie Antoinette to answer the charges, she responded with simplicity and grace, insisting on love for France and never wishing for anything but the nation's happiness. The prosecution, in turn, painted her as the merciless "scourge and the blood-sucker of the French people."[49]

At four o'clock in the morning, on October 16, 1793, the Revolutionary Tribunal found Marie Antoinette to be a "declared enemy of the French nation." They believed she was "the accomplice or rather the instigator of the majority of crimes in which the *ci-devant* king [Louis XVI] was found guilty."[50] Marie Antoinette "heard her sentence with much calmness."[51] Like her husband, she was sentenced to die on the scaffold at the Place de la Révolution. But unlike Louis, she was not allowed to say goodbye to her family. She would be executed that same day. Marie Antoinette's day of destiny had arrived, and it was time for her to be immortalized.

The trial lasted a staggering twenty hours, after which Marie Antoinette was taken to a holding cell instead of back to her room. Rather than sleep, she requested a candle, ink, and some paper at half-past four in the morning to compose a heart-wrenching farewell letter to Élisabeth:

> It is to you, my sister, that I write for the last time. I have just been sentenced, not to a shameful death...but to join your brother. Innocent like him, I hope to show the firmness he showed in these last moments. I am calm as one is when one's conscience is clear; I deeply regret having to abandon my poor children; you know that I lived only for them and for you, my good and loving sister. You who have out of friendship sacrificed everything to be with us. In what a position I leave you!...May my son never forget his father's last words, which I expressly repeat to him, that he never seek to avenge our deaths....

It remains for me to confide my last thoughts to you...I die in the Catholic, Apostolic and Roman religion, the religion of my fathers, the one in which I was brought up and which I always professed.... I forgive all my enemies the harm they have done me. I here bid farewell to my aunts and to all my brothers and sisters.... The thought of being separated from them forever and their sorrow is among my greatest regrets in dying; may they know, at least, that I thought of them up to the very last. Farewell, my good and loving sister, may this letter reach you! Think of me always. I embrace you with all my heart as well as those poor, dear children. My God! How heartbreaking it is to part with them forever. Farewell! Farewell!...[52]

This letter would never reach her sister-in-law in the Temple. As morning dawned, Marie Antoinette was resolved to her fate. "This, madame, is the moment in which you must arm yourself with courage," her priest told her. "Courage!" she replied, "I have been so long apprenticed to it, that there is little probability of its failing me at this moment."[53]

At eleven o'clock Marie Antoinette, carrying herself with the greatest dignity and grace, left the Conciergerie for the Place de la Révolution. The procession made its way through the streets of Paris on a "fine, slightly misty" day. Ahead of the cart, an actor on horseback waved his sword crying, "here she is, the infamous Antoinette, she is *foutue*, my friends!"[54]

For the trip to the scaffold, she was forced to ride in an open cart like a common criminal, yet she seemed to pay little attention to the crowd or the troops. Her appearance was "pathetic and contributed to [the] overall depiction of a hideous, haggard crone, justly deprived of all her *ci-devant* splendor."[55] She had "no sign of dejection on her face, nor yet of pride; she looked quite calm, and seemed hardly to notice the cries of *Vive la Républic! Down with tyranny!* that rose as she went by."[56]

When the procession finally reached the Place de la Révolution at noon, Marie Antoinette had gained enough composure to walk up to the scaffold with her head held high, but in the process accidentally stepped on the foot of the executioner. "Excuse me, sir," she apologized, "I did not do it on purpose." As she prepared to place her head in the guillotine, she cried out: "Adieu for ever, my children; I go to rejoin your father."[57] They were her last words.

With one swift motion it was done. The guillotine's blade fell, ending the life of the youngest, and undoubtedly the most famous, of all Maria Theresa's children. The execution of Queen Marie Antoinette of France hardly brought the public satisfaction it was intended to. The tens of thousands of people gathered along the banks of the Seine stood in utter silence, a sign of deep respect. There was a profound sense of pity from the crowd.

Years later, Marie Thérèse wrote of the day her mother died: "Then, having made the sacrifice of her life she went to death with courage, amid curses which the unhappy, misguided people poured forth against her. Her courage did not abandon her in the cart, nor on the scaffold; she showed as much in death as she had shown in life."[58]

Marie Antoinette's life was truly one of misfortune. Hers was "one of the most tragical to be encountered in the history of royalty. Born of a great house; married into a great house; beautiful, charming, amiable; she ended her life on the scaffold amid a storm of obloquy, after enduring every species of injury and insult possible to be offered to a high-spirited queen."[59]

PART IV

Empires at War

(1793—1814)

22

In Revolution's Shadow

y the end of 1793, only two of Maria Theresa's five special children were left: Queen Maria Carolina of Naples and Amalia, Duchess of Parma. Though her death was unspeakable, Marie Antoinette was spared the years of war that were about to engulf Europe, and in the process would topple Maria Theresa's reigning daughters.

Marie Antoinette's murder horrified Europe. Her nieces and nephews spread across the continent grieved for their aunt's tragic life. Archduchess Marianne, Leopold II's daughter who was born the same day Marie Antoinette left Austria forever, wrote to the Bishop of Nancy: "Monseigneur, I heard of the unfortunate Queen's death in some black-sealed letters I received from Dresden. It is a terrible event."[1]

In Naples, Queen Maria Carolina was devastated beyond words. Her daughter, Princess Maria Amelia, remembered the terrible day when the news arrived. With "her face bathed in tears," Charlotte took all of her children into the royal chapel for a special Mass to pray for Marie Antoinette.[2] The children "were awestruck as they saw their mother kneeling with bowed head before the altar making intercessions for her sister's soul."[3] Years later, Princess Marie Thérèse wrote to her aunt: "my mother often spoke of you…. She loved you more than all her other sisters." The broken queen took great comfort from this fact. Everyone recognized Marie Antoinette's deep affection for her Neapolitan sister.[4]

Maria Carolina was driven into a rage by the executions in Paris. One historian has noted that the "detestation of the

Sicilian Court for the new government of France was not exceeded in vehemence in any quarter of Europe."[5] Charlotte's hatred for the people who killed her sister ran so deep that she even tried to stop herself from speaking French, which was the official court language in Naples.

The French Revolution shattered Maria Carolina, and "destroyed her finest sensibilities." She was haunted by images of her sister at the guillotine and was overwhelmed with grief by the fact that Marie Antoinette was executed by people acting upon the principles of the same Enlightenment she herself was hoping to bring about in Naples. With her judgment and common sense gone, Charlotte's personality became unstable. She resorted to spies and secret police as a caution against conspiracies against the monarchy. An atmosphere of paranoia and anarchy was sweeping the country. Fears of a French invasion and of the Queen's secret police drove Neapolitan society to the edge of madness.

During this traumatic time in her life, Charlotte was pregnant for the seventeenth and final time.[*] The ships anchored in the Gulf of Naples fired their cannons for the last time in December 1793. At the age of forty-one, Charlotte gave birth to a daughter, Isabella. Like Prince Alberto who had been born while the court was grieving for Leopold II, Isabella's birth was celebrated in the midst of darkness. Naples was still mourning the death of Marie Antoinette, and nothing could raise the Queen's spirits. "My health is feeble and poor, and I think it will never be otherwise," she wrote near the end of December.[6]

The French Revolution was forcing Europe to the brink of panic. It did not take long for anxiety and paranoia to invade the Two Sicilies. Soon, Queen Maria Carolina found herself to be the subject of the same slander and innuendo that had been hurled at her sister in France.

One of the most popular rumors against her was that she had emptied the national treasury for one of her self-indulgent political schemes. Incensed by the mistrust her people had for

---

[*] Maria Carolina had given birth to a son, Alberto, on May 2, 1792.

her, Charlotte told a friend: "I have lived here thirty-one years...I do not even own a country house, a garden (a thing I have always desired), a jewel, no capital or anything. By now everyone has been able to ascertain the non-existence of my famous millions; I have not even been able to benefit those I wished to, having resolved not to depart from the strict rule of duty even in this respect." By the end of the year, there was little doubt of the Queen's unpopularity. Foreign diplomats like William Hamilton noticed that even though Ferdinand IV was as popular as ever, "the Queen of Naples is by no means popular, but as her power is evident, she is greatly feared."[7]

Ferdinand and the children tried to persuade Charlotte to visit the royal retreat at Pozzuoli on the Mediterranean coast for some rest and relaxation, but she adamantly refused to leave the capital in the midst of such chaos. With the Revolution in full swing, its destabilizing effects were beginning to be felt in the four corners of Europe. The Franco-Austrian War had turned into the War of the First Coalition, with more countries joining Emperor Francis II and King Frederick Wilhelm. But France's troops were strong, and smaller countries in Germany and southern Europe feared for their safety. Hundreds of refugees poured into Naples escaping the war in the north.

By the mid-1790s, Naples was wrought with revolutionary fever. Paranoia, show trials, and conspiracy theories were everywhere. People throughout the kingdom were affected, even members of Ferdinand and Charlotte's households. Siblings of valets, parents of chamberlains, and cousins of ladies-in-waiting were suspected and tried for treason. The Kingdom of Naples was beginning to cannibalize itself.

CB

For Amalia, Duchess of Parma, the past two years had been filled with tragedy, just like it had been for her sister Charlotte. She was sickened by the sudden deaths of her brothers, Joseph and Leopold, and the murder of her sister, Marie Antoinette.

At the court of Parma there was a genuine sense of grief over the events in Paris. Amalia's daughter Maria Antonietta ("Tognina") wept for the loss of her beloved aunt and godmother.

319

The Parmesan ambassador to France, Virieu, reported to Amalia that in the last moments of her life, Marie Antoinette "never failed for a single instant either her great soul or the illustrious blood of the House of Austria."[8]

The tragic loss of her siblings had turned Amalia into a care-worn, pessimistic woman, but her life was also marked by moments of joy. Her daughter Carolina was leading a contented life in Saxony with her husband Max. And when she told Amalia that she was going to be a grandmother, the Duchess was thrilled. Carolina gave birth to a daughter in Dresden in 1793. As a tribute to the baby's grandmother, Carolina and Max made Amalia the first of her fourteen names.* But Carolina's absence was hard on her mother, and it was made all the more difficult for the Duchess when her only son, Prince Luigi, packed up and set off for Spain.

The official story was that the prince, who had grown into a tall, handsome young man, was in Spain to finish his education away from the instability that was plaguing central Europe. This was only a half-truth though, because there was a secret arrangement for him to marry one of the daughters of his aunt, Queen Luisa. The agreement was kept quiet because the Spanish monarchs had become unpopular with the rest of Europe for expressing pro-French sympathies. Don Ferdinand wanted to avoid attracting any unfavorable attention when it came to his son's future, a sign of the wisdom he had acquired over the years.

Before Luigi had even arrived in Madrid, he decided to marry his cousin, who was ironically named María Amalia. But after only a short time at the Spanish court, it was clear to everyone that Luigi and the infanta were mismatched. She was timid and melancholy, and he was shy and reserved, a trait from his sheltered childhood that he never outgrew. As he spent more time in Spain, Luigi grew close with María Amalia's younger sister, María Luísa ("Luisetta"). This young girl, who was the complete opposite of Luigi in every way, enchanted the prince. Luisetta was only thirteen, but she was "of a more cheerful

---

* It was a long-standing tradition for German royalty to have names that were as lengthy as possible. At birth, Carolina's daughter was H.S.H. Maria Amalia Friederike Augusta Karolina Ludovica Josepha Aloysia Anna Nepomucena Philippina Vincentia Franziska de Paula Franziska de Chantal, Princess of Saxony.

disposition and somewhat better looking" than her sisters.[9] Luigi was quickly taken with his young cousin.

In the chaos of the Revolution and the subsequent Reign of Terror that was sweeping Paris, France was swooning over a new, young general who was making a name for himself. Originally from the small Mediterranean island of Corsica, he served in the French army after the fall of the monarchy. Napoleon Bonaparte was his name, and it was becoming famous in France and throughout the continent. The sound of it brought terror, because when it was heard, an invading army was not far behind.

By July 1795, around the same time that Amalia's son arrived in Madrid, France was looking for a way to hedge its bets in Europe. The Spanish House of Bourbon was already unpopular and had no reservations about doing whatever was necessary to preserve itself. The continent's royals were outraged when Amalia's sister-in-law and her husband, Queen Luisa and King Carlos IV, sold out to the murderers of the French royal family by signing a treaty with France. The agreement had a profound impact on the rest of Europe, because it meant that France's armies would continue moving east into Germany and Austria, and further south into Italy, rather than west into Spain.

Napoleon's army set its sights on the Italian peninsula and sped through at a staggering pace. Within a month, General Bonaparte had forced the King of Sardinia to surrender Nice and Savoy. French forces pressed on like a swarm of locusts. They quickly overcame Lombardy and granted an armistice to the Duke of Modena for "exorbitant ransoms."[10] Napoleon was leading his armies to resounding victories, forcing country after country to surrender. There was little surprise, then, that his next target was Parma. In truth, Napoleon had little interest in the tiny duchy beyond his desire to eliminate it as a potential threat.

Until that point, Don Ferdinand had worked to ensure his country remained untainted by the French Revolution. In fact, Parmesan society seemed little affected by it at all until 1795. Ferdinand had been "engrossed...in his religious observances, the Duchess in her flirtations, and society in its 'academies'."[11]

But in facing the challenges imposed by a full-scale European war, Parma embraced neutrality as its best chance for survival. After all, Spain had signed a treaty with France and was being left alone. But Parma was not Spain. The country's geographic position, coupled with its strategic importance as a buffer between France, Austria, and the rest of Italy, meant that the oncoming French army had set Parma directly in its crosshairs. All these factors placed the country's duke in the most unenviable, and ultimately disastrous, position.

Personally, the decision of neutrality had cost Ferdinand much. Amalia, like Charlotte of Naples, was fiercely anti-French for the executions of the royal family and the incursions into Austria. But her husband was also waging an intense internal battle because he considered himself as much of a Frenchman as he did an Italian. His mother, Madame Infanta, was French. So too was his tutor and first prime minister, Guillaume du Tillot. Now the Duke was being forced to choose between siding with his French brethren or stepping out in Parma's best interests.

In May 1796, French troops crossed the Po River into northern Parma. There, they met with resistance from royalist citizens. The French quickly and efficiently overpowered the Parmesans with a minimal loss of life. Napoleon sent an uncoded—meaning open and readable—message to the Spanish minister in the capital. It was obvious he wanted Ferdinand to see it: "I consent to suspend all hostilities against the Duke of Parma, and the march of my troops on Parma; but the Duke must send plenipotentiaries to me in the course of the night to conclude the armistice. I am marching several regiments of cavalry and one brigade to within three leagues of [Piacenza]; but this need not give the Duke of Parma the least uneasiness, from the moment he accepts the conditions we agree upon.[12] Ferdinand refused to be intimidated, and sent no response to the message. Hoping to use as little force as possible, Napoleon offered to give him the island of Sardinia as compensation, which he recently conquered, in exchange for Parma. Ferdinand refused to accept someone else's kingdom, and certainly refused to accept signing a treaty with Bonaparte.

Fuming that his "generous offer" was rejected, Napoleon retaliated in the most forceful way possible by sending ten thousand soldiers under the command of General Cervoni to seize the city of Parma. With the Ducal Palace overrun with troops, Ferdinand and Amalia had no choice but to accept French control of their country.

A few days after the invasion, Napoleon wrote to Ferdinand's foreign minister confirming Parma's surrender: "I have received, Sir, the ratification of the suspension of hostilities which you have accepted on the part of the Duke of Parma. I send General Cervoni to you, in order that you may arrange with him all the particulars of the execution of this treaty. You will deliver to him in the course of to-morrow the five hundred thousand francs which, according to the terms of the suspension, are to be paid within five days...and will take the necessary steps for the execution of the said suspension."[13]

In Spain, Prince Luigi was worried sick by the invasion of his homeland. But always the arch-intriguer, his aunt Queen Luisa was eager to distract him with "other matters." Along with her most trusted ally, the insidious Spanish Prime Minister Manuel de Godoy, she picked up on her nephew's interest in Luisetta almost right away. She and Godoy did everything they could to keep Luigi's attention focused on the infanta, and not on the current political atmosphere lest he become a threat to Spain's comfortable position with France. Luigi and Luisetta found themselves being seated together at parties, invited to the same salons, and practically thrust into each other's arms by the Queen and her henchman. Luisa approved of her nephew's interest, because the other four Spanish infantas were "short and plain," but Luisetta was "clever, lively and amusing. She had dark curly hair, brown eyes and a Greek nose," a fact that her mother exploited.[14]

Regardless of all the scheming done by Godoy and her mother, Luisetta genuinely cared for Luigi, and was a very kind, generous, and decent girl. It did not take the prince long to ask Luisetta to marry him. Once the couple had the approval of the King and Queen—which happened with very little prodding—plans for the wedding went ahead. They were married on August 25, 1795 at La Granja Palace in San Idelfonso, "surrounded by beautifully laid out parks high up in the Castilian Mountains."[15]

In the days and weeks after their wedding, the couple were extremely happy, even though they were very young; he was nineteen and she was only thirteen. Luisetta wrote in her memoirs after her wedding: "I continued, nevertheless, to reside in Spain, as Princess of Parma, with my parents and brothers—most happy in my union with a husband, whom I loved with the greatest tenderness, and who returned my affection."[16]

Luigi was quickly accepted into the Spanish royal family. He was nicknamed "El Niño" by the King and Queen, and granted the title and style of a Spanish infante. He also changed his name from Luigi to the more Spanish-sounding Lodovico.

Amalia's son and daughter-in-law were a perfect balance to one another. He was tall, blonde, and shy, while she was short, dark, and energetic. The only shadow that hung over their lives was Lodovico's health. His epileptic seizures had only gotten worse as he got older, leaving him almost completely dependant on Luisetta. This played perfectly into the hands of Queen Luisa, who had no intention of letting her daughter and son-in-law leave Spain.

❧

Once Napoleon's forces had control of Parma, there was little doubt that they would take the rest of Italy. In a matter of weeks, Tuscany fell. Charlotte's daughter, Grand Duchess Luisa, and her family were forced to flee to Austria under the protection of the Emperor. The King and Queen of Naples realized it was only a matter of time before their country was invaded. But unlike the other rulers in Italy, they refused to let Naples fall into the hands of the French.

The fight for the freedom of their country took on the mantle of a holy war. Standing on the balcony of the Royal Palace before a crowd numbering in the thousands, the royal couple cried out: "Our holy Religion, the State and the Throne are in danger; they require defense and defenders. Ready to spill our blood and perish for our subjects, we expect them to reciprocate." There were exhortations from pulpits and preachers to take up arms, and enrollment in the military skyrocketed. Even Prince Leopoldo, only five, was made a commander of the Royal Corps of Nobles, with the title Prince of Salerno.

Throughout Naples, troops on parade were "a gallant sight...in their white uniforms with blue velvet borders, plumes aflutter, like the paladins of Tasso come to life."[17]

King Ferdinand needed to stall for time while he prepared Naples for war, so he ordered his diplomats to negotiate a peace treaty with France. At the bargaining table, his ambassadors sat across from an unimpressed Napoleon. "Believe me," he told them, "in three weeks' time I shall be at Bologna, in a month perhaps at Rome. Now when I get there, will the King of Naples risk everything in a battle?"[18]

With little choice, Naples and France signed the Treaty of Brescia in October 1796. Far from helping Naples, it placed the country in an untenable position. The kingdom was forced to pay an indemnity of eight million *francs*. "On the 8th of December, 1796, arrived the news of peace for Naples with cursed France," wrote Emma Hamilton, wife of the British ambassador.[19] Queen Maria Carolina was outraged that Naples agreed to a peace treaty with France, and made no effort to hide her disapproval. She wrote to the Marquis de Gallo: "I am not and never shall be on good terms with the French...I shall always regard them as the murderers of my sister and the royal family."[20]

The Edge of Despair

Open war had reached the heart of Italy by 1797 as Napoleon's troops prepared to march on Rome. Like a bolt of lightning, they captured the Eternal City in February. When Rome fell, King Ferdinand ordered a mobilization of his troops along the border. A few days later, he personally took command of the armed forces on the front lines.

With her husband gone, Maria Carolina was left to rule in Naples, but on the home front she was facing an invasion of her own. Louis XVI's spinster aunts, Adélaïde and Victoire, had been living in Rome under the Pope's protection since escaping France in 1790. But after the invasion, *Mesdames Tantes* fled to Caserta and became a constant source of annoyance to Maria Carolina: "I have the awful torment of harbouring the two old Princesses of France with eighty persons in their retinue and every concievable impertinence... The same ceremonies are observed in the interior of their apartments here as were formerly at Versailles." She was even angrier because more than fifty families had to be turned out of the palace to make room for the princesses and their entourage.[1]

The greatest happiness in the Queen's life continued to be her family, which was about to receive an addition. The time had come for Prince Francesco to marry his fiancée, Archduchess Clementine of Austria. The youngest daughter of Leopold II was refined and sophisticated, and "her walk was that of a Queen," but Francesco was a simple man who enjoyed "agriculture and machines and preferred country life."[2] Though there were differences, Ferdinand and Charlotte approved of the match.

Clementine and Francesco were married in Foggia in June 1797. The wedding was simple, and could not compare to the magnificent ceremonies that took place in Vienna in the summer of 1790. In Maria Carolina' opinion, "luxury and ostentation are not proper at a time when all pay taxes which must last many years, even after the war [against France]." After the ceremony, the newlyweds seemed to be getting along well. Charlotte happily wrote: "My son loves her passionately and she reciprocates. It is a pleasure to see them harmonize so well... I am delighted with the Princess, gentle, fresh, sensible and accomodating [sic]." But soon there were signs of trouble for Francesco and Clementine. The new Duchess of Calabria was perennially homesick and, as the Queen observed, "she is discontented and everybody notices it." But Charlotte was committed to supporting her daughter-in-law as much as possible: "I will do everything for her happiness."[3]

By the end of the year, the war and the fate of Naples remained uncertain. Austria had found willing allies in Great Britain, Prussia, and the other European powers, but France's armies remained undefeated.

Rather than shrink back in the face of such overwhelming opposition, the indefatigable Queen Maria Carolina rallied to the cause. Her indomitable spirit rose up and refused to accept defeat. Taking matters into her own hands, in May 1798 she negotiated a secret treaty with her son-in-law, Emperor Francis II, for the defense of Naples should the Treaty of Brescia with France fail. By the summer, that looked like a very real possibility.

In June, France launched an unexpected assault on Egypt. This spelled trouble for Naples since the country was now surrounded. The French controlled nearly all of Italy, the islands in the Mediterranean, and now, the northern coast of Africa. In a plan to cut their enemies off, Great Britain diverted nearly fifteen thousand troops to Alexandria.

Sensing the tide was turning, Charlotte tried to convince Ferdinand to launch a pre-emptive strike against France. To help her make her case, she asked for the support of a British naval captain who frequented Naples, Lord Horatio Nelson. She trusted Nelson implicitly, and knew that if anyone could convince her husband to go to war, it was him. The Queen called a meeting of the state council where she outlined her plan to attack French-held Rome. It was too risky, Ferdinand argued. Realizing the queen was getting nowhere, Nelson stepped in and made a passionate speech. With voice bellowing and fists pounding the desk in front of him, Nelson declared: "Either advance, trusting to God and for His Blessings on a just cause, or remain quiet and be kicked out of [your] dominion."[4]

It was enough to convince Ferdinand. On November 29, 1798, he led an army of 30,000 men to liberate Rome. But instead of victory, the Neapolitan army was totally vanquished. The French commander, General Jean Championnet, anticipated the attack and withdrew his forces from Rome in order to strike back from a more strategic position. When Ferdinand's troops reached the city they were met by masses of people singing the king's praises who believed the French were gone for good. One witness to Ferdinand's triumphal entry, the Abate Benedetti, recalled that the "King of Naples arrived before noon…. The king was welcomed with the ringing of the bells, and great acclamations of the people, and has taken up his quarters in his magnificent Farnese palace."[5] The truth was that the French had completely surrounded the city and were closing in around Ferdinand's armies. They retook all of Rome in just two days. The Neapolitan army "lost all they had. Cannons, tents, baggage, all were left behind."[6]

With the courage of his troops annihilated, King Ferdinand IV "was seized with terror, fully expecting to be made a prisoner by his own officers" after the devastating defeat they suffered under his command.[7] To avoid being captured by the French, and fearing a mutiny by his own soldiers, Ferdinand fled Rome. One account claims that he only escaped after he exchanged clothes with his aide, the Duke d'Ascoli.

Enraged by this violation of the Treaty of Brescia, Napoleon ordered General Championnet and his army to invade Naples. News of the oncoming French army sent worried Neapolitans into a panicked frenzy. The King's advisors pushed for an immediate evacuation of the royal family, but Ferdinand refused to leave. With "a sudden burst of courage," he boldly declared "that he refused to be seen to run – that he would defend the palace and his family's lives to the end," but "Queen Maria Carolina would have none of it." She feverishly packed clothes and other valuables, using Emma Hamilton as a courier. Any items that were not sent directly to their ship in the harbor were kept for safekeeping at the British Embassy. One modern estimate claimed that "the queen was able to secrete some two-and-a-half million pounds, crowns jewels and treasure at the British embassy."[8] Lord Nelson and the British legation, who were prepared for the worst, made plans to evacuate both the royal family and all British citizens from Naples.

Five days before Christmas 1798, the crisis in Naples reached its flashpoint as terrified Neapolitans surrounded the royal palace and began shouting for arms to defend king and country. All night long, anti-republican sentiments could be heard echoing from the palace courtyard. "Death to the Jacobin!"[9] the mob shouted when one unfortunate palace servant was wrongfully suspected of spying for France. Ferdinand "disapproved with horror" as they tortured and killed the young man.[10] Inside the palace walls, the frightened royal family was trapped by a mob whose loyalty was bordering on madness. "You will not go! *We* will deal with the Jacobins!" the people cried.[11]

A terrified Charlotte wrote: "They want to keep us as hostages, and force us to make terms with those villains [the French]."[12] Horatio Nelson, who was with the Queen and her family that night, described the scene to Lord St. Vincent in Britain: "this day the 20th and 21st [of December], very large assemblies of people were in commotion, and several people killed, and one dragged by the legs to the palace. The mob by the 20th were very unruly, and insisted the Royal Family should not leave Naples; however, they were pacified by the King and Queen speaking to them."[13]

This pacification that Nelson spoke of was short-lived, and the city of Naples descended into a state of anarchy fueled by a strange mix of fear and patriotism. Nelson also noticed a frightening similarity between what was happening in Naples and what took place that dreaded night in 1791 when the French royal family tried to escape from the Tuileries to the town of Varennes. He noted that the "mob, like that of Paris, was bitterly opposed to their sovereign leaving the capital."[14] But what Nelson failed to realize was that the motivation of the mob in Naples was wholly different than in Paris. While the Parisians sought to make their king a prisoner of the state, the Neapolitans were bent on keeping Ferdinand from abandoning them to the invaders.

After nearly thirty-six hours of house arrest, the royal family finally escaped through a secret passage beneath the palace. Charlotte described their dramatic flight to her daughter Teresa: "We *descended*—all our family, ten in number, with the utmost secrecy, in the dark, without our ladies-in-waiting or other attendants. Nelson was our guide."[15] Once outside the palace walls, the royal family made their way to the harbor where Lord Nelson's flagship, the H.M.S. *Vanguard*, stood ready, accompanied by Portuguese and Neapolitan warships.

The pain of leaving Naples was hard on Maria Carolina. She was faced with the bitter prospect of never seeing her home again and settling in the smaller, secondary realm of the kingdom, the island of Sicily. But King Ferdinand was always an adventurous man, and the idea of sailing on the open sea to a new land appealed to him. One English passenger on the *Vanguard* observed that "the King seemed quite reconciled to his fate."[16]

The journey to the Sicilian capital of Palermo was a perilous one. The *Vanguard* was hit by the most powerful storm that Horatio Nelson had ever seen. He admitted that the winds "blew harder than I have ever experienced since I was at sea."[17] The *Vanguard* was nearly torn apart, and the passengers on board did not fair much better.

Christmas Day 1798 was especially tragic for Charlotte. Her son, Prince Alberto, six, fell ill from dehydration and seasickness. While Charlotte was caring for her baby daughter Isabella, Emma Hamilton held little Alberto in her arms as he suffered "heart-rending convulsions" all day.[18] As darkness fell and the sea grew calm, the six-year-old prince died in Emma's arms. That tragic moment stayed with Lady Hamilton for the rest of her life. Recalling the horrible scene, she told a friend a few days later:

We arrived on Christmas day at night, after having been near lost, a tempest that Lord Nelson had never seen the like for thirty years he has been at sea; all our sails torn to pieces... And poor I to attend and keep up the spirits of the Queen and the Princess Royall [*sic*], three young princesses, a baby six weeks old, and 2 young princes Leopold and Albert; the last, six years old, my favourite, taken with convulsion in the midst of the storm, and, at seven in the evening of Christmas day, expired in my arms, not a soul to help me, as the few women her Majesty brought on board were incapable of helping her or the poor royal children.[19]

The grief over losing her son was almost too much for the queen, who was gravely ill herself. Her own life appeared to be in danger. "I have lived long enough. I do not fear death," she said.[20] But for the sake of her family she rallied her strength and recovered.

When the *Vanguard* arrived in the Bay of Palermo, it had taken such a beating that it was a miracle the ship even made it into port. Everyone on board had suffered greatly during the voyage, and were "ill, miserable, and exhausted."[21] Once they disembarked, the royal family took up residence at the Colli Palace. A damp, empty, run-down building, it offered little comfort to Maria Carolina and her long-suffering family. Colli was so dank that when she saw it, she broke down in tears. "Life is over," she cried.[22] From that day on, the Queen isolated herself in the palace. With the exception of her family, Emma Hamilton, and a few ladies-in-waiting, she saw no one.

With Charlotte and Ferdinand gone, Naples fell to the French before the end of December. The *lazzaroni*—the country's working class—were fiercely devoted to the King and tried as best they could to fight a "wild, irregular, and unfortunate battle...against the French."[23] They even "broke open the prisons and let out the convicts" for the added manpower.[24]

When the news came that the Neapolitan armed forces eventually declared an armistice with France, riots and rebellions broke out across the country. The commander of the French troops announced upon his arrival:

Neapolitans, be free; if you know how to enjoy the gift of freedom, the French Republic will be amply rewarded in your happiness for her dead and for the war.... Your magistrates will, by their paternal administration, provide for the tranquillity [*sic*] and happiness of the citizens; …may you be as solicitous to serve us, as the perfidy of your fallen government was to injure us.[25]

Charlotte was almost forty-seven when she fled Naples; she had been queen for just over thirty years. But exile to Sicily did not bring any peace or tranquility. Instead, her family slipped into crisis. Francesco and Clementine, along with the rest of the children, were seriously ill. "My daughters and Leopold suffer but try to comfort me," she wrote. "But nothing can console me, I am in despair."[26] Even worse for Charlotte was the deep trouble into which her marriage was falling. King Ferdinand was never able to reconcile himself to the fact that, because his wife had prompted the attack on Rome, he blamed her for their circumstances.

The stress of a crumbling marriage and a failed reign worsened Charlotte's already delicate health in the damp, old Colli Palace. She was frequently plagued by fever, chills, and constant infections in her throat, chest, and head. Her doctors could do nothing for her, and Ferdinand used these illnesses as an excuse to see his wife as little as possible. She was morose and depressed all the time, so he wanted "to spare himself the tedium of his wife's tears."[27]

Life in Palermo was a nightmare for the royal family of Naples. "Every day the Queen frequented the churches for prayer and the convents for meditation. Each evening she poured out her heart to the helpful friend of her choice, whose sympathy lightened a load else insupportable."[28] Sicily was like a prison for Maria Carolina, one in which she was forced to watch her family suffer. The poor climate in the palace and the primitive culture in Sicily wreaked havoc on the health of her daughters Amélie and Toto; Clementine's health was so ruined that the doctors thought she would not live. The Queen wrote to a friend of her despair: "My daughters are all ill. As for my daughter-in-law, she is dying of consumption."[29]

In spite of the latest tragedies befalling her family, the Queen was happy to see her daughter Teresa doing so well in Austria. The one topic Charlotte always beamed about was her daughter in Vienna, who became the Holy Roman Empress in 1792 when Francis II ascended the throne. She was thrilled to see Teresa sit on the same throne as her grandmother and namesake, and many saw it as a good omen that for the second time in half a century, Francis and Teresa ruled Austria.

By the end of the eighteenth century, Queen Maria Carolina was glibly called the "mother-in-law of Europe." She had managed to engineer the marriages of her children so that her immediate family sat on thrones stretching across more than a third of Europe. Teresa was married to the Holy Roman Emperor, while her second daughter Luisa was married to the Grand Duke of Tuscany. And after all, her eldest son Francesco had married an Austrian archduchess.

As proud as Charlotte was of her children, the distance from her daughters left a profound emptiness in her life, especially since she could no longer count on her husband's love to support her. She and Ferdinand had since gone their separate ways, and when he found a comfortable villa along Sicily's coast, he relocated there permanently "to escape from his wife's sensibility."[30] Like her reigning siblings that went before her, Maria Carolina's life had become tragic. Felled by misery, she told Lady Hamilton, "I am neither consulted nor even listened to, and am excessively unhappy."[31]

The Neapolitan royal family completely fell apart in the winter of 1798-1799. Their allowance was cut from sixty thousand *ducats* per month down to ten thousand. And the King, who from time to time returned to Palermo to see his children, became a ghost. He spent all his time at the theatre and his country house by the sea. "He has forgotten Naples and all his old habits, and I am convinced that he never wishes to see it again and is very satisfied here," Charlotte wrote.[32]

As the Queen's life went from bad to worse, Naples was undergoing a drastic change under French occupation. With the help of local republicans, the French reorganized the country into the Parthenopean Republic in January 1799. But as events reached the edge of despair, an unexpected visitor walked onto the scene in Palermo, and would restore hope and change the fortunes of the royal family.

Cardinal Fabrizio Ruffo, a former member of Pope Pius VI's government in Rome, had retired to Naples before the Roman invasion. His distinguished reputation earned him the court title Prince of the Church, and he accompanied the royal family when they escaped to Palermo. Once there, he immediately began developing a plan to retake Naples from the Parthenopeans, beginning in his native Calabria. Ruffo's patriotism re-energized Charlotte, who threw all her support behind him. Before long, he had set sail with an army to re-conquer the mainland.

While Charlotte anxiously awaited updates from Ruffo, she occupied her time by being completely devoted to her family. She wrote continuously to Teresa. She tried not to make their situation sound as dire as it really was:

> As Queen-mother, woman I am unlucky. My children hide their grief in order not to sadden me, they merit a better fate. Mimi (Maria Christina) prays and does penance, hoping that God will take pity and change our circumstances. Amélie is the prettiest and has infinite tact and an excellent heart. Your father is well; whether from religious principle or resignation he is content. I admire him. Naples is like the Hottentots to him. He does not see it and therefore does not think of it.[33]

The Queen's spirits were lifted yet again when Clementine, Duchess of Calabria, not only recovered her health but also became pregnant with her second child.* She delivered a son, Ferdinando, in August 1800. But Charlotte was greatly concerned for her granddaughter and namesake, saying "their daughter is very pretty but shows little vivacity." She feared little Carolina's development was being stunted in the primitive Palermo. Even her favorite son, Leopoldo, was "losing his beauty and amiability." He was not yet ten, but the Prince of Salerno wanted to be taken seriously as an adult. This made him "less agreeable," which Charlotte chalked up to having to share a room with his sisters. The princesses were a continual source of strength for their mother. Maria Cristina ("Mimi") was "always the best and most vivacious soul alive." Toto and Amélie were "excellent children" as well.[34]

By summer 1799, Ruffo and his army of 20,000 men had succeeded in toppling the Parthenopean Republic. In June, a formal treaty was signed, ending France's occupation and

---

* Francesco and Clementine's first child, Princess Carolina of Calabria, was born in Naples on November 5, 1798.

restoring King Ferdinand IV and Queen Maria Carolina to the throne. But one of the conditions Ruffo agreed to was an amnesty for those who had collaborated with the French occupying force. Ferdinand and Maria Carolina were both incensed that Ruffo would agree to such a condition. Before they even considered returning to the mainland, the royal couple came together for the first time in a year to coordinate a counterstrike to eliminate the republicans within their kingdom. The Queen's desire for vengeance was tempered only by her desire to shy away from public life. She wrote to Lady Hamilton in July, "I am determined, on returning to Naples, to isolate myself entirely from the world."[35]

CB

The welfare of Amalia's daughter, Princess Carolina, continued to be a source of constant attention for the Duchess of Parma. Carolina's brother-in-law, the Elector Frederick August III of Saxony, had made a home for the Princess, her husband, and their family. As the eighteenth century drew to a close, Amalia could proudly boast of more grandchildren.

Having been relieved of much of her duties by the French occupation force, Amalia took an active interest in her German grandchildren and kept a closer eye on her daughter. Carolina had given birth to a healthy set of three daughters and two sons by the time she was twenty-nine. After Princess Amalia was born in 1794, Carolina expanded her family with Ferdinanda in 1796, Frederick August (the future king of Saxony) in 1797, Clemens in 1798, and Marianne in 1799.

The Duchess of Parma loved all of her German grand-children passionately, but when news reached her that Lodovico's wife was expecting a baby, she was overjoyed. In December 1799 Luisetta gave birth to a son in Madrid named Carlo after his grandfather. She wrote after the birth: "I had a son, to whom we gave the name of [Carlo]...my father having held him at the [baptismal] font."[36]

Once the baby was born, Amalia immediately began to pressure her son and daughter-in-law to return home. The Duke and Duchess had still not met Luisetta, and Ferdinand was eager for his grandson and heir to be raised in Parma, the land he was destined to rule. It had been four years since Amalia had last seen Lodovico, but King Carlos IV and Queen Luisa were deeply attached to their daughter and grandson, not to mention their son-in-law. They used every excuse they could think of to delay the couple's departure. No one could have ever imagined that by keeping them in Spain, they were opening the door for Lodovico to become a unified Italy's first modern king.

24

Italy's Unlikely King

*B*efore she retreated into a solitary existence, Charlotte revealed a new iron-willed facet of her personality that was set like stone against those who had threatened her family, her crown, and her country. From Palermo, she and Ferdinand launched a devastating attack on the republican elements within their kingdom.

In the days that followed, state trials ensued en masse, not unlike the Reign of Terror in Paris that had recently ended. According to a nineteenth century estimate, out of "8,000 political prisoners 105 were condemned to death, only six of whom were reprieved, 222 were condemned to life imprisonment, 322 to shorter terms, 288 to deportation, and 67 to exile." This brought the total punishment count to 1,004 out of 8,000.[1] The city of Naples saw innocent people crucified for allegations of being French sympathizers. "Defenceless [*sic*] men, women, and children were butchered in hundreds by the lazzaroni and by the provincial levies of Cardinal Ruffo."[2] Even "the ancient representation of the town and the kingdom were entirely abolished; the privileges of the city were materially diminished,"[3] giving the monarchy almost sole dictatorial control over the nation. Almost every measure of constitutional freedom for the Neapolitan people was swept away. Baron Louis de Viel-Castel wrote frighteningly, "one hardly calumniates this frightful epoch by comparing it to the Terror [in Paris] of 1793."[4]

Even after order was restored by force on the mainland, King Ferdinand IV still refused to leave Sicily. "Plain common sense points out that the King should return to Naples, but nothing can move him," Lord Nelson wrote with frustration. He highlighted the sad fact that one of the reasons for this was that "the King and Her Majesty do not, at this moment, draw exactly the same way."[5] She wanted an immediate return to Naples but he ordered the court to stay in Palermo.

No longer submissive to his wife's will, Ferdinand established his own dominance with a vengeance, becoming a family dictator in his Sicilian court. The impoverished lifestyle of the royal family now made the King painfully cheap and overwhelmingly controlling of the few servants they could still afford. The queen observed that her husband "supervises the royal household, the accounts. We are all kept so sparingly as to lack everything."[6]

As she approached middle age, Queen Maria Carolina's personality became more erratic. By October 1799, she had reached a precipice in her life. She declared: "Were it not for my daughters, I should wish to bid adieu to the world, and retire to a convent, there to terminate my days, a desire prompted by circumstances in which I am placed."[7] Her depression only made worse the deep pain that she had long held in her heart from being forced to leave Naples. But true to her Christian nature, she tried to show forgiveness: "I pardon all those who tear me to shreds, repeating humbly the words of my God: 'Lord, forgive them, for they know not what they do!'"[8]

The restoration of the monarchy did nothing to ease the lies being spread about the Queen on the mainland. Horatio Nelson continued to be among her staunchest supporters. "Do not believe a syllable the newspapers say, or what you hear," he wrote. "Mankind seems fond of telling lies."[9]

The list of Charlotte's allies grew even thinner when, after decades in Naples, William and Emma Hamilton were recalled to London, and Horatio Nelson's tour of duty in the Mediterranean came to an end. It was obvious to everyone the deep sadness that Charlotte felt at having to say goodbye to her dear friend Emma. Sir William observed that "the Queen is really so fond of Emma that the parting will be a serious business." And Emma herself admitted, "I am miserable to leave my dearest friend."[10] They decided to accompany Charlotte on one final voyage when she planned to visit Vienna that summer.

Charlotte was anxious beyond words to return to Austria, where her daughter and grandchildren lived. In June 1800, the Queen, the Hamiltons, the princesses, and Prince Leopoldo sailed from Palermo to Livorno. There, Charlotte made a visit to her daughter, Grand Duchess Luisa of Tuscany, who, along with her husband Ferdinand III, had been living under French occupation. Luisa was anxious to see her mother after ten long years, especially after her young son Franz (b. 1794) died earlier that year. Charlotte relayed the sad news of her grandson's death to Emma Hamilton: "My daughter Louise has lost in a few hours her six-year-old son, and she is much troubled, which is only natural. As for me, I envy the fortunate child for no longer being of this base world."[11]

After a three-month voyage, with stops in Florence, Parma, and Innsbruck, Maria Carolina and her companions finally arrived in Vienna in September. Though exhausted from a fever and fits of apoplexy, the Queen was thrilled to be back in Austria to see her daughter, and meet her grandchildren for the first time.

As the undisputed matriarch of two reigning houses, Charlotte was received with as much honor and stately dignity as Imperial Austria could extend to her "as daughter of the great Empress Maria Thérèsa, and mother of the reigning Empress and aunt to the Emperor."[12] Prince Leopoldo and his sisters were treaty just as grandly. They "basked in the affection of their northern cousins, and the royal palaces overflowed with the merriment of bouncing little Archdukes and Archduchesses."[13] In her journal, Princess Maria Amelia wrote of "the happiness of her life in Austria."[14]

For all the sadness she had endured, Charlotte's heart was touched to see how idyllic were the lives of her Austrian grandchildren. She was the proud grandmother of Marie Louise, Ferdinand, Leopoldina, Maria Clementina, and Joseph. Emperor Francis was a devoted father who "loved joking and playing with his children."[15] He and Charlotte got along very well at first. He was fond of calling her his "mother-in-law and three-fold aunt."[16]

Francis and Teresa had a loving, committed marriage, and frequently wrote love notes to one another. By the time the Queen arrived in 1800, Teresa enjoyed her husband's utmost confidence and wrote letters of love and loyalty to him:

Dearest best husband.

I reached for my quill with greatest joy in order to...assure you of my love. I hope that you...find yourself in the condition my heart wishes for you. Thinking of you constantly, I can enjoy nothing for everything seems dead without you. Thank God we are all fairly well and the weather is pleasant and warm.... The children kiss your hands and I pray you to preserve for me your dear love. Forever

Your most loving wife and friend
THERESE[17]

Empress Teresa was a loving mother who was famous for being "vivacious, gay and serene, particularly in times of crisis." She represented to her daughters, especially young Leopoldina,* "a lifelong example of self-denial, charity and goodness." Unfortunately for the Empress, she was criticized for being "extravagant with money" and "for the large amounts" she spent "on charity and family entertainments."[18]

This little piece of paradise in Maria Carolina's life did not last long. The time had finally come for her to bid farewell to William and Emma Hamilton, and to Horatio Nelson. In a parting letter to Emma, she poured out her heart, saying that "at all times and places, and under all circumstances, Emma, dear Emma, shall be my friend and sister, and this sentiment will remain unchanged."[19]

The peace that reigned after France was forced out of Naples did not last long. Less than two months after Charlotte arrived in Vienna, Europe was plunged into war again. Austria and France pointed their guns squarely at one another in what eventually became known as the War of the Second Coalition.

---

* Leopoldina, who was named for her grandfather Emperor Leopold II, was destined to sit on an imperial throne. She became Empress Consort of Brazil in 1822 when her husband, Crown Prince Pedro of Portugal, became Emperor.

In an undignified display, both Napoleon and Emperor Francis II partly blamed Maria Carolina's meddling political influence for this latest round of hostilities. She told a close friend that she was finding herself "abandoned by my own children, avoided and thrust aside by the rest of my family, who render me responsible for everything and make me bear the burden of everybody's hatred." Her son-in-law, Ferdinand III of Tuscany, urged her to flee to Brunn or Budapest to escape the tense atmosphere in Vienna. But for Charlotte, the notion of retreating was unimaginable, even in such dire straits. "I am the daughter of Maria Theresa," she declared, "and will rouse other jealousies in those who, to my misfortune, have no heart."[20]

By the end of 1800, Francis II was eager to get rid of his aunt. She was just as ready to distance herself from the increasingly unpopular Habsburg monarchy. She wrote prophetically before leaving Vienna: "I love the sovereigns, Vienna, its vicinity, this land where I was born, and the way of living here. But as for relying on them, never, never, never. I am certain, ultra-certain, of the collapse of this monarchy."[21]

The Vienna that Charlotte visited was a far cry from the one she had known. The glittering capital of Austria and the Habsburg realm that she grew up in was gone: "The numerous Archdukes lived quietly and retired. The aristocracy resided in the capitals of their provinces, or on their vast estates, and rarely came to Vienna.... In winter the Imperial family dwelt in the great gloomy pile of the Hofburg in the heart of the walled city [Vienna], surrounded by narrow streets. In summer they moved to Schönbrünn, or Laxenburg, a few miles outside."[22] There was little society, and no parties. Vienna was a city that had fallen asleep.

In November 1801, Charlotte and her family were dealt another blow. Messengers arrived in Vienna to inform the Queen and her children that her daughter-in-law, the Duchess of Calabria, eventually succumbed to her frequent bouts of consumption and died.

Clementine had led a sad life in Naples after her only son, Ferdinando, died in July 1801. Charlotte wrote to Lady Hamilton:

341

You have of course shared in the grievous misfortune I have experienced in losing my dear and good daughter-in-law. It destroyed the single happiness that remained to me, in a perfect union and domestic attachment. This dear and good princess died like a saint, and her husband is in the deepest despair. My dear children do nothing but mourn for their sister-in-law, who was a tender sister to them, and would at my death (which by reason of my troubles and griefs cannot be distant) have been a mother to them.[23]

Clementine's daughter, Princess Carolina of Calabria, recalled the death of her mother: "I was then too young to remember her; but I have found ineffaceable souvenirs of her in the hearts of all who were so happy as to be near her and admire her virtues.... How I would have cherished her!"[24]

This was the first in a series of misfortunes that forced the Bourbons of Naples to secure a rapprochement with Spain, which had been politically excommunicated from the rest of Europe after it signed its treaty with France in 1795.

The issue of the Duke of Calabria's remarriage came to the fore almost immediately after Clementine's death. King Ferdinand decided the time was also right for his daughter Princess Maria Antonietta ("Toto") to be married as well. Charlotte's strained relationship with her husband meant that she was not consulted when a double wedding was arranged for both Francesco and Toto with the family of King Carlos IV of Spain, while the princess was still with Charlotte in Austria!

According to the marriage contract, Francesco would marry the Infanta Isabel of Spain, and Toto would marry the Spanish heir, Prince Fernando of the Asturias. While Charlotte was anxious to find husbands for her daughters, she was deeply prejudiced against the Spanish Bourbons, hoping instead that all her children would marry "respectable Austrians." She wrote to the Marquis de Gallo about her aspirations for daughters, but "fate has willed otherwise. [Francesco] wishes to marry his cousin, the Infanta of Spain. I have seen it in his own hand-writing...only ten days after the death of his virtuous wife..." All this transpired while the Queen was in Vienna, but it was still not enough to prompt her to return home. "I am waiting for the King to express in writing his desire to see me again," she said even though her relatives in Vienna were making her feel she had overstayed her welcome.[25]

CB

As France's occupation of Parma dragged on, the situation became intolerable. The economy collapsed trying to support and maintain thousands of soldiers; hundreds were displaced from their homes; and the poor starved in the streets. Once French troops were firmly entrenched in the country, they proceeded to systematically bankrupt and dismantle Parma.

At Napoleon's order, entire convents and religious orders were emptied; royalist politicians were removed from office or fled into exile; and Don Ferdinand was ordered to pay France an indemnity of two million *francs* in silver, but the overall loss to the nation soared far above that.

Napoleon reasoned that since Parma had no military resources whatsoever that could be useful to France, the country should offer up its other assets as a ransom. According to the ceasefire that Ferdinand was forced to sign in May 1796, Parma lost, in addition to money already paid, "twelve hundred draught horses,...four hundred dragoon horses,...one hundred saddled horses,....ten thousand quintals of corn and five thousand of hay."[26]

Not only did French forces claim Parma's resources as their own, they even laid claim to sixteen "specially-selected" Renaissance paintings from the National Gallery.[27] One of those chosen was the famous *St. Jerome* by Coreggio. Ferdinand offered another million *francs* as a ransom for the priceless painting, but Napoleon declared: "The million which he offers us would soon be spent; but the possession of such a *chef-d'œuvre* at Paris will adorn that capital for ages, and give birth to similar exertions of genius."[28] To cover his country's losses and pay his "debts" with France, Don Ferdinand was forced to pawn what was left of the royal jewels and even melted down his grandmother Elizabeth Farnese's famous Golden Rose.

Ferdinand and Amalia continued to reign in title alone, and only at the pleasure of Napoleon Bonaparte, who was now the First Consul of France. They were forced to sit by and watch as Parma's infrastructure was demolished, their people levied with heavy taxes, and their State property sold, but the situation for the Duchess and her people was about to grow even worse.

In February 1801 the great powers of Europe assembled at Lunéville in northeastern France to decide the fate of the continent after this latest round of French aggrandizement. Parma and its Italian neighbors were offered up as lambs to the slaughter. France's invasion of Italy had left it with control of Tuscany, Parma, Savoy and Sardinia, Lucca, and Modena. The Treaty of Lunéville, which was signed on February 9, 1801, now recognized French instead of Bourbon authority in Parma, declaring that "the Duke of Parma has renounced his hereditary states."[29]

The Duke and Duchess were horrified and humiliated when they were stripped of their throne and their country. They were allowed to keep their styles and titles as a courtesy, but they now had little more than nominal authority. Amalia was enraged that her family lost everything simply because they were unable to speak for themselves with the same voices as Austria, Prussia, or Spain.

The treaty plotted a new course for Parma's future. It was agreed that the duchy would cease to exist on its own. Along with Lucca, Modena, and parts of Tuscany, Parma would make up Napoleon's new puppet brainchild, the Kingdom of Etruria. To ease the transition of power and to avoid a struggle with the Bourbon family, Napoleon decided not to go forward with Parma's integration until Ferdinand's death. To appease the Royal House of Bourbon in Spain, Napoleon offered Amalia's son, the Infante Lodovico, the throne of Etruria.

Luisetta recalled in her memoirs, "it was intimated to me, that a treaty had been made, by which my husband was appointed to the throne of Tuscany, with the title of King of Etruria."[30] The decision was part of a complicated strategic plan by Napoleon. In making Lodovico a king, it meant that the daughter of the Spanish monarchs would become a queen, placing yet another Bourbon on a throne who would be sympathetic to France. In exchange, Luisetta's father agreed to the Louisiana Purchase with France.

Once the treaty was ratified by the continental powers, Napoleon began bribing Italy's deposed rulers to accept his plan. Queen Maria Carolina's daughter and son-in-law, Luisa and

Ferdinand III, were exiled from Tuscany and compensated with the Grand Duchy of Salzburg. In Parma and Spain, French ambassadors tried to show the Bourbons how Etruria was "greater, richer and more important than Parma." For a low ranking prince of a greater royal house to be given such a prominent kingdom was an "enticing bargain," according to France. Queen Luisa of Spain, that master manipulator who wanted her daughter to sit on a throne, added further pressure to Lodovico and Luisetta to take the offer. In the meantime, the Duchess of Parma was being given no say in the matter. She knew that if her son accepted the throne, he would be little more than "a puppet Duke of Parma" for France.[31]

Don Ferdinand was greatly opposed to the plan. He may have been simple minded when it came to politics, but his greatest wish was that Parma would remain intact. He stayed "calm and sure of his subjects," and refused to give up his country to Etruria.[32] His resoluteness enraged his sister, Queen Luisa, who was determined to see her daughter become a queen. In one of Luisa's typical outburst, she launched a venomous attack on her brother: "What an egoist he is! his only concern is with his own good pleasure and his own sacred purposes; he refuses to submit to the smallest inconvenience or to be in anyone's debt for anything. What a man!"[33]

Ferdinand refused to be intimidated, and pleaded with his son to do likewise, but by 1801 Lodovico's health had made him weak-willed and even more easily manipulated by the people around him. He could not resist the pressure from his mother-in-law or the influential Manuel de Godoy. The Infante Lodovico accepted the throne of Etruria, but only on the condition that Luisetta agree to it as well.

The road Luisetta faced was a difficult one, but Amalia of Parma would have been proud of the manner in which her daughter-in-law conducted herself. She refused to blindly take Napoleon's offer without listening to her own feelings. This sensitive young woman was already opposed to the plan on the sheer principle of usurping other people's hereditary lands just to give her a kingdom. Napoleon also stipulated that for the accession to be official, the royal couple must go to Paris to be crowned king and queen by him. Luisetta loathed the idea of going there after the executions of Louis XVI and Marie

Antoinette, but always the obedient daughter, she obeyed her mother in the end and went to Paris.

The announcement that Lodovico was named King of Etruria sent shockwaves across Europe. Never before had a military leader done anything as ambitious as this. Lodovico of Parma was now finding himself on the receiving end of some very harsh criticism for accepting the throne. But more than that, he was now, like his mother, in a very select group of Maria Theresa's descendants. Like Amalia and her four siblings who were the ruling children of the Empress, Lodovico and his cousins in Austria and Naples were destined to reign as well. Of Maria Theresa's fifty-five grandchildren, only nine were born to rule. Lodovico now shared a special connection with his cousins, but unlike any of his relatives, he had to travel to Paris to receive his crown from the very man who deposed his own parents.

Lodovico, Luisetta, and their son left Madrid in April 1801. Luisetta confided in her memoirs: "My grief was excessive at this separation from my family, and from my native country, to which I was, and indeed am, most sincerely attached."[34] When they arrived in France in May, there were mixed reactions to the new king and queen. "You see what these princes are," Napoleon said to one of his aides, his voice dripping with disdain; "sprung from the old blood, and especially those who have been educated at the southern courts."[35] But Luisetta made a very different impression on Napoleon and the Parisians. The First Consul was deeply impressed by the way she cared for and nurtured her family. Lodovico's health was terrible during their entire time in Paris, making both himself and Prince Carlo dependent on Luisetta, who herself was suffering from chills and a high fever.

Amalia of Parma's son made a far more ambivalent impression on French society than his wife did. As Napoleon's *valet de chambre* put it, Lodovico of Etruria "was endowed with very little wit and still less charm." And even though Napoleon called him "a good little prince," he never failed to notice how Lodovico "grumbles in an undertone at having to owe his elevation to the head of this cursed French Republic."[36]

While Amalia and Ferdinand waited anxiously for news from Paris, their son and daughter-in-law were in constant meetings with Napoleon. Gala parties were thrown by the highest members of the French government, but there was a sad irony to it all. These extravagances were not out of reverence to the King and Queen, but out of a desire to please Napoleon, who wanted opportunities to be able to observe "the character of the man on whom he had bestowed a kingdom" and his consort, a woman "who proved to be very agreeable."[37]

The First Consul could easily see the great differences that existed between the King and Queen of Etruria. Lodovico had still not outgrown his awkwardness. An observer at one of the many meetings noticed "he could not answer the simplest questions...without embarrassment."[38] In these moments, he turned to Luisetta for strength. She was his rock in every situation when he did not know what to do. She always knew the right thing to say to sooth her husband's easily frazzled nerves.

The King's fragile health in Paris was a source of deep concern for his mother. Amalia was constantly afraid for her son's well being in the den of vipers that was France. Each day, she awaited patiently the arrival of letters from Paris to keep her up to speed on everything that was happening, but news from her son was few and far between.

The young king never seemed to earn a reprieve in his health. In fact, one of the worst episodes for Lodovico was during the final days he spent with his family in Paris. The new King and Queen were to dine with Napoleon and his wife one evening, but on the way to dinner Lodovico suffered a violent epileptic seizure. He survived, but not without giving his wife the scare of her life. She feared she would be widowed at only fifteen. Lodovico recovered his strength, but neither he nor Luisetta realized how true her premonition of widowhood would actually be.

Moments like these revealed to everyone Luisetta's magnificent talent for exerting grace under pressure. No matter what the circumstance, this daughter-in-law of Amalia of Parma always exuded temperance and dignity. Her abilities earned her the highest esteem from Napoleon. She was a young woman who so elegantly "promenaded in the garden with a diadem, or flowers on her head, and in a robe with a train that swept the sand of the alleys."[39] For Napoleon, there was undoubtedly no contest. The success of Etruria rested with its queen.

Once the legwork for the new kingdom had been completed, the now-officially crowned King Lodovico I and Queen María Luísa of Etruria left France and headed south to Lodovico's beloved Parma in June 1801. "This journey was not very beneficial to our health," Luisetta remembered. "My husband was never very well after his stay at Paris, and my fever still continued."[40] Before they left, all eyes were fixed on Lodovico and Napoleon, who had "a long secret interview." No one knew exactly what went on, but in the words of one witness, "neither of them looked satisfied on coming out of it."[41] The two rulers would not meet again.

When news reached the Parmesan Court that Lodovico and his family were returning, Amalia was speechless with joy, a first for the fifty-five-year-old duchess. She planned the details of the reunion down to the letter. In July, Amalia, Ferdinand, and their daughters Carlotta and Tognina, headed north to the cozy palace at Piacenza to await the arrival of their son, daughter-in-law, and grandson. It was a deeply moving scene when mother and son were reunited after six long years. The Duke and Duchess embraced their son and his family with all their hearts. They instantly fell in love with Luisetta and their adorable grandson.

Words could not express how happy Amalia was to have her only son home again. The King and Queen were only able to stay for three weeks before heading south to Tuscany, which had since been reorganized into Etruria. Florence would be their new capital, with Parma being added to the kingdom after Don Ferdinand's death. It was bittersweet for Amalia that her son was now ruling the land that had been taken from her own nephew—Leopold's son Ferdinand III—but the irony seemed lost on Lodovico.

During the time Amalia spent with her son, she began to notice subtle differences since he left for Spain. His personality was still kind and gentle, but when he spoke Italian, he did so with a noticeable Spanish accent. Luisetta made a good impression on her in-laws, but she spoke little Italian, and when she did speak, it was usually mixed with Spanish.

In Parma, Luisetta wrote that "the tenderness with which I was treated by my husband's parents, the Duke and Duchess of Parma, and by his sisters, the princesses, restored me...to the enjoyment of happiness."[42] The time that Lodovico spent in Parma was cluttered by festivities to honor the new king and queen (at Napoleon's insistence). During the daytime, Lodovico and Ferdinand held audiences with dignitaries from Florence, Modena, and the other countries that had been absorbed into Etruria. While the King and the Duke attended state affairs, Luisetta and Amalia spent quality time getting to know one another.

The Duchess barely had the chance to adjust to Luisetta or Prince Carlo before it was time for them to leave Parma. In her memoirs, Luisetta wrote: "after three weeks passed…we set off for Florence. I felt real affliction at parting from the duke and duchess, since I loved them sincerely, and was beloved by them in return."[43] This was the last time that Amalia would see King Lodovico I. But she would always keep a close eye on her beloved son, especially in the tumultuous years that lay ahead.

"The Mother of My People"

After three years in Palermo, debt and inflation prompted the Sicilian parliament to force King Ferdinand back to Naples. Even the modest budget of the royal court proved too damaging to the fragile Sicilian economy. In June 1802, Ferdinand sailed to the mainland, and rode on horseback from Portici to Naples.

Charlotte, who was still in Vienna, was unable to be in Italy for the royal procession because of "an excruciating operation" for a hemorrhoid infection "which she bore stoically." When the time finally came for her to leave Austria, she dreaded returning to Naples because she believed her time had passed: "I leave as one condemned to death and certainly to torment for the rest of my life... I shall attend the Council [of State]; I shall deliver my opinion; but my door will be closed to every class and rank, as I do not wish to be accused of dealing with spies." She later wrote from Trieste, "unless I had children to marry, no force human or divine would have brought me back."[1]

Queen Maria Carolina finally returned to Naples in August 1802, to deafening silence. She alone was blamed for the failures of the country. Her absence for the past three years had weakened her influence to only a mere fraction of what it had been. Added to this were disease and worry, which had aged her prematurely.

Shortly after her return to Naples, the Queen was dealt another devastating blow when her daughter, Luisa, died in September. The Grand Duchess had been pregnant with her sixth child, but the delivery claimed the life of both mother and infant. In a move that touched Charlotte's heart during her grief, Luisa's body was buried in the imperial crypt in Vienna with her baby wrapped in her arms.

Grief was a powerful motivator in Charlotte's life. Like Maria Theresa, it fueled her concern for her remaining children. In particular, she focused much of her time and energy on preparing her daughter Maria Antonietta for her marriage to the Spanish crown prince. The princess was ambitious and intelligent; the Duchess D'Abrantès described her as "a charming creature, beautiful and interesting, able to converse in seven or eight languages, an excellent musician and artist, and, in short, a highly-accomplished woman."[2]

Since Maria Antonietta already had a strong desire to be married, she departed Naples without any reluctance or regrets. For Charlotte, saying goodbye was especially painful since she knew that she would probably never see her daughter again. "I thought the grief would kill me," she told one of her ambassadors.[3]

Ↄ

Almost immediately upon his arrival in Etruria, there was trouble brewing for Amalia's son, King Lodovico I. His family's new home was none other than the Pitti Palace, which had once belonged to Lodovico's uncle, Leopold. According to one witness, Lodovico and Luisetta found the royal palace "ransacked, and so unfurnished, that they were obliged to have recourse to the Tuscan nobility, to supply, in this emergency, what was indispensible to the immediate use of the court."[4]

Beyond their immediate accommodations, many of the troubles facing the King and Queen were not political in nature. Instead, they were confronted with the strong but divided sense of nationalism within Etruria. When Napoleon formed the kingdom, he did so with several smaller, previously independent nations, each of which fiercely valued its own sovereignty. Now, as Etruria's first king, the shy and withdrawn Lodovico had to confront a population who resented being forced to surrender their diverse national identities.

With the exception of his parents, support was a luxury that Lodovico did not seem to have; the people did not trust the King and Queen. Luisetta recalled those difficult early days in Florence: "Our hearts were somewhat depressed, because the people, seeing that we entered the kingdom surrounded by French troops, believed that we were of the same party."[5] King Lodovico did the best he could, exercising "a gentle rule, treading in the footsteps of Leopold,"[6] but the international community refused to take him seriously as a ruler. In their eyes, Lodovico and Luisetta were little more than Napoleon's puppets.

King Louis XVI's sister, Queen Clothilde of Sardinia, was living in exile in Naples. In a letter to a friend in October, she relayed the seriousness of the situation in Etruria:

> You will no doubt have heard that the King and Queen of Etruria have arrived, and are now installed at Florence. They are so little masters of themselves that, when walking in the Boboli gardens, they are always accompanied by two dragoons; the gardens are always closed to the public, and when they go to the Cassine, they have fifteen dragoons following them....the new Sovereigns behave very well; they show much affability, and great interest in religion. Still, it is better to be compelled by poverty to beg [for] one's bread than to exercise a pretended sovereignty in such a condition of slavery [to the French].[7]

The intolerable circumstances that Lodovico and Luisetta faced were an echo of the situation in Parma. Amalia and Ferdinand could do nothing without a regiment of French soldiers following them, watching their every move. The couple still had the freedom to come and go in the capital city as the pleased, but even the tiny amount of independence they enjoyed was about to be taken away.

In the hopes of intimidating the Duke and Duchess, Napoleon dispatched Moreau de St. Méry to be the French-appointed prime minister. Officially, he was sent to put the government in order, but it was widely known that Napoleon wanted him to keep a close eye on Don Ferdinand's actions. This made Amalia fear for her husband's life, and rightfully so, for the moment that her husband died, Parma would be annexed to Etruria. The idea that French forces might conspire to assassinate Ferdinand haunted his wife day and night.

That fear, combined with the trials plaguing her son and daughter-in-law, nearly wrecked Amalia's fragile nerves. She was helpless to come to the rescue of Lodovico and his family in Florence; since the arrival of the French army, her power and influence in her own country had evaporated. She feared for her husband's life, and was worried sick by the worsening situation in Italy. Disease, famine, civil war, and bankruptcy fired up her son's subjects against him. Amalia felt the world around her was spinning out of control, but nothing could have prepared her for the disastrous events she would face in less than a year.

St. Méry served as prime minister of Parma for only a short time before he was replaced by a new governor named Jean-Andoche Junot. Tall and handsome, Junot was relatively young when he arrived in Parma (he was only thirty-years-old), but his reputation had preceded him. He was a ruthless soldier who had fought and conquered much of Italy in Napoleon's army. Once he arrived in Parma, he proved that his reputation for being harsh and temperamental was well earned. He immediately went to work eradicating any forces that still opposed French rule. The last remnants of the Parmesan rebellion were rounded up and "severely punished," while many religious orders were completely banned from the country.[8] Junot also made sure that Ferdinand and Amalia were practically placed under house arrest in the Ducal Palace. Their hope was hanging by a thread.

Like Queen Maria Carolina, Amalia of Parma drew strength from her daughters in her times of despair; Tognina and Carlotta never left their mother's side. The princesses had inherited much of their father's piety and their mother's determination. Tognina in particular, who had always been quiet and reserved, began studying as a postulant nun in early 1802.

As for Princess Carlotta, Governor Junot—owing to his unpredictable personality—decided to recognize her status as a Royal Highness within the French Consulate and even secured for her a government allowance. The Duchess D'Abrantès recalled in her memoirs: "Junot wrote immediately to the Emperor

[Napoleon] that the Princess of Parma was entitled to a certain establishment which she did not enjoy, and asked his orders upon the subject. The establishment was instantly granted."[9] The disregard France had for Amalia and Ferdinand did not seem to carry over to their children, who were apparently considered innocents.

As the citizens of Parma were suffering under French occupation, Amalia was enraged by the decadent Spanish court's continuing neutrality while Europe was engulfed in one war after another. The Duchess and her sister-in-law, Queen Luisa, had always been bitter enemies, so it came as no surprise that Amalia was not invited to Barcelona for the double weddings of the Spanish and Neapolitan crown princes to their respective brides. However, since Luisetta's brother, the Prince of the Asturias, was marrying Lodovico's cousin, Maria Antonietta of Naples, it only made sense that the Queen of Spain wanted her favorite daughter to return home for the ceremonies.

By September 1802, Luisetta was nearly nine-months pregnant with her second baby. She was hesitant to travel in such a condition, but her mother was a formidable force to be reckoned with and pressured her daughter to submit. One of Queen María Luísa's friends suggested another reason why she would risk such a treacherous journey in her condition: "it was important, I believe, that her offspring should be born in Spain, in order to insure the privileges and inheritence [sic] allotted to *infants* of that realm. There is no other way to account for the risk her majesty incurred by embarking at such a moment..."[10]

The King, Queen, and their court left Florence for Livorno at the end of September, where they boarded a ship bound for Spain. While the Etrurian royal family was at sea in the Mediterranean heading for Barcelona, Luisetta went into labor on October 2. The birth was extremely traumatic, and threatened to claim the life of both mother and child. Once again showing her incredible strength, Luisetta pulled through and delivered a baby girl, but everyone aboard the ship believed the Queen and her daughter would not survive the voyage.

The situation became even more perilous when their ship was struck by a storm and nearly destroyed. By the time they reached Spain, they were a month late and the weddings had already taken place. When the ship finally made anchor in

Barcelona, Luisetta was too weak to even go ashore, and rested on the ship for three days. In her memoirs, she recalled the difficulty of her first days back in Spain since she first left to reign at Lodovico's side in Etruria:

> Immediately on our arrival, my father came to visit me, and it was determined that I should be brought on shore the next day, which took place accordingly; and, as it was only three days after my delivery, they took me up on the bed in which I lay, and lowered me through one of the port-holes of the ship into the boat; and, on our landing, placed me in a sort of litter, and so carried me to the palace. The next day my daughter was baptized by the names of Louisa Charlotte, after my parents.[11]

The first few days in the life of Amalia of Parma's newest grandchild were certainly turbulent. Clotilda Stisted, a friend of Queen María Luísa's, wrote: "The Princess Charlotte Louisa,* first saw the light during that voyage [to Spain], as I remember her royal highness telling us, remarking, that she was of no country, having been born at sea."[12]

After the Etrurian royal family settled in Barcelona, Amalia was not at all surprised that the marriage of the Spanish crown prince to Maria Carolina's daughter was falling apart at an alarming rate. "Antoinette is in despair. The life there is abominable, like that of five centuries ago," Maria Carolina wrote.[13]

Lodovico described to his mother how Crown Princess Maria Antonietta was practically kept under lock and key. She was forced to submit her letters to the Neapolitan ambassador for Queen Luisa's approval before being sent to her mother in Naples. The ambassador even threatened to dismiss members of her suite if any whisper of the truth got out. It broke Luisetta's heart that neither she nor her husband could intervene on behalf of the Princess of the Asturias. Their own bad health, and the needs of their new baby, limited what they were able to do from day to day.

Amalia's relief at Luisetta's and her granddaughter's survival was shattered just a few days later in what was to become one of

---

* Her full given names were Maria Louisa Charlotte, so it remains unclear why Stisted refers to her as "Charlotte Louisa."

the most difficult moments in the Duchess's entire life. Stress had begun to take a toll on Don Ferdinand's health. On October 9, 1802, he decided to take a day trip in the hopes of reinvigorating himself. He visited the convent of St. Alessandro, and planned to spend the rest of the day at the healing baths of Fontevivo, in the countryside just outside the capital city. Shortly after he arrived at Fontevivo, Ferdinand, Duke of Parma, suddenly collapsed and died. He was fifty-one.

Ferdinand was deeply loved by all his subjects, even more so after the French invasion. His death sent the entire nation into deep mourning. Amalia was devastated by the loss of her husband. Their thirty-three year marriage had been a rocky one, but as the Duke and Duchess grew older together, they grew closer to each other, and were united into their devotion to Parma. Standing by the grieving duchess's side throughout the ordeal were her daughters Carlotta and Tognina. Dressed in black with long flowing veils, Amalia and her daughters followed Ferdinand's coffin as it wound its way through the packed streets of Parma to the Sanctuary of the Santa Maria della Steccata where he was buried.

The loss of Ferdinand was made all the more painful for Amalia when rumors began to circulate that his death had not been natural. Most people agreed that the Duke had been poisoned, but it was a more difficult question to answer of who was behind it. The most popular stories claimed that Amalia had murdered her husband in an effort to gain back her lost power. This story made little sense, because the moment Ferdinand died, Parma would be absorbed into Etruria. This gave credence to the most popular culprit, the French. To the wise and educated in Parma, it was only logical that Ferdinand had outlived his usefulness to the impatient Napoleon, who ordered his spies to murder the duke.

Whatever the rumors may have claimed, the moment King Lodovico got word of his father's death, he wanted to rush back to Italy immediately. Luisetta wrote about the harrowing days that followed for her husband: "A few days after our arrival, we received the news of the death of the Duke of Parma, my father-in-law. This was a great affliction to my husband, who was then extremely ill, his cough having so much increased, that the Spanish physicians thought it adviseable to send him back to

Florence immediately, where he might remain undisturbed."[14] Lodovico's troubling health, and the queen's slow recovery from her traumatic *accouchement* added even greater hardship for the couple. These issues, combined with pressure from King Carlos IV and Queen Luisa, forced Lodovico and his family to postpone their departure until at least December.

In Parma, Amalia and her court were given little time to grieve the loss of Ferdinand before Napoleon served them with an eviction notice. He did not care where they went, but Parma was now the property of the Kingdom of Etruria by the authority of France. The now-deposed duchess had no place in Italy. As 1802 drew to a close, she and her unmarried daughters packed up and left, destined to spend the short time they had left in exile. She said goodbye to the small country that had been her home for more than thirty years. There were few places in Europe that were willing to take in the infamous duchess, her family, and the handful of maids and servants that volunteered to join them. The only place left for them was in the Habsburg lands.

Emperor Francis II was never especially close to any of his aunts living abroad. During the French Revolution, he spoke with eloquent words but was generally indifferent to the plight of his aunt, Marie Antoinette. When Amalia informed her nephew that she and her family were fleeing into exile, the emperor sent them north to Prague on a journey that lasted months, out of his way and far from Vienna.

Their new home was the Hradschin Palace, part of the current Prague Castle complex. A dark, drafty, imposing fortress of a building, the only redeemable quality it possessed, in Amalia's eyes, was that it was reportedly the largest castle in the world. Besides that, there were few comforts to it. The Duchess spent most of her time locked up in her medieval-inspired bedroom writing, knitting, or sometimes simply staring out the window in silence. Her daughters spent most of their time in the castle's church complex, the world famous St. Vitus Cathedral. There, they spent hours in prayer surrounded by exquisite stained-glass windows and armored-covered tombs of old Bohemian kings.

Though she was finally free of the oppressive tyranny of the French occupying forces, Amalia's life in Prague was filled with

357

little joy. A few weeks after settling down at Hradschin, a messenger arrived at the castle with a piece of news that shattered what was left of her delicate emotional state. Her son, King Lodovico I of Etruria, had died "of an acute fever."[15] Recalling the most painful moment of her life, Lodovico's wife Luisetta wrote with her characteristic calm: "on the 27th of May, 1803, five months after our return from Spain, I was left a widow, at the age of twenty-one, with two infants."[16]

The death of her son pushed the Duchess to the point of collapse. Like her mother before her, Amalia started wearing only black. She rarely saw anyone except her daughters. She was utterly heartbroken, but also felt deep compassion and pity for her widowed daughter-in-law, whose life was becoming more difficult with each passing day. Luisetta was named queen-regent for her young son, who took the name King Lodovico II, but her seat on the Etrurian throne was now in a precarious position, since the rightful king was only a child.

CB

When Francesco, Duke of Calabria, returned from his wedding in Barcelona, public reaction to his new bride ranged from shock to indignation. Princess Isabel was a mere child, only thirteen, but for the sake of her son and the dynasty, Charlotte sought to find some good in her new daughter-in-law. She admitted that Isabel had "a fine, fresh healthy face, not Bourbon in the least," but "she is null in every respect, knowledge, ideas, curiosity." Charlotte summed up Isabel's personality simply: "Nothing, absolutely nothing."[17]

The problem was compounded by the fact that the new Duchess of Calabria spoke neither French nor Italian and only a little Spanish. Francesco enlisted tutors for his young wife, but Queen Maria Carolina believed Isabel had the intellectual capacity of her four-year-old granddaughter: "I have tried to praise and enliven her. She feels nothing; she merely laughs" like an "automaton."[18]

By contrast, Maria Antonietta's charming and vivacious personality was forcing her to suffer the wrath of her mother-in-law. The crown princess's life in Spain was only growing worse with time. She wrote to her mother: "you have been deceived.

358

For you are too good a mother to have sacrificed me like this if you had known."[19] Unlike Maria Theresa, Queen Maria Carolina's motherly instincts outweighed her sense of duty. In one of her last letters to Maria Antonietta, the Queen wrote:

> My daughter, I can scarcely conceive how you endure what you described to me....There is no throne that can be worth being purchased so dearly....Rather leave Spain and come back to me. But if you cannot resolve to leave [Fernando], from whom you derive the little share of happiness you enjoy in that country, then, my daughter, learn to be not a weak woman, but a great and courageous Princess. Recollect the words of Catherine II: *It is better to kill the devil than to let the devil kill us!*[20]

Her daughter's situation broke Charlotte's heart. She told one of her confidants, "I cannot have a moment's peace knowing my dear child to be so miserable."[21]

Maria Antonietta's cultivated and refined personality earned her daggers from her mother-in-law, Queen Luisa. The Duchess D'Abrantès explained what was at the root of the bitter relationship between the queen and the crown princess:

> A mother-in-law has not a mother's heart. A mother is proud of the merit of a daughter; a mother-in-law is jealous of it. The Queen of Naples...cherished an affection for her *learned* yet unaffected daughter; but the Queen of Spain contracted her black eyebrows, and from the first day she saw her [Maria Antonietta] conceived an antipathy which was soon converted into hatred of her charming daughter-in-law, who in the Court circle spoke to each Ambassador in the language of his nation. Alas! the hatred produced by the envy of a woman has something horrible in its results.[22]

The one bright spot in Maria Antonietta's unfortunate existence was her marriage. She and her husband, Prince Fernando, loved and cared for each other deeply. The happy marriage "of this unfortunate pair was the only consolation they experienced in a life full of continually renewed grief and trouble."[23]

By 1803, Europe was at the brink of war again. The complex series of treaties, armistices, and ceasefires had failed, and it appeared as if Napoleon were preparing to storm the continent for a second time. He had already annexed Poland and Elba and refused to abandon the territories he conquered in Germany. He also blatantly violated the Treaty of Lunéville by occupying neutral Switzerland. By the spring, France had all but disregarded its treaty with Naples. In May, French troops landed in Naples and occupied the strategically important seaports of Taranto and Brindisi. According to the French government, they were "obliged in self-defense to retake the territories [they] had held prior to the ratification of that treaty," which supposedly included the ports.[24]

Queen Maria Carolina did everything in her power to prevent a second invasion by France. She stayed in close contact with Lord Nelson, who told her that "my orders for the safety of the Two Sicilies will always be exactly executed, and to this end my whole soul goes in unison with my orders...I would rather fight twice our number of forces, than risk for a moment seeing your Royal person and family fall into the hands of the French."[25] Still, the rest of Europe seemed to take little interest in the plight of faraway Naples.

Eventually, Maria Carolina made a direct appeal to Napoleon himself:

> The entry of the French troops in our kingdom, which is at peace with France...ruins us above all with the enormous and unexpected burden of defraying their cost. Our country has suffered too much from war, the subsequent anarchy and the formidable price of peace... I speak as the mother of my children and my people. I ask you to relieve us of this burden of troops in a neutral company, and of the appalling expense of supporting them.[26]

Charlotte's plea fell on deaf ears, for Napoleon believed that anyone who was not with him was against him. She wrote to Empress Teresa in Austria, "it is as if we were assaulted on the public highway" by France. And later, she told a friend that Napoleon's actions were "worthy of Robespierre."[27]

☙

During her life in exile, Amalia continued to be plagued by one tragedy after another. In March 1804, her daughter Carolina died in Dresden. As an added insult, her son-in-law Prince Max of Saxony, who already was in no position to inherit the throne, was becoming famous for little more than "his faithful and devoted adherence to Napoleon."[28] Max's unwavering support for Napoleon was no less than a slap in the face to Amalia.

The former duchess continued as best she could to take an active interest in the welfare her German grandchildren. Now that she was in Prague, staying up to date on her grandchildren in nearby Dresden was a good deal easier. When their mother died, the little Princess Amalia and her siblings were looked after by their aunts, the Electress of Saxony and the Princess Theresa, Leopold II's daughter.

Amalia watched from Prague as her granddaughters were raised with "great strictness." Sadly, she would not live to see her namesake, Princess Amalia, become the "accomplished authoress" Amelia Heiter.[29] As one of the most famous German authors of the nineteenth century, this princess of Saxony would have made her grandmother proud by her willfulness and independence.

Two months after Carolina died, Napoleon dealt another bitter blow to the royals of Europe in May 1804 when he was crowned Emperor of the French. The ceremony in Paris, which lasted more than four hours, was presided over by Pope Pius VII and was intended to show the glory the emperor had brought back to France and the triumph over his enemies.

In Prague, the princesses Carlotta and Tognina continued to live with their mother, humbled and forgotten. The former duchess was suffering from poor health brought on by the stress of her circumstances; apoplexy was taking its course. In the last days of her life, Amalia was stripped of her titles, robbed of her ducal throne, and remained unacknowledged by her family in Austria as her nephew Francis II preoccupied himself with his war against Napoleon.

The empire in which Amalia lived her last days was a dream and a shadow of the thriving Habsburg realm in which she had grown up. Her parents and almost all of her siblings were gone. Her brother Ferdinand was living in Modena until he too was deposed by Napoleon; and Archduchess Elizabeth, now well into her sixties, was living at an abbey in Linz. Her brothers the emperors were dead, and she had no contact with Francis II or his family. Alone and forgotten, Amalia, Duchess of Parma, Piacenza, and Guastalla, died in Prague on June 18, 1804. Any number of maladies was attributed to her death, but this once scandalous and brazen consort succumbed to age and infirmity.

The funeral for Amalia was small and unremarkable. Carlotta and Tognina mourned their mother with as much stateliness as they could afford, but only a few members of Francis II's household represented the Emperor at her funeral, which was held at the Cathedral of St. Vitus. Her body was laid to rest in the church's cavernous mausoleum alongside some of the greatest kings in Bohemian history. Amalia, the eldest reigning daughter of Maria Theresa, took her rightful place in the halls of her ancestors that had gone before her, far away and out of sight from her beloved Vienna, never to return again.

The Passing of an Age

"Towards the close of 1805, the year of Trafalgar and Austerlitz, the affairs of the kingdom of Naples had reached a crisis; a remarkable series of events was soon to overtake it."[1] These were the words that one historian used to describe one of the most fateful years in Neapolitan history.

The situation on continental Europe had been perilous for some time. After the uneasy Treaty of Amiens was signed in March 1802, Europe was at peace for the first time in a decade. Not content to see French superiority in Europe, Great Britain declared war the following year. Unfortunately for England, Austria, and their allies, France's armies unleashed a deadly onslaught upon them. In 1805, Vienna fell to French troops, but the worst humiliation for the Habsburg empire was still to come.

On December 2, 1805, French, Austrian, and Russian forces collided in the historic Battle of Austerlitz on a lush, green field in eastern Bohemia. It was the most ambitious, critical battle of the Napoleonic Wars up until that point and promised to place Europe solely in the hands of the victors. Within a matter of hours, Napoleon's troops had dealt a crippling blow to the Austrian and Russian armies, and there was no choice for the two empires but to surrender. Napoleon wrote proudly to his wife Joséphine, "I have beaten the Austro-Russian army commanded by the two emperors."[2]

The French newspaper *Moniteur* proudly reported the details of the devastating battle: "Forty thousand prisoners. Seventy pieces of artillery. The Guard of the Emperor of Russia routed and a part captured, including several officers and a colonel. The two emperors of Russia and Austria on the point of being taken and ran away in all haste to Olmütz."[3] As a military leader, Francis II had "gambled by proxy" with his army "and lost every throw."[4] When Russia's Tsar Alexander realized his fate was now up to Napoleon, he uttered: "We are babies in the hands of a giant."[5]

Napoleon could think of nothing more fitting for the Holy Roman Empire than to dismantle it completely. At the Treaty of Pressburg on December 26, 1805, Napoleon abolished the empire that had been founded by Charlemagne himself. That body which had united the German nations of Europe for a thousand years was gone. Emperor Francis II was spared the humiliation of his country being downgraded to an insignificant archduchy. Instead, the Habsburg crown lands were unified into a single empire, with Maria Carolina's son-in-law being styled as His Imperial Majesty, Francis I, Emperor of Austria.[*]

Once Austria was vanquished, Napoleon set his sights on retaking Naples once and for all. He wrote to his brother on New Year's Eve that he planned "to take possession of the kingdom of Naples" and wanted to know the instant his forces had "driven out the treacherous Court, and subjected that part of Italy to our authority."[6] Napoleon made it clear that he wanted "to punish the Queen of Naples, and to cast from the throne that guilty woman who has so often and with so much effrontery profaned every law, human and divine."[7]

A day after he dismantled the Holy Roman Empire, Napoleon assembled his troops for a final assault on the Two Sicilies. He told them passionately: "The House of Naples has ceased to reign; its existence is incompatible with the repose of Europe, and with the honor of my crown.... Hasten to inform me that all Italy is ruled by my laws..."[8] Napoleon wanted his brother Joseph to reign once they were able to depose Ferdinand IV: "I intend my blood to reign in Naples, as long as it does in France: the kingdom of Naples is necessary to me."[9]

On January 23, 1806, King Ferdinand IV fled to Palermo ahead of the oncoming French army for the second time in less

---

[*] Francis was the second Holy Roman emperor with that name, but he was the first emperor of the new Austrian empire. This is why he is referred to as Francis I.

than ten years. The rest of the royal family stayed in Naples. Prince Francesco and his brother Leopoldo headed north to Calabria to represent the House of Bourbon to the occupying army. The Duke of Calabria and the Prince of Salerno wanted to make sure that as little damage as possible was done to Naples in the course of the takeover.

As she prepared her country for invasion, Queen Maria Carolina was transformed. For the first time in years, she was again truly the Daughter of Maria Theresa. She remembered her mother's role as Queen of Hungary and the prosperity and unity she brought to her lands during the most difficult days of her reign. Charlotte stayed on in Naples to organize the resistance movement, and her spirit was more indomitable than ever.

The royal family's final days in Naples were filled with sadness and heartache. In one of her last letters to Empress Teresa before leaving, Charlotte wrote: "We spend the days in all the horrors of packing and in tears. I am prepared for anything, but shall endeavour to die without remorse. My daughter-in-law [Isabel]...sees all the packing going on and everyone crying, and she is just like a log, understanding and feeling nothing. Her husband is all fire, preparation, honour, and courage, and I pity him. Leopold is also full of enthusiasm, but it can only end in horror."[10]

On February 11, 1806, Queen Maria Carolina bid farewell to Naples for the last time. Her daughter, Princess Maria Amelia, recalled in her journal how the entire court visited the palace chapel for Mass before leaving: "After the service mamma addressed the Court in touching words of farewell; nothing but tears and sobs were heard. I felt my heart breaking."[11] With those final acts, the Queen, her daughters, the Duchess of Calabria, her two granddaughters, and the royal suite embarked on the heavily escorted Neapolitan frigate *Archimede* bound for Sicily.

The Queen wrote to Teresa: "I fear we shall never see Naples again. This thought overwhelms me; it is a dreadful misfortune, a crying injustice, for which I hope God will give us compensation."[12] The city of Naples fell to the French three days later. Napoleon declared that the Bourbons had forfeited the crown, and went ahead with placing his brother Joseph on the throne. "By the legitimate right of conquest," France announced, "[Napoleon] having become lord of the kingdoms of Naples and Sicily, appointed his brother, Joseph Bonaparte, king."[13]

This second exile put King Ferdinand back on the throne of Sicily, but this time it was at the sole discretion of the British government, who had been keeping a very close eye on the Royal Family of Naples. Maria Carolina had once been a trusted friend and ally to Great Britain, but her meddlesome ambition forced her to outlive her usefulness to London. Britain's interest in Ferdinand and Charlotte was now purely political. Ferdinand IV had become little more than a puppet-king in Sicily.

Life in Palermo was much as it had been the first time. Ferdinand went hunting, Amélie and Mimi visited convents on the island and took up the causes of local charities, and Charlotte shut herself up in the bleak, bare Colli Palace. The only person who seemed to enjoy anything on the island was King Ferdinand. The British ambassador to Sicily, Hugh Elliot, wrote back to London that the King was "immensely enjoying this period of his life," when he could indulge his love of outdoor activities and not be burdened by the duties of ruling.[14] Charlotte found nothing enjoyable or pleasurable about her life in Sicily. In fact, over the next twelve months, her life would go from bad to worse.

In May 1806, her daughter in Spain, Maria Antonietta, died. The Princess of the Asturias contracted tuberculosis, and endured an agonizing death. "I could no longer endure the sound of her piercing shrieks," wrote her friend, the Duchess D'Abrantès.[15] Maria Antonietta's cries were so shattering that the only person who could endure remaining at her bedside was her husband, Fernando. When Charlotte was told the news, she was devastated. She did not even receive any kind of notification from Spain, but read her daughter's obituary in a Neapolitan newspaper, the *Moniteur*. "It *cannot* be true!" she cried; "there has been no messenger to announce it from Madrid; or would they have the infamy not to write to me?"[16]

Shortly after Maria Antonietta's death, rumors began to circulate that it was not tuberculosis that killed her. The Duchess D'Abrantès admitted: "Strange reports were circulated respecting the illness of the Princess of the Asturias. The affair was enveloped in mystery; but in confidential conversation the terrible word *poison* was hinted by persons attached to the Queen [of Spain]."[17] No doubt it was an attempt by Queen Luisa to find a daughter-in-law more to her liking.

As she mourned for her poor daughter, Charlotte consoled herself with the fact that her sons were joining the family in Sicily. Once it became obvious that Francesco and Leopoldo were of no use in Calabria, they sailed for Palermo. Leopoldo lived with his mother and sisters in the Colli Palace, and Francesco settled his wife and children on a small farm outside the city. The queen continued to be thankful for her eldest son's strong moral character, and praised the Duke of Calabria to his sister, Empress Teresa: "Franz is a thoroughly good man...he bears with resignation what is laid upon us." But time had not healed her relationship with Francesco's wife, Isabel. "Franz alone looks after the children, for his wife does not love them, but often says she hates children," she told Teresa.[18]

Charlotte used Isabel's failings as an excuse to take a more active role in caring for Francesco's children herself. She showered love and affection on all her grandchildren. She was especially close to her granddaughter, Carolina of Calabria, who was Francesco's daughter from his marriage to Clementine. Years later, Carolina remembered her relationship with her grandmother fondly: "I habitually received the tenderest care from my family. The Queen lavished continual attentions on me, for which I shall be eternally grateful."[19] Charlotte and her granddaughter developed a deep bond that would last for the rest of their lives. But it broke her heart that her grandchild "commenced her wandering life, by passing and repassing the sea, backwards and forewards to Sicily, in consequence of the foreign warfare and civil discord which then shook Italy from north to south."[20]

Maria Carolina was also deeply interested in her Austrian grandchildren, who continued to hold a special place in her heart. The archdukes and archduchesses were especially in her thoughts and prayers when tragedy struck in 1807. Empress Teresa had steadily produced "thirteen children in seventeen years,* without ever losing her composure," but during her fourteenth pregnancy she "was seized with a chill, which

---

* Since Maria Carolina's visit in 1800, Teresa had delivered Caroline (1802-1832), Franz Karl (1802-1878), Maria Anna (1804-1858), and Johann Nepomuk (1805-1809).

developed rapidly into inflammation of the lungs."[21] She went into premature labor and delivered a daughter named Amalia in April 1807, but the infant died three days later. The Empress died of her own illness within a week.

Teresa's death "severed Maria Carolina's closest tie with her native land." One historian believed that her passing "was perhaps the heaviest blow and deepest sorrow of her [Charlotte's] life."[22] She wrote to Emperor Francis a few days later, "God has chosen to bereave me of her upon whom I depended to take my place with my dear children."[23] After a state funeral, Empress Teresa was buried in the Capuchin Church in Vienna alongside the great Habsburg emperors and empresses who had gone before her.

Teresa's death came as a devastating loss to her entire family, both in Naples and in Vienna. Her daughter, Archduchess Marie Louise, wrote to a friend of the "terrible loss of our dear Mamma."[24] And when Charlotte's grandson, Archduke Joseph, died in June 1807, the imperial family was still grieving the loss of Teresa. "He [Joseph] is happy in having found in heaven our dear Mamma, whose death still causes us much grief," Marie Louise wrote.[25]

While Charlotte was grieving for her family in Austria, she was shocked when Emperor Francis remarried only ten months later, this time to Princess Maria Ludowika of Modena.* One contemporary noted that Francis had "lived with the Empress Theresa in the most happy union, but he bore the loss of the mother of his twelve children with singular apathy."[26] It came as a crippling blow to Maria Carolina when her Austrian grand-children so quickly "loved their young stepmother," who was not only "intelligent," but "agreeable and cultivated" too.[27]

The Neapolitan royal family had always been close knit, and when these latest tragedies struck, the Queen clung to her daughters Mimi and Amélie for support. What Maria Carolina did not realize was that changes were in store for her family once again.

Mimi had fallen in love with the Crown Prince of Sardinia, Carlo Felice. Charlotte was sad to lose any more of her daughters, but Carlo Felice was as devoted to God as Mimi was.

---

* Maria Ludowika was also a granddaughter of Maria Theresa. She was the daughter of Archduke Ferdinand, Duke of Modena. She and Emperor Francis were first cousins.

He was their highest priority. The queen heartily approved of the crown prince, and they had a magnificent wedding in March 1807 at the Romanesque cathedral in Palermo, followed by three days of celebrations. In September, the pair left Sicily for the court of Carlo Felice's uncle, the King of Sardinia.

Maria Carolina, now fifty-five, was saddened by Mimi's departure. For much of the next year, she was depressed and alone, save for her last unmarried daughter, Princess Maria Amelia. Amélie, as she was known within the family, had grown into a tall, elegant woman. Now twenty-five, she clearly took after her Habsburg relatives. She possessed the same aquiline nose, high forehead, and protruding bottom lip. Her role in the family changed once Mimi left. With no suitable bachelors in sight, she was expected to stay at her mother's side. No one, least of all Charlotte, could ever have believed that Amélie would soon fall in love, and with the son of the man who sentenced Louis XVI to death.

In June 1809, Palermo was energized by the arrival of Louis Philippe, Duc d'Orléans. This thirty-five-year-old member of the French royal family was none other than the son of Philippe Égalité, the *ci-devant* Duc d'Orléans who turned republican to save himself during the Revolution. Égalité was the same man who Princess Marie Thérèse of France believed incited the October Riot at Versailles, and who voted for executing King Louis and Queen Marie Antoinette.

Louis Philippe had come to Sicily to ask for Amélie's hand in marriage. As a naval officer, he made frequent stops to Palermo. In time, his acquaintance with the princess turned into a deep love and admiration for her. He also hoped to reinstate himself with his Bourbon cousins and erase the treachery of his father. He believed that "the greater the faults of my father, the more I am bound to prove that I do not share his errors; they have done too much evil in my family."[28] Charlotte had never forgiven Philippe Égalité for what he had done. Now, more than fifteen years later, she dreaded meeting his son. His very title, Duc d'Orléans, brought back bitterly painful memories for her.

Charlotte finally agreed to meet Louis Philippe, and it turned out to be a meeting neither of them would ever forget. An avid journal keeper (which was very popular among royals at the

369

time), Louis Philippe wrote an account of that fateful first meeting:

> The Queen awaited me at the top of the steps at the entrance of her residence at Tamastro; when I presented myself she took my hand and led me into her room; there, standing in the recess of a window, she held my head between her hands and gazed at me for some time without speaking. At last she said: "I ought to detest you and yet I feel a liking for you."[29]

The meeting went relatively smoothly from that point on. Louis Philippe said the Queen "was no angel, but was pleased with her."[30] In the end, she accepted this "very-Bourbon looking" young man for her daughter on the grounds he spoke frankly to her about the past. "I forgive you everything on the condition that I know everything," she told him.[31] The pair spent the rest of the afternoon locked in the Queen's apartments as he revealed the grisly truth about Marie Antoinette's tragic last years in France.

That evening, Charlotte finally allowed Louis Philippe to see her daughter. In her journal, Maria Amelia recorded her first meeting with him: "Mamma sent for Isabel and me, and presented the Duke of Orléans. He is of the ordinary height, rather inclined to be stout, in appearance neither handsome nor ugly. He has the features of the house of Bourbon, and is very polite and well-educated."[32] Amélie "had the good sense to see and appreciate his intellectual endowments, and the moral purity with which his character was elevated and adorned."[33]

Amélie quickly accepted his proposal, and they were married in Palermo on November 25, 1809. But outside the close-knit royal family, there was indignation at the marriage. When it came to her daughter's wedding, Charlotte recalled that "Europe was astounded to see one of the principle accomplices in the death of Louis XVI and of Marie Antoinette[,] all still fuming over their blood so precious, sharing the bed of the niece of these august victims of the faction of Orleans." The small, private ceremony was held in Ferdinand's bedroom because he was confined to his bed, the result of "a very dangerous fall."[34] The bride was dressed in white Sicilian fabric topped off with a diamond tiara. Years later, Amélie recalled her wedding day: "My legs trembled under me, knowing as I did the sanctity and the strength of the vows I was uttering." But the groom's resounding "Yes" filled her "heart with courage."[35]

One witness who was in Palermo for the wedding wrote of the celebrations that followed: "In Sicily they are all delighted.... The court there is very gay at present, the Duke of Orleans being lately married to the Princess Amelia, who appeared to be a mild and pleasing woman."[36] At the time of their wedding, the couple had almost nothing. Both Maria Amelia and Louis Philippe's families were deposed, but according to Queen Maria Carolina, they were "poor but happy, and love each other infinitely."[37] The Duc and Duchesse would share a happy, love-filled marriage for the rest of their lives.

As a wedding gift to his daughter, King Ferdinand IV gave the couple "a large and ancient villa" called Santa Teresa, which was later renamed the Palazzo d'Orléans. The following year, Amélie gave birth to a son there, Ferdinand Philippe, who was given the French title Duc de Chartres. Now that her last daughter was married, Charlotte could boast of being the "mother-in-law to an emperor [Francis I] of whom she was an aunt, as well as to two monarchs [the future kings of France and Sardinia]; while already she had been sister to two successive emperors."[38]

Amélie's wedding marked the last time that Queen Maria Carolina and King Ferdinand came together in an official capacity. He blamed her for every misfortune that had befallen him, and the strong marriage they once enjoyed had all but dissolved. "The King is very angry with her; his love is long gone by," wrote Lord Nelson.[39]

The last years of Maria Carolina's life were ones of abject humiliation. In 1810 she was publicly embarrassed when her granddaughter, Archduchess Marie Louise, married Napoleon Bonaparte to secure a new peace between France and Austria. She could not believe that Emperor Francis would offer up her own granddaughter as a bargaining chip for peace. The Queen remembered how the "whole Court was witness both to the surprise...and the profound sorrow that" was felt about the wedding.[40]

Europe's staunch royalists were appalled by the marriage, which helped legitimize Napoleon's claim as emperor. The Austrian ambassador to France admitted: "I pity the princess, but let her remember that it is a fine thing to bring peace to such good people!"[41] However offensive the idea of her grand-daughter marrying Napoleon might have been, it actually worked out for Charlotte's benefit. As Empress of the French, Marie Louise implored her husband to leave Sicily alone. Napoleon was now more than happy to oblige on behalf of his "grandmother, the Queen of Sicily."[42]

With Napoleon's anger turning away from her for the moment, Charlotte was forced to deal with another crisis, this one much closer to home. By 1813 Sicily's British allies had become tired of the queen's meddling influence. With only the slightest force of pressure, the British minister on the island, William Bentinck, convinced King Ferdinand to banish his wife from his kingdom forever.

When the British general delivered the news to Charlotte of her expulsion, she reacted "as tactfully as possible" with the expected flurry of emotions: rage, indignation, and accusations. "Was it for this that I helped Nelson to win the battle of the Nile?" she asked the British officer. "For this, that I brought your army to Sicily? General, is this your English honor?" Afterwards, the general observed, "the daughter of Maria Theresa, at all times a majestic woman, was terrible in her rage."[43]

Once Maria Carolina realized she had been beaten, she sent the British ministry "a proud and eloquent protest" denying the authority of Britain to separate her from her family and remove her status as queen, but yielded for the sake of her family. In a last gesture to the man she called husband for forty-three years, she wrote a letter to King Ferdinand IV. She pitied him, she forgave him, but she could never forgive the "wretches" that surrounded him. According to Maria Carolina, Ferdinand's reign sat upon the edge of a knife. She offered her prayers for his happiness and that of the kingdom.[44]

The only place Maria Carolina could think of to go in her exile was Austria. For the first time since Marie Louise married Napoleon, the Queen wrote to her nephew and son-in-law, Francis I: "Will your majesty grant me a refuge in one of your cities, Brünn, Graz, or Salzburg, to finish my unhappy life there?"[45] The Emperor had little sympathy for the aunt who had caused him so much grief. William Bentinck claimed that

Francis "approved very much what had been done in Sicily....He approved of the Queen being sent away from Sicily. He was embarassed [*sic*] by the Queen's letter asking for permission to go to Vienna," but at the same time, he "thought he could not refuse."[46] The Emperor sent a formal reply back to Palermo that the queen could take refuge in Vienna.

Once the arrangements had been made, the time came for Maria Carolina to say goodbye to her family. The separation from her children and grandchildren was heart wrenching for the sixty-year-old queen. "Pray for me my children, I stand in great need of your prayers," she told them.[47] Her granddaughter, Princess Carolina of Calabria, "loved her grandmother tenderly, and it was with profound grief that she saw her depart."[48] The Queen's one consolation came from the fact that Prince Leopoldo refused to be parted from his mother's side and was accompanying her into exile.

The journey to Vienna lasted eight exhausting months. Empress Teresa was dead, and Charlotte was no longer in good standing with her British allies. This daughter of Maria Theresa was now "a wanderer, an outcast,"[49] with nothing left but to journey home in disgrace. Her children pleaded with Emperor Francis to receive their mother hospitably. Maria Amelia wrote to Francis that her mother's "departure plunges me into the deepest affliction."[50] King Ferdinand, too, wrote a letter to the Emperor. He begged his nephew to receive his wife and son, because "for reasons very displeasing [to me], my dear wife being obliged to leave this kingdom...to avoid greater misfortunes to us both."[51]

The course of the journey was so erratic that Charlotte and Leopoldo traveled through the Ionian Sea and onto Istanbul and St. Petersburg before reaching the eastern border of the Habsburg lands. Her travelling companions were amazed at the Charlotte because "she had seen and suffered so much, and she lent herself so graciously to conversation! The Queen was most amiable and talkative," which caused those traveling with her to greatly enjoy her company. The voyage to Austria saw Maria Carolina become a Habsburg again after forty years as a Bourbon queen. On the long journey, she shared many stories from her turbulent life and reign,

She remembered her mother, the august Maria Theresa, whose children respected her deeply, she said, but who were very much afraid of her. And her brother Joseph: 'He had had love affairs with nearly all the beauties in Vienna!' And Marie Antoinette: 'Poor Sister! The world was at your feet…Hail Mary, full of grace… Alas, what became of all that!' And the Princess of Asturias her daughter, who died so young, poisoned!...[52]

Maria Carolina finally arrived in Vienna on February 2, 1814 and was granted the courtesy title Queen of Sicily by the imperial court. She settled into a quiet life at the pastoral Hetzendorf Castle near Schönbrunn. An old Baroque building with marble floors and gold artwork, Hetzendorf was a comfortable reminder to Charlotte of her happy childhood, and was a far cry from the squalid conditions she endured at the Colli Palace in Palermo. In Vienna, the Queen was determined to maintain her status and honors as much as she was allowed. Along with Prince Leopoldo and the bevy of servants that accompanied them, she maintained as dignified an atmosphere as possible at the picturesque Hetzendorf.

In the last major public appearance of her life, Queen Maria Carolina joined the imperial family at the theatre in Vienna ten days after her arrival. The Baroness du Montet, a lady-in-waiting to Empress Maria Ludowika, described the Queen's entrance in her memoirs:

The hall was brilliantly lighted, and the loudest acclamations announced the Empress, who saluted with infinite grace. Shortly after, in the same box, appeared the Queen of Naples, and it seemed that she was trying to hide behind the Empress so as not to distract the public from the double homage it rendered, both for the Emperor's anniversary and for the recent victory [of Blücher at Brienne]. But this delicate modesty could not restrain the enthusiastic applause with which everybody expressed sympathy for this last living daughter of Maria Theresa. The Queen of Naples bowed lightly in acknowledgement... I watched Maria Carolina with attention and curiosity... How old she had grown! How bent and curved by the blows of sorrow!

That night at the theatre, the Baroness saw a very different woman than the one who had so bravely travelled to Naples at the tender age of sixteen to fulfill her destiny. As she stood before Vienna's high society surrounded by her family, Maria Carolina had become an elderly, white-haired woman hardly able to "bear the weight of her crown." Here was a woman who "seemed to be tenderly interested" in the grandchildren surrounding her, especially the shy and awkward Crown Prince Ferdinand.[53]

Maria Carolina's days in Vienna brought a renewed energy to her life, and her spirits were lifted tremendously when it was announced that a series of disastrous campaigns led to the collapse of the armies of France. Prussia, Austria, Great Britain, and Russia allied in a final assault to topple Napoleon once and for all. The Queen wrote to a friend in August 1814: "my health is much improved since I have been at Hetzendorf and the pure air combined with a little more quiet has done me a lot of good. Here we are expecting the Congress [of Vienna] and the great powers who will settle it."[54]

Napoleon's defeat was heralded with the greatest exuberance across Europe. *The Times* in London reported that the "most hateful of Tyrants has finished by proving himself the most infamous of cowards."[55] Now that Napoleon was defeated and exiled, Europe could be reformed. The delicate peace process brought together the greatest diplomats in the world to decide the fate of France, and promised an historic gathering of rulers.

The Congress of Vienna marked the first major display of the new European royal order after it was reshaped by the Napoleonic Wars. One estimate claimed that over a hundred thousand royals, dignitaries, and aristocrats had flooded into Vienna for the momentous event. One witness called it "the most important, and certainly the most brilliant assemblage that ever met in Europe."[56] It brought together Emperor Francis I of Austria and Tsar Alexander I of Russia; the Kings Frederick Wilhelm III of Prussia, Frederick August I of Saxony, Frederick VI of Denmark, Maximilian I of Bavaria, Frederick I of Württemberg; the Grand Dukes Charles of Baden, Charles August of Saxe-Weimar-Eisenach, Ludwig I of Hesse-Darmstadt, Wilhelm IX of Hesse-Cassel; and the Dukes Frederick Wilhelm of Brunswick, Ernst I of Coburg, and Frederick Wilhelm of Nassau-Weilburg, not to mention the hundreds of other dignitaries who represented Spain, Portugal, Sweden, the Netherlands, Great Britain, Hanover, Switzerland,

Naples, Sardinia, and even the Iroquois Confederacy from Canada.

The Congress also brought a renewed interest in the former queen of Naples from many of those in attendance. After an exhaustive day of visitors and courtiers on September 7, 1814, Maria Carolina retired to bed at Prince Leopoldo's insistence. She asked her servants to let her sleep past seven o'clock to get some rest. Sometime around midnight, the maid thought she had been called, and rushed into the Queen's room. When she entered, she found Maria Carolina lying dead, her hand grasping for the bell-rope. A fit of apoplexy had suddenly ended the life of Maria Theresa's last surviving daughter.

The body of Queen Maria Carolina of Naples and Sicily, dressed in a black taffeta gown, veil, lace cap, and silver fabric shoes, was taken to lie in state before the funeral. The Baroness du Montet described her visit to the Queen's memorial on September 10:

> In the Queen's last sleep there is a trace of sadness, of infinite weariness. Maria Carolina, who thought she would die in Naples, had had her portrait set up on a tomb in the Capuchin convent in Vienna together with a tender and moving inscription, a gentle testimony of the poor lady's desire to be buried near her august parents. A sensitive but vain precaution, since the Queen's mortal remains have been buried on the spot.[57]

Strict mourning for no less than six months was ordered in Naples and Sicily. Churches in Palermo overflowed with parishioners who came to offer prayers for Maria Carolina's soul. King Ferdinand instructed his secretary to read the following statement after he was informed of his wife's death: "The dreadful blow struck at my soul by the fatal news which came as a thunder-bolt on the morning of the 22nd left me so dispirited that I could do nothing but retire to the country plunged in the most extreme affliction."[58]

Maria Carolina's death echoed Empress Maria Theresa's by earning the praise of her most bitter enemy. Napoleon Bonaparte, even as he faced his own demise, paid homage to the Queen by admitting: "That woman knew how to think and act like a queen, while preserving her rights and her dignity." Her granddaughter, Princess Carolina of Calabria, was deeply affected by her death. She later recalled that the "Queen's death, in 1814, affected me keenly. In her I lost a support, a mother, and I still regret not having been able to attend upon her."[59]

The death of Queen Maria Carolina marked a turning point in history. The historian John Cordy Jeaffreson perhaps best described the significance of her death with the following words:

> Thus Maria Carolina passed from the world at the moment of the restoration of that old order of things, for whose preservation and recovery she had made so many efforts and endured such serious reverses. From the outbreak of the French revolution till overwhelming calamities weakened her mind and ruined her fortunes, she had fought resolutely for the legitimate sovereigns and thrones of Europe.[60]

Maria Carolina's death closes out the unique story of Maria Theresa's five special children. Joseph of Austria, Amalia of Parma, Leopold of Tuscany, Maria Carolina of Naples, and Marie Antoinette of France lived very different lives that were strikingly similar in so many respects. They each sat on tumultuous thrones shaken by triumph and tragedy. They were each deeply committed to family, both to their own and to the welfare of that great imperial family of which they were all a part, the Habsburgs. And to their very core, they each remained Austrian.

None of them could escape the awe, reverence, and fear of the woman who was queen, empress, and mother to them, Maria Theresa. Each of these five individuals lived their lives through a unique filter of their experiences growing up at their mother's side, and each of them were saddled with a different expectation of what role they would play in adulthood.

Destiny had chosen these five individuals to rule and change history, but also to lead tragic lives. Their august mother was the arbiter of their different fates. Her maternal love was mixed with imperial ambition. She sent each of her children out into the world with the greatest expectations attached to them, but in the end, all five of them came to sad fates. Joseph, Antoine, Poldy, Amalia, and Charlotte reigned over the end of their empires and witnessed the closing stages of one of the most formative periods in European history. Their deaths marked the end of an era, and the passing of an age.

Epilogue

"A nobler brood of princes never came from the same parents; and it is one of Maria Theresa's titles to historic homage that she was no less exemplary as a mother than admirable as ruling woman. Most of these stately children of a statelier mother have passed, in Time's tragic course, from human regard; but [five] of them...live, and will continue to live, amongst the momentous personages of European story."[1]

-John Cordy Jeaffreson, historian

One twentieth-century author went a step further and described the Habsburgs as "the greatest dynasty of modern history, and the history of central Europe revolves around them, not they around it."[2] The five special children of Maria Theresa were the embodiment of these words. They defined the most pivotal moments in their nations' histories, and left a deep and lasting legacy on the face of Europe.

Two months after Queen Maria Carolina's death, King Ferdinand married the Duchess di Floridia, one of his late wife's ladies-in-waiting, in a morganatic ceremony in November 1814. Two years later, he united the Neapolitan and Sicilian thrones into the Kingdom of the Two Sicilies. King Ferdinand ruled until his death in 1825. He was succeeded by his son and daughter-in-law, King Francesco I and Queen Isabel.

Prince Leopoldo continued to live in Vienna after his mother's death and married Emperor Francis I's daughter, Archduchess Maria Clementina, in 1816. The Prince and Princess of Salerno had two children. Each of Maria Carolina's surviving daughters followed in their mother's footsteps and reigned as queen consorts. Mimi became Queen of Sardinia in 1824 when her husband, Carlo Felice, ascended the throne. Six years later, in 1830, Maria Amelia, Duchesse d'Orléans, became Queen of the French when her husband Louis Philippe was chosen as king after France following the abdication of King

Charles X.* The King and Queen reigned until 1848 when they were overthrown by a mild revolution. They lived out their days in exile in Great Britain. The descendants of their ten children make up the members of the modern French royal family.

At the Congress of Vienna, Parma was given to Maria Carolina's granddaughter, Marie Louise, until her death in 1847. She was allowed to keep her title and style for the rest of her life, being known as Her Imperial Majesty, the Empress of the French. Amalia's grandson, Lodovico II, reigned as King of Etruria under the regency of Luisetta until 1807 when he was deposed by Napoleon. From 1824 until 1847, he was known the Duke of Lucca. Upon Marie Louise's death, he returned to Parma and ruled as Duke Carlo II. A year later, he abdicated in favor of his twenty-five year-old son, Carlo III.

Amalia's two unmarried daughters, Maria Antonietta and Carlotta, went their separate ways after their mother died. Carlotta moved to Rome and died there in 1813. A year before her mother's death, on April 22, 1803, Princess Maria Antonietta completed her training as a nun and took the veil of the ursuline order as Sister Louise Marie. She returned to the ursuline convent in Parma after the fall of Napoleon and lived almost entirely in seclusion until 1831, when she moved to the Convent of St. Agatha in Rome. She died there in 1841.

After the Revolution of 1789, France alternated between a republic and a monarchy. Queen Marie Antoinette's daughter, Marie Thérèse, was held captive until December 1795 when her relatives in Austria and Naples arranged a deal for her release. She fulfilled her mother's wish and married her cousin, Louis-Antoine, Duc d'Angoulême, in 1799. Her brother, Prince Louis Charles, who was hailed by most of Europe as King Louis XVII after his father's death, died in the Temple in 1795. After he was taken from his mother, he was placed under the care of an abusive bootmaker named Antoine Simon whose mistreatment of the child king would have broken Marie Antoinette's heart. The exact cause of his death still remains a mystery, but the general opinion is that he died from malnourishment. Marie

---

* King Charles X of France is more famously remembered as Charles, Comte d'Artois, the younger brother of Louis XVI. Both he and his brother, the Comte de Provence, reigned as kings of France after the fall of Napoleon. The Comte de Provence ruled as King Louis XVIII.

Antoinette's sister-in-law, Princess Élisabeth, never received the Queen's emotional last letter. She was held in the Temple until 1794 when she was executed as a royalist threat to the Republic. Many believed she died simply for being the sister of the king.

After years of bloodshed in the Revolution, France enjoyed peace during the reign of King Louis Philippe and Queen Maria Amelia. As members of the Orléans branch of the French royal family, they were not directly descended from Louis XVI and Marie Antoinette, whose own descendants died out when the Duchesse d'Angoulême died childless in 1851. In 1815, the remains of King Louis XVI and Queen Marie Antoinette were exhumed and reburied in the Bourbon vault in the Cathedral of St. Denis by order of King Louis XVIII.

Emperor Leopold's son, Francis, ruled Austria until his death in 1835. He married four times and fathered thirteen children. Francis tasted the bitterness of defeat and the exultation of triumph throughout his long reign. He was stripped of the millennial title of Holy Roman Emperor but returned Austria to a place of prominence and strength at the Congress of Vienna in 1814.

Leopold II was connected with Maria Carolina through the marriage of Francis and Teresa; Ferdinand and Luisa; and Francesco and Clementine; but he also became connected with Amalia of Parma when his granddaughter, Archduchess Caroline, married Amalia's grandson, Crown Prince Frederick August of Saxony. Frederick August became King of Saxony in 1819.

Maria Theresa had a vision for her children and the future of their dynasties, but not a single one of these countries remains a monarchy today. Tuscany, Parma, and the Two Sicilies were annexed to Italy during its unification in 1859. France became an empire under Napoleon III in 1852, but the Franco-Prussian War of 1870-71 stripped France of its imperial status, making it a republic for the third and final time. The Austrian Empire (and later Austria-Hungary) remained intact until the conclusion of World War I in 1918, but its influence in Europe began declining during the reign of Leopold II's great-grandson, Emperor Franz Joseph, in 1848.

The golden era of European monarchies has long been over, but its effects can still be seen in the twenty-first century. Some of the most illustrious royal families in the world can trace their lineage back to Joseph, Amalia, Poldy, Charlotte and Antoine. The rulers of Austria, Germany, France, Saxony, Portugal, Brazil, Mexico, Belgium, Romania, Bulgaria, Spain, Luxembourg, and Italy were descended from the five special children of Maria Theresa.

The lives of these five rulers have been documented numerous times over the past two hundred years. Their stories have made for some of the most memorable literary, musical, artistic, and cinematic experiences of our time. But through whatever medium their lives are viewed, their stories are timeless and give us greater glimpses than we ever could have thought possible into some of the most pivotal moments in history. Utterly compelling, their lives were truly in destiny's hands.

Notes

Introduction
[1] Antonia Fraser, *Marie Antoinette: The Journey* (New York: Anchor Books, 2001), p. 439.

Part I: Destined to Reign (1741-1765)

Chapter 1: Queen, Empress, Mother
[1] S.K. Padover, *The Revolutionary Emperor: Joseph the Second* (London: Jonathan Cape, LTD., 1934), p. 17.
[2] Frank A.J. Szabo, *Kaunitz and Enlightened Absolutism, 1753—1780* (Cambridge: Cambridge University Press, 1994), p. 3.
[3] Albert, Duc de Broglie, et al., *Frederick the Great and Maria Theresa*, vol. I (London: Sampson Low, Marston, Searle, & Rivington, 1883), pp. 80-81.
[4] Andrew Wheatcroft, *The Habsburgs: Embodying Empire* (London: Penguin Books, 1996), p. 219.
[5] Lily Constance Morris, *Maria Theresa: The Last Conservative* (London & New York: Alfred A. Knopf, 1937), p. 81.
[6] John S. Jenkins, *The Heroines of History* (Auburn: Alden, Beardsley & Company, 1859), p. 199.
[7] Voltaire, *The Age of Louis XV*, vol. I (London: G. Kearsly, 1774), p. 156.
[8] Julia P. Gelardi, *In Triumph's Wake: Royal Mothers, Tragic Daughters, and the Price They Paid for Glory* (New York: St. Martin's Press, 2008), p. 137.
[9] R. Nisbet Bain, *The Daughter of Peter the Great* (New York: E.P. Dutton & Co., 1900), p. 128.
[10] Carolly Erickson, *To the Scaffold: The Life of Marie Antoinette* (New York: St. Martin's Press, 1991), pp. 28-29.
[11] J. Alexander Mahan, *Maria Theresa of Austria* (New York: Thomas Y. Crowell Company, 1932), p. 239.
[12] Fraser, *Marie Antoinette*, pp. 14-15.
[13] Evelyne Lever, *Marie Antoinette: The Last Queen of France*, trans. Catherine Temerson (New York: St. Martin's Press, 2000), p. 6.
[14] Fraser, *Marie Antoinette*, p. 16.

[15] Wheatcroft, *The Habsburgs*, p. 222.

[16] Catherine Mary Bearne, *A Sister of Marie Antoinette: The Life-story of Maria Carolina, Queen of Naples* (London: T. Fisher Unwin, 1907), pp. 27-28.

[17] Edward Crankshaw, *Maria Theresa* (London & Harlow: Longmans, Green, & Co., 1969), p. 25.

[18] Walter Sichel, ed., *Memoirs of Emma, Lady Hamilton, The Friend of Lord Nelson, and the Court of Naples* (New York: P.F. Collier & Son, 1910), p. 99.

[19] William J. McGill, Jr., *Maria Theresa* (New York: Twayne Publishers, Inc., 1972), p. 74.

[20] Anna Jameson, *Memoirs of Celebrated Female Sovereigns*, vol. II (London: Henry Colburn and Richard Bentley, 1831), p. 243.

Chapter 2: "The Empress and Her Children Are the Court"

[1] Erickson, *To the Scaffold*, p. 33.

[2] Derek Beales, *Joseph II*, vol. I: *In the Shadow of Maria Theresa, 1741-1780* (Cambridge: Cambridge University Press, 1991), p. 43.

[3] Crankshaw, *Maria Theresa*, p. 253.

[4] *Ibid*, p. 250.

[5] Fraser, *Marie Antoinette*, p. 23.

[6] Beales, *Joseph II*, vol. I, p. 67.

[7] Maurice Boutry, *Le Mariage de Marie-Antoinette* (Paris: Émile Paul, 1904), p. 19.

[8] Gelardi, *In Triumph's Wake*, p. 173.

[9] Fraser, *Marie Antoinette*, p. 3.

[10] C.A. Macartney, *Maria Theresa and the House of Austria* (Mystic, Connecticut: Lawrence Verry, Inc., 1969), p. 96.

[11] Padover, *The Revolutionary Emperor*, p. 19.

[12] Gelardi, *In Triumph's Wake*, pp. 178-179.

[13] Madame (Jeanne Louise Henriette) Campan, *Memoirs of the Court of Marie Antoinette, Queen of France*, vol. I (Philadelphia: Parry & McMillan, 1854), p. 78.

[14] Dr. E. Vehse, *Memoirs of the Court, Aristocracy, and Diplomacy of Austria*, trans. Franz Demmler, vol. II (London: Longman, Brown, Green, & Longmans, 1856), p. 256.

[15] Erickson, *To the Scaffold*, p. 27.

[16] Comtesse d'Armaille, *Marie-Thérèse et Marie Antoinette*, 3rd ed. (Paris: Perrin & Co., 1893), p. 32.

[17] Charles Duke Young, *The Life of Marie Antoinette, Queen of France* (New York: Harper & Brothers, 1856), p. 23.

[18] Leopold Mozart to Lorenz Hagenauer, 16 October 1762, L. 2, in Emily Anderson, ed., *The Letters of Mozart & His Family*, vol. I (London: Macmillan & Co., 1938), p. 8.

[19] Fraser, *Marie Antoinette*, p. 23.

[20] Jameson, *Memoirs*, vol. II, p. 259.

[21] Jenkins, *Heroines*, p. 213.

[22] Fraser, *Marie Antoinette*, p. 20.

[23] Erickson, *To the Scaffold*, p. 17.

[24] Fraser, *Marie Antoinette*, p. 21.

[25] Lady Catherine Charlotte Jackson, *The French Court and Society. Reign of Louis XVI and First Empire*, vol. I (Boston: I.C. Page & Company, 1897), p. 200.

[26] Gelardi, *In Triumph's Wake*, p. 176.

[27] ("An affair of the heart, not a political affair"); Henry Schoellkopf, *The Enlightened Despotism of the Eighteenth Century: Charles III in Spain*, thesis (B.A.), (Ithaca, N.Y.: Cornell University, 1902), p. 16.

Chapter 3: The Etiquettes of Greatness

[1] A letter of Sir Nathaniel Wraxall, 4 March 1779, in Sir Nathaniel Wraxall, *Memoirs of the courts of Berlin, Dresden, Warsaw, and Vienna in the years 1777, 1778, and 1779*, vol. II (London: A. Strahan, 1800), p. 391.

[2] Margaret Goldsmith, *Maria Theresa of Austria* (London: Arthur Baker, Ltd., 1936), p. 200.

[3] Morris, *Maria Theresa*, p. 268.

[4] Jenkins, *Heroines*, p. 212; Bearne, *A Sister of Marie Antoinette*, p. 30.

[5] Fraser, *Marie Antoinette*, p. 46.

[6] Diana Fontescu, ed., *Americans and Queen Marie of Roumania: A Selection of Documents* (Iași: The Center for Romanian Studies, 1998), p. 137.

[7] Padover, *The Revolutionary Emperor*, p. 33.

[8] Morris, *Maria Theresa*, p. 268.

[9] Erickson, *To the Scaffold*, pp. 33-34.

[10] Goldsmith, *Maria Theresa*, p. 201.

[11] *Ibid.*

[12] Bearne, *A Sister of Marie Antoinette*, p. 31.

[13] Dr. John Doran, *'Mann' and Manners at the Court of Florence, 1740—1786*, vol. II (London: William Clowes & Sons, 1876), p. 106.

[14] Fraser, *Marie Antoinette*, p. 50.

[15] *Ibid*, p. 23.

[16] Erickson, *To the Scaffold*, pp. 33-36.

[17] Fraser, *Marie Antoinette*, p. 176.

[18] *Ibid*, pp. 23-24.

[19] Harold Acton, *The Bourbons of Naples* (London: Prion Books Ltd., 1998 [1957]), p. 131.

[20] H.R.H. Princess Michael of Kent, *Crowned in a Far Country: Portraits of Eight Royal Brides* (New York: Touchstone Books, 2007 [1986]), p. 68.

[21] Acton, *The Bourbons of Naples*, p. 131.

[22] Lever, *Marie Antoinette*, p. 5.

[23] Campan, *Memoirs*, vol. I, p. 70.

[24] Goldsmith, *Maria Theresa*, p. 201.

[25] Morris, *Maria Theresa*, p. 269.

[26] Queen Victoria to Princess Victoria of Prussia, 16 May 1860, in Christopher Hibbert, ed., *Queen Victoria in Her Letters and Journals* (Stroud, Glos.: Sutton Publishing, 2000), p. 104.

[27] Goldsmith, *Maria Theresa*, p. 201.

[28] Erickson, *To the Scaffold*, p. 34.

[29] Goldsmith, *Maria Theresa*, pp. 201-202. In reality, Isabella's I.Q. was probably off the charts. Her manic depression combined with her vast intellect suggests a

highly developed mind. Joseph, on the other hand, was most likely only moderately above average.

[30] Fraser, *Marie Antoinette*, pp. 23-24.

[31] Goldsmith, *Maria Theresa*, p. 205.

[32] Morris, *Maria Theresa*, p. 276.

[33] Goldsmith, *Maria Theresa*, pp. 212-213.

[34] Gelardi, *In Triumph's Wake*, p. 186.

Chapter 4: "I Have Lost All"

[1] A letter of Sir Nathaniel Wraxall, 4 March 1779, in Wraxall, *Memoirs*, vol. II, p. 393.

[2] Moritz Bermann, *Maria Theresia und Joseph II in ihrem Leben und Wirken* (Vienna: Hartleben, 1881), p. 709.

[3] Bearne, *A Sister of Marie Antoinette*, p. 36.

[4] Mahan, *Maria Theresa*, p. 279.

[5] Bearne, *A Sister of Marie Antoinette*, p. 37.

[6] Empress Maria Theresa to Prince Wenzel Kaunitz, 26 November 1763, in Morris, *Maria Theresa*, p. 277.

[7] Padover, *The Revolutionary Emperor*, p. 40.

[8] Morris, *Maria Theresa*, p. 277.

[9] Archduke Joseph to Philip, Duke of Parma, 11 December 1763, in Beales, *Joseph II*, vol. I, p. 77.

[10] Johann von Goethe, *Truth and Poetry: From My Own Life*, trans. John Oxenford, vol. I (London: George Bell & Sons, 1891), p. 161.

[11] *Ibid*, p. 169.

[12] Goldsmith, *Maria Theresa*, p. 215.

[13] *Ibid.*

[14] Erickson, *To the Scaffold*, p. 34.

[15] Empress Maria Theresa to Archduchess Maria Christina, undated, May 1764, in Goldsmith, *Maria Theresa*, p. 217.

[16] *Ibid.*

[17] Padover, *The Revolutionary Emperor*, p. 48; Erickson, *To the Scaffold*, p. 34.

[18] Beales, *Joseph II*, vol. I, p. 150.

[19] Emperor Joseph II to Grand Duke Leopold I, 26 September 1765, in *ibid.*

[20] William J. McGill, Jr., *Maria Theresa* (New York: Twayne Publishers, Inc., 1972), pp. 99-100.

[21] J. Franck Bright, *Maria Theresa* (London: Macmillan & Co., 1897), p. 201.

[22] John S.C. Abbott, *Maria Antoinette* (New York & London: Harper & Brothers Publishers, 1904), p. 23.

[23] Fraser, *Marie Antoinette*, p. 25.

[24] Campan, *Memoirs*, vol. I, p. 69.

[25] Crankshaw, *Maria Theresa*, p. 265.

[26] William Coxe, *History of the House of Austria*, vol. I, 3rd ed. (London: Bell & Dalby, 1873), p. 435.

[27] Jenkins, *Heroines*, p. 210.

[28] Alfred Michiels, *Secret History of the Austrian Government, and of its Systematic Persecution of Protestants. Compiled from Official Documents* (London: Chapman & Hall, 1859), p. 267.

[29] Wheatcroft, *The Habsburgs*, p. 227.

[30] Morris, *Maria Theresa*, p. 280.

[31] Crankshaw, *Maria Theresa*, p. 266.

[32] Gelardi, *In Triumph's Wake*, p. 182.

[33] *Ibid.*

[34] Padover, *The Revolutionary Emperor*, p. 53.

[35] Gelardi, *In Triumph's Wake*, p. 182.

[36] *Ibid*, p. 183.

[37] Maxime de la Rocheterie, *The Life of Marie Antoinette*, trans. Cora Bell Hamilton, vol. I (New York: Dodd, Mead & Co., 1893), pp. 5-6.

Part II: An Empire Divided (1765—1780)

Chapter 5: One Empire, Two Crowns

[1] Gelardi, *In Triumph's Wake*, p. 182.

[2] *Ibid.*

[3] Padover, *The Revolutionary Emperor*, p. 66.

[4] Wheatcroft, *The Habsburgs*, p. 228.

[5] T.C.W. Blanning, *Joseph II* (New York: Longman Publishing, 1994), p. 10.

[6] Empress Maria Theresa to Emperor Joseph II, undated, July 1777, in Gelardi, *In Triumph's Wake*, p. 187.

[7] *Ibid.*

[8] Jameson, *Memoirs*, vol. II, p. 246.

[9] Charles W. Ingrao, *The Habsburg Monarchy, 1618-1815*, 2nd ed. (Cambridge: Cambridge University Press, 1994), p. 183.

[10] Mahan, *Maria Theresa*, p. 289.

[11] Crankshaw, *Maria Theresa*, p. 264.

[12] Mahan, *Maria Theresa*, p. 289.

[13] Erickson, *To the Scaffold*, p. 136.

[14] Padover, *The Revolutionary Emperor*, p. 49.

[15] Fraser, *Marie Antoinette*, p. 25.

[16] *Ibid.*

[17] Empress Maria Theresa to Countess Sophie Enzenberg, 9 November 1765, in W. Fred, ed., *Briefe der Kaiserin Maria Theresia*, vol. I, (Vienna: n.p., 1881) p. 207.

[18] Bearne, *A Sister of Marie Antoinette*, p. 44.

[19] Fraser, *Marie Antoinette*, p. 27.

[20] *Ibid*, p. 26.

[21] James Breck Perkins, *France Under Louis XV*, vol. II, (Boston and New York: Houghton Mifflin Company, 1897) p. 241.

[22] Empress Maria Theresa to Grand Duke Leopold, undated, August 1765, Alfred von Arneth, ed., *Briefe der Kaiserin Maria Theresia an ihre Kinder und Freunde*, vol. I (Vienna: Wilhelm Braumuller, 1881), pp. 14-18.

[23] Sir Horace Mann to Sir Horace Walpole, undated, September 1765, in Doran, *'Mann' and Manners*, vol. II, p. 144.

[24] Sir Horace Mann to Sir Horace Walpole, 14 September 1765, in *ibid.*

[25] McGill, *Maria Theresa*, p. 118.

[26] Eric Cochrane, *Florence in the Forgotten Centuries: 1527-1800*, (Chicago: The University of Chicago Press, 1973) p. 423

[27] Georgina Masson, *Italian Villas and Palaces*, (London: Harry N. Abrams, Ltd., 1959) p. 172.

[28] Julia de Wolf Addison, *The Art of the Pitti Palace*, (Boston: L.C. Page & Company, 1903) p. 30.

[29] Robert Joseph Kerner, *Bohemia in the Eighteenth Century: A Study in Political, Economic and Social History With Special Reference to the Reign of Leopold II, 1790-1792* (New York: The Macmillan Company, 1934), p. 55.

[30] Walter Consuelo Langsam, *Francis the Good: The Education of an Emperor, 1768-1792*, 1st ed. (New York: The Macmillan Company, 1949), p. 3.

[31] Henry Edward Napier, *Florentine History, from the Earliest Authentic Records to the Accession of Ferdinand the Third, Grand Duke of Tuscany*, vol. VI (London: Edward Moxer, 1847), p. 48.

[32] Langsam, *Francis the Good*, p. 7.

[33] Doran, *'Mann' and Manners*, vol. II, p. 180.

[34] *Ibid.*

[35] James Whiteside, *Italy in the Nineteenth Century* (London: Longman, Green, Longman, and Roberts, 1860), p. 143.

[36] Cochrane, *Florence in the Forgotten Centuries*, p. 423.

[37] Beales, *Joseph II*, vol. I, p. 152.

[38] Goldsmith, *Maria Theresa*, p. 227.

[39] Padover, *The Revolutionary Emperor*, p. 63.

[40] Empress Maria Theresa to Count Francis Thurn, 29 November 1765, in Beales, *Joseph II*, vol. I, p. 152.

[41] Conte Egan Caesare Corti, *Ich, ein Tochter Maria Theresias: ein Lebensbild der Königin Marie Karoline von Neapal* (Munich: Bruckmann, 1950), p. 24.

[42] Fraser, *Marie Antoinette*, p. 24.

[43] *Ibid*, pp. 26-27.

[44] Gelardi, *In Triumph's Wake*, p. 183.

[45] Virginia Rounding, *Catherine the Great: Love, Sex, and Power* (New York: St. Martin's Griffin, 2006), p. 205.

[46] Fraser, *Marie Antoinette*, pp. 27-28.

[47] Alfred von Arneth, ed., *Geschichte Maria Theresias*, vol. VII (Vienna: n.p., 1876), p. 551.

Chapter 6: "I Remain True to My Dear Vienna

[1] Arneth, ed., *Geschichte Maria Theresias*, vol. VII, p. 551.

[2] Empress Maria Theresa to King Carlos III of Spain, undated, November 1767, in Corti, *Ich, ein Tochter*, p. 30.

[3] Doran, *'Mann' and Manners*, vol. II, p. 187.

[4] Langsam, *Francis the Good*, p. 1.

[5] Whiteside, *Italy in the Nineteenth Century*, p. 145.

[6] Emperor Joseph II to Grand Duke Leopold I, undated, February 1768, in Beales, *Joseph II*, vol. I, p. 177.

[7] Crankshaw, *Maria Theresa*, p. 140.

[8] Doran, *'Mann' and Manners*, vol. II, p. 189.

[9] Emperor Joseph II to Empress Maria Theresa, 12 April 1769, in Langsam, *Francis the Good*, p. 6.

[10] Emperor Joseph II to Empress Maria Theresa, 14 April 1769, in *ibid*, p. 7.

[11] Cochrane, *Florence in the Forgotten Centuries*, p. 423.

[12] *Ibid.*

[13] Beales, *Joseph II*, vol. I, p. 195.

[14] Acton, *The Bourbons of Naples*, pp. 131-132.

[15] Fraser, *Marie Antoinette*, p. 53.

[16] Queen Maria Carolina to Countess Marie Lerchenfeld, 17 April 1768, in Fraser, *Marie Antoinette*, pp. 43-44.

[17] Corti, *Tochter Maria Theresias*, pp. 32-34.

[18] Empress Maria Theresa to Archduchess Maria Carolina, 19 August 1767, in Bearne, *A Sister of Marie Antoinette*, pp. 54-55. There are conflicting reports to the date when this letter was written. Bearne references it in 1767, but Goldsmith and more recent authors claim it was not written until Maria Carolina was queen of Naples, in 1768. In this context, it is treated as having been written in 1768, but the above date is cited as a reference point from the original work.

[19] Empress Maria Theresa to Queen Maria Carolina, undated, April 1768, in W. Fred, ed., *Briefe der Kaiserin Maria Theresia*, vol. III (Vienna, n.p., 1881), p. 37.

[20] Bearne, *A Sister of Marie Antoinette*, p. 65.

[21] Acton, *The Bourbons of Naples*, p. 132.

[22] Queen Maria Carolina to Countess Marie Lerchenfeld, undated, 1768, in *ibid*, p. 133.

[23] Grand Duke Leopold I to Empress Maria Theresa, 29 April 1768 in Bearne, *A Sister of Marie Antoinette*, pp. 68-69.

[24] Queen Maria Carolina to Countess Marie Lerchenfeld, 10 May 1768, in *ibid*.

[25] Grand Duke Leopold I to Empress Maria Theresa, 10 May 1768, in Morris, *Maria Theresa*, p. 286.

Chapter 7: The Two Ferdinands
[1] Elizabeth, Margravine of Anspach, *Memoirs*, vol. I (London: Henry Colburn, 1826), p. 291.

[2] Louis Dutens, *Memoirs of a Traveller, Now in Retirement*, vol. II (London: Blackfiars, and Dulau and Co., 1806), p. 155.

[3] Clara Erskine Clement, *Naples the City of Parthenope and its Environs* (Boston: Estes and Lauriat, 1894), p. 147.

[4] Queen Maria Carolina to Countess Marie Lerchenfeld, 12 May 1768, in Bearne, *A Sister of Marie Antoinette*, p. 71.

[5] Queen Maria Carolina to Countess Marie Lerchenfeld, 13 August 1768, in Erickson, *To the Scaffold*, p. 37.

[6] John Cordy Jeaffreson, *The Queen of Naples and Lord Nelson* vol. I, (London: Hurst and Blackett, Ltd., 1889), p. 106.

[7] Princess Michael, *Crowned in a Far Country*, pp. 70-71.

[8] Empress Napoleon I to King Joseph of Spain, 11 May 1808, in John S.C. Abbott, ed., *Confidential Correspondance of the Emperor Napoleon and the Empress Josephine* (New York: Mason Brothers, 1856), p. 212.

[9] R.M. Johnston, *The Napoleonic Empire in Southern Italy and the Rise of Secret Societies*, vol. I (London: Macmillan and Co., Ltd., 1904), p. vii.

[10] Anna Challice, *Illustrious Women of France, 1790-1873* (London: Bradbury, Agnew & Co., 1873), p. 218.

[11] King Ferdinand IV to King Carlos III, undated, in Constance H.D. Giglioli, *Naples in 1799: An Account of the Revolution of 1799 and of the Rise and Fall of the Parthenopean Republic* (London: John Murray, 1903), p. 6.

[12] Goldsmith, *Maria Theresa*, p. 152. SEE: *Chapter 6, note 33.*

[13] Giglioli, *Naples in 1799*, p. 5.

[14] Acton, *The Bourbons of Naples*, pp. 135-136.

[15] Princess Michael, *Crowned in a Far Country*, pp. 70-71.

[16] Acton, *The Bourbons of Naples*, p. 137-138.

[17] *Ibid*, pp. 138-139.

[18] Princess Michael, *Crowned in a Far Country*, pp. 72-73.

[19] *Ibid.*

[20] Emperor Joseph II to Empress Maria Theresa, 8 April 1769, in Acton, *The Bourbons of Naples*, pp. 151-152.

[21] Princess Michael, *Crowned in a Far Country*, p. 74.

[22] Emperor Joseph II to Empress Maria Theresa, 16 May 1769, in Beales, *Joseph II*, vol. I, p. 262.

[23] Fraser, *Marie Antoinette*, p. 29.

[24] Goldsmith, *Maria Theresa*, p. 241.

[25] Julia P. Gelardi, "The World of Maria Theresa," email to the author, 22 May 2007.

[26] Morris, *Maria Theresa*, p. 287

[27] Fraser, *Marie Antoinette*, p. 29.

[28] Bearne, *A Sister of Marie Antoinette*, p. 61.

[29] Empress Maria Theresa to Maria Amalia, Duchess of Parma, undated, June 1769, in C. Krack, ed., *Briefe einer Kaiserin. Maria Theresia an ihre Kinder und Freunde* (Berlin: Verlag, 1910), pp. 61-63.

[30] Philippe Amiguet, ed., *Lettres de Louis XV à sons petit-fils l'Infant Ferdinand de Parme* (Paris: B. Grassett, 1938), p. 115.

[31] Bearne, *A Sister of Marie Antoinette*, p. 61.

[32] Doran, *'Mann' and Manners*, vol. II, p. 393.

[33] S.K. Padover, *The Life and Death of Louis XVI* (New York & London: D. Appleton Century Co., 1939), p. 28.

[34] Caroline Weber, *Queen of Fashion: What Marie Antoinette Wore to the Revolution* (New York: Henry Holt and Company, 2006), p. 7.

[35] Weber, *Queen of Fashion*, p. 12.

Chapter 8: "Farewell, My Dearest Child"

[1] Weber, *Queen of Fashion*, p. 13.

[2] Marcel Brion, *Daily Life in the Vienna of Mozart and Schubert*, trans. Jean Stewart (London: George Weidenfeld & Nicholson, Ltd., 1961), p. 18.

[3] Emperor Joseph II to Grand Duke Leopold I, undated, in Padover, *The Revolutionary Emperor*, p. 62.

[4] Goldsmith, *Maria Theresa*, p. 224.

[5] Erickson, *To the Scaffold*, p. 137.

[6] Ingrao, *The Habsburg Monarchy*, pp. 183-184.

[7] Erickson, *To the Scaffold*, p. 137.

[8] Ingrao, *The Habsburg Monarchy*, p. 184.

[9] Cornelia Knight, *The Autobiography of Miss Cornelia Knight, Lady Companion to the Princess Charlotte of Wales. With Extracts From Her Journals and Anecdote Books*, 3rd ed., vol. I (London: W.H. Allen & Co., 1861), p. 72.

[10] Ingrao, *The Habsburg Monarchy*, p. 184.

[11] Jameson, *Memoirs*, vol. II, p. 243.

[12] Rev. J. Franck Bright, *Joseph II* (London: Macmillan and Co., 1905), p. 81.

[13] Wheatcroft, *The Habsburgs*, pp. 226-227.

[14] *Ibid.*

[15] Langsam, *Francis the Food*, pp. 2-3.

[16] Gelardi, *In Triumph's Wake*, pp. 190-191.

[17] *Ibid.*

[18] Empress Maria Theresa to Marie Antoinette, Dauphine of France, 4 May 1770, in Olivier Bernier, *Imperial Mother, Royal Daughter: The Correspondance of Marie Antoinette and Maria Theresa* (London: Sidgwick & Jackson, 1969), p. 35.

[19] Francine du Plessix Gray, "The Child Queen," *The New Yorker*, 7 August 2000, p. 81.

[20] Rocheterie, *The Life of Marie Antoinette*, vol. I, p. 7.

[21] Imbert de Saint-Amand, *Women of Versailles: Last Years of Louis XV*, trans. Elizabeth Gilbert Martin (New York: Charles Scribner's Sons, 1893), p. 120.

[22] *Gazette de France*, 16 April 1770.

[23] Fraser, *Marie Antoinette*, p. 53.

[24] Weber, *Queen of Fashion*, p. 11.

[25] Thomas Carlyle, *The French Revolution*, 2nd ed. (New York: The Modern Library, 1932), p. 627.

[26] Weber, Joseph. *Memoirs of Maria Antoinetta, Archduchess of Austria, Queen of France and Navarre*, trans. R.C. Dallas, vol. I (London: C. Rickaby, 1805), p. 4.

[27] Rocheterie, *The Life of Marie Antoinette*, vol. I, p. 12.

[28] Fraser, *Marie Antoinette*, p. 53.

[29] Weber, *Queen of Fashion*, pp. 16-18.

[30] Gelardi, *In Triumph's Wake*, p. 192.

[31] Empress Maria Theresa to Marie Antoinette, Dauphine of France, undated, April 1770, Regina Schulte, ed., *The Body of the Queen: Gender and Rule in the Courtly World, 1500-2000* (New York: Berghahn Books, 2006), p. 158.

[32] Lillian C. Smythe, ed., *The Guardian of Marie Antoinette: Letters from the Comte de Mercy-Argenteau, Austrian Ambassador to the Court of Versailles, to Marie Thérèse, Empress of Austria 1770-1780*, vol. I (London: Hutchinson & Co., 1902), p. 17.

[33] Empress Maria Theresa to Marie Antoinette, Dauphine of France, 21 April 1770, in Suzanne Burkard, ed., *Mémoires de la Baronne d'Oberkirch sur la cour de Louis XVI et la societé français avant 1789* (Paris: Mercure de France, 1970 [1853]), p. 56.

[34] Gelardi, *In Triumph's Wake*, p. 192.

Chapter 9: France's Charming Dauphine

[1] Weber, *Queen of Fashion*, p. 22.

[2] Paul Gaulot, *A Friend of the Queen (Marie Antoinette—Count Fersen*, trans. Mrs. Cashel Hoey, 2nd ed. (London: William Heinemann, 1895), p. 2.

[3] Weber, *Queen of Fashion*, pp. 22-23.

[4] Constantia Maxwell, *The English Traveler in France 1698-1815* (London: George Routledge & Sons, 1932), p. 111.

[5] Dorothy Moultron Mayer, *Marie Antoinette: The Tragic Queen* (New York: Coward-McCann, 1968), p. 22.

[6] P. Cunningham, ed., *Letters of Horace Walpole*, vol. IV (London: n.p., 1891), p. 414.

[7] Ian Dunlop, *Marie Antoinette: A Portrait* (London: Sinclair Stevenson, 1993), p. 18.

[8] Gelardi, *In Triumph's Wake*, p. 193.

[9] Blanning, *Joseph II*, p. 200.

[10] Padover, *The Revolutionary Emperor*, p. 97.

[11] Beales, *Joseph II*, vol. I, p. 197; Adam Wandruszka, *Leopold II*, vol. II (Herold: Vienna, 1965), p. 342.

[12] Beales, *Joseph II*, vol. I, p. 320.

[13] Fraser, *Marie Antoinette*, p. 70.

[14] Princess Michael, *Crowned in a Far Country*, p. 40.

[15] Weber, *Queen of Fashion*, p. 43.

[16] John Lough, ed., *France on the Eve of Revolution: British Travellers' Observations, 1763-1788* (London: Croom Helm, 1987), p. 263.

[17] Weber, *Queen of Fashion*, p. 49.

[18] John Lewis Soulavie, *Historical and Political Memoirs of the Reign of Lewis XVI. from His Marriage to His Death*, vol. II (London: G. & J. Robinson, 1802), p. 50.

[19] Fraser, *Marie Antoinette*, p. 82.

[20] Rocheterie, *Marie Antoinette*, vol. I, p. 28.

[21] Saint-Amand, *Women of Versailles*, p. 132.

[22] Florimond Claude, Comte Mercy d'Argenteau, to Empress Maria Theresa, 20 August 1770, in Smythe, ed., *Guardian of Marie Antoinette*, vol. I, p. 37.

[23] Florimond Claude, Comte Mercy d'Argenteau, to Empress Maria Theresa, 23 January 1771, in *ibid*, p. 78.

[24] Florimond Claude, Comte Mercy d'Argenteau, to Empress Maria Theresa, undated, 1770, in Alfred, Ritter von Arneth, & M.A. Geoffrey, eds., *Marie-Antoinette: Correspondance Secrète entre Marie-Thérèse et le Comte de Mercy-Argenteau*, vol. I (Paris: Firmon Didot Brothers, Sons, & Co., 1874), pp. 10-14.

[25] Empress Maria Theresa to Marie Antoinette, Dauphine of France, 31 October 1771, in Saint-Amand, *Women of Versailles*, p. 170.

[26] Gelardi, *In Triumph's Wake*, p. 197.

[27] Florimond Claude, Comte Mercy d'Argenteau, to Empress Maria Theresa, 26 November 1771, in Bernier, *Imperial Mother, Royal Daughter*, p. 84.

[28] Lever, *Marie Antoinette*, p. 38.

[29] Empress Maria Theresa to Marie Antoinette, Dauphine of France, undated, April 1770, in Schulte, ed., *The Body of the Queen*, p. 158.

[30] Edith E. Cuthell, *An Imperial Victim: Marie Louise, Archduchess of Austria, Empress of the French, Duchess of Parma*, vol. II (London: Stanley Paul & Co., 1911), pp. 94-95.

[31] Bearne, *A Sister of Marie Antoinette*, p. 61.

[32] Gelardi, *In Triumph's Wake*, p. 195.

[33] Bearne, *A Sister of Marie Antoinette*, p. 61.

[34] Arneth & Geoffrey, eds., *Marie Antoinette*, vol. I, p. 20.

Chapter 10: An Austrian Carnival

[1] Empress Maria Theresa to Archduke Ferdinand, 30 January and 13 February 1777, in Gelardi, *In Triumph's Wake*, p. 184.

[2] Ingrao, *The Habsburg Monarchy*, p. 186.

[3] Padover, *The Revolutionary Emperor*, p. 85.

[4] Emperor Joseph II to Grand Duke Leopold I, 21 February 1771, in Beales, *Joseph II*, vol. I, p. 340.

[5] Gelardi, *In Triumph's Wake*, p. 184.

[6] Bright, *Maria Theresa*, p. 221.

[7] Fraser, *Marie Antoinette*, pp. 100-101.

[8] Bearne, *A Sister of Marie Antoinette*, p. 85.

[9] Gelardi, "The World of Maria Theresa."

[10] Bright, *Maria Theresa*, p. 221.

[11] Doran, *'Mann' and Manners*, vol. II, p. 233.

[12] McGill, *Maria Theresa*, p. 108.

[13] Empress Maria Theresa to Maria Christina, Duchess of Saxe-Teschen, undated, in Eugen Guglia, *Maria Theresa*, vol. II (Berlin: n.p., 1917), p. 270.

[14] Empress Maria Theresa to Maria Amalia, Duchess of Parma, undated, June 1769, in Krack, ed., *Briefe einer Kaiserin*, pp. 61-62.

[15] Goldsmith, *Maria Theresa*, p. 241.

[16] Charles Nisard, *Guillaume du Tillot: Un valet ministre et secrétaire d'état* (Paris: Paul Ollendorff, 1887), p. 293.

[17] Cuthell, *An Imperial Victim*, vol. II, p. 125.

[18] Amalia, Duchess of Parma, to Marquis Cavriani, 9 November 1771, in Nisard, *Tillot*, p. 244.

[19] Princess Michael, *Crowned in a Far Country*, p. 72.

[20] Campan, *Memoirs*, vol. I, p. 170.

[21] Erickson, *To the Scaffold*, p. 350n.

[22] A letter of Lady Anne Millar, 25 January 1771, in Lady Anne Millar, *Letters from Italy*, vol. II (London: Edward & Charles Dilly, 1776), p. 234.

[23] Anspach, *Memoirs*, vol. I, p. 292.

[24] Guglielmo Pépé, *Memoirs of General Pépé*, vol. I (London: Richard Bentley, 1846) p. 9.

[25] Pietro Colletta, *History of the Kingdom of Naples: 1734—1825*, trans. S. Horner, vol. I (Edinburgh: T. Constable and Co., 1858), p. 119.

[26] Acton, *The Bourbons of Naples*, p. 155.

[27] *Ibid.*

[28] A letter of Lady Anne Millar, 25 January 1771, in Millar, *Letters from Italy*, vol. II, p. 235.

[29] Acton, *The Bourbons of Naples*, p. 149.

[30] Bearne, *A Sister of Marie Antoinette*, pp. 86-87.

[31] Jeaffreson, *The Queen of Naples and Lord Acton*, vol. I, p. 115.

[32] Bearne, *A Sister of Marie Antoinette*, pp. 86-87.

[33] Marie Antoinette, Dauphine of France, to Empress Maria Theresa, 15 December 1772, in Young, *Marie Antoinette*, p. 71.

[34] Langsam, *Francis the Good*, p. 6.

[35] *Ibid*, p. 3.

[36] Wheatcroft, *The Habsburgs*, p. 233.

[37] *Ibid.*

[38] Langsam, *Francis the Good*, p. 4.

[39] Emperor Joseph II to Grand Duke Leopold I, 9 June 1774, in *ibid*, p. 8.

[40] *Ibid*, p. 10.

[41] Empress Maria Theresa to Queen Marie Antoinette, 30 May 1774, in Smythe, ed., *The Guardian of Marie Antoinette*, vol. II, p. 376.

[42] Florimond Claude, Comte Mercy d'Argenteau, to Empress Maria Theresa, 21 February 1772, in Saint Amand, *Women of Versailles*, p. 171.

[43] Erickson, *To the Scaffold*, pp. 78-79.

[44] Gelardi, *In Triumph's Wake*, pp. 194-195.

[45] Empress Maria Theresa to Emperor Joseph II, 24 December 1775, in Moritz von Landwehr, ed., *Aus dem Briefwechsel Maria Theresias mit Josef II* (Liepzig & Vienna, U. Hasse, 1917), pp. 23-24.

[46] Erickson, *To the Scaffold*, pp. 78-79.

[47] Gelardi, *In Triumph's Wake*, p. 217.

[48] Emperor Joseph II to Grand Duke Leopold I, undated, in Blanning, *Joseph II*, p. 27.

[49] Cuthell, *An Imperial Victim*, vol. II, p. 124.

[50] Morris, *Maria Theresa*, p. 288.

[51] *Ibid.*

[52] Empress Maria Theresa to Florimond Claude, Comte Mercy d'Argenteau, 2 August 1773, in Krack, ed., *Briefe einer Kaiserin*, p. 67.

[53] Empress Maria Theresa to Count Rosenberg, undated, March 1772, in *ibid*, p. 65.

[54] Nisard, *Tillot*, p. 252.

[55] Fraser, *Marie Antoinette*, pp. 100-101.

[56] Goldsmith, *Maria Theresa*, p. 241; Morris, *Maria Theresa*, p. 289.

[57] Gelardi, "The World of Maria Theresa."

[58] Gelardi, *In Triumph's Wake*, p. 195.

[59] Goldsmith, *Maria Theresa*, p. 242.

[60] Jeaffreson, *The Queen of Naples and Lord Acton*, vol. I, p. 115.

[61] Princess Michael, *Crowned in a Far Country*, p. 80.

[62] Acton, *The Bourbons of Naples*, p. 169.

Chapter 11: "We Are Too Young to Reign"

[1] Erickson, *To the Scaffold*, p. 99.

[2] Weber, *Queen of Fashion*, p. 59.

[3] Campan, *Memoirs*, vol. I, pp. 81-82.

[4] Marie Antoinette, Dauphine of France, to Empress Maria Theresa, undated, 1770, in Maxime de la Rocheterie & Marquis de Beaucourt, eds., *Lettres de Marie Antoinette*, vol. I (Paris: A. Picard et fils, 1895), p. 8.

[5] Jean-François Léonard, *The Souvenirs of Léonard: Hairdresser to Queen Marie-Antoinette*, trans. A. Teixera de Mattos, vol. I (London: n.p., 1897), p. 74.

[6] Weber, *Queen of Fashion*, p. 60.

[7] Erickson, *To the Scaffold*, p. 142.

[8] Empress Maria Theresa to Florimand Claude, Comte Mercy d'Argenteau, 4 January 1772, in Smythe, ed., *Guardian of Marie Antoinette*, vol. I, p. 177.

[9] Empress Maria Theresa to Florimand Claude, Comte Mercy d'Argenteau, 11 February 1771, in Saint-Amand, *Women of Versailles*, p. 167.

[10] Empress Maria Theresa to Marie Antoinette, Dauphine of France, undated, in Arneth & Geoffrey, eds., *Marie Antoinette*, vol. I, p. 104.

[11] Marie Antoinette, Dauphine of France, to Empress Maria Theresa, undated, in Philippe Delorme, *Marie Antoinette: Épouse de Louis XVI, mère de Louis XVII* (Paris: Pygmalion/Gérard Watelet, 1999), p. 65.

[12] Empress Maria Theresa to Marie Antoinette, Dauphine of France, undated, in Arneth & Geoffrey, eds., *Marie Antoinette*, vol. I, p. 104.

[13] Marie Antoinette, Dauphine of France, to Empress Maria Theresa, 13 January 1773, in Smythe, ed., *Guardian of Marie Antoinette*, vol. I, p. 277.

[14] Fraser, *Marie Antoinette*, p. 115.

[15] Queen Marie Antoinette to Empress Maria Theresa, 14 May 1774, in Smythe, ed., *Guardian of Marie Antoinette*, vol. I, p. 365.

[16] Campan, *Memoirs*, vol. I, p. 96.

[17] Fraser, *Marie Antoinette*, p. 116.

[18] Jacques de Norvins, *Mémorial*, vol. I (Paris, n.p., 1896), p. 56.

[19] H. Noel Williams, *Memoirs of Madame Du Barry, Of the Court of Louis XV* (New York: P.F. Collier & Son, 1910), p. 260.

[20] Emperor Joseph II to Queen Marie Antoinette, undated, May 1774, in Padover, *The Revolutionary Emperor*, p. 115.

[21] Queen Marie Antoinette to Empress Maria Theresa, 14 May 1774, in Young, *Marie Antoinette*, p. 89.

[22] Empress Maria Theresa to Florimand Claude, Comte Mercy d'Argenteau, undated, May 1774, in Jackson, *French Court and Society*, p. 42.

[23] Empress Maria Theresa to Florimand Claude, Comte Mercy d'Argenteau, 18 May 1774, in Smythe, ed., *Guardian of Marie Antoinette*, vol. II, p. 370.

[24] Gelardi, *In Triumph's Wake*, p. 205.

[25] Empress Marie Theresa to Queen Marie Antoinette, undated, May 1774, in Smythe, ed., *Guardian of Marie Antoinette*, vol. I, p. 371.

[26] Lever, *Marie Antoinette*, p. 55 ("Louis the Desired One").

[27] Rocheterie, *The Life of Queen Marie Antoinette*, vol. I, pp. 96-97.

[28] Empress Maria Theresa to Queen Marie Antoinette, undated, 1774, in *ibid*, p. 98.

[29] Ethel Colburn Mayne, *Enchanters of Men*, 2nd ed. (London: Methuen & Co., 1909), p. 159.

[30] Emperor Joseph II to Grand Duke Leopold I, undated, 1774, in Rocheterie, *The Life of Queen Marie Antoinette*, vol. I, p. 102.

[31] Campan, *Memoirs*, vol. I, p. xxvi.

[32] Florimand Claude, Comte Mercy d'Argenteau to Empress Maria Theresa, 18 May 1775 (mistakenly dated in source as 1875), in Vincent W. Beach, "The Count of Artois and the Coming of the French Revolution," in *The* Journal *of Modern History*. Vol. 30, no. 4 (December, 1958), p. 314.

[33] Amanda Foreman, *Georgiana: Duchess of Devonshire* (London: Harper Perennial, 1998), p. 40.

[34] Empress Maria Theresa to Queen Marie Antoinette, undated, in Schulte, ed., *The Body of the Queen*, p. 159.

[35] Florimand Claude, Comte Mercy d'Argenteau to Empress Marie Theresa, 18 March 1775, in *ibid*, p. 315.

[36] Fraser, *Marie Antoinette*, p. 127.

[37] Acton, *The Bourbons of Naples*, p. 177.

[38] *Ibid*, p. 171.

[39] Dutens, *Memoirs*, vol. II, p. 154.

[40] C.C. Dyson, *The Life of Marie Amélie: Last Queen of the French, 1782-1866* (New York: D. Appleton & Company, 1910), p. 47.

[41] A letter of Johann von Goethe, 15 March 1787, in Nathan Haskell Dole, ed., *Letters from Switzerland and Italy*, trans. A.J.W. Morrison, et al (New York: International Publishing Company, 1902), p. 322.

[42] Princess Michael, *Crowned in a Far Country*, p. 75.

[43] A letter of Johann von Goethe, 25 February 1787, in Dole, ed., *Letters*, p. 295.

[44] A letter of Johann von Goethe, 16 March 1787, in *ibid*, p. 323.

[45] Princess Michael, *Crowned in a Far Country*, pp. 76-77.

[46] Acton, *The Bourbons of Naples*, p. 173.

Chapter 12: Friendship, Family, and Alliances

[1] Rocheterie, *The Life of Marie Antoinette*, vol. I, pp. 127-128.

[2] Campan, *Memoirs*, vol. I, p. 124; Weber, *Queen of Fashion*, p. 96; Jackson, *French Court and Society*, vol. I, p. 122.

[3] Vicomte de Grouchy & Paul Cottin, eds., *Journal inédit du Duc de Croÿ 1718-1784*, vol. III (Paris: E. Flammarion, 1907), pp. 181-182.

[4] Lever, *Marie Antoinette*, p. 74.

[5] Weber, *Queen of Fashion*, p. 95.

[6] Étienne-Léon, Baron de Lamothe-Langon, *Souvenirs sur Marie Antoinette et la Cour de Versailles*, vol. II (Paris: Bourgogne et Martinet, 1836), p. 268.

[7] Lever, *Marie Antoinette*, p. 75.

[8] Gelardi, *In Triumph's Wake*, p. 204.

[9] Queen Marie Antoinette to Emperor Joseph II, undated, in Queen Marie Antoinette of France, *Correspondance de Marie-Antoinette*, vol. I (Clermont-Ferrand: Paléo, 2004), pp. 204-205.

[10] Weber, *Queen of Fashion*, p. 79.

[11] Emperor Joseph II to Grand Duke Leopold I, undated, in Erickson, *To the Scaffold*, p. 142.

[12] Morris, *Maria Theresa*, p. 289.

[13] *Ibid*, p. 290.

[14] Guglia, *Maria Theresa*, vol. II, p. 271.

[15] Morris, *Maria Theresa*, p. 290.

[16] Guglia, *Maria Theresa*, vol. II, p. 271.

[17] Hyde, ed., *Secret Memoirs*, p. 97.

[18] Wheatcroft, *The Habsburgs*, p. 233.

[19] Langsam, *Francis the Good*, p. 9.

[20] *Ibid.*

[21] Dyson, *Life of Marie Amélie*, p. 26.

[22] Sir Henry Swinburne to Sir Edward Swinburne, 12 February 1777, in Henry Swinburne, *Secret Memoirs of the Courts of Europe: Letters at the End of the Eighteenth Century*, vol. I (Philadelphia: George Barrie & Sons, 1840), p. 131.

[23] Princess Michael, *Crowned in a Far Country*, p. 81.

[24] Acton, *The Bourbons of Naples*, p. 182.

[25] Sir Henry Swinburne to Sir Edward Swinburne, 20 August 1777 in Swinburne, *Secret Memoirs*, vol. I, p. 157.

[26] Erickson, *To the Scaffold*, p. 137.

[27] Jackson, *French Court and Society*, vol. I, p. 189.

[28] Casimir Stryienski, *The Eighteenth Century*, trans. H.N. Dickinson (London: William Heinemann, 1916), p. 251.

[29] Lever, *Marie Antoinette*, p. 106.

[30] Young, *Marie Antoinette*, p. 134.

[31] Rocheterie, *The Life of Marie Antoinette*, vol. I, p. 189.

[32] Weber, *Memoirs*, vol. I, p. 45.

[33] Rocheterie, *The Life of Marie Antoinette*, vol. I, p. 200.

[34] Jackson, *French Court and Society*, vol. I, p. 192.

[35] Fraser, *Marie Antoinette*, p. 140.

[36] Emperor Joseph II to Grand Duke Leopold I, 9 July 1777, in Lever, *Marie Antoinette*, p. 109.

[37] Weber, *Queen of Fashion*, p. 139.

[38] Emperor Joseph II to Empress Maria Theresa, 3 July 1777, in Gelardi, *In Triumph's Wake*, p. 218.

[39] Corti, *Mariage de Marie Antoinette*, p. 140.

[40] Grouchy & Cottin, eds., *Journal inédit*, vol. IV, pp. 11-13.

[41] Louis Xavier, Count of Provence, to King Gustav III of Sweden, undated, April 1777, in Rocheterie, *The Life of Marie Antoinette*, vol. I, p. 205.

[42] Weber, *Queen of Fashion*, p. 139.

[43] Campan, *Memoirs*, vol. I, pp. 166-67.

[44] Emperor Joseph II to Empress Maria Theresa, undated, May 1777, in Rocheterie, *The Life of Marie Antoinette*, vol. I, p. 207.

[45] Queen Marie Antoinette to Empress Maria Theresa, 14 June 1777, in Young, *Marie Antoinette*, p. 137.

[46] Emperor Joseph II to Maria Christina, Duchess of Saxe-Teschen, 9 June 1777, in Rocheterie, *The Life of Marie Antoinette*, vol. I, p. 211.

[47] Coxe, *History of the House of Austria*, p. 458.

[48] Campan, *Memoirs*, vol. I, p.178.

[49] Rounding, *Catherine the Great*, p. 355.

[50] Emperor Joseph II to Prince Kaunitz, 1 January 1778, in Beales, *Joseph II*, vol. I, p. 392.

[51] Emperor Joseph II to Grand Duke Leopold I, undated, January 1778, in Rocheterie, *The Life of Marie Antoinette*, vol. I, p. 216.

[52] Arneth & Geoffrey, eds., *Marie Antoinette*, vol. I, p. 38.

[53] Empress Maria Theresa to Florimond Claude, Comte Mercy d'Argenteau, undated, July 1777, in Smythe, ed., *Guardian of Marie Antoinette*, vol. II, p. 533.

[54] Empress Maria Theresa to Emperor Joseph II, 2 January 1778, in Rocheterie, *The Life of Marie Antoinette*, vol. I, pp. 216-217.

[55] Bright, *Joseph II*, pp. 94-95.

[56] Emperor Joseph II to Grand Duke Leopold, 24 January 1778, in Harold Temperley, *Frederick the Great and Kaiser Joseph* (London: Frank Cass Publishers, 1968), p. 89.

[57] Fraser, *Marie Antoinette*, p. 160; Ingrao, *The Habsburg Monarchy*, p. 196.

Chapter 13: "Only in Tears"

[1] Thomas Campbell, *Frederick the Great, His Court and Times*, vol. IV (London: Henry Colburn, 1834), p. 375.

[2] King Frederick II to Count von Goltz, 11 February 1778, in Rocheterie, *The Life of Marie Antoinette*, vol. I, p. 220.

[3] Empress Maria Theresa to Emperor Joseph II, 14 March 1778, in Beales, *Joseph II*, vol. I, p. 398.

[4] Campbell, *Frederick the Great*, vol. IV, p. 377.

[5] Empress Maria Theresa to Florimond Claude, Count Mercy d'Argenteau, 7 July 1778, in Smythe, ed., *Guardian of Marie Antoinette*, vol. II, pp. 591-592.

[6] Empress Maria Theresa to Archduke Ferdinand, undated, July 1778, in Rocheterie, *The Life of Marie Antoinette*, vol. I, p. 222.

[7] Prince Charles-Joseph de Ligne, *The Prince de Ligne: His Memoirs, Letters, and Miscellanious Papers*, trans. Katherine Prescott Wormeley, vol. I (New York: Brentano's Publishers, 1899), p. 216.

[8] Empress Maria Theresa to Queen Marie Antoinette, undated, July 1778, in Rocheterie, *The Life of Marie Antoinette*, vol. I, p. 223.

[9] Queen Marie Antoinette to Empress Maria Theresa, undated, October 1778, in Gaulot, *Friend of the Queen*, p. 234.

[10] Empress Maria Theresa to Queen Marie Antoinette, undated, 1778, in Schulte, ed., *The Body of the Queen*, p. 165.

[11] *Ibid*.

[12] Fraser, *Marie Antoinette*, pp. 161-162.

[13] Erickson, *To the Scaffold*, p. 151.

[14] *Ibid*, p. 152.

[15] Campan, *Memoirs*, vol. I, p. 186.

[16] Florimond Claude, Comte Mercy d'Argenteau, to Empress Maria Theresa, 20 December 1778, in Smythe, ed., *Guardian of Marie Antoinette*, vol. II, p. 614.

[17] A letter of Sir Nathaniel Wraxall, 30 December 1778, in Wraxall, *Memoirs*, vol. II, pp. 220-221.

[18] Queen Marie Antoinette to Empress Maria Theresa, undated, January 1779, in Pierre de Nolhac, *Marie Antoinette the Queen* (Paris: Goupil & Co., 1898), p. 27.

[19] Lever, *Marie Antoinette*, p. 127.

[20] Empress Maria Theresa to Queen Marie Antoinette, undated, April 1779, in Schulte, ed., *The Body of the Queen*, p. 166.

[21] Empress Maria Theresa to Emperor Joseph II, 14 April 1778, in Krack, ed., *Briefe einer Kaiserin*, p. 41.

[22] Emperor Joseph II to Grand Duke Leopold, 18 July 1778, in Beales, *Joseph II*, vol. I, p. 409.

[23] Beales, *Joseph II*, vol. I, p. 420.

[24] Wraxall, *Memoirs*, vol. II, p. 164.

[25] Lydia Hoyt Farmer, *The Girl's Book of Famous Queens* (New York: Thomas Y. Crowell & Co., 1887), p. 300.

[26] Ingrao, *The Habsburg Monarchy*, p. 196.

[27] Empress Maria Theresa to Emperor Joseph II, 25 July 1778, in Krack, ed., *Briefe einer Kaiserin*, pp. 41-42.

[28] Sir Henry Swinburne to Sir Edward Swinburne, 8 January 1779, in Swinburne, *Secret Memoirs*, vol. I, p. 223.

[29] *Ibid.*

[30] Hilda Gamlin, *Nelson's Friendships*, vol. I (London: Hutchinson & Co., 1899), p. 33.

[31] Morris, *Maria Theresa*, p. 328.

[32] *Ibid.*

[33] Empress Maria Theresa to Prince Francis of Tuscany, undated, February 1890, in Langsam, *Francis the Good*, p. 27.

[34] Empress Maria Theresa to Grand Duke Leopold, 5 October 1780, in Arneth, ed., *Briefe der Kaiserin Maria Theresia*, vol. I, p. 42.

[35] Gelardi, *In Triumph's Wake*, p. 221.

[36] Empress Maria Theresa to Queen Marie Antoinette, 30 June 1780, in Krack, ed., *Briefe einer Kaiserin*, p. 146.

[37] Empress Maria Theresa to Queen Marie Antoinette, 3 November 1780, in Fraser, *Marie Antoinette*, p. 184.

[38] Gelardi, *In Triumph's Wake*, p. 222.

[39] Coxe, *History of the House of Austria*, p. 482.

[40] Smythe, ed., *Guardian of Marie Antoinette*, vol. II, p. 678.

[41] Empress Maria Theresa to Grand Duke Leopold, undated, November 1780, in Elizabeth McFarland, ed., *Familienbriefe. Mit einem biographischen Anhang von Maria Theresia* (Berlin & Vienna: Ullstein & Co., 1920), p. 152.

[42] Rocheterie, *The Life of Marie Antoinette*, vol. I, p. 241.

[43] Bright, *Joseph II*, p. 126.

[44] Coxe, *History of the House of Austria*, p. 481.

[45] McGill, *Maria Theresa*, p. 152.

[46] Jameson, *Memoirs*, vol. II, p. 283.

[47] Empress Catherine II of Russia to Emperor Joseph II, 2 December 1780, in Alfred von Arneth, ed., *Joseph II. und Katharina von Russland. Ihr Briefwechsel* (Vienna: W. Braumüller, 1869), p. 25.

[48] John Aikin, *Annals of the Reign of King George the Third; From its Commencement in the Year 1760 to the Death of His Majesty in the Year 1820*, 2nd ed., vol. I

(London: Longman, Hurst, Rees, Orme, and Brown, 1820), p. 272; Farmer, *Famous Queens*, p. 300.

[49] Rocheterie, *The Life of Marie Antoinette*, vol. I, p. 241.

[50] Henriette Louise, Baroness d'Oberkirch, *Memoirs of the Baroness d'Oberkirch, Countess de Montbrison*, vol. I (London: Colburn and Co., 1852), p. 167.

[51] Gelardi, *In Triumph's Wake*, p. 222.

[52] Doran, *'Mann' and Manners*, vol. II, p. 376.

[53] Bearne, *A Sister of Marie Antoinette*, p. 101.

[54] Baron Etienne Léone de Lamothe-Langon, ed., *Memoirs of Louis the Eighteenth*, vol. II (London: Saunders & Otley, 1832), p. 184.

[55] Queen Marie Antoinette to Emperor Joseph II, 10 December 1780, in Rocheterie, *The Life of Marie Antoinette*, vol. I, p. 242.

[56] Weber, *Queen of Fashion*, p. 158.

[57] Campan, *Memoirs*, vol. I, p. 191.

Part III: The Flames of Revolution (1780—1793)

Chapter 14: The Philosopher King

[1] Campbell, *Frederick the Great*, vol. IV, p. 385.

[2] Robin Okey, *The Habsburg Monarchy c. 1765—1918: From Enlightenment to Eclipse* (New York: Palgrave Macmillan, 2002), p. 40.

[3] Bright, *Joseph II*, p. 127.

[4] John S.C. Abbott, *The Monarchies of Continental Europe. The Empire of Austria; Its Rise and Present Power* (New York: Mason Brothers, 1859), p. 491.

[5] Ingrao, *The Habsburg Monarchy*, p. 197.

[6] *Ibid*, p.198.

[7] A.J. Grant, *The French Monarchy (1483—1789)*, 4th ed., vol. II (Cambridge: Cambridge University Press, 1931), p. 276.

[8] Philip Mazzei to Grand Duke Leopold, undated, May 1781, in Howard R. Marraro, "Mazzei's Correspondance with the Grand Duke of Tuscany during His American Mission," in *William and Mary College Quarterly Historical Magazine*. 2nd ser., vol. 22, no. 3 (July, 1942), p. 277.

[9] Weber, *Queen of Fashion*, p. 172.

[10] Queen Marie Antoinette to Princess Louise of Hesse-Darmstadt, undated, 1781, in Rocheterie, *The Life of Marie Antoinette*, vol. I, p. 242.

[11] *Ibid*, p. 243.

[12] Campan, *Memoirs*, vol. I, p. 192.

[13] Rocheterie, *The Life of Marie Antoinette*, vol. I, pp. 243-244.

[14] Angélique de Bombelles to Marc, Marquis de Bombelles, 22 October 1781, in Imbert de Saint-Amand, *Marie Antoinette and the End of the Old Regime*, 2nd ed.,(London: Hutchinson & Co., 1892), p. 15.

[15] Emperor Joseph II to Grand Duke Leopold, 29 October 1781, in Alfred von Arneth, ed., *Joseph II. und Leopold von Toscana. Ihr Briefwechsel von 1781 bis 1791*, vol. I (Vienna: Braunmüller, 1872), p. 60.

[16] Emperor Joseph II to Grand Duke Leopold, 1 November 1781, in *ibid*.

[17] Angélique de Bombelles to Marc, Marquis de Bombelles, 29 October 1781, in *ibid*, p. 16.

[18] Victoire M. Montagu, *The Celebrated Madame Campan, Lady-in-Waiting to Marie Antoinette and Confidante of Napoleon* (Philadelphia: J.B. Lippincott Company, 1914), p. 58.

[19] Rocheterie, *The Life of Marie Antoinette*, vol. II, p. 3.

[20] Weber, *Queen of Fashion*, p. 151.

[21] Langsam, *Francis the Good*, p. 75.

[22] *Ibid*, p. 74.

[23] Empress Catherine II of Russia to Emperor Joseph II, 22 January 1781, Letter XIX, in Arneth, ed., *Joseph II. und Katharina*, p. 40.

[24] Langsam, *Francis the Good*, p. 74.

[25] *Ibid*, p. 75.

[26] Empress Maria Theresa to Count Bliimegen, 19 June 1777, in Henry Wickham Steed, *The Habsburg Monarchy*, 4th ed. (London: Constable & Company, Ltd., 1919), p. 85.

[27] Empress Maria Theresa to Emperor Joseph II, 5 July 1777, in Gelardi, *In Triumph's Wake*, p. 183.

[28] Ingrao, *The Habsburg Monarchy*, p. 199.

[29] Max Beloff, *The Age of Absolutism: 1660—1815* (New York: Harper & Brothers, 1962), p. 129.

[30] Ingrao, *The Habsburg Monarchy*, p. 199.

[31] Beloff, *Age of Absolutism*, p. 129.

[32] Ingrao, *The Habsburg Monarchy*, p. 199.

[33] James, Viscount Bryce, *The Holy Roman Empire* (London: Macmillan and Co., Limited: 1897), p. 355n.

[34] Ingrao, *The Habsburg Monarchy*, p. 199.

[35] Blanning, *Joseph II*, p. 97.

[36] Sir Horace Rumbold, *The Austrian Court in the Nineteenth Century* (London: Methuen & Co., 1909), p. 15.

[37] Bryce, *The Holy Roman Empire*, p. 355n; Doran, *'Mann' and Manners*, vol. II, p. 392.

[38] Ingrao, *The Habsburg Monarchy*, p. 199.

[39] Brion, *Daily Life*, p. 21.

[40] Ritchie Robertson, "Joseph II: The Tragedy of an Enlightened Despot," in *St. John's College Alumni: Magazine* (2006, accessed 20 November 2006, http://www.sjc.ox.ac.uk/alumni/display/magazine.php?textId=83&pageNo=3&PHPSESSID=4f3ebfcf87be1c678ee039f446e).

[41] Ingrao, *The Habsburg Monarchy*, p. 197.

[42] Blanning, *Joseph II*, p. 49.

[43] A.J.P. Taylor, *The Habsburg Monarchy 1809—1918: A History of the Austrian Empire and Austria-Hungary* (London: Hamish Hamilton, Ltd., 1948), p. 10.

[44] Bright, *Joseph II*, p. 191.

[45] *Ibid*, p. 196.

[46] Robertson, "Joseph II," *St. John's College Alumni*.

[47] *Ibid*.

[48] *Ibid*.

[49] Taylor, *The Habsburg Empire*, p. 17.
[50] Beloff, *Age of Absolutism*, p. 119.
[51] Emperor Joseph II to Grand Duke Leopold, 31 October 1784, in Arneth, ed., *Joseph II. und Leopold von Toscana*, vol. I, p. 227.
[52] Fraser, *Marie Antoinette*, p. 197.
[53] J.F. Labourdette, *Vergennes: Ministre Principal de Louis XVI* (Paris: Desjonquères, 1990), p. 276.
[54] Cuthell, *An Imperial Victim*, vol. II, p. 123.

Chapter 15: "The White Elephant"
[1] Campan, *Memoirs*, vol. II, p. 14.
[2] *The Times*, 5 September 1785.
[3] Campan, *Memoirs*, vol. II, p. 15.
[4] *Ibid*, p. 16.
[5] Montagu, *Madame Campan*, p. 68.
[6] *Ibid*.
[7] Emperor Joseph II to Queen Marie Antoinette, 9 September 1783, Letter XI, in Alfred von Arneth, ed., *Marie Antoinette, Joseph II. und Leopold II. - Ihr Briefwechsel* (Leipzig: K.F. Köhler, 1866), p. 34.
[8] Queen Marie Antoinette to Emperor Joseph II, 29 September 1783, Letter XII, in *ibid*, p. 36.
[9] Erickson, *To the Scaffold*, p. 168.
[10] Blanning, *Joseph II*, p. 14.
[11] "Considerations concerning the Education of the Archduke Francis," Emperor Joseph II, 18 August 1784, in Vehse, *Memoirs*, p. 376.
[12] Blanning, *Joseph II*, p. 14.
[13] *Ibid*, p. 60.
[14] Wheatcroft, *The Habsburgs*, p. 235.
[15] Blanning, *Joseph II*, p. 60.
[16] Wheatcroft, *The Habsburgs*, p. 236.
[17] Bearne, *A Sister of Marie Antoinette*, p. 111.
[18] *Ibid*, p. 112.
[19] Catherine Hyde, Marquise de Gouvion Broglie Scolari, ed., *Private Anecdotes of Foreign Courts*, vol. I (London: Henry Colburn, 1827), p. 408.
[20] Acton, *The Bourbons of Naples*, pp. 187-188.
[21] *Ibid*, pp. 188-189.
[22] Clement, *Naples*, p. 149.
[23] Princess Michael, *Crowned in a Far Country*, p. 82.
[24] Bearne, *A Sister of Marie Antoinette*, p. 104.
[25] Campan, *Memoirs*, vol. I, p. 218.
[26] *Ibid*, pp. 218-219.
[27] Henry Swinburne, *At the Close of the Last Century*, vol. II (London: H.S. Nichols and Co., 1895), pp. 33-34.
[28] Campan, *Memoirs*, vol. I, p. 219.
[29] Giglioli, *Naples in 1799*, p. 19.
[30] *Ibid*, p. 78.

[31] Queen Maria Carolina to Lady Emma Hamilton, 6 December 1801, Jeaffreson, *The Queen of Naples and Lord Nelson,* vol. II, p. 146.

[32] Campan, *Memoirs,* vol. I, p. 218.

Chapter 16: Overturning the Throne

[1] *The Times,* 5 September 1785.

[2] R. Storry Deans, *The Trial of Five Queens: Katherine of Aragon, Anne Boleyn, Mary Queen of Scots, Marie Antoinette and Caroline of Brunswick,* 2nd ed. (London: Methuen & Co., 1910), p. 201.

[3] Montagu, *Madame Campan,* p. 75.

[4] *The Times,* 5 September 1785.

[5] Queen Marie Antoinette to Emperor Joseph II, 22 August 1785, in Rocheterie, *The Life of Marie Antoinette,* vol. I, p. 309.

[6] An address of King Louis XVI, 5 September 1785, in Saint-Amand, *End of the Old Regime,* p. 104.

[7] Rocheterie, *The Life of Marie Antoinette,* vol. I, p. 311.

[8] Deans, *Five Queens,* p. 202.

[9] Mayne, *Enchanters,* p. 160.

[10] Imbert de Saint-Amand, *The Youth of the Duchess of Angoulême,* trans. Elizabeth Gilbert Martin (New York: Charles Scribner's Sons, 1892), p. 9.

[11] Campan, *Memoirs,* vol. I, p. 229.

[12] Imbert de Saint-Amand, *The Youth of the Duchess of Angoulême,* trans. Elizabeth Gilbert Martin (New York: Charles Scribner's Sons, 1892), p. 9.

[13] Weber, *Queen of Fashion,* p. 173.

[14] Princess Élisabeth of France to Angélique de Bombelles, 25 June 1787, in Princess Élisabeth of France, *The Life and Letters of Madame Élisabeth de France, Sister of Louis XVI* (New York: H.P. & Co., 1899), p. 37.

[15] Gelardi, *In Triumph's Wake,* p. 226.

[16] Ernest Daudet, *Madame Royale, daughter of Louis XVI and Marie Antoinette, her youth and marriage* (London: William Heinemann, 1913), p. 2.

[17] Nolhac, *Marie Antoinette the Queen,* p. 44.

[18] Grand Duke Leopold to Emperor Joseph II, 7 January 1787, in Arneth, ed., *Joseph II. und Leopold von Toscana,* vol. II, p. 60.

[19] Grand Duke Leopold to Maria Christina, Duchess of Saxe-Teschen, 28 January 1789, Letter XXXVIII, in Adam Wolf, ed., *Leopold II. und Marie Christine. Ihr Briefwechsel (1781—1792)* (Vienna: Carl Gerold's Sohn: 1867), p. 46.

[20] Grand Duke Leopold to Maria Christina, Duchess of Saxe-Teschen, 6 February 1789, Letter XXXVIX, in *ibid,* p. 47.

Chapter 17: "Anguish and Deep Despair"

[1] Queen Marie Antoinette to Emperor Joseph II, 10 November 1785, Letter XLIX, in Arneth, ed., *Marie Antoinette, Joseph II. und Leopold II.,* p. 100.

[2] A Letter of Emperor Joseph II, undated, September 1787, in Campan, *Memoirs,* vol. I, pp. 319-320.

[3] King Louis XVI to Emperor Joseph II, 20 January 1788, Letter LIX, in Arneth, ed., *Marie Antoinette, Joseph II. und Leopold II.,* pp. 111-112.

[4] Ingrao, *The Habsburg Monarchy,* p. 207.

[5] Maynard Solomon, *Mozart: A Life*, (New York: Harper Perennial: 1995), pp. 432-433.

[6] Bright, *Joseph II*, pp. 174-176.

[7] Acton, *The Bourbons of Naples*, p. 212.

[8] Campan, *Memoirs*, vol. I, p. 283.

[9] Ingrao, *The Habsburg Monarchy*, p. 207.

[10] Schoellkopf, *Enlightened Despotism*, p. 131.

[11] Acton, *The Bourbons of Naples*, p. 226.

[12] Schoellkopf, *Enlightened Despotism*, pp. 137-138.

[13] Letter of the Austrian ambassador to Naples, name unknown, 3 January 1789, in Bearne, *A Sister of Marie Antoinette*, p. 112.

[14] Grand Duke Leopold to Maria Christina, Duchess of Saxe-Teschen, 28 January 1789, Letter XXXVIII, in Wolf, ed., *Leopold II. und Marie Christine*, pp. 46-47.

[15] Bearne, *A Sister of Marie Antoinette*, p. 113.

[16] Queen Maria Carolina to the Marquis de Gallo, 10 February 1789, in Acton, *The Bourbons of Naples*, p. 226

[17] Emperor Joseph II to Grand Duke Leopold, undated, 1789, in Padover, *The Revolutionary Emperor*, p. 381.

[18] Wheatcroft, *The Habsburgs*, p. 228.

[19] Volkmar Braunbehrens, *Mozart in Vienna* (New York: Grove Weidenfeld, 1990), pp. 311-312.

[20] Bright, *Joseph II*, p. 195.

[21] *Ibid*, p. 196.

Chapter 18: A Pale Sun

[1] Gelardi, *In Triumph's Wake*, p. 207.

[2] *Ibid*, p. 229.

[3] Sophia H. MacLehose, *From the Monarchy To the Republic in France 1788—1792* (Glasgow: James MacLehose and Sons, 1904), p. 59.

[4] Charles M. Andrews, *The Historical Development of Modern Europe, From the Congress of Vienna to the Present Time*, vol. I: 1815-1850 (London & New York: G.P. Putnam's Sons, 1896), p. 10.

[5] Diary entry of Queen Marie Antoinette, 22 February, 1788, in Rocheterie, *The Life of Marie Antoinette*, vol. II, p. 9.

[6] Dyson, *Life of Marie Amélie*, pp. 35-36.

[7] Diary entry of King Louis XVI, 4 June 1789, in Louis Nicardot, ed., *Journal de Louis XVI* (Paris: E. Dentu, 1873), p. 135.

[8] Reginald Secher, & Yves Murat, *Un Prince Méconnu: Le Dauphin Louis-Joseph, Fils Aîné de Louis XVI* (Paris: R.S.E., 1998), p. 197.

[9] Lady Catherine Charlotte Jackson, *The French Court and Society. Reign of Louis XVI and First Empire*, vol. II (Boston: I.C. Page and Company, 1897), p. 18.

[10] Weber, *Queen of Fashion*, p. 197.

[11] Rocheterie, *The Life of Marie Antoinette*, vol. I, p. 325.

[12] Fraser, *Marie Antoinette*, p. 277.

[13] Gelardi, *In Triumph's Wake*, p. 227.

[14] King Louis XVI to Charles, Comte d'Artois, 13 July 1789, Letter XIX, in Helen Maria Williams, ed., *The Political and Confidential Correspondence of Lewis XVI*, vol. I (New York: n.p., 1803), p. 170.

[15] Colletta, *Kingdom of Naples*, vol. I, p. 172.

[16] John Emerich Edward Dalbert-Acton, *Lectures on the French Revolution* (London: Macmillan and Co., 1910.), p. 84.

[17] *Ibid*, p. 87.

[18] Lever, *Marie Antoinette*, p. 212.

[19] A. Aulard, *The French Revolution: A Political History, 1789—1804*, trans. Bernard Miall, vol. I: *The Revolution Under the Monarchy, 1789—1792* (New York: Charles Scribner's Sons, 1910), p. 142.

[20] Gaulot, *Friend of the Queen*, pp. 123-124.

[21] Katharine Prescott Wormeley, ed., *The Ruin of a Princess* (London: T. Werner Laurie, Ltd., 1912), p. 212.

[22] Anonymous, *The Sufferings of the Royal Family During the Revolution in France* (London: Smithers Hampden and Co., 1902), p. 27.

[23] Gelardi, *In Triumph's Wake*, p. 231.

[24] Fraser, *Marie Antoinette*, p. 295.

[25] *Ibid*.

[26] Eckard, *King Who Never Reigned*, p. 23.

[27] MacLehose, *Monarchy to the Republic in France*, p. 199.

[28] Fraser, *Marie Antoinette*, pp. 296-297.

[29] Maclehose, *Monarchy to the Republic*, p. 199.

[30] Weber, *Queen of Fashion*, p. 216.

[31] Maclehose, *Monarchy to the Republic*, p. 200.

[32] Princess Élisabeth to Angélique de Bombelles, 8 October 1789, in Princess Élisabeth, *Life and Letters*, p. 42.

[33] Fraser, *Marie Antoinette*, p. 302.

[34] Imbert de Saint-Amand, *Marie Antoinette at the Tuileries, 1789-1791*, trans., Elizabeth Gilbert Martin (New York: Charles Scribner's Sons, 1891), p. 4.

[35] *Ibid*, p. 6.

[36] *Ibid*, p. 24.

[37] Emperor Joseph II to Grand Duke Leopold, 4 January 1790, in Bright, *Joseph II*, p. 217.

[38] Emperor Joseph II to Grand Duke Leopold, undated, February 1790, in Langsam, *Francis the Good*, p. 83.

[39] *Ibid*.

[40] Grand Duke Leopold to Maria Christina, Duchess of Saxe-Teschen, undated, Letter LXIX, in Wolf, ed., *Leopold II. und Marie Christine*, p. 110.

[41] *Ibid*.

[42] Emperor Joseph II to Grand Duke Leopold, 21 January 1790, in Beales, *Joseph II*, vol. I, p. 5.

[43] Padover, *The Revolutionary Emperor*, p. 388.

[44] Vehse, *Memoirs*, p. 347.

[45] Langsam, *Francis the Good*, p. 82.

[46] Padover, *The Revolutionary Emperor*, p. 389.

[47] Robertson, "Joseph II," *St. John's College Alumni*.

[48] Catherine Elisabeth von Goethe to Friedrich von Stein, 1 March 1790, in Alfred S. Gibbs, ed., *Goethe's Mother* (New York: Dodd, Mead, and Company, 1880), p. 180.

[49] *The Times*, 9 April 1790.

[50] Brion, *Daily Life*, pp. 22-23.

[51] Prince Charles-Joseph de Ligne to Empress Catherine II, 12 February 1790, in Ligne, *Memoirs*, trans. Katherine Prescott Wormeley, p. 124.

Chapter 19: Weights of the Crown

[1] Grand Duke Leopold to Prince Francis of Tuscany, 25 February 1790, in Langsam, *Francis the Good*, p. 86.

[2] Grand Duke Leopold to Queen Marie Antoinette, 27 February 1790, Letter LXV, in Arneth, ed., *Marie Antoinette, Joseph II. und Leopold II.*, p. 120.

[3] Queen Marie Antoinette to Grand Duke Leopold, undated, March 1790, in Young, *Marie Antoinette*, p. 294.

[4] Grand Duke Leopold to Maria Christina, Duchess of Saxe-Teschen, 15 March 1790, Letter LXXIII, in Wolf, ed., *Leopold II. und Marie Christine*, p. 119.

[5] Grand Duke Leopold to Maria Christina, Duchess of Saxe-Teschen, 2 May 1790, Letter XC, in *ibid*, p. 143.

[6] Grand Duke Leopold to Maria Christina, Duchess of Saxe-Teschen, 16 May 1790, Letter XCII, in *ibid*, p. 144.

[7] Langsam, *Francis the Good*, p. 87.

[8] *Ibid*, p. 90.

[9] Acton, *The Bourbons of Naples*, p. 227.

[10] *Ibid*.

[11] Grand Duke Leopold to Maria Christina, Duchess of Saxe-Teschen, 2 May 1790, Letter XC, in Wolf, ed., *Leopold II. und Marie Christine*, pp. 142-143.

[12] Acton, *The Bourbons of Naples*, p. 237.

[13] Grand Duke Leopold to Maria Christina, Duchess of Saxe-Teschen, 12 June 1790, Letter XCIX, in Wolf, ed., *Leopold II. und Marie Christine*, pp. 156-157.

[14] Fraser, *Marie Antoinette*, p. 312.

[15] Emperor Leopold II to Maria Christina, Duchess of Saxe-Teschen, 24 October 1790, Letter CXXIX, in Wolf, ed., *Leopold II. und Marie Antoinette*, p. 201.

[16] Coxe, *History of the House of Austria*, p. 544.

[17] *Ibid*, p. 106.

[18] Fraser, *Marie Antoinette*, pp. 320-321.

[19] Flora Fraser, *Princesses: The Six Daughters of George III* (London: John Murray, 2004), p. 126.

[20] Queen Marie Antoinette to Emperor Leopold II, 27 December 1790, in Reeve, ed., *Royal and Republican France*, vol. I, pp. 291-292.

[21] Saint-Amand, *Marie Antoinette at the Tuileries*, p. 34.

[22] Deans, *Five Queens*, p. 204.

[23] Daudet, *Madame Royale*, pp. 4-5.

[24] Coxe, *History of the House of Austria*, p. 555.

[25] Langsam, *Francis the Good*, p. 94.

[26] Ingrao, *The Habsburg Monarchy*, p. 221.

[27] Albert Mousset, *Un témoin ignoré de la Révolution: Le comte Fernan Nuñez, ambassadeur d'Espagne à Paris* (Paris: Éduoard Champion, 1924), p. 244.

[28] Emperor Leopold II to Albert, Duke of Saxe-Teschen, and Maria Christina, Duchess of Saxe-Teschen, 5 July 1791, Letter CLX, in Wolf, ed., *Leopold II. und Marie Christine*, p. 240.

[29] Queen Marie Antoinette to Emperor Leopold II, 22 May 1791, Letter XCIV, in Arneth, *Marie Antoinette, Joseph II. und Leopold II.*, p. 166.

[30] Queen Marie Antoinette to François Hue, undated, August 1791, in Saint-Amand, *Marie Antoinette at the Tuileries*, p. 250.

[31] Fraser, *Marie Antoinette*, p. 324.

[32] Rocheterie, *The Life of Marie Antoinette*, vol. II, p. 169.

[33] Emperor Leopold II to Albert, Duke of Saxe-Teschen, and Maria Christina, Duchess of Saxe-Teschen, 5 July 1791, Letter CLX, in Wolf, ed., *Leopold II. und Marie Christine*, p. 240.

[34] Emperor Leopold II to King Frederick Wilhelm II, undated, 1790, in Abbott, *Monarchies*, p. 500.

Chapter 20: "The Most Blessed Monarch"

[1] Emperor Leopold II to Archduke Maximilian, undated, 1791, in Andrews, *Historical Development*, vol. I, p. 18.

[2] Emperor Leopold II to Maria Christina, Duchess of Saxe-Teschen, 30 July 1791, Letter CLXVII, in Wolf, ed., *Leopold II. und Marie Christine*, p. 256.

[3] W. Miller, "Europe and the Ottoman Power before the Nineteenth Century," in *The English Historical Review*, vol. 16, no. 63 (July, 1901), p. 459.

[4] Langsam, *Francis the Good*, p. 101.

[5] Archduchess Teresa to Archduke Francis, 3 August 1791, in *ibid*.

[6] Acton, *The Bourbons of Naples*, p. 248.

[7] Queen Maria Carolina to Archduchess Teresa, undated, December 1791, in Cuthell, *An Imperial Victim*, vol. I, p. 13.

[8] Queen Maria Carolina to the Marquis of Gallo, undated, 1791, in Acton, *The Bourbons of Naples*, p. 249.

[9] Saint-Amand, *Marie Antoinette at the Tuileries*, p. 248.

[10] Kerner, *Bohemia in the Eighteenth Century*, p. 190.

[11] Pillnitz Declaration, 27 August 1791, in Rocheterie, *The Life of Marie Antoinette*, vol. II, p. 170.

[12] Emperor Leopold II to Maria Christina, Duchess of Saxe-Teschen, 5 September 1791, Letter CLXXIV, in Wolf, ed., *Leopold II. und Marie Christine*, p. 265.

[13] Maclehose, *Monarchy to the Republic*, p. 372.

[14] F. de Bourgoing, *Histoire Diplomatiques Pendant la Révolution Français*, vol. II (Paris n.p., 1831), p. 451.

[15] Gaulot, *Friend of the Queen*, p. 276.

[16] Archduke Francis to Alexander, Prince Palatine of Hungary, 1 March 1792, in Langsam, *Francis the Good*, pp. 105-106.

[17] Archduke Francis to Archduke Karl, 1 March 1792, in *ibid*.

[18] *Ibid.*

[19] Bearne, *A Sister of Marie Antoinette*, p. 139.

[20] Acton, *The Bourbons of Naples*, p.250.

[21] Frederick Adams Woods, *The Influence of Monarchs: Steps in a New Science of History* (New York: The Macmillan Company, 1913), p. 176.

[22] Langsam, *Francis the Good*, pp. 106-107.

Chapter 21: Oppressed Innocence

[1] Bearne, *A Sister of Marie Antoinette*, p. 158.

[2] Princess Élisabeth to Angélique de Bombelles, 5 August 1791, in Saint-Amand, *Marie Antoinette at the Tuileries*, p. 250.

[3] Aulard, *The French Revolution*, vol. I, p. 353.

[4] Fraser, *Marie Antoinette*, p. 365.

[5] Queen Marie Antoinette to Florimand Claude, Comte Mercy d'Argenteau, 30 April 1792, in Rocheterie, *The Life of Marie Antoinette*, vol. II, pp. 221-222.

[6] Fraser, *Marie Antoinette*, p. 357.

[7] Weber, *Queen of Fashion*, pp. 244-245.

[8] Fraser, *Marie Antoinette*, p. 351.

[9] King Louis XVI to Mesdames Tantes, 25 March 1792, Letter LII, in Williams, ed., *Political and Confidential Correspondence*, vol. II, p. 246.

[10] King Louis XVI to M. Montmorin, 1 August 1792, Letter XVI, in *ibid*, vol. III, p. 23.

[11] King Louis XVI to Louis Xavier, Comte de Provence, 11 August 1792, Letter XVIII, in *ibid*, vol. III, p. 42.

[12] King Louis XVI to Louis Xavier, Comte de Provence, 12 August 1792, Letter LXIX, in *ibid*, vol. III, p. 46.

[13] Lever, *Marie Antoinette*, p. 278.

[14] Saint-Amand, *The Youth of the Duchess of Angoulême*, p. 14.

[15] *Ibid*, p. 280.

[16] *Ibid*, p. 281.

[17] *Ibid*, p. 51.

[18] Jean-Baptise Cléry, *A Journal of Occurrences at the Temple, During the Confinement of Louis XVI, King of France*, trans. R.C. Dallas (London: Baylis, 1798), p. 149.

[19] Bearne, *A Sister of Marie Antoinette*, pp. 119-120.

[20] Anonymous, *The Sufferings of the Royal Family*, p. 103.

[21] Diary entry of Princess Marie Thérèse, undated, October 1795, in Théodore Gosslin (pseud. G. Lenotre), *The Daughter of Louis XVI. Marie-Thérèse-Charlotte de France Duchess d'Angoulême*, trans. J. Lewis (London & New York: John Lane, 1908), p. 145.

[22] Diary entry of Gouverneur Morris, 21 September 1792, in Beatrix Cary Davenport, ed., *The Diary of the French Revolution by Gouverneur Morris 1752-1816, Minister to France During the Terror*, vol. II (Boston: Houghton Mifflin Company, 1939), p. 547.

[23] Gouverneur Morris to Thomas Jefferson, 21 December 1792, in Davenport, ed., *Gouverneur Morris*, vol. II, p. 591.

[24] Hilaire Belloc, *The Last Days of the French Monarchy* (London: Chapman & Hall Ltd., 1916), p. 204.

[25] *The Times*, 25 January 1793.

[26] Diary entry of Marie Thérèse, undated, October 1795, in Gosselin, *Daughter of Louis XVI*, p. 154.

[27] Eckard, *King Who Never Reigned*, pp. 72-73.

[28] *Ibid.*

[29] *The Times*, 25 January 1793.

[30] Fraser, *Marie Antoinette*, p. 399.

[31] Weber, *Queen of Fashion*, p. 267.

[32] Gouverneur Morris to Thomas Jefferson, 25 January 1793, in Davenport, ed., *Gouverneur Morris*, vol. II, p. 602.

[33] Eckard, *King Who Never Reigned*, p. 74.

[34] Crown Princess Clothilde of Sardinia to the Prince de Condé, 18 February 1793, in Louis Léopold D'Artemont, *A Sister of Louis XVI: Marie-Clotilde de France, Queen of Sardinia (1759-1802)* (London: John Murray, 1911), p. 68.

[35] Weber, *Queen of Fashion*, p. 271.

[36] King George III of Great Britain to William Pitt the Younger, 2 February 1793, in John Heneage Jesse, *Memoirs of King George the Third: His Life and Reign*, vol. IV, (Boston: L.C. Page & Company, 1902), p. 409.

[37] Queen Marie Antoinette of France, *Correspondance de Marie-Antoinette*, vol. II (Clermont-Ferrand: Paléo, 2004), p. 180.

[38] Weber, *Queen of Fashion*, p. 273.

[39] *Ibid.*

[40] Delorme, *Marie Antoinette*, p. 301

[41] Phoebe Allen, *The Last Legitimate King of France: Louis XVII* (New York: E.P. Dutton & Co., 1912), p. 14.

[42] Weber, *Queen of Fashion*, p. 273.

[43] *Ibid.*

[44] *Le Moniteur*, 27 March 1793.

[45] Diary entry of Princess Marie Thérèse, 2 August 1793, in Saint-Amand, *The Youth of the Duchess of Angoulême*, pp. 49-50.

[46] Queen Marie Antoinette to Princess Marie Thérèse, undated, August 1793, in André Castelot, *Marie Antoinette* (Paris: Hacette, 1967), p. 470.

[47] Deans, *Five Queens*, p. 210.

[48] Young, *Marie Antoinette*, p. 455.

[49] Weber, *Queen of Fashion*, pp. 282-283.

[50] *Ibid*, pp. 283-284.

[51] Wormeley, ed., *Ruin of a Princess*, p. 277.

[52] Queen Marie Antoinette to Princess Élisabeth of France, 16 October 1793, in Lever, *Marie Antoinette*, p. 303.

[53] Annie Forbes Bush, *Memoirs of the Queens of France*, 2nd ed., vol. II (London: Henry Colburn, 1843), p. 303.

[54] Fraser, *Marie Antoinette*, p. 439.

[55] Weber, *Queen of Fashion*, p. 287.

[56] Théodore Gosselin (pseud. G. Lenotre), *The Last Days of Marie Antoinette*, trans. Rodolph Stawell (London: William Heinemann, 1907), p. 249.

[57] Bush, *Queens of France*, vol. II, p. 303.

[58] Wormeley, ed., *Ruin of a Princess*, pp. 277-278.

[59] Deans, *Five Queens*, p. 197.

Part IV: Empires at War (1793—1814)

Chapter 22: In Revolution's Shadow

[1] Archduchess Marianne to Louis Henri de La Fare, Bishop of Nancy, undated, October 1793, in Daudet, *Madame Royale*, p. 11.

[2] Bearne, *A Sister of Marie Antoinette*, p. 200.

[3] Dyson, *Life of Marie Amélie*, p. 39.

[4] Fraser, *Marie Antoinette*, pp. 443-444.

[5] Johnston, *Napoleonic Empire*, vol. I, p. 40.

[6] Acton, *The Bourbons of Naples*, p. 271.

[7] Princess Michael, *Crowned in a Far Country*, p. 85.

[8] Fraser, *Marie Antoinette*, p. 440.

[9] Catherine Mary Bearne (as Catherine Bearne Charlton), *A Royal Quartette* (London: T. Fisher Unwin, 1908), p. 282.

[10] Acton, *The Bourbons of Naples*, p. 289.

[11] Cuthell, *An Imperial Victim*, vol. II, p. 125.

[12] General Napoleon Bonaparte to the Minister of Spain in Parma, 6 May 1796, in Emperor Napoleon I of the French, *Memoirs of the History of France During the Reign of Napoleon*, vol. IV (London: Henry Colburn, and Martin Bossange and Co., 1824), p. 475.

[13] General Napoleon Bonaparte to the Foreign Minister of Parma, 13 May 1796, in *ibid*, pp. 475-476.

[14] Bearne, *A Royal Quartette*, p. 364.

[15] Julia P. Gelardi, *Born to Rule: Five Reigning Consorts, Granddaughters of Queen Victoria* (New York: St. Martin's Griffin, 2005), p. 143.

[16] Queen Maria Louisa of Etruria, *Memoir of the Queen of Etruria, Written by Herself* (London: J.F. Dove, 1814), pp. 3-4.

[17] Acton, *The Bourbons of Naples*, p. 289.

[18] *Ibid*, p. 292.

[19] Bearne, *A Sister of Marie Antoinette*, p. 236.

[20] Queen Maria Carolina to the Marquis de Gallo, 8 November 1796, in *ibid*, p. 298.

Chapter 23: The Edge of Despair

[1] Acton, *The Bourbons of Naples*, p. 300.

[2] *Ibid*, pp. 302-303.

[3] *Ibid*.

[4] Nathan Miller, *Broadsides: The Age of Fighting Sail, 1775-1815* (Edison, NJ: Castle Books, 2005), p. 213.

[5] Diary entry of Abate Benedetti, 29 November 1798, in Giglioli, *Naples in 1799*, pp. 83-84.

[6] Miller, *Broadsides*, p. 213.

[7] Giglioli, *Naples in 1799*, p. 85.

[8] Leigh Eduardo, *Mistresses: True Stories of Seduction, Power and Ambition* (London: Michael O'Mara Books, Ltd., 2005), pp. 95-96.

[9] Acton, *The Bourbons of Naples*, pp. 327-328.

[10] Giglioli, *Naples in 1799*, p. 91.

[11] Walter Sichel, ed., *Emma Lady Hamilton* (London: Archibald Constable, 1905), p. 244.

[12] Acton, *The Bourbons of Naples*, pp. 327-328.

[13] Lord Horatio Nelson to Lord St. Vincent, 28 December 1798, in Jeaffreson, *The Queen of Naples and Lord Nelson*, vol. II, p. 29.

[14] Giglioli, *Naples in 1799*, p. 93.

[15] Sichel, ed., *Emma Lady Hamilton*, p. 252.

[16] Acton, *The Bourbons of Naples*, pp. 329-331.

[17] Miller, *Broadsides*, p. 213.

[18] Acton, *The Bourbons of Naples*, pp. 329-331.

[19] Sichel, ed., *Emma Lady Hamilton*, p. 257.

[20] Acton, *The Bourbons of Naples*, p. 331.

[21] Bearne, *A Sister of Marie Antoinette*, p. 256.

[22] Eduardo, *Mistresses*, p. 96.

[23] Alfred de Reumont, *Carafas of Maddaloni: Naples Under Spanish Dominion* (London: Henry G. Bohn, 1854), p. 418.

[24] Oscar Browning, "Queen Caroline of Naples," in *The English Historical Review*, vol. 2, no. 7 (July, 1887), p. 483.

[25] Clement, *Naples*, p. 155.

[26] Acton, *The Bourbons of Naples*, p. 348.

[27] *Ibid.*

[28] Sichel, ed., *Emma Lady Hamilton*, p. 259.

[29] Acton, *The Bourbons of Naples*, p. 351.

[30] *Ibid*, p. 365.

[31] Queen Maria Carolina to Lady Emma Hamilton, 1 January 1799, in Jeaffreson, *The Queen of Naples and Lord Nelson*, vol. II, p. 52.

[32] Acton, *The Bourbons of Naples*, p. 365.

[33] Queen Maria Carolina to Empress Teresa, undated, 1799, in Dyson, *Life of Marie Amélie*, p. 57.

[34] Acton, *The Bourbons of Naples*, p. 366.

[35] Queen Maria Carolina to Lady Emma Hamilton, 7 July 1799, in Acton, *The Bourbons of Naples*, p. 423.

[36] Queen María Luísa, *Memoir*, p. 4.

Chapter 24: Italy's Unlikely King

[1] Acton, *The Bourbons of Naples*, pp. 424-425.

[2] Johnston, *Napoleonic Empire*, vol. I, p. 40.

[3] Reumont, *Carafas of Maddaloni*, p. 419.

[4] Imbert de Saint-Amand, *Duchess of Berry and the Court of Louis XVIII*, trans. Elizabeth Gilbert Martin (New York: Charles Scribner's Sons, 1898), p. 4.

[5] Acton, *The Bourbons of Naples*, p. 431.

[6] *Ibid*, pp. 431-432.

[7] Gamlin, *Nelson's Friendships*, vol. I, p. 92.

[8] Acton, *The Bourbons of Naples*, p. 443.

[9] A Letter of Lord Horatio Nelson, 27 May 1804, in Jeaffreson, *The Queen of Naples and Lord Nelson*, vol. II, p. 216.

[10] Sichel, ed., *Emma Lady Hamilton*, p. 321n.

[11] Queen Maria Carolina to Lady Emma Hamilton, undated, 1800, in Jeaffreson, *The Queen of Naples and Lord Nelson*, vol. II, p. 108.

[12] Dyson, *Life of Marie Amélie*, p. 59.

[13] Acton, *The Bourbons of Naples*, p. 457.

[14] Bearne, *A Sister of Marie Antoinette*, p. 330.

[15] Princess Michael, *Crown in a Far Country*, p. 89.

[16] Bearne, *A Sister of Marie Antoinette*, p. 123.

[17] Empress Teresa to Emperor Francis II, 9 May 1805, in Langsam, *Francis the Good*, pp. 159-160.

[18] Princess Michael, *Crowned in a Far Country*, pp. 89-90.

[19] Sichel, ed., *Emma Lady Hamilton*, p. 332.

[20] Queen Maria Carolina to the Marquis de Gallo, undated, December 1801, in Acton, *The Bourbons of Naples*, pp. 459-460.

[21] Acton, *The Bourbons of Naples*, p. 461.

[22] Cuthell, *An Imperial Victim*, vol. I, p. 19.

[23] Queen Maria Carolina to Lady Emma Hamilton, 6 December 1801, in Jeaffreson, *The Queen of Naples and Lord Nelson*, vol. II, p. 145.

[24] Saint-Amand, *Duchess of Berry*, p. 5.

[25] Queen Maria Carolina to the Marquis de Gallo, undated, in Acton, *The Bourbons of Naples*, pp. 469-471.

[26] Treaty of Suspension of Arms Between Parma and France, 9 May 1796, in Napoleon, *Memoirs*, vol. IV, pp. 481-482.

[27] Cuthell, *An Imperial Victim*, vol. II, pp. 125-126.

[28] Sir Archibald Alison, *History of Europe from the Commencement of the French Revolution to the Restoration of the Bourbons in MDCCCXV*, vol. IV (Edinburgh and London: William Blackwood and Sons, 1860), p. 64.

[29] Jacques Chastenet, *Godoy: Master of Spain, 1792-1808*, trans. J.F. Huntington (London: The Batchworth Press, 1953), p. 104.

[30] Queen María Luísa, *Memoir*, p. 4.

[31] Acton, *The Bourbons of Naples*, p. 460.

[32] Cuthell, *An Imperial Victim*, vol. II, p. 126.

[33] Chastenet, *Godoy*, p. 104.

[34] Queen María Luísa, *Memoir*, p. 5.

[35] D'Auvergne, *Godoy*, p. 134.

[36] Louis Constant Wairy, *Memoirs of Constant, first valet de chambre of the emperor, on the private life of Napoleon, his family and his court*, trans. Elizabeth Gilbert Martin, vol. I (New York: The Century Company, 1907), p 94.

[37] Laure Junot, Duchess d'Abrantès, *Memoirs of the Emperor Napoleon: From Ajaccio to Waterloo, As Soldier, Emperor, Husband*, vol. II (Washington & London: M. Walter Dunne, 1901), p. 128.

[38] Wairy, *Memoirs*, vol. I, p. 94.

[39] *Ibid*, p. 97.

[40] Queen María Luísa, *Memoir*, p.7.

[41] Wairy, *Memoirs*, vol. I, p. 99.

[42] Queen María Luísa, *Memoir*, pp. 7-8.

[43] *Ibid.*

Chapter 25: "The Mother of My People"

[1] Acton, *The Bourbons of Naples*, p. 474.

[2] Duchess D'Abrantès, *The Home and Court Life of the Emperor Napoleon and His Family*, vol. III (New York: Charles Scribner's Sons, 1894), p. 78.

[3] Acton, *The Bourbons of Naples*, p. 477.

[4] Clotilda Elizabeth Stisted to the Dowager Lady Knowles, undated, Letter IX, in Clotilda Elizabeth Stisted, *Letters from the Bye-Ways of Italy* (London: John Murray, 1845), p. 103.

[5] Queen María Luísa, *Memoir*, p. 9.

[6] Carlo Botta, *History of Italy During the Consulate and Empire of Napoleon Buonaparte*, vol. I (London: Baldwin and Cradock, 1828), p. 233.

[7] D'Artemont, *A Sister of Louis XVI*, p. 193.

[8] Duchess D'Abrantès, *Emperor Napoleon*, p. 368.

[9] Duchess D'Abrantès, *Home and Court Life*, p. 227.

[10] Clotilda Elizabeth Stisted to the Dowager Lady Knowles, undated, Letter IX, in Stisted, *Letters*, p. 104.

[11] Queen María Luísa, *Memoir*, p. 14.

[12] Clotilda Elizabeth Stisted to the Dowager Lady Knowles, undated, Letter IX, in Stisted, *Letters*, p. 104.

[13] Acton, *The Bourbons of Naples*, p. 478.

[14] Queen María Luísa, *Memoir*, p. 14.

[15] Botta, *History of Italy*, vol. I, p. 257.

[16] Queen María Luísa, *Memoir*, p. 16.

[17] Acton, *The Bourbons of Naples*, p. 479.

[18] *Ibid.*

[19] *Ibid.*

[20] Queen Maria Carolina to Princess Maria Antonietta of the Asturias, undated, 1806, in Duchess D'Abrantès, *Home and Court Life*, p. 194.

[21] Acton, *The Bourbons of Naples*, p. 479.

[22] Duchess D'Abrantès, *Home and Court Life*, p. 91.

[23] *Ibid*, p. 92.

[24] Frederick W. Kagan, *The End of the Old Order: Napoleon and Europe 1801-1805* (Cambridge: Da Capo Press, 2006), pp. 54-55.

[25] Lord Horatio Nelson to Queen Maria Carolina, 29 December 1803, in Nicholas Harris Nicolas, ed., *The Dispatches and Letters of Vice Admiral Lord Viscount Nelson*, vol. V: *January 1802, to April 1804* (London: Henry Colburn, 1845), p. 338.

[26] Acton, *The Bourbons of Naples*, pp. 490-491.

[27] *Ibid.*

[28] Princess Amalie of Saxony, *Six Dramas Illustrative of German Life, From the Original of the Princess Amalie of Saxony* (London: John W. Parker, 1848), p. v.

[29] *Ibid.*

Chapter 26: The Passing of an Age

[1] Johnston, *Napoleonic Empire*, vol. I, p. 1.

[2] Emperor Napoleon I to Empress Joséphine, undated, December 1805, in David G. Chandler, *The Campaigns of Napoleon* (New York: Simon and Schuster, 1995), pp. 432-433.

[3] Robert Goetz, *1805: Austerlitz—Napoleon and the Destruction of the Third Coalition* (London: Greenhill Books, 2005), p. 304.

[4] Masson, ed., *Private Diaries*, p. 16.

[5] Todd Fisher & Gregory Freemont-Barnes, *The Napoleonic Wars: The Rise and Fall of an Empire* (Oxford: Osprey Publishing, Ltd., 2004), p. 54.

[6] Emperor Napoleon I to Joseph Bonaparte, 31 December 1805, in Anonymous, *The Confidential Correspondance of Napoleon Bonaparte with His Brother Joseph, Sometime King of Spain*, vol. I (London: John Murray, 1855), p. 69.

[7] Saint-Amand, *Duchess of Berry*, p. 6.

[8] Clement, *Naples*, p. 165.

[9] Emperor Napoleon I to Joseph Bonaparte, 31 January 1806, in Anonymous, *Confidential Correspondance*, p. 77.

[10] Bearne, *A Sister of Marie Antoinette*, p. 375.

[11] Dyson, *Life of Marie Amélie*, p. 66.

[12] Queen Maria Carolina to Empress Teresa, undated, February 1806, in Acton, *The Bourbons of Naples*, p. 554.

[13] Royal Decree of Emperor Napoleon I, 30 March 1806, in Pietro Colletta, *History of the Kingdom of Naples: 1734—1825*, trans. S. Horner, vol. II (Edinburgh: T. Constable & Co., 1858), p. 16.

[14] A Letter of Ambassador Hugh Elliot, undated, 1806, in Giglioli, *Naples in 1799*, p. 7.

[15] Duchess D'Abrantès, *Home and Court Life*, p. 193.

[16] Bearne, *A Sister of Marie Antoinette*, p. 383.

[17] Duchess D'Abrantès, *Home and Court Life*, p. 194.

[18] Bearne, *A Sister of Marie Antoinette*, p. 392.

[19] Saint-Amand, *Duchess of Berry*, p. 7.

[20] Alfred Nettement, "Mémoirs Historiques de S.A.R. Madame la Duchesse de Berri, depuis sa naissance jusqu'à ce jour," in *The Foreign Quarterly Review*, 3 vols., 8 vo. (Paris, 1837), p. 247.

[21] Princess Michael, *Crowned in a Far Country*, p. 90; Cuthell, *An Imperial Victim*, vol. I, p. 40.

[22] Bearne, *A Sister of Marie Antoinette*, p. 396.

[23] Queen Maria Carolina to Emperor Francis I, undated, April 1807, in Acton, *The Bourbons of Naples*, p. 579.

[24] Archduchess Marie Louise to Victoire de Poutet, undated, April 1807, in Cuthell, *An Imperial Victim*, vol. I, p. 41.

[25] Archduchess Marie Louise to Victoire de Poutet, undated, June 1807, in *ibid*.

[26] Cuthell, *An Imperial Victim*, vol. I, p. 16.

[27] Acton, *The Bourbons of Naples*, p. 580.

[28] Nettement, "Mémoires Historiques," p. 248.

[29] Dyson, *Life of Marie Amélie*, p. 70.

[30] Acton, *The Bourbons of Naples*, p. 585.

[31] Fraser, *Marie Antoinette*, p. 444.

[32] Diary entry of Princess Maria Amelia, 22 June 1809, in Bearne, *A Sister of Marie Antoinette*, p. 403.

[33] John S.C. Abbott, *Kings and Queens; or, Life in the Palace* (New York: Harper and Brothers, 1850), p. 72.

[34] R.M. Johnson, ed., *Mémoire de Marie Caroline, Reine de Naples* (London & Cambridge, MA: Oxford University Press, 1912), p. 28.

[35] Challice, *Illustrious Women of France*, p. 233.

[36] Lord Cuthbert Collingwood to Mr. Blackett, undated, November 1809, in Rev. G.N. Wright, *The Life and Times of Louis Philippe, King of the French* (London & Paris: Fisher, Son, & Co., 1848), p. 378.

[37] Acton, *The Bourbons of Naples*, p. 592.

[38] Wichel, ed., *Memoirs*, p. 100.

[39] A Letter of Lord Horatio Nelson, 27 May 1804, in Jeaffreson, *The Queen of Naples and Lord Nelson*, vol. II, p. 216.

[40] Johnson, ed., *Mémoire*, p. 34.

[41] Imbert de Saint-Amand, *The Happy Days of the Empress Marie Louise*, trans. Thomas Sergeant Perry (New York: Charles Scribner's Sons, 1898), p. 5.

[42] Bearne, *A Sister of Marie Antoinette*, p. 409.

[43] *Ibid.*

[44] Queen Maria Carolina to King Ferdinand IV, undated, 1813, in Acton, *The Bourbons of Naples*, p. 630.

[45] Queen Maria Carolina to Emperor Francis I, 30 August 1813, in Browning, "Queen Caroline of Naples," p. 489.

[46] Johnson, ed., *Mémoire*, p. 135.

[47] Browning, "Queen Caroline of Naples," p. 489.

[48] Saint-Amand, *The Duchess of Berry*, p. 9.

[49] Jeaffreson, *The Queen of Naples and Lord Nelson*, vol. II, p. 245.

[50] Maria Amelia, Duchesse d'Orléans, to Emperor Francis I, undated, 1813, in Bearne, *A Sister of Marie Antoinette*, p. 421.

[51] *Ibid.*

[52] Acton, *The Bourbons of Naples*, p. 636.

[53] *Ibid*, p. 640.

[54] Queen Maria Carolina to Roger de Damas, 3 August 1814, in Acton, *The Bourbons of Naples*, p. 653.

[55] *The Times*, 11 April 1814.

[56] W.K.W. Blumenbach to William, Viscount Melbourne, undated, in W.K.W. Blumenbach, *Austria and the Austrians*, vol. II (London: Henry Colburn, 1837), p. 61.

[57] Acton, *The Bourbons of Naples*, p. 654.

[58] *Ibid*, p. 655.

[59] Saint-Amand, *Duchess of Berry*, p. 11.

[60] Jeaffreson, *The Queen of Naples and Lord Nelson*, vol. II, p. 250.

Epilogue
[1] *Ibid*, vol. I, pp. 65-66.

[2] Taylor, *The Habsburg Monarchy*, p. 9.

Illustrations

Emperor Francis I; formerly Duke of Lorraine and Grand Duke of Tuscany, by Martin van Meytens, 1745 (*Kunsthistorisches Museum, Vienna*).

Maria Theresa, Holy Roman Empress, Queen of Hungary and Bohemia, Archduchess of Austria, by Jean-Étienne Liotard, c. 1760 (*Lviv State Picture Gallery, Ukraine*).

A portrait of the Imperial family. *Left to right*: Francis I, Marianne, Amalia, Joseph, Leopold, Elizabeth, Maria Theresa, and Karl, by Martin van Meytens, 1755 (*Hulton Archive/ Kunsthistorisches Museum, Vienna*).

Maria Carolina ("Charlotte") and her brother Ferdinand, by Anton Raphael Mengs, 1754 (*AISA*).

Archduchess Maria Antonia (later Marie Antoinette). She was widely considered one of Maria Theresa's most beautiful daughters, by Martin van Meytens, 1767 (*Schloss Schönbrunn*).

Archduchess Amalia. She was the eldest of Maria Theresa's reigning daughters, but as the Duchess of Parma, she ranked the lowest of all her siblings, by anonymous, 1765 (*Hulton Archive*).

Grand Duke Leopold (*left*) and Emperor Joseph II (*right*) together in Rome, by Pompeo Batoni, 1769 (*Kunsthistorisches Museum, Vienna*).

Joseph II's first wife, Isabella of Parma (1741-1763). Isabella's brother was Amalia's husband Ferdinand, Duke of Parma. Her sister, Luisa, became queen consort of Spain, by Jean-Marc Nattier, 1758 (*Kunsthistorisches Museum, Vienna*).

Archduchess Theresa of Austria (1762-1770). She was the only surviving child of Joseph of Austria and Isabella of Parma, by anonymous, c. 1768 (*Kunsthistorisches Museum, Vienna*).

Schönbrunn Palace outside Vienna. This was the Habsburgs' main summer residence, by Bernardo Bellotto, c. 1760 (*Kunsthistorisches Museum, Vienna*).

The Royal Palace of Naples. This was Maria Carolina's main home in Naples. It paled in comparison to the awe-inspiring Caserta palace, photograph by anonymous, 2007.

The Palace of Versailles, built by Louis XIV. It was the home of Marie Antoinette and her family from 1770 until 1789, photograph by Michael Shade, 2006.

King Louis XV of France, grandfather of Louis XVI. Along with Carlos III and Maria Theresa, he was one of the architects of the Family Pact, by Louis Michel van Loo, c. 1768 (*Library and Archives Canada*).

King Carlos III of Spain (1716-1788). He was the father of King Ferdinand IV of Naples, Empress María Luísa, and King Carlos IV of Spain, by Anton Raphael Mengs, c. 1760 (*Museo Lazaro Galdiano, Madrid*).

King Ferdinand IV of Naples and Sicily at the age of nine. He was seventeen when he married Archduchess Maria Carolina in 1767, by Anton Raphael Mengs, 1759 (*Prado, Madrid*).

Emperor Joseph II. His idealism and desire to reform Austria, though well-meaning, nearly tore the Habsburg monarchy apart, by Joseph Hickel, c. 1780 (*Hutton Archive*).

Empress María Luísa, wife of Leopold II. She remained her husband's closest friend and confidante during their entire twenty-seven-year marriage, by Anton Raphael Mengs, 1765 (*Kunsthistorisches Museum, Vienna*).

Pitti Palace. *Left to right:* Theresa, Karl, Clementine, Marianne, María Luísa (holding Joseph), Leopold, Francis, and Ferdinand. *Seated in the front row:* Alexander, by Johann Zoffany, c. 1777 (*Kunsthistorisches Museum, Vienna*).

Emperor Francis II, Leopold's son and successor. In addition to being Maria Carolina's nephew, he also became her son-in-law in 1790 when he married her daughter, Teresa, anonymous, c. 1790 (*Kunsthistorisches Museum, Vienna*).

Amalia, Duchess of Parma. There was a profound contrast between her volatile, early years in Parma, and her subdued, melancholy later years, by Johann Zoffany, c. 1780 (*Galleria Nazionale, Parma*).

Ferdinand, Duke of Parma. It took him nearly twenty years to mature as a ruler. He spent the last years of his life fighting French suzerainty in Italy, by Pietro Melchiorre Ferrari, c. 1780 (*Galleria Nazionale, Parma*).

Maria Carolina, Queen of Naples. Of all Maria Theresa's children, she most emulated her mother, both as a ruler and a mother. She was the undisputed ruler of Naples, and also delivered 19 children, by Johann Georg Weikert, 1768 (*Kunsthistorisches Museum, Vienna*).

The Royal Family of Naples. *Left to right:* Teresa, Francesco, King Ferdinand, Queen Maria Carolina, Maria Cristina, Carlo, and Luisa (holding Amélie).

Despite giving birth nineteen times, only seven of Maria Carolina's children survived into adulthood, by Angelica Kauffmann, 1783 (*Museo e Gallerie Nazionali di Capodimonte, Naples*)

King Louis XVI, husband of Marie Antoinette. Despite being hampered by timidity and indecisiveness, Louis was a kind and good-natured king, by Joseph-Siffred Duplessis, c. 1775 (*AKG Berlin*).

Queen Marie Antoinette of France, by Élisabeth Louise Vigée Le Brun, 1779 (*Kunsthistorisches Museum, Vienna*).

Marie Antoinette with her children, Marie Thérèse, Louis Charles, and Louis Joseph, by Élisabeth Louise Vigée Le Brun, 1787 (*Château de Versailles/Giraudon*).

Princess Marie Thérèse. As the daughter of Marie Antoinette and Louis XVI, she was known as "Madame Royale" at the French court, by Heinrich Friedrich Füger, 1795 (*State Hermitage Museum, St. Petersburg*).

Napoleon I, Emperor of the French. He was directly responsible for the ultimate fates of Queen Maria Carolina and Amalia, Duchess of Parma, by Jacques-Louis David, 1812 (*National Gallery of Art, Washington, D.C.*).

Empress Marie Louise, wife of Napoleon Bonaparte, and their son, Napoleon II. Marie Louise was the daughter of Emperor Francis II and Teresa of Naples, making her a granddaughter of both Leopold II and Maria Carolina. She was also a double-great-grandchild of Maria Theresa, by François Gérard, 1812 (*Château de Versailles*).

Maria Amelia of Naples ("Amélie"), Queen of the French, with her sons Ferdinand Philippe and Louis, by Louis Hersent, 1835 (*Château de Versailles*).

The author and publisher are grateful to the WikiMedia Foundation, Inc., for permission to use the above images under the GNU Free Documentation License Agreement and the Common Reuse of PD-Art Photographs.

Bibliography

PRIMARY SOURCES

UNPUBLISHED LETTERS

H.I. & R.H. Crown Prince Otto of Austria, to the author, 28 April 2007.
H.R.H. Ferdinand, Duke of Parma, to H.M. King Ferdinand IV of Naples & Sicily, 29 September 1795.

UNPUBLISHED ACADEMIC SOURCES

Cornell University
Schoellkopf, Henry. *The Enlightened Despotism in the Eighteenth Century: Charles III in Spain.* Thesis, B.A. Ithaca, N.Y.: Cornell University, 1902.

UNPUBLISHED EMAILS

Gelardi, Julia P., to the author. "The World of Maria Theresa." 22 May 2007.
H.I. & R.H. Archduke Géza of Austria, to the author. "History of Austria." 16 April 2007.

PUBLISHED DIPLOMATIC & POLITICAL DOCUMENTS

Burant, Stephen R., ed. "Enlightened Absolutism," in *Hungary: A Country Study.* Washington, D.C.: GPO for the Library of Congress, 1989.
Francis I, Emperor of Austria. *Austrian Declaration Against France. Aug. 1813. Manifesto of His Majesty the Emperor of Austria, King of Hungary and Bohemia.* Broxbourne: Watts, 1813.
Leopold, Grand Duke of Tuscany. *Edict of the Grand Duke of Tuscany, For the reform of criminal law in his dominions: translated from the Italian: together with the original.* Warrington: W. Eyres, 1789.
Michiels, Alfred. *Secret History of the Austrian Government, and of its Systematic Persecution of Protestants. Compiled from Official Documents.* London: Chapman & Hall, 1859.
The Annual Register, or a View of the History, Politics, and Literature, for the Year of 1768. 6th ed. London: G. Woodfall, 1800: John Davis Batchelder Collection, Library of Congress.

PERIODICALS

Gazette de France
Le Moniteur
The Times
Wiener Zeitung

PUBLISHED LETTERS & MEMOIRS

Abbott, John S.C., ed. *Confidential Correspondence of the Emperor Napoleon and the Empress Josephine.* New York: Mason Brothers, 1856.

Abrantès, Laure Junot, Duchess d'. *Memoires of the Duchess d'Abrantès.* Vol. III. London: Henry Colburn, 1832.

———. *Memoirs of the Emperor Napoleon: From Ajaccio to Waterloo, As Soldier, Emperor, Husband.* Vol. II. Washington & London: M. Walter Dunne, 1901.

———. *The Home and Court Life of the Emperor Napoleon and His Family.* Vol. III. New York: Charles Scribner's Sons, 1894.

Amiguet, Philippe, ed. *Lettres de Louis XV à sons petit-fils l'Infant Ferdinand de Parme.* Paris: B. Grassett, 1938.

Anderson, Emily, ed. *The Letters of Mozart and His Family.* Vol. I. London: Macmillan & Co., 1938.

Arneth, Alfred von, ed. *Briefe der Kaiserin Maria Theresia an ihre Kinder und Freunde.* Vols. I & III. Vienna: Wilhelm Braumüller, 1881.

———. *Geschichte Maria Theresias.* Vol. VII. Vienna: n.p., 1876.

———. *Joseph II. und Katharina von Russland. Ihr Briefwechsel.* Vienna: Wilhelm Braumüller, 1869.

———. *Joseph II. und Leopold von Toscana. Ihr Briefwechsel von 1781 bis 1791.* Vols. I & II. Vienna: Braunmüller, 1872.

———. *Maria Theresia und Joseph II. Ihre correspondenz sammt Briefen Joseph's bruder Leopold.* Vienna: Druck, Verlag, & Carl Gerhold's Sons, 1868.

———. *Marie Antoinette, Joseph II. und Leopold II. Ihr Briefwechsel.* Leipzig: K.F. Köhler, 1866.

Beer, A., ed. *Leopold II., Franz II. und Catharina. Ihre Correspondenz nebst einer Einleitung: Zur Geschichte der Politik Leopolds II.* Leipzig: Duncker & Humblot, 1874.

Bernier, Olivier. *Imperial Mother, Royal Daughter: The Correspondence of Marie Antoinette and Maria Theresa.* London: Sidgwick & Jackson, 1969.

Broglie, Albert, Duc de, et al. *Frederick the Great and Maria Theresa.* Vol. I. London: Sampson Low, Marston, Searle, & Rivington, 1883.

Burkard, Suzanne, ed. *Mémoires de la Baronne d'Oberkirch sur la cour de Louis XVI et la societé français avant 1789.* Paris: Mercure de France, 1970 [1853].

Campan, Madame (Jeanne Louise Henriette). *Memoirs of the Court of Marie Antoinette, Queen of France.* Vols. I & II. Philadelphia: Parry & McMillan, 1854.

Cléry, Jean-Baptiste. *A Journal of Occurrences at the Temple, During the Confinement of Louis XVI, King of France*, trans. R.C. Dallas. London: Baylis, 1798.

Crack, E., ed. *Briefe einer Kaiserin: Maria Theresia an ihre Kinder un Freunde.* Berlin: Verlag, 1910.

Cunningham, P., ed. *Letters of Horace Walpole.* Vol. IV. London: n.p., 1891.

Davenport, Beatrix Cary, ed. *The Diary of the French Revolution by Gouverneur Morris 1752-1816, Minister to France During the Terror.* Vol. II. Boston: Houghton Mifflin Company, 1939.

Dole, Nathan Haskell, ed. *Letters from Switzerland and Italy*, trans. A.J.W. Morrison, et al. New York: International Publishing Company, 1902.

Doran, Dr. John. *'Mann' and Manners at the Court of Florence, 1740-1786.* Vol. II. London: William Clowes & Sons, 1876.

Dutens, Louis. *Memoirs of a Traveller, Now in Retirement.* Vol. II. London: Blackfiars, Dulau, & Co., 1806.

Eckard, Jean. *The King Who Never Reigned, Being Memoirs Upon Upon Louis XVII.* London: Eveleigh Nash, 1908.

Élisabeth, Princess of France. *The Life and Letters of Madame Élisabeth de France, Sister of Louis XVI.* New York: H.P. & Co., 1899.

Elizabeth, Margravine of Anspach. *Memoirs.* Vol. I. London: Henry Colburn, 1826.

Fontescu, Diana, ed. *Americans and Queen Marie of Roumania: A Selection of Documents.* Iaşi: The Center for Romanian Studies, 1998.

Fred, W., ed. *Briefe der Kaiserin Maria Theresia.* Vols. I & III. Vienna: n.p., 1881.

Geoffrey, M.A., and Alfred von Arneth, eds. *Marie-Antoinette: Correspondance Secrète entre Marie-Thérèse et le Comte de Mercy-Argenteau.* Vol. I. Paris: Firmont Didot Brothers, Sons, & Co., 1874.

Gibbs, Alfred S., ed. *Goethe's Mother.* New York: Dodd, Mead, and Company, 1880.

Goethe, Johann von. *Truth and Poetry: From My Own Life*, trans. John Oxenford. Vol. I. London: George Bell & Sons, 1891.

Grouchy, Vicomte de and Paul Cottin, eds. *Journal inédit du Duc de Croÿ 1718-1784.* Vols. III & IV. Paris: E. Flammarion, 1907.

Hibbert, Christopher, ed. *Queen Victoria in Her Letters.* Stroud, Glos.: Sutton Publishing, 2000.

Hyde, Catherine, Marquise de Gouvion Broglie Scolari, ed. *Private Anecdotes of Foreign Courts.* Vol. I. London: Henry Colburn, 1827.

———. *Secret Memoirs of Princess Lamballe, Being, Her Journals, Letters, and Conversations During Her Confidential Relations with Marie Antoinette.* Washington & London: M. Walter Dunne, 1901.

Jameson, Anna. *Memoirs of Celebrated Female Sovereigns.* Vol. II. London: Henry Colburn & Richard Bentley, 1831.

Jesse, John Heneage. *Memoirs of King George the Third: His Life and Reign.* Vol. IV. Boston: L.C. Page & Company, 1902.

Krack, C., ed. *Briefe einer Kaiserin. Maria Theresia an ihre Kinder und Freunde.* Berlin: Verlag, 1910.

Knight, Cornelia. *The Autobiography of Miss Cornelia Knight, Lady Companion to the Princess Charlotte of Wales.* Vol. I. 3rd ed. London: W.H. Allen & Co., 1861.

Lamothe-Langon, Étienne-Léon, Baron de. *Memoirs of Louis the Eighteenth.* Vol. II. London: Saunders & Otley, 1832.

——. *Souvenirs sur Marie Antoinette et la Cour de Versailles.* Vol. II. Paris: Bourgogne et Martinet, 1836.

Landwehr, Moritz von, ed. *Aus dem Briefwechsel Maria Theresias mit Josef II.* Leipzig & Vienna: U. Hasse, 1917.

Léonard, Jean-François. *The Souvenirs of Léonard: Hairdresser to Queen Marie-Antoinette*, trans. A. Teixera de Mattos. Vols. I & II. London: n.p., 1897.

Ligne, Charles-Joseph, Prince de. *The Prince de Ligne: His Memoirs, Letters, and Miscellanious Papers*, trans. Katherine Prescott Wormeley. Vols. I & II. New York: Brentano's Publishers, 1899.

Lough, John, ed. *France on the Eve of Revolution: British Travellers' Observations, 1763-1788.* London: Croom Helm, 1987.

María Luísa, Queen of Etruria. *Memoir of the Queen of Etruria, Written by Herself.* London: J.F. Dove, 1814.

Marie Antoinette, Queen of France. *Correspondance de Marie-Antoinette.* Vols. I & II. Clermont-Ferrand: Paléo, 2004.

Masson, Frédéric, ed. *The Private Diaries of the Empress Marie Louise, Wife of Napoleon I.* New York: D. Appleton & Co., 1922.

McFarland, Elizabeth, ed. *Familienbriefe. Mit einem biographischen Anhang von Maria Theresia.* Berlin & Vienna: Ullstein & Co., 1920.

Millar, Lady Anne. *Letters from Italy.* Vol. II. London: Edward & Charles Dilly, 1776.

Mousset, Albert. *Un témoin ignoré de la Révolution: Le comte Fernan Nuñez, ambassadeur d'Espagne à Paris.* Paris: Éduoard Champion, 1924.

Napoleon I, Emperor of the French. *Memoirs of the History of France During the Reign of Napoleon.* Vol. IV. London: Henry Colburn, & Martin Bossange & Co., 1824.

Nathan Miller, *Broadsides: The Age of Fighting Sail, 1775-1815.* Edison, NJ: Castle Books, 2005.

Nicardot, Louis, ed. *Journal de Louis XVI.* Paris: E. Dentu, 1873.

Nicolas, Nicholas Harris, ed. *The Dispatches and Letters of Vice Admiral Lord Viscount Nelson.* Vol. V: *January 1802, to April 1804.* London: Henry Colburn, 1845.

Norvins, Jacques de. *Mémorial.* Vol. I. Paris, n.p., 1896.

Oberkirch, Henriette Louise, Baroness d'. *Memoirs of the Baroness d'Oberkirch, Countess de Montbrison.* Vol. I. London: Colburn & Co. 1852.

Pépé, Guglielmo. *Memoirs of General Pépé.* Vol. I. London: Richard Bentley, 1846.

Pulszky, Theresa. *Memoirs of a Hungarian Lady.* Vol. I. London: Henry Colburn, 1850.

Reeve, Henry, ed. *Royal and Republican France.* Vol. I. London: Longmans, Green, and Co., 1872.

Rocheterie, Maxime de la, and the Marquis de Beaufort, eds. *Lettres de Marie Antoinette*. Vol. I. Paris: A. Picard & fils, 1895.

Schlitter, Dr. Hanns, ed. *Briefe der Erherzogin Marie Christine Statthalterin der Niederlande an Leopold II.* Vienna: Carl Gerold's Sohn, 1896.

Sichel, Walter, ed. *Memoirs of Emma, Lady Hamilton, Friend of Lord Nelson, and the Court of Naples.* New York: P.F. Collier & Son, 1910.

Soulavie, John Lewis. *Historical and Political Memoirs of the Reign of Lewis XVI. from His Marriage to His Death.* Vol. II. London: G. & J. Robison, 1802.

Smythe, Lillian C., ed. *The Guardian of Marie Antoinette: Letters from the Comte de Mercy-Argenteau, Austrian Ambassador to the Court of Versailles, to Marie Thérèse, Empress of Austria 1770-1780.* Vols. I & II. London: Hutchinson & Co., 1902.

Stisted, Clotilda Elizabeth. *Letters from the Bye-Ways of Italy.* London: John Murray, 1845.

Stryienski, Casimir. *The Eighteenth Century*, trans. H.N. Dickinson. London: William Heinemann, 1916.

Swinburne, Henry. *At the Close of the Last Century.* Vol. II. London: H.S. Nichols & Co., 1895.

———. *Secret Memoirs of the Courts of Europe: Letters at the End of the Eighteenth Century.* Vol. I. Philadelphia: George Barrie & Sons, 1840.

Vehse, E., Dr. *Memoirs of the Court, Aristocracy, and Diplomacy of Austria* , trans. Franz Demmler. Vol. II. London: Longman, Brown, Green, & Longmans, 1856.

Wairy, Louis Constant. *Memoirs of Constant, first valet* de chambre *of the emperor, on the private life of Napoleon, his family and his court,* trans. Elizabeth Gilbert Martin. Vol. I. New York: The Century Company, 1907.

Weber, Joseph. *Memoirs of Maria Antoinetta, Archduchess of Austria, Queen of France and Navarre*, trans. R.C. Dallas. Vol. I. London: C. Rickaby, 1805.

Williams, Helen Maria, ed. *The Political and Confidential Correspondence of Lewis XVI.* Vol. I. New York: n.p., 1803.

Williams, H. Noel. *Memoirs of Madame Du Barry, Of the Court of Louis XV.* New York: P.F. Collier & Sons, 1910.

Wolf, Adam, ed. *Leopold II. und Marie Christine. Ihr Briefwechsel (1781—1792).* Vienna: Carl Gerold's Sohn: 1867.

Wraxall, Sir Nathaniel. *Memoirs of the Courts of Berlin, Dresden, Warsaw, and Vienna in the years 1777, 1778, and 1779.* Vol. II. London: A. Strahan, 1800.

SECONDARY SOURCES

BOOKS

Abbot, John S.C. *Maria Antoinette.* New York & London: Harper & Brothers Publishers, 1904.

————. *The Monarchies of Continental Europe. The Empire of Austria; Its Rise and Present Power.* New York: Mason Brothers, 1859.

Acton, Harold. *The Bourbons of Naples.* London: Prion Books, Ltd., 1998 [1957].

Addison, Julia de Wolf. *The Art of the Pitti Palace.* Boston: L.C. Page & Co., 1903.

Agnew, Hugh LeCaine. *The Czechs and the Lands of the Bohemian Crown.* Stanford: Hoover Institution Press, 2004.

Aikin, John. *Annals of the Reign of King George the Third: From its Commencement in the Year 1760 to the Death of His Majesty in the Year 1820.* 2nd ed. Vol. I. London: Longman, Hurst, Rees, Orme, & Brown, 1820.

Alison, Sir Archibald. *History of Europe from the Commencement of the French Revolution to the Restoration of the Bourbons in MDCCCXV.* Vol. IV. Edinburgh and London: William Blackwood and Sons, 1860.

Allen, Phoebe. *The Last Legitimate King of France: Louis XVII.* New York: E.P. Dutton & Co., 1912.

Amalia, Princess of Saxony. *Six Dramas Illustrative of German Life, From the Original of the Princess Amalia of Saxony.* London: John W. Parker, 1848.

Andrews, Charles M. *The Historical Development of Modern Europe, From the Congress of Vienna to the Present Time.* Vol. I: *1815-1850.* London & New York: G.P. Putnam's Sons, 1896.

Anonymous. *The Sufferings of the Royal Family During the Revolution in France.* London: Smithers Hampden and Co., 1902.

Armaille, Comtesse d'. *Marie-Thérèse et Marie Antoinette.* 3rd ed. Paris: Perrin & Co., 1893.

Artemont, Louis Léopold D'. *A Sister of Louis XVI: Marie-Clotilde de France, Queen of Sardinia (1759-1802).* London: John Murray, 1911.

Aulard, A. *The French Revolution: A Political History, 1789—1804,* trans. Bernard Miall. Vol. I: *The Revolution Under the Monarchy, 1789—1792.* New York: Charles Scribner's Sons, 1910.

Auvergne, Edmund B. D'. *Godoy: The Queen's Favourite.* Boston: The Gorham Press, 1913.

Bain, R. Nisbet. *The Daughter of Peter the Great.* New York: E.P. Dutton & Co., 1900.

Beales, Derek. *Joseph II.* Vol. I: *In the Shadow of Maria Theresa, 1741-1780.* Cambridge: Cambridge University Press, 1991.

Bearne, Catherine Mary (as Catherine Bearne Charlton). *A Royal Quartette.* London: T. Fisher Unwin, 1908.

————. *A Sister of Marie Antoinette: The Life of Maria Carolina, Queen of Naples.* London: T. Fisher Unwin, 1907.

Belloc, Hilaire. *The Last Days of the French Monarchy.* London: Chapman & Hall Ltd., 1916.

Beloff, Max. *The Age of Absolutism: 1660—1815.* New York: Harper & Brothers, 1962.

Bermann, Moritz. *Maria Theresia und Joseph II in ihrem Leben und Wirken.* Vienna: Hartleben, 1881.

Blanning, T.C.W. *Joseph II.* New York: Longman Publishing, 1994.

Botta, Carlo. *History of Italy During the Consulate and Empire of Napoleon Buonaparte*. Vol. I. London: Baldwin and Cradock, 1828.

Bourgoing, F. de. *Histoire Diplomatiques Pendant la Révolution Français*. Vol. II. Paris n.p., 1831

Boutry, Maurice. *Le Mariage de Mare-Antoinette*. Paris: Émile Paul, 1904.

Braunbehrens, Volkmar. *Mozart in Vienna*. New York: Grove Weidenfeld, 1990.

Bright, J. Franck. *Joseph II*. London: Macmillan & Co., 1905

———. *Maria Theresa*. London: Macmillan & Co., 1897.

Brion, Marcel. *Daily Life in the Vienna of Mozart and Schubert*, trans. Jean Stewart. London: George Weidenfeld & Nicholson, Ltd., 1961.

Bryce, James, Viscount. *The Holy Roman Empire*. London: Macmillan & Co., Ltd., 1897.

Bush, Annie Forbes. *Memoirs of the Queens of France*. 2nd ed. Vol. II. London: Henry Colburn, 1843.

Campbell, Thomas. *Frederick the Great, His Court and Times*. Vol. IV. London: Henry Colburn, 1834.

Čapek, Thomas, ed. *Bohemia Under Hapsburg Misrule*. London et al: Fleming H. Revell Company, 1915.

Carlyle, Thomas. *The French Revolution*. 2nd ed. New York: The Modern Library, 1935.

Castelot, André. *Marie Antoinette*. Paris: Hacette, 1967.

Challice, Anna. *Illustrious Women of France, 1790-1873*. London: Bradbury, Agnew, & Co., 1873.

Chastenet, Jacques. *Godoy: Master of Spain, 1792-1808*, trans. J.F. Huntington. London: The Batchworth Press, 1953.

Clement, Clara Erskine. *Naples and the City of Parthenope and its Environs*. Boston: Estes & Lauriat, 1894.

Cochrane, Eric. *Florence in the Forgotten Centuries: 1527-1800*. Chicago: The University of Chicago Press, 1973.

Colletta, Pietro. *History of the Kingdom of Naples: 1734-1825*, trans. S. Horner. Vol. I. Edinburgh: T. Constable & Co., 1858.

Corti, Conte Egan Ceasare. *Ich, ein Tochter Maria Theresias: ein Lebensbild der Königin Marie Karoline von Neapal*. Munich: Bruckmann, 1950.

Coxe, William. *History of the House of Austria*. Vol. I. 3rd ed. London: Bell & Dalby, 1873.

Crankshaw, Edward. *Maria Theresa*. London & Harlow: Longmans, Green, & Co., 1969.

Cuthell, Edith E. *An Imperial Victim: Marie Louise, Archduchess of Austria, Empress of the French, Duchess of Parma*. Vols. I & II. London: Stanley Paul & Co., 1911.

Daudet, Ernest. *Madame Royale, daughter of Louis XVI and Marie Antoinette, her youth and marriage*. London: William Heinemann, 1913.

Deans, R. Storry. *The Trial of Five Queens: Katherine of Aragon, Anne Boleyn, Mary Queen of Scots, Marie Antoinette and Caroline of Brunswick*. 2nd ed. London: Methuen & Co., 1910.

Delorme, Philippe. *Marie Antoinette: Épouse de Louis XVI, mere de Louis XVII*. Paris: Pygmalion/Gérard Watelet, 1999.

Dunham, S.A. *History of the Germanic Empire.* Vol. III. London: Longman, Rees, Orme, Brown, Green, & Longman, 1835.

Dunlop, Ian. *Marie Antoinette: A Portrait.* London: Sinclair Stevenson, 1893.

Dyson, C.C. *The Life of Marie Amélie: Last Queen of the French, 1782-1866.* New York: D. Appleton & Co., 1910.

Eduardo, Leigh. *Mistresses: True Stories of Seduction, Power and Ambition.* London: Michael O'Mara Books, Ltd., 2005.

Emerich, John and Edward Dalbert-Acton. *Lectures on the French Revolution.* London: Macmillan and Co., 1910.

Erickson, Carolly. *To the Scaffold: The Life of Marie Antoinette.* New York: St. Martin's Press, 1991.

Farmer, Lydia Hoyt. *The Girl's Book of Famous Queens.* New York: Thomas Y. Crowell & Co., 1887.

Foreman, Amanda. *Georgiana: Duchess of Devonshire.* London: Harper Perennial, 1998.

Fraser, Antonia. *Marie Antoinette: The Journey.* New York: Anchor Books, 2001.

Fraser, Flora. *Princesses: The Six Daughters of George III.* London: John Murray, 2004.

Gamlin, Hilda. *Nelson's Friendships.* Vol. I. London: Hutchinson & Co., 1899.

Gaulot, Paul. *A Friend of the Queen (Marie Antoinette—Count Fersen),* trans. Mrs. Cashel Hoey. 2nd ed. London: William Heinemann, 1895.

Gelardi, Julia P. *Born to Rule: Five Reigning Consorts, Granddaughters of Queen Victoria.* New York: St. Martin's Press, 2005.

———. *In Triumph's Wake: Royal Mothers, Tragic Daughters, and the Price They Paid for Glory.* New York: St. Martin's Press, 2008.

Giglioli, H.D. *Naples in 1799: An Account of the Revolution of 1799 and of the Rise and Fall of the Parthenopean Republic.* London: John Murray, 1903.

Goldsmith, Margaret. *Maria Theresa of Austria.* London: Arthur Baker, Ltd., 1936.

Gosslin, Théodore (pseud. G. Lenotre). *The Daughter of Louis XVI. Marie-Thérèse-Charlotte de France Duchess d'Angoulême,* trans. J. Lewis. London & New York: John Lane, 1908.

———. *The Last Days of Marie Antoinette,* trans. Rodolph Stawell. London: William Heinemann, 1907.

Grant, A.J. *The French Monarchy (1483—1789).* 4th ed. Vol. II. Cambridge: Cambridge University Press, 1931.

Guglia, Eugen. *Maria Theresa.* Vol. II. Berlin: n.p., 1917.

H.R.H. Princess Michael of Kent. *Crowned in a Far Country: Portraits of Eight Royal Brides.* New York: Touchstone Books, 2001 [1986].

Horner, Susan. *A Century of Despotism in Naples and Sicily.* Edinburgh: Edmonston & Douglas, 1860.

Ingrao, Charles W. *The Habsburg Monarchy, 1618-1815.* 2nd ed. Cambridge: Cambridge University Press, 1994.

Jackson, Lady Catherine Charlotte. *The French Court and Society. Reign of Louis XV and First Empire.* Vols. I & II. Boston: I.C. Page & Co., 1897.

Jeaffreson, John Cordy. *The Queen of Naples and Lord Nelson.* Vols. I & II. London: Hurst & Blackett, Ltd., 1889.

Jenkins, John S. *The Heroines of History*. Auburn: Alden, Beardsley & Co., 1859.

Johnston, R.M. *The Napoleonic Empire in Southern Italy and the Rise of Secret Societies*. Vol. I. London: Macmillan & Co., Ltd., 1904.

Kagan, Frederick W. *The End of the Old Order: Napoleon and Europe 1801-1805*. Cambridge: Da Capo Press, 2006.

Kann, Robert A. *A History of the Habsburg Empire 1526—1918*. Berkley: University of California Press, 1980.

Kerner, Robert Joseph. *Bohemia in the Eighteenth Century: A Study in Political, Economic, and Social History With Special Reference to the Reign of Leopold II, 1790-1792*. New York: The Macmillan Company, 1934.

Labourdette, J.F. *Vergennes: Ministre Principal de Louis XVI*. Paris: Desjonquères, 1990.

Langsam, Walter Consuelo. *Francis the Good: The Education of an Emperor, 1768-1792*. 1ˢᵗ ed. New York: The Macmillan Company, 1949.

Lever, Evelyne. *Marie Antoinette: The Last Queen of France*, trans. Catherine Temerson. New York: St. Martin's Press, 2000.

Macartney, C.A. *Maria Theresa and the House of Austria*. Mystic, Connecticut: Lawrence Verry, Inc., 1969.

MacLehose, Sophia H. *From the Monarchy To the Republic in France 1788—1792*. Glasgow: James MacLehose and Sons, 1904.

Mahan, J. Alexander. *Maria Theresa of Austria*. New York: Thomas Y. Crowell Company, 1932.

Marek, George R. *The Eagles Die: Franz Joseph, Elisabeth, and Their Austria*. New York: Harper & Row, 1974.

Masson, Georgina. *Italian Villas and Palaces*. London: Harry N. Abrams, Ltd., 1959.

Maxwell, Constantia. *The English Traveler in France 1698-1815*. London: George Routledge & Sons, 1932.

Mayer, Dorothy Moultron. *Marie Antoinette: The Tragic Queen*. New York: Coward-McCann, 1968.

Mayne, Ethel Colbert. *Enchanters of Men*. 2ⁿᵈ ed. London: Metheun & Co., 1902.

McGill, William J., Jr. *Maria Theresa*. New York: Twayne Publishers, Inc., 1972.

Menzel, Wolfgang. *The History of Germany, From the Earliest Period to the Present Time*, trans. Mrs. George Horrocks. Vol. III. London: Henry G. Bohn, 1854.

Montagu, Victoire M. *The Celebrated Madame Campan, Lady-in-Waiting to Marie Antoinette and Confidante of Napoleon*. Philadelphia: J.P. Lippincott Company, 1914.

Morris, Lily Constance. *Maria Theresa: The Last Conservative*. London & New York: Alfred A. Knopf, 1937.

Napier, Henry Edward. *Florentine History, from the Earliest Authentic Record to the Accession of Ferdinand the Third, Grand Duke of Tuscany*. Vol. VI. London: Edward Moxer, 1897.

Nisard, Charles. *Guillaume du Tillot: Un valet ministre et secrétaire d'état*. Paris: Paul Ollendorff, 1887.

Nolhac, Pierre de. *Marie Antoinette the Queen*. Paris: Goupil & Co., 1898.

Okey, Robin. *The Habsburg Monarchy c. 1765—1918: From Enlightenment to Eclipse.* New York: Palgrave Macmillan, 2002.

Padover, S.K. *The Life and Death of Louis XVI.* New York & London: D. Appleton Century Co., 1939.

———. *The Revolutionary Emperor: Joseph the Second.* London: Jonathan Cape, LTD., 1934.

Perkins, James Breck. *France Under Louis XV.* Vol. II. Boston & New York: Houghton Mifflin Company, 1897.

Pick, Robert. *Empress Maria Theresa: The Early Years, 1717-1751.* London: Harper & Row, 1966.

Reumont, Alfred de. *Carafas of Maddaloni: Naples Under Spanish Dominion.* London: Henry G. Bohn, 1854.

Rocheterie, Maxime de la. *The Life of Marie Antoinette,* trans. Cora Bell Hamilton. Vols. I & II. New York: Dodd, Mead & Co., 1893.

Roider, Karl A., Jr. *Baron Thugut and Austria's Response to the French Revolution.* Princeton, New Jersey: Princeton University Press, 1987.

Rounding, Virginia. *Catherine the Great: Love, Sex, and Power.* New York: St. Martin's Press, 2006.

Rumold, Sir Horace. *The Austrian Court in the Nineteenth Century.* London: Methuen & Co., 1909.

Saint-Amand, Imbert de. *Marie Antoinette and the End of the Old Regime.* 2nd ed. London: Hutchinson & Co., 1892.

———. *Marie Antoinette at the Tuileries, 1789-1791,* trans. Elizabeth Gilbert Martin. New York: Charles Scribner's Sons, 1891.

———. *The Youth of the Duchess of Angoulême,* trans. Elizabeth Gilbert Martin. New York: Charles Scribner's Sons, 1892.

———. *Women of Versailles: Last Years of Louis XV,* trans. Elizabeth Gilbert Martin. New York: Charles Scribner's Sons, 1893.

Schulte, Regina, ed. *The Body of the Queen: Gender and Rule in the Courtly World, 1500-2000.* New York: Berghahn Books, 2006.

Secher, Reginald and Yves Murat. *Un Prince Méconnu: Le Dauphin Louis-Joseph, Fils Aîné de Louis XVI.* Paris: R.S.E., 1998.

Sichel, Walter, ed. *Emma Lady Hamilton.* London: Archibald Constable, 1905.

Solomon, Maynard. *Mozart: A Life.* New York: Harper Perennial: 1995.

Steed, Henry Wickham. *A Short History of Austria-Hungary and Poland.* London: The Encyclopaedia Britannica Company, Ltd., 1914.

———. *The Habsburg Monarchy.* 4th ed. London: Constable & Company, 1919.

Szabo, Frank A.J. *Kaunitz and Enlightened Absolutism, 1753—1780.* Cambridge: Cambridge University Press, 1994.

Taylor, A.J.P. *The Habsburg Monarchy 1809—1918: A History of the Austrian Empire and Austria-Hungary.* London: Hamish Hamilton, Ltd., 1948.

Temperley, Harold. *Frederick the Great and Kaiser Joseph.* London: Frank Cass Publishers, 1968.

Voltaire. *The Age of Louis XV.* Vol. I. London, G. Kearsly, 1774.

Von Horn, W.D. *Maria Theresa,* trans. by George P. Upton. Chicago: A.C. McClurg & Co., 1905.

Wandruska, Adam. *Leopold II.* Vols. I & II. Vienna: Herold, 1965.

Weber, Caroline. *Queen of Fashion: What Marie Antoinette Wore to the Revolution.* New York: Henry Holt & Co., 2006.

Wheatcroft, Andrew. *The Habsburgs: Embodying Empire.* London: Penguin Books, 1996.

Whiteside, James. *Italy in the Nineteenth Century.* London: Longman, Green, Longman, & Roberts, 1860.

Woods, Frederick Adams. *The Influence of Monarchs: Steps in a New Science of History.* New York: The Macmillan Company, 1913.

Wormeley, Katharine Prescott, ed. *The Ruin of a Princess.* London: T. Werner Laurie, Ltd., 1912.

Young, Charles Duke. *The Life of Marie Antoinette, Queen of France.* New York: Harper & Brothers, 1856.

ARTICLES & ESSAYS

Beach, Vincent W. "The Count of Artois and the Coming of the French Revolution," in *The Journal of Modern History.* Vol. 30, no. 4 (December, 1958).

Browning, Oscar. "Queen Caroline of Naples," in *The English Historical Review.* Vol. 2, no. 7 (July, 1887).

Gray, Francine du Plessix. "The Child Queen," *The New Yorker,* 7 August 2000.

Marraro, Howard R. "Mazzei's Correspondence with the Grand Duke of Tuscany during His American Mission," in *William and Mary College Quarterly Historical Magazine.* 2nd ser. Vol. 22, no. 3 (July, 1942).

Miller, W. "Europe and the Ottoman Power before the Nineteenth Century," in *The English Historical Review.* Vol. 16, no. 63 (July, 1901).

Robertson, Ritchie. "Joseph II: The Tragedy of an Enlightened Despot," in *St. John's College Alumni: Magazine* (2006). http://www.sjc.ox.ac.uk/alumni/display/magazine.php?textId=83&pageNo=3&PHPSESSID=4f3ebfcf87be1c678ee039f446e (accessed 20 November 2006).

Weis, Eberhard. "Enlightenment and Absolutism in the Holy Roman Empire: Thoughts on Enlightened Absolutism in Germany," in *The Journal of Modern History.* Vol. 58: *Supplement: Politics and Society in the Holy Roman Empire, 1500-1806.* December, 1986.

Index

Bonaparte, Napoleon (con't)
conquests of, in Italy, 321-323, 324-325, 326, 328, 343-344, 352, 353-354
    defeat and exile of, 375-376
    early years of, 325
    forms Etruria and names Lodovico as king, 345-348, 351, 352
    marriage to Marie Louise, 371-372
    relationship with Maria Carolina, 341, 360, 365-366, 376
Bosnia, 250
Bourbon dynasty,
    in France, 53, 100, 113, 125, 168, 181, 199, 214, 229, 243, 245, 260, 264, 267, 306, 358, 370, 381
    in Parma, 111, 185, 344-345
    in Naples and Sicily, 253, 342, 365, 369, 374
    in Spain, 48, 69, 253, 321, 342
Bozen, 69
Brenner Pass, 83
Breteuil, Louis Auguste, Baron de, 242
Brindisi, 360
Brook-Shepherd, Gordon, 37
Brunn, 341
Bubonic plague, 91
Budapest, 341
Bulgaria, 32, 283, 382

Calabria, 234, 334, 365, 367
Campan, Madame (Jeanne Louise), 127, 130, 208, 241
Canada, 113, 375
Capet, Louis. See Louis XVI
Capuchin Church, 207, 250, 271, 289, 368, 376
Caramenico, Prince, 236
Carlo (son of Maria Carolina), 252, 255-256
Carlo, Duke of Calabria (son of Maria Carolina), 176, 177, 203
Carlo II, Duke of Parma. See Lodovico II, King of Etruria
Carlo III, Duke of Parma, 380

Carlos III, King of Spain, 47-48, 49, 53-54, 64, 88-91, 92, 99-100, 106, 110, 136, 137, 153, 157, 164, 175-176, 187, 236-237, 238, 252
    final years and death of, 254-255
Carlos IV, King of Spain, 321, 336, 342, 357
Carlo Felice, Crown Prince of Sardinia (later King of Sardinia), 369, 379
Carlotta of Parma (daughter of Amalia), 227, 348, 353, 356, 361, 362, 380
Carniola (duchy). See Slovenia
Carolina of Calabria, Duchess de Berry (daughter of Francesco I), 342, 367, 373, 376
Carolina of Parma (daughter of Amalia), 136-137, 149, 150, 184, 227, 305-306, 320, 335, 361
Caserta Palace (Naples), 99, 100-101, 105, 156, 166, 177, 255, 325
Catherine II (the Great) of Russia, 160-161, 232, 250, 253, 359
    friendship with Joseph II, 192-193, 207, 217-218, 271
Cavriani, Marquis, 153
central European famine (1770-1772), 147-148
Cervoni, General, 323
Chaisse-Dieu, la (abbey of), 243
Championnet, Jean, General, 328
Charlemagne, 39, 211, 364
Charles of Zweibrücken, Prince. 46, 107
Charles, Archduke (son of Maria Theresa), 34, 37, 40, 52
Charles, Comte d'Artois, 169, 174, 279, 280-281, 286, 304, 309, 380n
Charles, Grand Duke of Baden, 375
Charles VI, Holy Roman Emperor, 32, 33, 38-39, 52, 273
    adopts Spanish court style, 35, 115
    drafts the Pragmatic Sanction, 32, 39
    empire ruled by, 32

Charles Albert, Elector of Bavaria (Holy Roman Emperor), 33-34, 65

Charles August, Grand Duke of Saxe-Weimar-Eisenach, 375

Charles Theodore, Elector of the Rhine, 63

Charlotte, Queen Consort of England, 278

Charlotte of Hesse-Darmstadt, 54

Charlotte of Lorraine (sister of Emperor Francis I), 70

Christianity. See Roman Catholicism, Protestantism

Christina, Archduchess (daughter of Joseph II), 61

Church of the Augustine Friars (Vienna), 51, 95, 108, 122, 275

Church of the Madeleine (Paris), 132

City of Lights. See Paris

Clemens, Prince of Saxony, 335

Clementine, Duchess of Calabria ("Marie," daughter of Leopold II), 247, 274-275, 326-327, 332, 334n, 342, 367

Clothilde, Queen Consort of Sardinia (sister of Louis XVI), 182, 309, 352

Clotilda (daughter of Maria Carolina), 252

Clovis I, King of France, 180

Colli Palace (Palermo), 331, 332, 366, 367

Colloredo, Francis, Count, 159-160, 185-186, 234, 250

Colorno, 110-111, 150-151, 153, 165

Commission on Spiritual Affairs (CSA), 220

Comte Mercy. See Mercy d'Argenteau, Florimond Claude, Comte

Conciergerie (Paris), 311, 313

Congress of Vienna (1814), 375-376, 380, 381

Constantinople. See Istanbul

consumption (tuberculosis), 333, 342

Convent of St. Agatha (Rome), 380

Corsica, 321

Council of Electors (Holy Roman Empire), 63, 78, 276

Council of State (Neapolitan), 176, 186-187, 328, 350

Count Falkenstein (alias of Joseph II), 116, 189

Couvent des Feuillants, 304

Cristina Amelia (daughter of Maria Carolina, twin sister of Maria Cristina), 252

Croatia, 32, 78, 283

Croÿ, Duc de, 129, 180, 191

Crusades, the, 220

Cunegunde of Saxony, 65-66

Czech Republic, 32

Damiens, Robert, 113

Danton, Georges, 306

Danube, 224

Day of the Dead, 42

Declaration of Pillnitz (1791), 286-287

diamond necklace, the, 230-231, 242

Diana (Roman goddess), 184

diet, 78, 267, 280, 299

Diplomatic Revolution (1756), 47

Dolfijn, 255

Dresden, 246, 248, 274, 284, 305, 317, 320, 361

Ducal Palace (Parma), 111-112, 136, 149, 150, 153, 163, 165, 184, 227, 323, 353

Durfort, Marquis de, 114

Dutch Republic, the, 225-226, 232-233, 249

Dutens, Louis, 177

Easter, 91, 243

Égalité, Philippe (Duc d'Orléans), 264, 279, 369

Egypt, 326

Elba, 359

Élisabeth, Duchess of Parma ("Madame Infanta," daughter of Louis XV), 49, 58, 106, 322

436

Frederick II (the Great), King of Prussia ("Fritz"), 33-34, 63, 160-161, 195-196, 207, 211, 218, 253

Frederick III, Prince of Salm-Kyburg, 225

Frederick VI, King of Denmark, 375

Frederick August of Saxony (later Frederick August I, King of Saxony), 335, 375, 381

Frederick August III, Elector of Saxony, 63, 335

Frederick Wilhelm, Duke of Brunswick, 302, 375

Frederick Wilhelm, Duke of Nassau-Weilburg,

Frederick Wilhelm of Prussia, Prince, 375

Frederick Wilhelm II, King of Prussia, 253-254, 282, 283, 286

Frederick Wilhelm III, King of Prussia, 375

Freiburg, 123

French Revolution, the (*See* Louis XVI, Marie Antoinette), 63, 201, 263-264, 266, 280, 285, 287, 299, 304, 309, 311-312, 318, 319, 321, 322, 357, 369, 376, 380-381
buildup to, 217, 245, 263

Gabriel, Infante of Spain (son of King Carlos III), 254

Galicia, 78, 161

Gallo, Marquis de, 256, 325, 342

Gazzette de France, 121

Gennaro (son of Maria Carolina), 252, 255

George III, King of England, 207, 214, 309

Germany, 32, 63, 201, 211, 217, 224, 300, 319, 321, 360, 382

Gibbon, Edward, 236

Girondins, 301, 306, 307

Giuseppe (son of Maria Carolina), 232n

Godoy, Manuel de, 323, 345

Goethe, Johann von, 64, 178

Golden Fleece, 252

Goltz, Count von, 195

Grand Cross of Carlos III, 252

Graz, 373

Great Britain, 47, 56, 156, 176, 213-214, 225, 236, 237, 238, 278, 309, 327, 329, 363, 366, 372, 375, 380

Greek Orthodoxy, 219

Gresset, Jean Baptiste, 173

Guastalla, 78, 150

guillotine, 307, 314, 318

Gulf of Naples, 166, 176, 252, 318

Gustav III, King of Sweden, 191

Habsburg dynasty (Austria), 32, 35, 37 39, 40, 41, 44, 46, 51, 52, 54, 78, 92, 129, 213, 219-220, 247, 248, 377, 379
and the Holy Roman Empire, 38, 63, 66, 78
conflicts of, with other European nations, 32-33, 38, 39, 62-63, 107, 173, 233, 253, 276, 341
history and traditions of, 34, 61, 69, 88, 100, 136, 147, 205, 258
territories belonging to the, 32, 53, 109, 229, 257, 267, 272, 364
titles of heads of the, 78

Habsburg dynasty (Spain), 47-48

Hackert, Philip, 166, 177

Hall of Mirrors (Versailles), 113, 130

Hamilton, Lady Emma, 238, 325, 329-331, 338-339, 340

Hamilton, Sir William, 104, 156, 166-167, 176, 237, 319, 338-339, 340

Hanover, 375

Harcourt, Duc d', 261

Hasse, Johann Adolf, 46

Heiter, Amalie. *See* Amalia of Saxony

Henry IV, King of France, 114, 264

Herder, Johann, 211, 270

Hermannsschlact, 211

Herzelles, Marquise d', 118

CPSIA information can be obtained at www.ICGtesting.com
Printed in the USA
266414BV00002B/29/P